IBERIAN AND LATIN AMERICAN STUDIES

Shakespeare in Catalan

Series Editors
Professor David George (University of Wales, Swansea)
Professor Paul Garner (University of Leeds)

Editorial Board
David Frier (University of Leeds)
Laura Shaw (University of Liverpool)
Gareth Walters (University of Exeter)
Rob Stone (University of Wales, Swansea)
David Gies (University of Virginia)
Catherine Davies (University of Nottingham)

IBERIAN AND LATIN AMERICAN STUDIES

Shakespeare in Catalan

Translating Imperialism

HELENA BUFFERY

UNIVERSITY OF WALES PRESS
CARDIFF
2007

© Helena Buffery, 2007

All rights reserved. No part of this book may be reproduced, stored in a retrieval system, or transmitted, in any form or by any means, electronic, mechanical, photocopying, recording or otherwise, without clearance from the University of Wales Press, 10 Columbus Walk, Brigantine Place, Cardiff, CF10 4UP.
www.wales.ac.uk/press

British Library Cataloguing-in-Publication Data
A catalogue record for this book is available from the British Library.

ISBN 978–0–7083–2011–2

The right of Helena Buffery to be identified as author of this work has been asserted by her in accordance with sections 77 and 79 of the Copyright, Designs and Patents Act 1988.

Typeset by Columns Design Ltd, Reading RG4 7DH
Printed in Great Britain by Antony Rowe Ltd, Wiltshire

Contents

List of Plates	vii
Series Editors' Foreword	ix
Acknowledgements	xi
Note to the Reader	xiii
Introduction	1
Chapter 1: Constructing a History of Shakespeare Translation in Catalonia	19
Chapter 2: Why Shakespeare? Critical Positionings	61
Chapter 3: The Catalan Shakespeare	101
Chapter 4: Shakespeare and the Catalan Language – 'La llengua més shakespeariana del món'	143
Chapter 5: The Politics of Storytelling: the Case of *Coriolanus/Coriolà*	179
Conclusions	223
Appendix A Catalan Translations of Shakespeare	227
Appendix B Shakespeare's Works and their Translators into Catalan	249
Appendix C Productions	257
Bibliography	279
Index	295

List of Plates

Fig. 1. Garavaglia cartoon in *L'Esquella de la Torratxa*, 1909. Reproduced with the permission of the Biblioteca de Catalienya.

Fig. 2. Adrià Gual's sketch for his production of *A Midsummer Night's Dream*, 1908. From the on-line visual archive in Barcelona's Institut del Teatre.

Fig. 3. Scene from *Titus Andrònic*, directed by Fabià Puigserver at the Teatre Lliure in Gràcia, 1977. © Ros Ribas 1977.

Fig. 4. Scene from *Titus Andrònic*, directed by Fabià Puigserver. © Ros Ribas 1977.

Fig. 5. Francesc Orella as Prospero in Lluís Pasqual's 2005 production of *La tempestad*. © Ros Ribas 2005.

Fig. 6. Free promotional postcard for Calixto Bieito's 1997 production of *La Tempesta*.

Fig. 7. One of the 'ghosts' of Shakespeare haunting Alex Rigola's *Richard III*. © Ros Ribas 2005.

Fig. 8. Actresses in costumes for Adrià Gual's production of *El somni d'una nit d'estiu*, as reproduced in the women's magazine *Feminal*, 1909. Reproduced with the permission of the Biblioteca de Catalunya.

Fig. 9. A cartoon representation of the 'crusade' for Catalan Theatre, in *L'Esquella de la Torratxa*, 1909, 480. Reproduced with the permission of the Biblioteca de Catalunya.

Fig. 10. Garavaglia's Hamlet presents his advice to the key players in Catalan Theatre, *L'Esquella de la Torratxa*, 1909, 356. Reproduced with the permission of the Biblioteca de Catalunya.

Fig. 11. Eduard Fernàndez's Hamlet gives advice to Anna Lizaran's player who is wearing a badge calling for freedom of speech in Basque. From Lluís Pasqual's production of *Hamlet*. © Ros Ribas 2004.

Fig. 12. Anna Lizaran's decidedly earthy representation of Ariel in Lluís Pasqual's production of *La Tempestad*. © Ros Ribas 2004.

Fig. 13. Frontispiece of Magí Morera i Galícia's 1918 translation of *Coriolanus* for the Editorial Catalana.

Fig. 14. The women in the 1977 production of *Coriolà* at the Teatre Casal Catòlic de Sant Andreu. Reproduced with the permission of the Institut del Teatre.

Fig. 15. Section of promotional poster for Georges Lavaudant's 2002 production of *Coriolà* at the Teatre Nacional de Catalunya with Lluís Homar as Coriolanus.

Fig. 16. The Macbeths according to Calixto Bieito. © Ros Ribas 2002.

Senior Editors' Foreword

Over recent decades, the traditional 'languages and literatures' model in Spanish departments in universities in the United Kingdom has been superceded by a contextual, interdisciplinary and 'area studies' approach to the study of the culture, history, society and politics of the Hispanic and Lusophone worlds – categories which extend far beyond the confines of the Iberian Peninsula, not only to Latin America but also to Spanish-speaking and Lusophone Africa.

In response to these dynamic trends in research priorities and curriculum development, this series is designed to present both disciplinary and interdisciplinary research within the general field of Iberian and Latin American Studies, particularly studies which explore all aspects of **Cultural Production** (*inter alia* literature, film, music, dance, sport) in Spanish, Portuguese, Basque, Catalan, Galician and the indigenous languages of Latin America. The series also aims to publish research on the **History and Politics** of Hispanic and Lusophone worlds, both at the level of region and that of the nation-state, as well as on **Cultural Studies** which explore the shifting terrains of gender, sexual, racial and postcolonial identities in those same regions.

Acknowledgements

Much of the research for this volume was undertaken with funds from Batista i Roca scholarships awarded by the Catalan government in 1995 and 2001. In addition, I received invaluable support from the School of Humanities and the Department of Hispanic Studies at the University of Birmingham, and I am especially grateful to Aengus Ward, Trevor Dadson, Derek Flitter and Patricia Odber de Baubeta for their kind words and good counsel over the years. I gratefully acknowledge the staff of the Biblioteca de Catalunya, the Hermeroteca at Casa L'Ardiaca and the Biblioteca de Teatre and later Institut del Teatre libraries, amongst the many libraries and archives to which I have had recourse over the years researching this volume. I must also thank Josep Ros Ribas for permission to reproduce some of his legendary photographs of Catalan Shakespeare productions, and the family of Adrià Gual for allowing me to use one of his paintings for the front cover of this book (*Romeo and Juliet*, 1920). In order to uncover the full range of traces of Shakespeare in Catalonia, I was dependent from the first on the advice and friendship of colleagues and companions in the Catalan-speaking countries. I would never have stumbled on this subject without the early encouragement of Miquel Ruiz Lacruz, Ricard Jordana and Sílvia Coll-Vinent who introduced me to the world of Catalan Studies. It was Lluís Cabré and Marcel Ortin Rull who put me on to the importance of translation in Catalonia, and Neus Real, Jordi Sala and Francesca Bartrina who accompanied me on my initial readings of the texts. I was fortunate to receive the input of translators and scholars, such as Joan Jaumà, Salvador Oliva, Enric Gallén and Eva Espasa, as well as insights from the world of the theatre in conversations with Lluís Soler, Lluís Homar, Rosa Novell and Joan Sellent.

As a member of the Anglo-Catalan Society since 1996, I have had the privilege to present and discuss my work at annual conferences with friends and colleagues from different fields of expertise. Dominic Keown, Jordi Larios, Alan Yates and Richard Mansell have fed my interest in the field of translation; Montserrat Roser i Puig, Josep-Anton Fernàndez and Louise Johnson have been invaluable interlocutors on questions of comparative literature and contemporary cultural studies; and David George and Maria Delgado inspired my love of Catalan theatre and performance. Above all I am grateful for the enthusiasm with which Joan Gili and Arthur Terry engaged with my work; I have sorely missed their wise words in the years since their deaths. Amèlia Trueta and Elizabeth Gili remain an inspiration to me in their unwavering commitment to the Society's aims of promoting the understanding of Catalan culture.

To fellow lecturers, researchers and postgraduate students at Birmingham, I owe both a spirit of fellowship and my continuing interest in comparative work within Hispanic Studies. They are too numerous to name, but particular thanks across the years are due to David and Jo Mackenzie, Patrick Quinn, Damian Smith, Manolo Puga, Manolo Hijano, Jules Whicker, Carmen Millán, Peter Holland and Conrad James. Amongst my postgraduate students, I have found sparring partners in Athena Mandis, Miriam Haddu, Stuart Davis, Patricia Plaza, José Luis Bellón, Sílvia Mas and Elisenda Marcer, and am glad that I am still able to count them amongst my friends.

It is, of course, to close friends and family that I am most indebted for their patience and support at all times. To Adrian Hunt, Liza Dimbleby, Stephanie Gard, Diana Boyd, Ivan Birks, Reyahn King and Constanza Lezama I owe many hours of conversations and friendship in spite of the silences. Andrew Dowling, Brad Epps and Graham Pollock I must thank for mad round-the-clock debates in the bars of Barcelona, whilst Veronica Barry and Sally Mallard have been my surrogate sisters in recent years. My parents Wilfred Buffery and María Teresa Manjón Vilas have given me more than they could ever know, and than I could ever repay. My family and close friends in Barcelona, Pablo Manjón, Paquita Vilas, Elena Manjón, Josep and Marc Ponz, and Pura Puchal, have provided me with entertainment and sustenance on many a flying visit. As for Vicky Buffery and Liam O'Toole, I look forward to spending the rest of my life in their gratitude, and hope that my children, Dylan and Carolina, will forgive the hours I spent on this at their expense.

Note to the Reader

Because this history is largely about words, and how they take on different meanings at different times and in different places, I felt it was important to include those words in the language in which they were originally spoken or written. Thus, I have not standardized any of the Catalan quotations which were found in what would now be considered an archaic or non-standard form. Whilst I have provided selective translations of these quotations, I have deliberately allowed Catalan keywords to become part of the texture of a book that is ultimately about how Shakespeare figures *in* Catalan. In contrast, I have standardized quotations from Castilian in the few instances where I have had recourse to nineteenth-century texts. I have also standardized the spelling of names, to avoid confusion; except, of course, the name of Shakespeare himself, the variant spellings of which are part and parcel of his multiple figurations.

Introduction

At the very heart of every imperialism there is a story of translation. (Godard)

Un impérialisme culturel tend à oublier son histoire, donc à méconnaître le rôle historique de la traduction et des emprunts dans sa culture. Cet oubli est le corollaire de la sacralisation de sa littérature. (Meschonnic)

This is not just another book about Shakespeare. Whilst it does indeed reveal the existence of a Catalan 'Shakespeare' to add to the numerous 'alternative' Shakespeares that now inhabit the bookshelves of every academic library,[1] its scope is at once wider and narrower than the Shakespeare industry would normally allow. It takes the author often considered the ultimate 'dead white male' and explores how he travels beyond British shores, not in terms of how he is served by a foreign culture nor in terms of his appropriation, but as a study of the diverse effects of translation in creating and deciding the afterlives of a canonical text.[2] It focuses on a minority language, estimated to be spoken by over 6.5 million speakers, and a minority culture, that is still only partially recognized within the Spanish state itself, let alone beyond Spain's borders. It tells the story of a minority Shakespeare employed to achieve cultural majority; of a 'universal', imperial Shakespeare used to wield cultural authority; and of a rebellious, counter-imperialist Shakespeare deployed against colonial domination.

Thus, whilst the practised 'postcolonial reader' might expect to find a narrative of cultural transgression, in which Shakespeare's stories are revised for political ends, overturning the narratives of colonialism, or indeed an oppositional Shakespeare, devised for the purpose of countering imperialism, the Shakespeare found here is, more often than not, an 'establishment' Shakespeare, born of a desire for cultural normality and universality. The

Catalan Shakespeare might then be more properly held to exemplify hypotheses about the function of translation in a minority culture formulated by Gideon Toury, demonstrating a preponderance of source-orientated rather than target-orientated translation practice, and thus revealing a relationship of subordination between the languages in the translation equation.[3] However, as recent empirical studies of different minority cultural systems have shown, the norms governing translation policy and practice are rarely quite so predictable. Indeed, the case of Shakespeare in Catalan reveals diverse and shifting trends and practices, according to individual taste, group interests and aesthetic fashions, but also to cultural and linguistic consciousness, historical accident and inter-cultural contact. Hence, whilst on one level what we will find reconstructed here is an imperial Shakespeare, standing as a supreme and exclusive model of culture and civilization, we will also see his imperialism positioned and his empire adjusted to exclude problematic aspects (such as its relationship with colonialism and with models of political imposition) and to include Catalan and Catalonia. Equally, although we will certainly see glimpses of 'postcolonial' Shakespeares, their significance is not always as easy to identify as that of Caribbean rereadings of *The Tempest*, for instance.[4] This is partly because Shakespeare does not directly address, nor indeed elide, the domination experienced historically by the Catalans, but mainly because Catalonia's and the Catalan-speaking regions' relationship to colonialism and imperialism is a multivalent one, reminding us that colonial and postcolonial experiences can and should only be read relationally, with clear reference to social and historical context.

Many critics have observed the awkward fit in trying to apply postcolonial models and approaches to Catalan culture, and even today it is a theoretical transplantation that continues to require some defence.[5] This is primarily because of the confusion about the location of culture exposed when language, territory and political legitimacy do not fully overlap, leading to differential affiliations and different understandings of community identity. However, it is also undeniable that in the Catalan case, according to class, location and linguistic relation, imperialism can be experienced as colonial domination, class distinction or cultural endowment, whether separately or simultaneously. It was the economic growth and urban expansion of the late eighteenth and nineteenth centuries that provided the conditions for the cultural revival underpinning Catalan regionalism and the development of a nationalist consciousness, and these were fed by colonialist exploitation of the Americas, in particular the Spanish Caribbean. Yet whereas for some critics this disqualifies Catalonia and all Catalans (transumed into a uniform culture) from anything resembling postcolonial experience, this is to forget the role of other variables in the equation that created a communal sense of Catalan identity, not least the central Spanish administration of the peripheral regions, the political and cultural relations between Spain's different urban centres, and class and labour relations in a burgeoning industrial area, which led to immigration as well as population shifts between countryside and city. Part of the impetus behind this book is the sense that the concept of imperialism is central to understanding the development of a Catalan cultural space, helped by the fact that unlike other cultures, its presence is often actually named and debated, and not just by canny postcolonial readers.[6] The changing Catalan understandings of imperialism will here be read in relation to and through Shakespeare, as a figure often held to contain the different values and aspects associated with imperial power.

Thus, Barbara Godard's perception that 'at the heart of every imperialism there is a story of translation' is to be taken in a rather peculiar sense.[7] Her words reflect a common postcolonial view of translation as a process that has aided cultures to reinforce their own dominance by assimilation, as a form of cultural and linguistic control. For Godard, translation both underpins the language shift that takes place in the encounter between dominant and dominated in the colonial equation, and contributes to cultural transvaluation through appropriation of the language of the dominated peoples to disseminate the dominant cultural forms. Whereas Venuti originally associated such uneven power relations with domestication and with a poetics of 'transparency' in the translation process, he was subsequently able to recognize their effects to be far less predictable.[8] Likewise, instead of imposing a model of translational interaction, translation will be explored here in the context of and as a by-product of imperialism, in full recognition of the relationship between culture and imperialism.[9] Just as Meschonnic shows that a feature of cultural dominance depends on the effacement of this history to present the original self-sufficiency of the imperial culture, here it will be explored how far this might apply to any cultural construction and, indeed, in the case of Catalan culture we will see continued debate over the expediency of translation in the struggle for cultural definition.[10] Translating imperialism should, then, be seen as the process by which a particular culture is shaped by others, whilst hiding and showing aspects of the relationships and transactions into which it enters with others. It is to be understood here as a figurative process, by which a national culture persuades of its distinctness and distinction through positioning itself in relation to other cultures.[11]

My own study began in response to the call of materialist approaches to the history of Catalan literature, as detected in such a seminal work as the modern volumes of the *Història de la Literatura Catalana*, to account for the social and historical fields in which what can be described as 'autonomous' art is developed, and its role in underpinning a particular cultural ideology, here the existence of a separate identity.[12] Any such account depends on an encounter with formulations of Catalan culture undertaken from a wide range of critical positionings and positions of production. These 'histories', predicated on the basis of underlining difference, also ride on the ascription of value, in the creation of a canonical structure that can stand as a monument of cultural reference. In recent years, there has been increasing interest in areas of cultural contact (where Catalan culture has participated in 'sameness', in perpetuating and reinforcing a world canon), and how this, in turn, has influenced Catalonia's own cultural development.

The potential significance of such a revision of cultural history can be found in the words of Cèsar August Jordana, reclaimed fifty years after their first publication to reflect a common concern of the 1930s and the 1980s:

> ... un exercici saludable per als que creuen, o pretenen fer-nos creure, que la cultura catalana és un camp clos seria de dreçar el catàleg de les bones traduccions que s'han fet al català. ... la llista mostraria en la novella, i encara delicada, cultura catalana un desig d'enriquir-se mirant enfora i portant endins, [desig] que altres cultures plenes d'orgull podrien envejar-li ...[13]

(... a salutary exercise for those who believe, or would have us believe, that Catalan culture is a limited field would be to redraw the catalogue of good translations into Catalan.... the list would show a desire in the new, and still delicate, Catalan culture, to enrich itself by looking beyond its borders and bringing things in, [a desire] that other cultures full of pride might envy...).

Since the 1990s, there has been increasing attention to the role of translation and transfer in the cultural programme developed by *Noucentisme* and its after-effects up to the end of the Spanish Civil War, with studies of particular institutions and individual translators, as well as the recovery of translations and studies of translation published in the early decades of the twentieth century.[14] Indeed, my own project, to trace the influence, representation and participation of Shakespeare in Catalan cultural life, how he figures and is transfigured, fits into the process of recuperating texts previously considered to be marginal, or of interest only in plotting the development of key, canonical writers.

The reason for pinpointing Shakespeare can be defended pragmatically in terms of the sheer number of Shakespeare translations undertaken since the Catalan *Renaixença*, many of them by writers who were or would subsequently become key players in Catalan cultural life, and yet whose translations are usually consigned to a paragraph or a footnote in accounts of their total output.[15] Yet the aim of this book is not simply to produce a catalogue of translations, a chronological history that might prove the role of Shakespeare translation in helping to forge a modern poetic language for Catalan writers, or as a surrogate father for modern Catalan theatre. Such approximations have already been attempted, to differing degrees of accuracy, and two scholars in particular, Ramon Esquerra and Alfons Par, have proved invaluable in my own collection of data, as well as in that of other briefer histories of Catalan and Spanish approximations to the Bard.[16] My approach depends on a more complex model of cultural interaction than that of traditional histories of influence and translation, a model necessary to allow for the overdeterminacy of Shakespeare in twentieth-century society.

In many ways, then, my starting point, like the works of Alfons Par and Ramon Esquerra, is that formulated by Bergnes de las Casas in 1840: 'He aquí un objeto de este artículo: la lejana influencia de la inteligencia sobre las inteligencias' ('Here is one of the objects of this article: the distant influence of intelligence on intelligences'). These words are taken from an article entitled 'Comparación entre las literaturas de los diversos países del globo' in 1840, and hence might be associated with the histories of influence usually undertaken within the field of comparative literature.[17] The study begins with consideration of Cervantes before going on to describe and compare the influence of Shakespeare on world literature, and the history of his critical reception. Immediately preceding the above outline of Bergnes' project comes the following affirmation: 'La última obra de Shakespeare es Walter Scott, el último vástago de la grande influencia shaksperiana' ('Shakespeare's latest work is Walter Scott, the last offspring of the great Shakespearian influence'). Alfons Par, in his *Shakespeare en la literatura española*, draws attention to this statement as reinforcing the sentiments of an earlier Bergnes article about Scott's influence on the wealth, morality and happiness of modern society in which he first identifies the Scottish novelist as Shakespeare's literary successor.[18]

This preoccupation with Scott reflects the aesthetic concerns of the Spanish Romantic movement, in particular within Catalonia, driven to revive past cultural forms and traditions. Bergnes does not question the importance of Scott, unlike Par in his later study of literary reception, but he does further determine the nature of his influence by revealing the influence of Shakespeare before him.[19] Such extension of the poetic family romance, which began to have some interest for other writers of the Catalan school, such as Milà i Fontanals and Piferrer, points to a more general lack of appreciation of Shakespearian influence in Catalonia, a lack which Par suggests might in some ways be countered by Bergnes' comparative approach.[20] The reasons for this lack are explained by Par as a heavy Catalan emphasis on Scott to encourage a revival of the national culture and, in a wider context, Spain (notwithstanding its openness to other more diverse Romantic influences, at times perceived to be 'immoral' by writers such as Bergnes, Milà i Fontanals and Piferrer) was felt to have failed to look beyond Scott and other foreign models to a more original influence: here, 'la inteligencia'. An object of the article could then be viewed as the recognition of the faraway influence (both in diachronic and synchronic terms) of 'la inteligencia' –

Shakespeare – on other 'inteligencias' – the English and German Romantics, followed by Spanish writers of the nineteenth century.

This gap in the tradition of cultural criticism in Catalonia, expressed by Par as a lack of adequate evaluations of Shakespeare, forms a position which anticipates later Catalan expressions of a neglect of Shakespeare, formulated in terms of a lack or a gap in Catalan culture. So, in the introduction to his translation of *King Lear* into an approximation to medieval Catalan, Par signals a lack of critical approaches to Shakespeare, both in Catalonia and in Spain as a whole.[21] His judgement reflects a common theme in articles and essays appearing in the early twentieth-century press, lamenting what was perceived to be the poverty of Catalan theatre at this time, and proposing the possibly regenerative role of Shakespeare translations as they began to appear.[22] In 1937, by which time there had been a number of translations of Shakespeare into Catalan, Ramon Esquerra takes stock of the English dramatist's status within the Catalan territories in *Shakespeare a Catalunya*. Compared to other linguistic communities the contribution of Catalonia to Shakespeare studies is perceived in his opening statement to be 'poc afalagadora' ('not very flattering'), for the Catalans have not concerned themselves with acquiring direct knowledge of his work.[23] Esquerra goes on to write of the causes of this 'manca d'interès' ('lack of interest'), identifying a livelier preoccupation with more contemporary foreign writers, an observation which might remind us of Par's comments in *Shakespeare en la literatura española*. Although there is recognition of an improvement in Shakespeare reception, Esquerra goes on to point out that a lot of work is still to be done, hoping that his 'inventory' will show exactly where the gaps lie:

> Implícitament ja queda dit en el que segueix, i hom veurà en cada període el que s'ha fet i com s'ha fet, i també el molt que s'ha deixat de fer, tot i que a Catalunya s'hagin fet proves en tots els sentits: des de la publicació de col·leccions d'obres completes i la impressió de textos anglesos, fins a la lliure interpretació dels temes shakespearians i la mutilació amb criteri escènic.

> (This is implicit in what follows, and one will see what has been done in each period and how it has been done, as well as all that has not been done, even though in Catalonia there have been attempts of all kinds: from the publication of complete works and

the printing of English texts, to the free interpretation of Shakespearian themes and mutilation of texts for the stage, p. 9).

Shakespeare translation was to continue after the Spanish Civil War, but it is only in critical introductions and reviews of translations and productions from the mid 1950s onwards that Shakespeare criticism can be found. The situation was such that the entry on Shakespeare in Joaquim Molas' dictionary of Catalan literature in 1979 is basically a summary of Esquerra's 1937 work, with the addition of references to the translations of Josep Maria de Sagarra and Terenci Moix's *Hamlet*.[24] By 1984 and the 'año Shakespeare', a collection of articles on Shakespeare's 'universal' influence were published by the Escola Universitària de Traductors i Intèrprets in Bellaterra. Many of the articles are in Castilian, but there is one dedicated to 'Crítiques, comentaris i interpretacions sobre Shakespeare i les seves obres'. Once again we find the familiar plaint:

> Malauradament, avui, aquí a Catalunya, el panorama respecte a la publicació d'obres de crítica shakespeariana, és decebedor. Gairebé a tots els pròlegs de les traduccions del dramaturg anglès, d'ençà que va començar a traduir-se, tant a l'estat espanyol, com a Catalunya, trobem estudis crítics. Però, això, i les notes a peu de pàgina és tot. I és molt poc per tota la gamma d'erudits [. . .] que motiva Shakespeare.[25]

> (Unfortunately, today, here in Catalonia, the situation with respect to the publication of works of Shakespeare criticism is disappointing. In almost every prologue to translations of the English dramatist, from the first time he was translated, both in Spain and in Catalonia, we find critical studies. But these, and the footnotes, are all there is. And that's not much considering the range of intellectuals [. . .] who are inspired by Shakespeare).

It might then be expected that a study of representations of Shakespeare in Catalonia would be a rather fruitless task. However, alongside this and other perceptions of a Shakespeare lacuna in Catalan culture, there is a seemingly conflicting drive, in the search for influences to prioritize Catalan perceptions and criticism of Shakespeare, to overdetermine the Bard's universal 'cultural' value in Catalan and hence trace his origins to something Catalan. The following comments from Alfons Par's 1931 essay on *Shakespeare y el folklore español* could be read in such a light:

Tot quant anticipa i mèna a Shakespeare es de valua preuadíssima y convé que les terres hispàniques hi facin llur debuda aportació. No constituim pas nosaltres excepció y segur soch que nostres investigadors poden descelar filiacions nostrades a molts passatges shakespearians que les comentaristes estrangers, mancats de la informació debuda, cerquen debades per altres regions.[26]

(All that which anticipates and leads to Shakespeare is of very great value and it is fitting that the Spanish territories should make the contribution they owe. We ourselves are no exception and I am sure that our researchers can uncover home-grown connections with many Shakespearian passages that foreign critics, lacking the necessary information, vainly seek in other regions).

In my study of critical approaches to and representations of Shakespeare I am to concentrate on one particular region, defined situationally according to the use of a particular language, and its relationship to other languages, in particular the dominant language of the Spanish state. My interest lies in revealing how exactly Shakespeare figures in Catalan, is figured by and perhaps transfigures Catalan cultural production. Any approximation to the status of Shakespeare in Catalan cannot be limited to a description of historical changes, flux in popularity or reception, whether popular or academic. As has been made clear in philosophical approaches to translation, fuelled by deconstructivist readings of Walter Benjamin's 'The Task of the Translator', these terms or discourses can never be fixed. There is not a single 'universal' appreciation of Shakespeare to be detected and reproduced according to the ability of the translator, for if there were, then translation would be unnecessary. Instead to be apprehended is a Shakespeare who is open to and feeds upon dialogue, intertextual relationships and other terms of cultural description.

In order to account for the complexity of these rhetorical relationships, the full scope of Shakespeare's signification in Catalan, his 'lejana influencia' ('distant influence'), I have divided the study into five main chapters, each telling a different Shakespeare story. The first, 'Constructing a History of Shakespeare in Catalonia', focuses on the translation and representation of his body of works into Catalan, drawing on a wide range of bibliographies and earlier studies, as well as original research, in order to present as complete an overview of Shakespeare's different entry points into Catalan culture as possible. Complete data on the translations and productions is available in appendices at the back of the book, but I have given a representative overview, stopping to comment on paradigmatic moments. Chapter 2 will consider how Shakespeare gains cultural reference in Catalan, the kind of figure he becomes, as part of a dialogue with cultural commentary on Shakespeare outside Catalonia, the discourses of international Shakespeare studies. By tracing different instances of the 'lejana influencia de la inteligencia sobre las inteligencias' – of cultural borrowing, as well as evidence of critical debate and divergence – I intend to map out the place of Catalan Shakespeare studies within a wider context, the kind of 'universal' Shakespeare that is chosen from amidst the many Shakespeares on offer. Once it becomes clear which attributes are foregrounded in Catalan formulations of Shakespeare's status, Chapter 3 will trace this figure's synchronic relationship with Catalan culture, particularly during the time in which he was most bespoken – the *Noucentista* period – before going on to explore the status of his linguistic referents, the language which he comes to speak, Catalan, to which I have dedicated chapter 4. The final chapter will read across translations of Shakespeare's works produced in the past century, focusing on versions of *Coriolanus*, in order to gauge their importance in giving meaning to Shakespeare, and to Catalan culture.

There are three types of Shakespeare which have been traced in their Catalan manifestations: the first is Shakespeare as man (and the kind of figure he cuts in Catalan); the second is Shakespeare as body of works; the third is Shakespeare as cultural pound sign. These manifestations have all been deliberately historicized in order to offer a picture of areas of recognition and difference. They are the types underlined in importance by Michael Bristol, although his conceptualization of the relative importance of the three has had to be modified according to the nature of each manifestation.[27] The most important parameters and changes to be traced are, however, linguistic (both in terms of figurative and 'literal' meanings) and hence not fully transparent, as Bristol would seem to suggest in some of his examples and analysis. In order to explore how Shakespeare is represented in Catalan, how he represents in Catalan, and the hierarchy of figuration with respect to these three categories, it has been necessary to read his manifestations in terms of other aesthetic, cultural, social and political discourse of the time in Catalan, as well as in relation to other European movements and aesthetics. Recognition of the continual interplay of new and old, centre and margins, behind the seeming solidity of a classic monument, leads to a sense of how a genealogy of Shakespeare translation and the translation of 'Shakespeare' can reveal hidden cultural histories and movements, revealing links between seemingly antagonistic groups and ideological positions.

The period in which Shakespeare was most invoked in support of imperialism was also the period in which translation was overtly identified as central to achieve the perceived cultural needs of an emerging Catalan nation. Indeed, whilst there were some translation attempts in the latter half of the nineteenth century, the seeds of a Catalan Shakespeare were really sown by *Noucentisme*.[28] Thus, whilst many translations of Shakespeare in Catalonia are accompanied by paratexts to justify their existence, the most visible contextualizations of this type can be associated with the *Noucentista* programme, an authoritative discourse, both cultural and political, which informed the writing of a large number of translations, including many published after the period usually ascribed to *Noucentisme*. The texts are often perceived as collaborations with a source author or concordances to source texts, contributing to the 'reciprocal' process of universalizing Catalan through texts of recognized cultural value and appropriating the imperialist values of other cultures so approved in the dominant nationalist political discourse of the early decades of the twentieth century.

In view of such a trend, it may not be surprising that I have chosen the subtitle 'Translating Imperialism', especially when one considers the potency of the second of the terms in descriptions of the process of, and political imperatives which underlie, translation. A further nod to the cultural theorist would be the association of this translation formula with figurations of Shakespeare, in the light of recent deconstruction of his sacred – and hence for many non-political – role in culture.[29] However, my choice of subtitle is deliberately ambiguous. On one level, it presents the study of Shakespeare's translation and figuration in Catalonia as a process that involves interaction with imperialism, where Shakespeare is taken to stand as a synecdoche for High Culture or even a metonym for British Empire, in which the individual translator or translating culture may opt for positions of resistance or slavery. Yet it may also be held to represent the description of the translation enterprise itself in Catalonia as a form of cultural imperialism, whose history can be traced in particular encounters with Shakespeare. What is clear is that it depends on how 'imperialism', 'Shakespeare' and 'translation' are to be interpreted.

Thus, the story to be told here is the way in which Shakespeare's imperialism is constructed and translated in the context of Catalan culture, and how this has contributed to creating the Shakespeares we see there today. It is a story that reveals the role of Shakespeare in Catalan culture, but also allows us to read Catalan culture through Shakespeare. Above all, it will show once more the power of meaning by Shakespeare, whilst exploring the ways in which that meaning can be apprehended in all its valencies.[30] As with all forms of imperialism, ours is to be a double-sided story; on the one hand it is a story of Catalan culture, and the way in which the process of translation and interpretation contributed to the creation of a national literature (and, hence, how the translation of imperialism has contributed to different degrees of cultural autonomy and independence); on the other hand, it is a story of Shakespeare, and how his interaction with Catalan culture tells us of his afterlives, of Shakespeare's remains.[31]

NOTES

[1] See for instance Gary Taylor, *Reinventing Shakespeare. A Cultural History from the Restoration to the Present* (London: Vintage, 1991), Graham Holderness (ed.); *The Shakespeare Myth* (Manchester: Manchester University Press, 1988); John Drakakis, *Alternative Shakespeares* (London/New York: Routledge, 1989); and Peter Erickson, *Rewriting Shakespeare, Rewriting Ourselves* (Berkeley/Los Angeles/London: University of California Press, 1994), amongst the many titles on offer.

[2] In Susan Bennett's *Peforming Nostalgia. Shifting Shakespeare and the Contemporary Past* (London/New York: Routledge, 1996), he is described as 'the ultimate Dead White Male: the pinnacle of an oppressive canonical hierarchy and ally of conservative elitism, patriarchal sovereignty, and colonial imperialism' (p. 21). For the concept of 'afterlives' in translation, I am of course indebted to Walter Benjamin, 'The Task of the Translator' (1923), *Illuminations*,

ed. Hannah Arendt, trans. Harry Zohn (London: Fontana, 1992), pp. 70–82.
3   Gideon Toury, *Descriptive Translation Studies and Beyond* (Amsterdam: John Benjamins, 1995).
4   See Ania Loomba and Martin Orkin (eds), *Postcolonial Shakespeares* (London and New York, Routledge, 1998) and Peter Hulme (ed.), *'The Tempest' and its Travels* (London: Reaktion Books, 2000).
5   Amongst others, see the introduction to Stewart King, *Escribir la catalanidad. Lengua e identidad culturales en la narrativa contemporánea de Cataluña* (Woodbridge: Tamesis, 2005), pp. 1–7.
6   Recent debate over the location of Catalan culture has often culminated in what might be called 'crisis' discourse, in which the impossibility of constituting a hegemonic culture in the Catalan language is lamented. Yet, whilst many critics see this as a contemporary phenomenon caused by the devastating historical experiences of the Spanish Civil War and its aftermath, others have identified it as a long-term failing of the Catalan cultural imagination. Just as in a recent article Edgar Illas controversially identifies the sense of imminent linguistic death at the heart of Catalan linguistic consciousness as a value to be embraced, as recognizing something that is elided in other, apparently 'healthier' linguistic communities, this book will explore the discomfiting presence of imperialism, often associated with *Noucentisme*, as a named pathology at the heart of Catalan cultural discourse. See E. Illas, 'Visca la mort del català! Una proposta modesta per a les llengües minoritàries', *Dissidences. Hispanic Journal of Theory and Criticism*, 1. On line. Internet: 15/09/05 (*http://www.dissidences/mortdelcatala.html*).
7   Barbara Godard, 'Language Policy and the configuration of Culture', Conference on *Translation and Power*, University of Warwick, 15 July 1997.
8   In his paper at the same conference, Laurence Venuti expressed his dissatisfaction with the dialectic between innovation and resistance on which his own *The Translator's Invisibility* (London/New York: Routledge, 1994) is largely based. He was, in effect, calling for histories to embrace the unpredictable effects of translation.
9   Edward Said, *Culture and Imperialism* (London: Vintage Books, 1993) is, of course, the classic exposition of the relationship between literature and the modes of distinction that underpin imperial domination, as well as providing insight into the appropriation of forms of cultural imperialism by postcolonial cultures.
10 Henri Meschonnic, *Pour la poétique: Épistémologie de l'écriture. Poétique de la traduction*, II (Paris: Gallimard, 1973), p. 301.
11 The model of rhetorical relations devised by Bloom has informed my own readings of Shakespeare in translation, primarily *The Anxiety of Influence* (Oxford: Oxford University Press, 1973) and *A Map of Misreading* (Oxford: Oxford University Press, 1975), but also *Ruin the Sacred Truths* (Cambridge, Massachussetts and London: Harvard University Press, 1991). His tropography of influence has been

further systematized by Peter de Bolla, *Harold Bloom: Towards Historical Rhetorics* (London and New York: Routledge, 1988) and suggestively applied to translation in Douglas Robinson, *The Translator's Turn* (John Hopkins' University Press, 1991). Obviously, in translation there is not so much an attempt to persuade of originality as of 'origins', as recognized in readings of Benjamin's 'The Task of the Translator'.

12 M. de Riquer, A. Comas and J. Molas (eds), *La Història de la Literatura Catalana*, 11 vols, (Barcelona: Ariel, 1964–88). I will refer to J. Molas (ed.), *HLC* vols VII–XI, 1986–8. These later volumes aim to account for the modern tradition in Catalan literature, in all its manifestations from journalism to theatre. What is meant here by 'autonomous' art is that which is felt to represent the Catalan-speaking regions rather than anywhere else. Materialist approximations to literary history would not suggest art was in any way 'autonomous' from other social fields and institutions.

13 Quoted in J. Fontcuberta i Gel, 'Als cinquanta anys de 'L'Art de Traduir' de C. A. Jordana', *Revista de Catalunya*, 36 (December 1989), 129.

14 Until recently most studies of the role of translation in Catalan culture, apart from the article mentioned, have tended to be descriptive lists of translations. Since the 1990s, there has been a proliferation of studies on different aspects of translation in the first thirty years of the twentieth century, publication of various Catalan translation readers, as well as interest in translation policy since the transition period of the 1970s and 1980s. Of particular significance is the series published by EUMO, with titles such as *L'art de traduir. Reflexions sobre la traducció al llarg de la història* and *Cent anys de traducció al català*.

15 Shakespeare figures in the work of many of the writers who were to become central to the *Història de la Literatura Catalana*: Joan Maragall, Eugeni d'Ors, Josep Carner, Josep Maria López-Picó, Carles Riba, Cèsar August Jordana, Marià Manent, Josep Maria de Sagarra, Gabriel Ferrater, Terenci Moix, Eduardo Mendoza, Manuel Desclot as well as translators and Hispanic Shakespeare scholars such as Alfons Par, Joan Jaumà, Salvador Oliva, Joan Sellent. In performance, he has been staged by almost every important director in the twentieth century, including Adrià Gual, Maria Aurèlia Capmany, Ventura Pons, Lluís Pasqual, Sergi Belbel, Xavier Albertí, Calixto Bieito and Alex Rigola, as well as being linked to the birth of emblematic theatre companies, such as the Teatre Lliure.

16 Ramon Esquerra, *Shakespeare a Catalunya* (Barcelona: Institució del Teatre, September 1937). First published in *La Revista*, XXI (January–June 1935), 78–111. Henceforward, references will be to the 1937 volume. Alfons Par, *Contribución a la bibliografía española de Shakespeare* (Barcelona: Instituto del Teatro Nacional–Diputación Provincial de Barcelona, March 1930); *Shakespeare en la literatura española*, 2 vols, (Madrid: Victoriano Suárez; Barcelona: Balmes,

1935), and *Representaciones shakespearianas en España*, 2 vols, (Madrid: Victoriano Suárez; Barcelona: Balmes, 1936 and 1940).

17 *El Museo de Familias*, Barcelona: A. Bergnes, 1838–41, IV (1840), 10. Henceforward, *Museo*, volume and year.

18 Par, *Shakespeare* . . ., I, pp. 338–9. The Bergnes article can be found in *Museo*, I (1838), 354. Par places strong emphasis on Bergnes' erudition in comparison with other nineteenth-century commentators on the life and work of Shakespeare, in particular in Catalonia. 'Muy superior, por su sólido conocimiento de las literaturas extranjeras, a cuantos catalanes hasta aquí nos han ocupado y a la mayoría de los que nos ocuparán, nos aparece la venerable figura de Antonio Bergnes de las Casas.' Par, *Shakespeare* . . ., I, p. 331.

19 In another article, 'Shakespeare', *Museo*, II (1839), 381–9, Bergnes appears to qualify the nature of Shakespeare's influence, suggesting the centrality of the Bard is limited to England. Although Shakespeare's greatness for other cultures is reaffirmed, his influence is not considered to be on a par with that of the Classics.

20 Par, *Shakespeare* . . ., I, p. 338. Even where Shakespeare is mentioned, knowledge of him tends to be mediated by other foreign versions. This is the conclusion of Ermanno Caldera in 'L'Influenza di Shakespeare sul Romanticismo spagnolo (A proposito di "Romeo y Julieta" di Solis Ducis)', *Letterature*, III (1980), 41–56. 'È certamente curioso pensare che la fama e l'influenza di Shakespeare durante il romanticisme spagnolo furono in molti casi il prodotto dell'umile attività di letterati aperti alle suggestioni del loro tempo che non avevano mai letto una sola pagina del drammaturgo elisabettiano e che in comune con lui avevano poco puì del titolo di un'opera' (56).

21 Alfons Par, *Lo Rei Lear. Tragedia de Guillem Shakespeare. Traducció de* . . . (Barcelona: Associació Wagneriana, 1912). In his preface to this work, Par accounts for this neglect of Shakespeare by referring to the problematic status of the original texts, evidenced by the heated critical debate surrounding the authenticity of parts of Shakespeare's *oeuvre* at the turn of the century. The role of the New Shakspere Society (*sic*) and the 'British disintegrators' in laying the path for a professionalization of Shakespeare studies, and in fuelling counter claims for the authenticity and continuing centrality of the Bard as cultural 'God' can be further explored in the 'Modernizing Shakespeare' chapter of Hugh Grady, *The Modernist Shakespeare. Critical Texts in a Material World* (Oxford: Clarendon Press, 1994), pp. 28–73.

22 Particular consternation was shown in the tricentenary year of Cervantes' and Shakespeare's death in 1916, which was hardly marked in the case of the latter. Other than Par's *Lear* of 1912 the only Shakespeare translation activity in that decade was Morera i Galícia's publication of some of the sonnets, and there was little extensive commentary, particularly after 1912. In some ways, renewal of interest seems to have come as a result of the neglect of Shakespeare in 1916, which was noted by a number of critics, in

particular Par in the preliminary notes to a study of the life of Shakespeare: 'Per a mi no ha passat pas debades la data del centenari de Shakespeare: ço mateix pugui ésser dit dels lletraferits catalans'. Alfons Par, *Vida de Guillem Shakespeare* (Barcelona: Verdaguer–Domènech, 1916), p. viii. An exception to prove the rule can be found in *El Teatre Català*, 218 (29 April 1916) 152–5, comprising a comparative sketch of the importance of Shakespeare and Cervantes, a bibliographical note on Shakespeare and some miscellaneous considerations on the essence of Shakespeare by Ambrosi Carrión.

23 Esquerra, *Shakespeare* . . ., p. 7. References to further pages will be given within the text.

24 Carles-Jordi Guardiola, 'Shakespeare als països catalans', in J. Molas (ed.), *Diccionari de la Literatura Catalana* (Barcelona: Edicions 62, 1979), pp. 673–4. Just as Esquerra's work is indebted to Par, so are a number of subsequent sketches of the history of Shakespeare translation in Catalonia indebted to Esquerra.

25 Rosa Maria Martínez Ascaso, 'Diàriament, periòdica, sempre Shakespeare', *Cuadernos de traducción e interpretación/Quaderns de traducció i interpretació*, 5–6 (1985), 139.

26 Alfons Par, Shakespeare y el folklore español Palma de Mallorca: Círculo de Estudios, 1931, p. 3. The statement may be compared with the early remark of Eduardo Julià Martínez, 'En España no se ha estudiado ni se estudia a Shakespeare como su inmensa figura merece, y es lo más sensible que semejante afirmación tiene una base cierta: en cantidad no son pocos los que han hablado del vate de Stratford; empero son escasos los que han producido cosa digna de tenerse en cuenta', *Shakespeare en España* (Madrid: Revista de Archivos, Bibliotecas y Museos, 1918), p. 9. Also quoted in Angeles Serrano Ripoll, *Bibliografía shakespeariana en España: crítica y traducción* (Alicante: Instituto de Estudios Alicantinos, 1983), p. 20, before commentary on the continuing shortcomings of Spain in this respect.

27 Michael Bristol, *Shakespeare's America – America's Shakespeare* (London/New York: Routledge, 1990). It is, for instance, often impossible to separate the figuration of Shakespeare as man from Shakespeare as cultural pound sign, and the meaning of the latter has 'multiple and equivocal valences', as Bristol recognizes in his later work, *Big time Shakespeare* (London–New York: Routledge, 1996), p. ix.

28 There are of course always problems with periodization in literature and history, as it is often based on criteria which do not necessarily hold for all the fields of discourse described within a particular period. It is however a useful shorthand to present trends and paradigm shifts in history, as long as it is treated as a shorthand. For periodization of this type I have followed the *HLC* divisions, although my own rewriting of Catalan cultural history in terms of Shakespeare translation will show the boundaries to be far more fluid. *Noucentisme*, for instance, is usually presented as embracing the years 1906–23. Yet it is clear that some of the features associated with the movement can

be traced to a number of nineteenth-century discourses, and that in many ways the model of culture represented by *Noucentisme* remains current long after the dictatorship of Primo de Rivera.

29 One example of the employment of Shakespeare as a symbol of the value and dominance of the English (rather than British) Empire is the fact that in India candidates for the Civil Service were required to sit Shakespeare examinations. See F. Barker, 'Nationalism, nomadism and belonging in Europe: *Coriolanus*', in J. Joughin (ed.), *Shakespeare and National Culture* (Manchester: Manchester University Press, 1997), p. 263, n. 12.

30 Different ways of 'meaning by Shakespeare' are explored by Terence Hawkes in *Meaning by Shakespeare* (London/New York: Routledge, 1992).

31 For the idea of Shakespeare's remains, I am indebted to Courtney Lehmann, *Shakespeare Remains. Theater to Film, Early Modern to Postmodern* (Ithaca/London: Cornell University Press, 2002).

Chapter 1

Constructing a History of Shakespeare Translation in Catalonia

It is just over two hundred years since the first Shakespeare translation was published in Barcelona, heralding a long and surprisingly fruitful relationship between Catalan culture and the Bard. Many of the key Catalan intellectuals of the Romantic period, such as Bergnes de las Casas and Milà i Fontanals, saw in Shakespeare the aesthetic support for a revival in peninsular literature, and it was their work in raising the consciousness of a national spirit in literary culture that ultimately underpinned the Catalan *Renaixença*.[1] At the same time, the economic, demographic and urban expansion of Barcelona in the nineteenth century meant that the French and Italian productions and adaptations of the Englishman's plays that toured Europe were showcased there as well as in Madrid. Indeed, it was in Barcelona that they received the greatest welcome, so much so that by the end of the nineteenth century the main sphere of Shakespeare's influence on the Spanish stage had shifted to Catalonia. Although the first Catalan-language adaptations, many of them comic and popular, did not appear until the last quarter of the nineteenth century, the increase in number and significance of critical responses, and in visits by European companies, paved the way for the first full translations into Catalan. From the 1880s there is not a decade without a new translation of Shakespeare into Catalan, making him the most translated author in the language. Even during the early years of the Franco dictatorship, clandestine editions of new Shakespeare translations were published in Barcelona, and he has continued to be translated, performed and celebrated right up to the present day.

The Catalan fascination with Shakespeare is plain from any survey of the number of translations, adaptations and performances. However, nowadays there is a tendency to see the extent and depth of his reception as self-evident, an inevitable by-product of his unquestionable canonicity, when the path of his incorporation has been far more idiosyncratic. Moreover, the studies that exist of Shakespeare translation in Catalonia tend to take an exclusionary view of the activity, judging translations in terms of how much they live up to the greatness of the original, or as part of a narrative that tests how far Catalan culture has done justice to Shakespeare.[2] Here, I will present a rather different narrative; one that will attempt to incorporate the full range of manifestations of a Catalan Shakespeare, without dismissing non-standard translations or representations. However, whilst I have sought to produce as complete a database of Catalan translation and performance as possible in the appendices at the end of the book, in preparing this chapter I have approached the data from a functional perspective, to identify paradigmatic moments, texts or performances that have influenced subsequent representations. It is these that provide the structure of this chapter.

My study is not, then, the first to attempt to reconstruct a history of Shakespeare translation in Catalonia. In fact there are many texts to which I am both indebted, and hope to have complemented and corrected. To begin to trace the range of translations, I had early recourse to Julià Martínez, Ruppert y Ujaravi and Par, the latter being one of the most important sources of Shakespeare translation bibliography, certainly for the period up to 1935.[3] Par's work also stands out for attempting to contextualize Shakespearian reception and influence, an endeavour which was taken up by Ramon Esquerra in serial form in 1935, producing a volume that was published the year after Par's death. Esquerra's *Shakespeare a Catalunya* was an impressive work of comparative criticism that employed lucid and systematic criteria in evaluating translation quality. Alongside his *Lectures europees*, it is a study that provides ample evidence of the critical sophistication and comparative awareness of the period.[4] More recent bibliographies have added little to the work of Par and Esquerra, except to cite works published after 1936.[5] Some contributions even fail to acknowledge their reliance on earlier sources, or do not fully recognize the extent of their borrowings. Inaccuracies are reproduced, generalizations are rife and many later works contribute to perpetuate certain positivist 'myths' of translation quality. This is the case with Esquerra, Fàbregas and Pessarrodona, all of whom seem to identify unproblematically chronological 'progress' with improvement in the quality of Shakespeare translations. Fàbregas, for instance, reproduces what is basically a precis of Esquerra's work, before adding two or three lines on 'Shakespeare, de 1939 a 1971': 'Després de 1939 es produeix el fet més important en les relacions entre l'obra de Shakespeare i la nostra cultura: les traduccions de Josep Maria de Sagarra' ('After 1939 came the most important event in the relationship between Shakespeare's work and our culture: the translations of Josep Maria de Sagarra').[6] Even today this tendency can be observed in projects such as the 'Shakespeare was here' exhibition, commissioned by the Teatre Lliure for the third Santa Susanna Shakespeare Festival in August 2005, whose main objective was to show the pioneering nature of Shakespearian productions at the Lliure since 1977, and hence the theatre's proximity to the Bard.

These types of evaluations cannot be anything but culturally constructed, a fact which in the case of translation at least has long been recognized. Translations with long afterlives are often linked to shifts in cultural paradigms which have lasting influence. A famous Shakespeare example would be the case of the influence enjoyed by the German Schlegel-Tieck translations on the German literary system in the nineteenth century and on theatrical productions right up to the present day.[7] A comparable case in Catalonia, as I will argue later in this chapter, would have to be Josep Maria de Sagarra and his translations of twenty-eight Shakespeare plays, which for at least two decades following the death of Franco held more cultural weight than Sagarra's original works. With the more recent translations of Salvador Oliva, there have been signs of impending canonization. However, these coincide with a marked proliferation of new translators, adapters and rewriters in the twenty-first century that might indicate a paradigm shift in Shakespeare reception.

In constructing my own chronology, I have sought to present as complete a list as possible of Catalan translations and adaptations of Shakespeare, including prose versions, theatrical productions, fragments in anthologies and magazines as well as full published versions, in order to show the range and extent of Shakespeare translation and reception. The appendices prove the range of versions of Shakespeare to be phenomenal. There are parodies or travesties, prose versions, poetic versions, restructurings, free versions, arrangements, adaptations, variations on a theme, children's versions, popular versions, as well as a long list of theatre collaborations and productions. I have not included all the 'original' works based on Shakespearian themes unless they involved a deliberate recasting of the language of part of the original play or poem, as is the case with Ignasi Iglésias or Josep Millàs-Raurell before the Civil War, and Albert Boadella and Manuel Molins today.[8] Examples of works that have not been included in Appendix A are poems on Shakespearian themes or characters by Josep Carner, Josep Maria de Sagarra and Feliu Formosa amongst others, and novels such as Dídac Ruiz's *Lo boig Macbeth, sacerdot* (1907), Eugeni d'Ors' *Gualba, la de mil veus* (1915) and the more recent *La segona mort de Shakespeare* (1999) by Jordi Mata and *L'ombra de Hamlet* (2000) by Antoni Torreño. Other celebrated revisionings include Joan Perucho's short story, 'Sheyton Barrett, el fantasma de Shakespeare' (1987), and Josep Palau i Fabre's plays *Avui Romea i Julieta* (1986) and *Els mots de Yorick* (1990).

Where possible I have relied on primary evidence to ratify the existence of specific translations, although certain texts, such as one of the nineteenth-century parodies of *Othello*, one or two children's versions and two arrangements of *The Taming of the Shrew*, have been included on the strength of reports in secondary sources. Where adaptations for performance have been used, I have included the author of the adaptation in the table of performances, but have not added the version to the list of translations unless it clearly constitutes a new translation of the play concerned. Of the unpublished translations, available in manuscript or typescript, I have had access to Jaume Massó i Torrent's *Otello* (1906) and a Batiste–Sagarra version of *Un somni d'una nit d'estiu* reconstructed by Josep Anton Codina (1992), as well as Gabriel Ferrater's *Coriolà* (1971), Sagarra's *Les alegres comares* (1959) and Maseras' *Somni d'una nit d'estiu* (1923), which were published. Other unpublished texts included in my chronology have been drawn almost entirely from evidence in periodicals, although Magí Morera i Galícia's two unpublished translations are mentioned in a number of bibliographies, mainly of his work, and I am indebted to Maria Campillo for information on the existence of Cèsar August Jordana's translation of the sonnets during the Civil War, and to Richard Mansell for information and access to some Balearic versions. Such texts are very rarely authoritatively dated, and once again I have had to date them from external references to their completion or projected productions. Whenever I have been unable to verify the existence of certain texts, I follow the secondary source. In certain cases this has caused uncertainty over dating. These infrequent problems will be indicated.

Appendix A offers what I would consider to be the most complete chronological picture of Shakespeare translation in Catalan, in that it includes different editions of the same translation in order to show the cultural durability of certain versions, translators or particular plays. In a similar fashion, where published translations have had prepublication influence on Catalan cultural life, whether in magazine excerpts, projected performances or actual performance, I have dated and included these events in most cases. A problematic case is, of course, that of Sagarra, whose versions should perhaps be dated from the early 1940s, but records are understandably anecdotal. I will reproduce this 'invisible' history here, as the case of Sagarra is perhaps that which has produced most mystification of historical data. Appendix B lists the translators by play, to give a more accessible picture of the relative numbers of versions of each of the plays, within the standard categories: Comedies, Tragedies, Histories, Roman Plays, Problem Plays, Late Plays, Poems. Such exhaustive presentation of data will not be repeated here; instead, the main focus of the chapter will be on broad trends and paradigmatic moments.

Appendix C is a table of Shakespeare productions in Catalan, ordered by date and title of the version. As far as theatrical productions are concerned, the record is far less complete. In some periods there are theatre magazines that provide details even of productions outside Barcelona. In other periods, Catalan theatre magazines are not available or have more limited scope and I have had to rely on other newspapers or periodicals, catalogues from the Institut del Teatre library, the electronic performance database for the 1990s, or monographs and memoirs on theatre history in Catalonia. Record of early performances of Sagarra translations has been drawn from published accounts of Sagarra's life or daily cultural life in Catalonia during the early post-war years of most stringent anti-Catalan censorship. There are a variety of source texts for the Sagarra story, ranging from his own memoirs to books written by his friends. It is one of the few cases where information is often legitimized on an emotional level, and such information is reproduced religiously in essays and articles that consider Sagarra's achievements as a translator. There may indeed have been more clandestine productions, but their current inaccessibility makes it difficult to gauge the extent of their influence on the figuration of Shakespeare in Catalonia, just as it has been impossible fully to uncover the history of amateur productions. I am relying mainly on 'official' or 'market' Shakespeares, Shakespeares who can be clearly identified as having some significant relationship with the cultural process in Catalonia (the process of constructing and reinforcing a Catalan cultural identity), and especially Barcelona. In defence of what might be considered rather a partial version of Catalan transfigurations of Shakespeare, it should be made plain that the construction of cultural and national identity from the second half of the nineteenth century onwards very much centred on Barcelona, and the significance of the city. Such a troping of the city should of course be considered within the context of European modernism, although its origins may be traced to demographic changes from the industrial revolution onwards.[9] Indeed, it is Barcelona's increasing function as a 'desired' metropolis, in particular in relation to the rest of the Catalan-speaking territories and as an alternative to Madrid, that most complicates postcolonial readings of Catalan culture.

Whilst I have endeavoured to include instances of translations and productions in the rest of the Catalan-speaking territories, these contribute only a very small percentage of the overall reception of Shakespeare in Catalan, and for historical reasons have not enjoyed the same cultural weight as those produced in Catalonia. To help contextualize the Catalan story, there is a thesis which compares Shakespeare productions and reception in Barcelona and Madrid.[10] However, it contains many errors of detail and gaps in production history, and does not identify major trends so that, in fact, the true extent of rewritings of the Bard is not shown. The list of translations into Catalan given is also incomplete for the period considered – up to 1970. It is because of the patchy nature of present histories that I have decided to reproduce an accessible overview in this chapter, before going on to trace a fuller historical picture of the figuration of Shakespeare in Catalonia, and its political and cultural significance.

Early Catalan Shakespeares

Alfons Par clearly traces the influence of Shakespeare in Spain to the late eighteenth century; however, the first translation of Shakespeare into Catalan does not come until a century after the first Castilian version. The pioneer Shakespeare was a *Hamlet* by Ramón de la Cruz (1777), although the translation which really brought the English playwright to the attention of late eighteenth and early nineteenth-century Spain is Leandro Fernández de Moratín's rendering of the same play (1798). The reasons for this Catalan 'latecoming' may be attributed in the main to the particular diglossic structure of language use in Catalonia in the early nineteenth century.[11] Although there was interest in Shakespeare, this, like most published cultural criticism, was written down and expressed in Castilian, and for a long period the revival of a literary culture in Catalan was limited to the realms of poetry and the restoration of the medieval tradition of the *Jocs Florals*.[12] Barcelona's increasing importance as a publishing centre, with numerous new ventures springing up alongside traditional houses and printers during the nineteenth century, is reflected in the number of Castilian versions of Shakespeare's plays published from 1804 onwards. Furthermore, the work of Romantic critics helped to pave the way for wider Shakespeare reception. However, notwithstanding the place of Shakespeare in the libraries and schooling of the educated classes, it is the world of theatre that offered the main entry point for the English dramatist. Indeed, it is within the comic tradition of *sainets* that we can perceive perhaps the earliest manifestations of Catalan Shakespeares.[13]

Throughout the century there were visiting tours by foreign theatre companies, usually from Italy but sometimes France, and certain Shakespeare-inspired operas – usually versions of *Othello* or *Macbeth* but sometimes *Romeo and Juliet* or *Falstaff* – would be performed. These in turn led to a spate of parodies or what are often known as 'travesties' of certain plays. In Castilian, Piquet did comic versions of *Othello, Romeo and Juliet, King John* and *Richard III*, but the first Catalan travesties are based on *Othello*.[14] Unlike many Castilian travesties which were based on operatic versions, Catalan versions were largely presented as recastings or spoofs of Italian productions, using what was termed 'macarronic' Italian. They were not then marketed as Catalan-language versions, but were very dependent on the relationships between languages. Generally they pick up on the carnivalesque *charivari* aspects of *Othello* which have been more recently explored in materialist readings of Shakespeare's politics, focusing on food, cultural stereotypes and the grotesque nature of the relationship between Othello and Desdemona, hence the emphasis on the ending of the play.[15] One particular rewriting, that of Antonio Ferrer y Codina became a multipurpose play, which could be contextualized according to the place in which it was performed. Usually staged as *Otel·lo o il moro di Sarrià*, it also appeared in Sant Gervasi as late as 1909 as *Otel·lo o el moro de Sant Gervasi*.

Productions of this comic version thus remained popular into the early years of the twentieth century, and may be held to represent a rather racialist focus on the moor's foreignness in Catalan cultural circles.[16] We can see this type of reading in the carnivalesque reproductions of Enric Borràs' appearance in his numerous performances in Castilian of the role of Othello, as well as in a later anecdote attributed to a theatre in Lleida which was said to have advertised a production of *Othello* followed by a short play called 'Fuera' as 'OTELLO CON LA PIEZA FUERA' ('Othello with his piece out'). Reports occur in the Barcelona press of racist outrage at performances of *Othello* in the United States but these tend to be used to exemplify the stupidity of identifying or mistaking the theatre for real life. However, certainly for the early period of modern Catalan theatre and Shakespeare pseudo-reception, *Othello* is associated far more with the character and particularly the character as embodied by Italian actors. The character is in many ways a fetishized object, whose foreignness is underlined by the language used in the parodies. The play is not in any way considered a model for the Catalan language. In contrast, Shakespeare is credited with being the source for one of the earliest incursions into serious theatre in Catalan in this period, with Victor Balaguer's tragedies: first *Les esposalles de la morta* with its alleged recasting of scenes from *Romeo and Juliet*, then *Coriolanus* and, even more tenuously, *Julius Caesar*.[17] Balaguer's importance in the history of Catalan theatre is attributed by Fàbregas to his mini-tragedies of the late 1870s onwards, a judgement itself authorized by recourse to Balaguer: 'El Balaguer de maduresa només es responsabilitza de la seva obra dramàtica a partir de les *Tragèdies*. En elles plasma l'intent de donar al teatre català unes obres, si breus en extensió, d'un gruix intel·lectual i cultural suficient perquè hom pugui arrenglar-les costat per costat amb el teatre que la burgesia europea consumeix en aquell moment' ('Balaguer later only recognizes his dramatic works from the Tragedies onwards. In these he succeeds in his attempt to give Catalan theatre some plays which, though brief in length, have a cultural and intellectual depth comparable with bourgeois theatre in the rest of Europe').[18]

Even so, none of the plays lays unambiguous claim to Shakespeare as its source, mentioning instead Bandello and Plutarch in many editions.[19] This is surprising given the growing importance of Shakespeare in nineteenth-century Catalan culture, but it may signal a deliberate and calculated omission, especially in the case of the Romeo and Juliet story, which would certainly have been recognized, and of which Balaguer had published an earlier version in Castilian.[20] Like the 'travesties', the version would to a certain extent depend on the audience's knowledge of the legend, the romantic love motif par excellence, and on their recognition of the name of Shakespeare. However, it would also clearly offer an alternative, Catalan version rather than one based on the authoritative intentionality of the Bard that we find in subsequent critical positionings and in translation aesthetics, most of which, however the cultural critic might feel to the contrary, are based on notions of and claims towards fidelity. Thus, the deliberate occlusion of Shakespeare might be seen as a strategy for prioritizing the 'Catalanness' of the texts. As for Shakespeare's *Coriolanus*, this was only once performed in Spain in the nineteenth century, and to no great acclaim, perhaps because of the problematically political nature of its conflict.[21] Its thematic dealings with the legitimacy of government, in particular republican government, set against the impositions of military power and the revolt of the plebeians would have had widespread resonance in the Barcelona of the latter decades of the nineteenth century. There is no evidence that Balaguer's versions of this play and *Julius Caesar* were identified with Shakespeare in that period, although later references are equivocal.

Hamletism and Hamletologies

The beginnings of Shakespeare translation proper focus on a play which might seem unusual given general performance trends in the nineteenth century, and that is *Hamlet*, although it is important to remember that the first Spanish translations of Shakespeare in the 1770s and 1790s were versions of that tragedy, based in turn on French translations, and the first French versions of Shakespeare also took *Hamlet* as their starting point.[22] A review of performance history in Spain shows a significant increase in productions – mainly Italian – of *Hamlet* from the 1850s onwards, especially in Barcelona.[23] Ernesto Rossi was the pioneer Hamlet on the Spanish stage, and his performance of the play in 1868, accompanied by a lecture at the Ateneu Barcelonès, stimulated Shakespeare reception in Barcelona.[24] Versions of excerpts from *Hamlet* were reproduced in periodicals and in the first thesis critiquing a Shakespeare translation (namely, Moratín's *Hamlet*) in the 1880s and 1890s, as well as two book-length translations of the play, one by Arthur Masriera who announced his intentions to translate the complete works into Catalan, the other by Gaietà Soler for the *Escena catòlica*. One of the *Hamlets* rivals Tate's eighteenth-century happy-ending *Lear* in which Cordelia is paired off with Kent. The Catholic priest Gaietà Soler, writing under the pseudonym of Angel Guerra, has his Prince of Denmark reconciled to his uncle and excludes the 'lewd' Ophelia and Gertrude altogether. Both versions were published in 1898, the year that marked the final loss of Spain's empire; only a few years later, *Hamlet* was to be identified by Joan Maragall with the situation of Spain at the *fin de siècle*, its indecision, inability for action and entrapment in the past, associated with critique and philosophy of the 1898 generation.[25] There was a third translation undertaken in the late nineteenth century by Antoni Bulbena i Tosell, which was eventually published in 1910 and reprinted in a popular edition in 1918. Only Gaietà Soler's version was performed in 1898, although there continued to be a number of foreign performances, and it was undoubtedly these that were responsible for the early influence of *Hamlet*. The 'censored' *Hamlet* continued to be played on local stages and in amateur productions long into the twentieth century, as a text fully domesticated using disambiguating language and Catalan verse forms.

There were, however, no mainstream productions of *Hamlet* in Catalan until Terenci Moix's translation was first televised in 1979, although there is record of a number of amateur and provincial productions in Catalan, including one using Morera i Galícia's 1920 translation for the Editorial Catalana.[26] None the less, *Hamlet* remained one of the most cited plays throughout the first three decades of the twentieth century and afterwards. It is, then, perhaps surprising that there were no further translations of *Hamlet* until the publication of Moix's version in 1980, sixty years after that of Morera. This gap, only filled by the reprint of Morera i Galícia's translation in 1964 to coincide with the quatercentenary of Shakespeare's birth, is variously attributed to historical contingency, the length of the play, and even the existence of a Hamlet complex in Catalan culture. Certainly it is a play which seems to attract anxiety about lack and plenitude, absence and excess in the Catalan cultural field, behaving rather like a synecdoche of the figure of Shakespeare, as we shall see in the next chapter. Fascination with *Hamlet* leads to numerous reprints in the late twentieth century, both of Morera's translation and of the 1984 version by Salvador Oliva, and reproductions, to coincide with key productions, anniversaries, and more recently film releases. It may also be perceived as a shadow over the 1930s, with comparison of Francesc Macià's return from exile in 1931 with the shadow of Hamlet.[27] Unsurprisingly, there are numerous plays inspired by the Hamlet story, whether by its thematic content, its cultural impact or the shadow of the eponymous protagonist. Ignasi Iglésias' *L'encís de la glòria* (1917), Millàs-Raurell's *La mare de Hamlet* (1930) and Ramon Vinyes' *Hamlet, dramaturg* (1940s) all confront readers or actors of *Hamlet* with their own experience of 'Hamletic' situations; Josep Palau i Fabre's *Els mots de Yorick* (1990), like Valle-Inclán in *Luces de Bohemia*, and indeed Iglésias, draw on *Hamlet* as a *memento mori* whereas Xavier Albertí (1996) and Manuel Molins' *Una altra Ofèlia* (Another Ophelia, 2003) focus on representation of the relationship with Ophelia, seeking to uncover other voices from the interstices of the Hamlet story; finally, Albert Boadella and *Els Joglars* question the status of *Hamlet* as a model for representation in *Visanteta la Favara* (1989) whilst Albert Munt (2004) looks for Hamlet in the slaughterhouses and Alex Rigola seeks his remains in the *European House* (2005–6).[28] All of these plays appeal to the tradition of popular and amateur representation of the classics, exploring their meaning in a Catalan context, and thus form part of a long-running tradition of readings of *Hamlet* that pull against official cultural forms.

Even so, in commercial terms it was not *Hamlet* that appealed to Catalan audiences in the early decades of the twentieth century and later. Notwithstanding continuing tours by Italian companies (see fig. 1), Catalan periodicals bemoaned the poor turnout by Barcelona theatregoers. *Les esposalles de la morta*, on the other hand, was regularly performed throughout Catalonia, and the early twentieth century marked increasing interest in Shakespeare's comedies. The most popular of these in Catalonia was probably *The Taming of the Shrew*, although the comedies performed in the main Catalan theatres of Barcelona were *Twelfth Night*, *A Midsummer Night's Dream* and *The Merry Wives of Windsor*. The latter are of historical importance because of their association with the figure of Adrià Gual, considered one of the most important theatre practitioners in Catalonia.[29]

Comic Shakespeares

The first decade of the twentieth century has often been identified with interest in a Catalan comic Shakespeare, although there were translations of parts of *Othello* and some of the poems, as well as two translations of *Macbeth* in 1907, one of which, that of Cebrià Montoliu, was particularly successful. The publications of this period were cheap, popular editions, and this appeared to coincide with popular theatrical interest in Shakespeare. The two main publishers of such cheap pocket-library editions were the Biblioteca Popular de l'Avenç and the Biblioteca Popular dels Grans Mestres (BPGM). The first published only Cebrià Montoliu's *Macbeth* in its list of Shakespeare plays, although there were plans to add at least *The Taming of the Shrew* and *Othello* to its collection of world classics.[30] The fact that these plans went unrealized may in part be due to the rival enterprise of the

Biblioteca Popular dels Grans Mestres, which was to publish sixteen Shakespeare translations between 1907 and 1910, by a range of authors many of whom would later become big names in Catalan literature.³¹ Cheap and accessible, many of the BPGM volumes ran to second or third editions. Some translations had been completed before the project started so that in the first year or so they were published almost monthly and marketing was helped by the success of productions of the comedies. The popularity of *The Taming of the Shrew* both in Castilian and Catalan can be observed in the number of versions projected in this period. As well as Farran i Mayoral's, there is record of a performance version by Carles Capdevila and notification of a further translation to be published by Bulbena i Tosell in 1910, although the latter never appeared.³²

The participation of Shakespeare in a revolution in popular publishing was paralleled by the success of versions of some of his plays in the theatre. The fact that the first mainstream Catalan Shakespeare productions were conceived by Adrià Gual led to the identification of Shakespeare with projects to renew Catalan theatre. Usually linked to the aesthetics of Modernisme, Gual's 1898 production of a Goethe play – *Iphigenia in Tauris* – revolutionized the theatrical world, and he subsequently set up the Teatre Intim to put into practice his theatrical ideals. The programmes he chose to influence and renew theatrical practice and taste in Barcelona reflected both advances in modern European theatre and reappropriation of the Classics. Most critics stress the importance of late nineteenth-century dramatists and Molière in his work, but his interest in Shakespeare was strong, and he was inspired by Novelli in his choice of repertoire. The first Shakespeare production by the Teatre Intim was *Nit de reis* in January 1904.³³ The play was put on again in June of the same year, and reproduced in the 1905–6 season. In between, in 1905, came a production of Gual's own play *Les alegres comediantes*, based on *The Merry Wives of Windsor*. This was not to be his only play inspired by one of Shakespeare's stories, as in 1920 he wrote a *Scherzo tràgic* based on the balcony scenes in *Romeo and Juliet*.³⁴ A polymath, his versatile paintings and drawings are both indicative of the long-lasting symbolist flavour of his work and present an original aesthetic vision of Shakespeare in Catalonia.

Perhaps Gual's most important contribution to Shakespeare reception was his production of *El somni d'una nit d'estiu* in

October 1908 (see fig. 2). Translated by Josep Carner, one of the most influential writers of the period, the publication and performance of the *Dream* met with sustained interest in the local press. In part, this was because of the symbolic value invested in the play by Carner, who identified it overtly with the dream of Catalan cultural normality, identifying a number of key areas in which the play could help to shape cultural taste.[35] Mediated by French symbolist readings of Shakespeare's *Dream*, Carner's version tuned in to the dream literature that was rife at the time, and coincided with the romantic, symbolist aesthetic favoured by Gual. Directed and produced by Gual, the *Somni d'una nit d'estiu* was the centrepiece of the Teatre Intim's 1908–9 season, and undoubtedly the most significant Catalan-language spectacle of the year, with numerous references in the press to its exemplary value for Catalan theatre, poetry, diction, decorum and taste. Even in the weeks following the *Setmana Tràgica* in 1909, Eugeni d'Ors advocates the 'civilizing' value of reading Carner's translation.[36] However, it also raised concern about the capabilities of Catalan actors and performers, who at times struggled with the poetic language used by Carner, and about the capacity of Catalan audiences to understand the poetry. Nevertheless, the play's run was extended in the 1908–9 season, to popular acclaim, and it was put on again in 1911. Furthermore, it features prominently in writers' memoirs as providing a glimpse of the cultural heights that could be achieved in the Catalan language.[37]

Another comic production in 1911 was that of *The Merry Wives of Windsor*, also in Carner's translation for the BPGM. Meeting with similar criticism to the *Somni*, it was a flop by comparison. In spite of this, Gual continued to promote Shakespeare through his role as director of the Escola Catalana D'Art Dramàtic (forerunner of the present Institut del Teatre), with a series of readings, conferences and sketches, including a 1915 enactment of Mark Antony's funeral speech from *Julius Caesar*.[38] There is record in the press of projected productions of Shakespeare with the Teatre Intim and the Escola in the 1910s and 1920s, including *The Tempest*, *The Taming of the Shrew*, *Coriolanus* and later *A Midsummer Night's Dream* and *Julius Caesar*.[39] Indeed, Gual even commissioned translations of these plays, including a new *Somni* by Alfons Maseras, suggesting that he responded to the changing linguistic and aesthetic paradigms of the period.[40] However, none of these productions came to fruition, as the never-ending crises in Catalan theatre were exacerbated by epidemics during the First World War, labour struggles after the war, financial hardship during the 1920s, general funding problems and continual complaints of the lack of a regular audience. Moreover, Gual's position as a pioneer of Catalan theatre was, for many, seriously undermined by his perceived willingness to switch to Castilian during the Primo de Rivera dictatorship. The extent and regularities of these crises in Catalan theatre can best be traced in *La Esquella de la Torratxa*, which often contains cartoons or jokes reflecting the latest problem or flop. Indeed, any scrutiny of the press and theatre magazines in the first three decades of the twentieth century shows continuing debate about the future of Catalan theatre, reference to each new crisis, as well as brief eulogies of theatrical oases. Some of these oases were perceived to be the few Shakespeare productions of the period. In subsequent chapters I will explore precisely how Shakespeare was recruited and figured in the debate over Catalan theatre.

Although the Biblioteca Popular dels Grans Mestres enterprise has historical importance, few of the translations outlived their moment, even in cultural memory. Puig i Ferreter's translation of *A Merchant of Venice* was reprinted in 1924, Farran i Mayoral corrected *The Taming of the Shrew* for a production in 1938, yet it was Carner's version of the *A Midsummer Night's Dream* which was to be most cited as a life-changing experience. Even though the series was discontinued after 1910, this did not indicate a sudden lack of interest in Shakespeare. Sections of *Hamlet* were reproduced in debates on theatre, Magí Morera i Galícia published version of the sonnets and longer poems in this period, and there continued to be evidence of interest in staging the plays, although the periodical theatre crises – and hard criticism from other cultural institutions – made such ventures difficult. Most remarkable of all versions of Shakespeare in the period was a rather idiosyncratic translation of *King Lear*, published in 1912, by Alfons Par, in an approximation to medieval Catalan.[41] Although strongly admired for its critical apparatus, and cited along with Cebrià Montoliu's *Macbeth* as the only 'erudite' translations of Shakespeare, Par's *Lo rei Lear* has been generally felt to be unreadable. Indeed, Par is primarily identified and remembered as an academic rather than a 'live' translator.[42] It is tempting to associate this translation with Eugeni D'Or's *Gualba, la de mil veus*, a text which points to the unsatisfactory nature of individual cultural engagement unless attached to wider cultural ideals. The incest motif in the novella must surely be significant here, and it should be noted that the main protagonist is called Alfons.[43]

Noucentisme to Normality?

The next important moment in Shakespeare translation in Catalonia came with the foundation of the Editorial Catalana and its publication of four plays translated by Magí Morera i Galícia between 1918 and 1924. The first, *Coriolà*, although completed in 1915 was finally published a year after another version, that of Joan Perpiñà in 1917.[44] Morera i Galícia's version aroused great critical excitement, unlike that of Perpiñà. The reason for this may be attributed to the former translator's acceptance in the political and cultural circles associated with *Noucentisme*, as well as the publication of the work as part of the Biblioteca Literària, run by Josep Carner.[45] Like Carner's *Somni d'una nit d'estiu* before it, *Coriolà* found itself recruited as the kind of universal value required by Catalan culture in this period. The other three plays in order of publication were *Hamlet*, *Romeo and Juliet* and *The Merchant of Venice*, and homages to Morera i Galícia after his death in 1927 indicate that he intended to translate the complete works. Two further translations were completed, one of which, *Macbeth*, was planned for production in the 1925–6 season after the success of his *El marxant de Venècia*, performed by the Vila–Daví company in 1925.[46] The other unpublished translation, *Julius Caesar*, was commissioned for production by Adrià Gual and there is record that he held the text after Morera i Galícia's death. However, because of the many economic problems Gual experienced during the Primo de Rivera dictatorship and his acquiescence to work in Castilian, he was unable to find the necessary backing for another Shakespeare play. Magí Morera i Galícia by this time was mainly remembered for his Shakespeare translations, and was often presented in histories as the official Catalan translator of Shakespeare. His translations continued to be published throughout the 1920s, and there was even an edition of the sonnets in 1931; however, there was increasing evidence of a shift in paradigm. On the one hand, there was work on translations specifically commissioned for the stage, such as those of Maseras and Farran i Mayoral (who also translated an excerpt of *Henry IV* in 1913); on the other, there was a simultaneous shift towards a new generation of writers, with pioneering focus on adaptations and children's versions. Josep Lleonart published an excerpt translated from *Much Ado about Nothing* in 1925 and other writers of his generation turned their pen to new readings of Shakespeare and his influence. Translations of Lamb's *Tales of Shakespeare* appeared in the popular periodical *Llegiu-me* from 1926 to 1927 and Cèsar August Jordana's produced a children's version of *Macbeth* (which is, incidentally, the only one of his Shakespeare translations to be republished after the Civil War). The late 1920s and early 1930s was also the period of most original adaptations, ranging from the costumed comedies of Salvador Vilaregut and Duran i Tortajada to the tragedy-inspired drama of Millàs-Raurell, to be followed a decade later by Ramon Vinyes's *Hamlet, dramaturg*.[47] The freedom indicated by these adaptations was soon to be lost in Catalonia, and it is notable that apart from translations of European adaptations such as Heiner Müller's *Hamletmachine*, there were no further free Catalan adaptations of the plays, except for children's versions, until the 1980s and the return of democracy.

Again, like the 1980s, one of the main features of the cultural situation in the 1930s was the sense of a break with the past, by which the contributions to Catalan culture of the first three decades of the twentieth century could be re-evaluated. Translation was perceived as having played an important role in the Catalan cultural revival, and for this reason there were calls for new editions of older translations, as well as new translations to fill in the gaps left by the past and to replace pre-1913 orthography. In 1928 Carme Montoriol published a complete translation of all of the sonnets, a full sixteen years before the first translation of the entire cycle into Castilian. In the 1930s, she translated *Cymbeline* and *Twelfth Night*, the second of which was performed in 1935. In some respects, she reflects the more individualistic approach to translation, focusing in the paratexts accompanying her versions on her personal choice of the two plays and reproducing a critical apparatus based on wider reading. Yet she can also be seen as an indication of the increasing participation of women on the literary scene, a scenario which is not repeated again until much later in the twentieth century. The most noteworthy exceptions were Maria Aurèlia Capmany's reimagining of Shakespeare's women in the 1960s,[48] as well as her contribution to the recovery of the Bard's work on the Catalan stage in the 1950s with the Agrupació Dramàtica de Barcelona, and, as an actress, the work of Núria Espert, who played Juliet in Catalan (1953) and then Hamlet in Castilian (1960) in the post-war period. Espert's co-direction of *The Tempest* with the Argentine director Jorge Lavelli at the Romea in 1983 holds the distinction of being one of the most expensive and, because it was funded from the public purse, controversial theatre productions of the decade. Espert played Prospero as a cloaked prestidigitator, projecting Ariel onto the box-like set with reflected lighting from a hand mirror. Whilst Espert was the first Prospero to tread the boards in Barcelona, the first Catalan Lear was also played by a woman, Anna Lizaran, indicating the strength of the Catalan female acting tradition. Women have been responsible for children's versions, focusing on critique of sexual and racial prejudice and have directed some of the more successful productions since the 1990s.[49] Furthermore, there have been one or two recent translators, Sara Mañero and Julia McLucas in Valencia, Aurora Díaz Plaja in Catalonia, as well as Lluïsa Cunillé's rewriting of *Troilus and Cressida* with Xavier Albertí in 2002.

Alongside the individual translations, adaptations and rewritings of the 1930s, which perhaps reflect increasing cultural normality in terms of quantity, there is the somewhat different project of Cèsar August Jordana, associated with a more collective effort to fill cultural gaps, in order to obtain uniformity. His assault on the complete works in the 1930s (which we might compare with Luis Astrana Marín's of the same period) both reflects a change in the literary polysystem and of translation's position within it.[50] His approach indicates less concern with reproducing the style of the original, rather prioritizing the meaning in prose. Most important of all is the ideological aim of demonstrating that Catalan too could have its version of the complete works.[51] Just as wider commentary on the enterprise of translation in this period set it in the context of European thinking on the subject, Shakespeare reception was recontextualized with wide reference to film, foreign productions and criticism. The editions of Jordana's translations were published in hardback, showing professional production values and indicating the buoyancy of the Catalan cultural market. There was a clear expansion in Catalan publishing houses in this period, and this too might be reflected in the desire for new versions, although lack of access to old ones remained an important reason. All of these factors helped to contribute to the situation at the time of the Spanish Civil War, by which time Shakespeare was by far the most translated author into Catalan.[52]

Civil War and its aftermath

As many cultural historians have shown, the outcome of the Spanish Civil War was a disaster for Catalan culture, in particular for cultural expression in the Catalan language. Whilst the Catalan *Generalitat* continued to promote Catalan literature during the conflict, no more translations were published apart from versions of some of the poems by Marià Manent. There was only one production, of *The Taming of the Shrew* in 1938, which once again led to musing on the political possibilities of Shakespeare. Jordana translated the sonnets during the war but these have never been published. His translations of the plays continued to be in print long after the end of the war and were probably known more widely than the subsequent Sagarra translations.[53] The imposition of the Franco regime in Catalonia meant the suppression of the Catalan language and culture, and the destruction of Catalan books in bookshops and publishing houses. Indeed, there was a concerted attempt to reduce Catalan culture to the realm of folklore. However, Shakespeare was to play a part in the clandestine attempts to maintain a Catalan cultural presence, in journals such as *Ariel* and *Poesia*, theatre groups and, above all, in the beginning of a new translation of the complete works by Josep Maria de Sagarra.

An eclectic writer with an aristocratic background, Sagarra had already shown interest in Shakespeare in articles in the 1920s. He was a well-practised playwright by the time of the Civil War, and had discussed the possibility of translating Shakespeare. Appropriately, his first-published poem (1911) was on Ophelia although, as subsequent chapters will show, he was by no means the only Catalan writer to have fallen under the spell of Shakespeare in his youth.[54] Many bibliographies date the Sagarra versions to before the Civil War, as 1935 is the date which appears on the volumes themselves and in Palau.[55] In fact he began the translations early in the 1940s, after his return from Paris, where he spent much of the Civil War. The publication dates of the seven volumes (comprising twenty-eight plays) for the Editorial Calíope are between 1945 and 1953, five of them having been circulated by 1949.[56] The volumes were dated incorrectly because Catalan literary production was severely repressed in the immediate post-war period. However, the volumes themselves are impressively edited and bound considering their illegality. According to contemporary sources, when Sir Henry Thomas showed a volume to a representative of the BBC, he could not believe it was clandestine.[57]

In many ways, then, the translations denote an act of resistance against domination. Their value is celebrated by Sir Henry Thomas in a speech broadcast by BBC radio in London, to alert Catalan exiles there to the enterprise: 'Cinc volums han sortit ja de les traduccions [...] permeteu-me que feliciti coralment Catalunya, ... Sagarra pel seu esplèndid assoliment i ... també tots els qui aneu a sentir les mostres del seu art' ('Five volumes of the translations have already come out ... allow me to heartily congratulate Catalonia, ... Sagarra for his splendid achievement and ... as well as all those who will listen to the examples of his art'). Thirty years on this speech was presented as a landmark in the Catalan struggle to defend the language from 'un veritable genocidi' ('a veritable genocide'), and Henry Thomas himself as an 'il·lustre anglès que es dedicà a aprendre la nostra llengua i a defensar-la' ('illustrious Englishman who applied himself to the learning and defence of our language').[58] On a more personal level, for a time the volumes were Sagarra's only real source of regular income during the post-war period.[59] The translations were commissioned by Salvador Martí, but his later loss of interest in bringing out the volumes (Sagarra had been translating one per month due to financial hardship) led the writer to rebuy and renegotiate the rights with Félix Millet, hence the creation of the publishing house Calíope and their eventual publication.

Although individual translations were completed before the publication dates for each volume, I have decided not to reproduce separate dates for each play. There are a number which can be dated from anecdotal evidence, but it is clear that the only ones that had any immediate cultural significance, apart from the very fact of their enforced clandestinity, were those which gave rise to readings or private productions before 1946. The most quoted example is that of a performance of *The Merchant of Venice* in 1944, although there is also record of a version of *The Tempest* and plans to put on *Love's Labour's Lost* and *Richard III*.[60] The print run of the volumes themselves was so small that the existence of the translations would not have been widely known, and they were slow to sell.[61] Yet they symbolized the attempts to continue the cultural heritage recovered before the Civil War by many intellectuals who remained in Catalonia, and gave hope to those in exile. Josep Manyé remembers how his purchase of the clandestine translations in England fuelled his faith in the future of Catalonia in a particularly dark period, and this underpins his answer to the question 'Per què Shakespeare en Català?'. The only other Shakespeare of the period, Vinyes' reimagining of the Hamlet story would not have been known at all, as it was written in exile and remained unpublished until the late 1980s.[62] It has, however, been included in appendix A, because of its historical importance as a record of the political and cultural significance of *Hamlet* in Catalonia and the conflict it throws into relief between the different actors in that culture. Set within the realist environment of a petit-bourgeois comedy of manners, rather like Millàs-Raurell's *La mare de Hamlet* and the Vilaregut versions of Shakespeare, Vinyes presents an embryonic *Hamlet* situation, revolving around issues of a mother's unfaithfulness, a son's ambiguous love, questions of origins, identity and inheritance. For the Hamlet of this play, one of the main anxieties is the fact of his name, leading to reflection upon the question of how far our destiny is within our control. This Hamlet learns to struggle against the material world around him, including that of the Professor of Literature who only values repetition of the past, and ultimately stands for the search for spiritual autonomy to match the recognition of one's difference. The political implications of such a process, in the context in which the play was composed, are unavoidable, for just as Vinyes' Hamlet is met with misunderstanding and criticism, the play itself is destined to over forty years of silence.

The Age of Sagarra

The lifting of the the worst of the repressive measures in the 1950s meant that there was more scope for publishing in Catalan in that decade, with versions of Shakespeare's poems by Marià Manent and Joan Triadú, as well as the publication of three volumes of

Sagarra's translations (comprising only nine plays). However, there was not a dramatic increase in performances, only *Romeo i Julieta* in 1953, with Núria Espert, and *Les alegres casades de Windsor* in two separate productions, one of which, by the *Agrupació Dramàtica de Barcelona*, amongst the earliest examples of *Teatre Independent* in Barcelona, is often remembered by actors of that generation as a formative moment in post-war Catalan theatre. The 1960s brought the quatercentenary of the birth of Shakespeare; the decade when there was least translation activity, but a notable increase in theatrical productions. None the less, few of these dramatic encounters were considered particularly fruitful apart from the 1964 staging of *The Merchant of Venice*, directed by Maria Aurèlia Capmany, and Josep Anton Codina's 1968 production of *Julius Caesar*.[63] Núria Espert's performance of the role of Hamlet in 1964 was a source of controversy, leading to an audience revolt on one night. Although the production was in Castilian, it contributed to consolidate Espert's fame as the foremost Catalan actress, and was remembered as a valuable precursor by Lluís Homar when he directed and took the lead in a Catalan version of the play in 1999.[64] The centenary year also saw the revised publication of Morera i Galícia's *Hamlet*, and an English-language performance of *Othello* at the British Institute in Barcelona. 1968 brought an attempt to recuperate one of the earliest players in Shakespeare's history in Catalan, with Fàbregas' edition of Balaguer's *Les esposalles de la morta*. In 1969, eight years after the death of his father, Joan de Sagarra brought out an edition of *Ricard III*, with a view to republishing all twenty-eight translations with the Editorial Selecta. However, he would have to wait until the end of the 1970s to see his dream realized, via the cheaper editions co-produced by the Editorial Bruguera and the Institut del Teatre.

In the 1970s there was an increase in productions, mainly using Sagarra's translations. However, divided opinion over the value of his translations both delayed publication of accessible new editions of individual plays, with accompanying critical apparatus, and led to the development of some projects to produce alternative versions.[65] By the early 1990s, these reservations had been overcome by the extent of the Sagarra myth, in particular his popularity amongst actors seeking a classical Catalan-language repertoire to compare with other national theatres. Until relatively recently, many booksellers had only heard of

Shakespeare translations by Sagarra although, when pushed, they would often be able to produce versions by Salvador Oliva. Joan Triadú's sonnets were reprinted in 1970, as were Carme Montoriol's in a specialist facsimile edition in 1980. Other translations of the 1970s include Gabriel Ferrater's *Coriolà*, commissioned for performance but incomplete at the time of his death, Jordi Voltas' and Aurora Díaz Plaja's versions of *The Taming of the Shrew*, *The Merchant of Venice* and later *A Midsummer Night's Dream* for children, some of them based on *Cavall Fort* projects, and a new *Macbeth*, by Jordi Pujol Cofan, performed outside Barcelona.

The early 1970s saw a number of productions for children in conjunction with the children's magazine *Cavall Fort*, clearly marketed as part of an important educational programme and signalling an expansion in ways of popularizing the theatre.[66] Marià Villangómez translated some sonnets in the late 1970s and Terenci Moix produced two translations of *Hamlet*, in poetry and prose. Whilst there are many anecdotes about the idiosyncrasies of the poetic version, and Moix's publisher persuaded him to publish a prose translation, the productions of the play caused a great stir as a multimedia event that was recognized throughout Spain. The translation has had few subsequent outings, partly due to the general lack of stage *Hamlets* in Catalan, partly due to the baroque nature of the version. It was used for a television film broadcast in 1979, which became one of the emblematic productions of the newly-created *Televisió de Catalunya*. Like other Shakespeare firsts, it was broadcast on a key cultural date, Easter Monday. The early 1980s broadcasts in the BBC Shakespeare series translated by Salvador Oliva were also given holiday screenings.

At the same time, Sagarra's reputation in the world of theatre was slowly being consolidated, mainly with productions of the comedies, although *Othello*, *Coriolanus* and *Titus Andronicus* were also staged in the 1970s. The 1977 Teatre Lliure production of the *Titus* was repeated on a number of occasions, and even went on tour to Madrid (see figs. 3–4). Directed by Fabià Puigserver, it is the only Catalan production to merit an entry in *Looking at Shakespeare*, and has achieved legendary status.[67] Both *Titus* and the later version of *As You Like It*, directed by Lluís Pasqual, were explicitly marketed as a Shakespeare for a new generation, with up-to-date sets and dynamic dramaturgy. Similar policies were shown in some productions of the 1990s, ranging from *The Merchant of Venice* (Sergi Belbel) to *El rei Joan* (Calixto Bieito) and even the Catalan version of the *Abridged Works of Shakespeare* in 1996, although it continued to be the romantic comedies which attracted the most popular acclaim. If by 1977, Xavier Fàbregas was able to write of the period from 1968 onwards as one in which Shakespeare's influence on the Catalan stage was unbroken, this was amply confirmed in the decades that followed.[68] There has hardly been a year since when there was not at least one production of a Shakespeare play in Catalan, and certain years, notably 1996, 2001–2 and 2004, have seen numerous versions.

It was not until the end of the 1970s that there was a return to Sagarra in the publishing world. Joan de Sagarra regained the rights to his father's translations from *Selecta*, and having allowed *King John* to be published with *Estudios escénicos*, agreed to the publication of a series of all twenty-eight plays by the Institut del Teatre, with the Editorial Bruguera (although he had originally hoped for a classic edition of the Complete Works). From 1977 onwards there was regular propaganda underlining the value of the Sagarra translations being re-released in popular versions for Catalonia's cultural recovery. Xavier Fàbregas, for instance, denounced the unavailability of the Sagarra translations, answering the question of where they might be with the following: 'Les tenim tancades amb pany i clau . . . Si fòssim a l'Edat mitjana, ja tindríem un equip de monjos benedictins traient còpies; ara els monjos han estat substituits per les fotocopiadores, que surten més bé de preu, encara que no il·luminin' ('We have them hidden away under lock and key . . . If we lived in the Middle Ages, we would already have a team of Benedictine monks taking copies of them; now the monks have been substituted by photocopiers, which are cheaper, although they don't illuminate the texts').[69] The intention of Xavier Fàbregas at the Institut del Teatre was to make the translations available once more in editions accessible to schoolchildren and university students: 'I és a partir d'ells que hem de guanyar la normalitat nostra de cada dia, no a partir de l'especialista' ('And it is from them that we will achieve our daily normality, not from the specialist').[70] Terenci Moix explicitly added his work in translating *Hamlet* to the enterprise associated with Sagarra.[71] Furthermore, in the same year that publication of the series began, with *Romeo and Juliet* (also the first of Salvador Oliva's translations of the complete

Constructing a History of Shakespeare Translation in Catalonia 43

works of Shakespeare to be published), there was an exhibition celebrating Shakespeare, which ran for twenty-six days at the Saló Tinell in 1979, and was accompanied by a number of lectures, articles and other events at various venues, including the British Council, intended to bring Shakespeare – and mainly Sagarra – back to the attention of the Catalan public. These *Dies de Shakespeare a Barcelona* were celebrated in the Catalan press as follows:

> Confiem que aquesta cortesia de Barcelona en acollir Shakespeare fructifiqui en un interés per la seva obra, però sobretot que a hores d'ara comenci un renaixement de traduccions al català del gran clàssic. D'aquest moviment pot ser el punt de partida la reimpressió en edicions a l'abast de tothom, de les traduccions d'en Sagarra, a punt de publicar-se, i la versió que Terenci Moix ha fet de *Hamlet*.[72]

> (We trust that this courtesy shown by Barcelona in receiving Shakespeare might bear fruit in an interest in his work, but above all that there should now begin to be a renaissance of translation of this great classic into Catalan. The starting point for this movement might be the imminent publication of Sagarra's translations in cheap and accessible editions, as well as Terenci Moix's version of *Hamlet*).

Fàbregas' original plan to publish each play with a prologue by an important Catalan writer was not fulfilled when the series eventually began to appear in 1979. The plays do have introductions, but these tend to be rather superficial and even inaccurate at times. Still it seemed that the 'etapa de provisionalitat' had not been overcome, and Fàbregas' 1977 call for funds was not fully heard.[73]

1980s and 1990s

A glance at Appendix A for the 1980s shows quite a remarkable situation in which there are three translators published as classic series, Sagarra, Morera and, most importantly, Salvador Oliva, who began publication of his translations in 1984. In many ways, this situation gives the lie to the old adage that each generation requires its own translation of the classics. What the example of Shakespeare in contemporary Catalonia shows is that different translations are used or redeployed for different purposes. Oliva was commissioned by TV3 and translated the plays with the BBC versions in mind, for his texts were to be used as the basis for dubbing and subtitling.[74] The plays themselves were broadcast twice, first with subtitles then dubbed a month later, and the transmission schedule was originally fixed by the BBC for the whole of Europe at a play every two months. Although at first 'Vicens Vives' intended to publish the ten most popular plays only, they finally decided to release the complete works, with the publication of each play taking place in parallel to the television broadcasts. Significantly, the first play, *Romeo and Juliet*, was scheduled for 23 April 1984, Saint George's Day, one of the most important celebrations in the Catalan cultural calendar, but also the day on which Shakespeare is supposed to have died.[75] The publication of the remaining volumes soon fell out of step with the broadcasts, the final play coming out in 1992. All the versions were and remain fairly accessible in price and availability. The Sagarra volumes were originally priced at 175 pesetas and hence were significantly cheaper than the 'Vicens Vives' ones at 495 pesetas, although the prices of both on the open market have risen significantly. The 'Vicens Vives' collection could also be ordered by subscription, and is far more reminiscent in its binding of the book club or encyclopaedia classic. The Morera i Galícia versions were published in the cheap paperback editions of the 'Millors Obres de la Literatura Universal', co-financed by 'La Caixa', primarily for accessibility. The popular marketing of the Sagarra and Oliva translations is surely no better signalled than by the fact that both series begin with *Romeo and Juliet*. According to John Beattie the most readily available versions of Shakespeare in Spain in the 1990s were those of Sagarra, Oliva and Valverde.[76]

Translations of the sonnets and poems from the plays were reproduced in anthologies – including a Catalan version of the anthology which went on sale after the film *Dead Poets Society* (1989). Increasingly in the 1990s, publication of specific works responded to other theatre or media events, such as the release of Mel Gibson's and subsequently Kenneth Branagh's film versions of *Hamlet*, and specific productions in Barcelona theatres.[77] Re-evaluation of Sagarra led to his translations being republished as part of his complete works in hardback and, after the commemoration of the centenary of his birth, in paperback. Second editions of the single plays have been published in the

1990s with more attractive covers and Oliva has revised his own translations for publication with the Universitat Pompeu Fabra. The editorial battle as to who is *the* Shakespeare translator continues, although Sagarra was easily the winner, at least until the end of 1990s. Whilst Oliva won prizes for his translations, Sagarra's versions were by far the most popular in the theatre. Late twentieth-century interest in Morera i Galícia is harder to explain. On the one hand, it should be seen as part of the growing trend to recuperate and re-evaluate the past, filling in gaps in the Catalan cultural tradition. Yet it might also reflect a marketing ploy, to cash in on a translation that is out of copyright, as in the case of the MOLU edition of Morera's *Hamlet*, which was brought out in hardback for the release of Branagh's film. Most importantly, it reminds us of the different expectations and associations with the name of Shakespeare.[78]

Notwithstanding the increasing criticism of Sagarra's versions, many actors continue to cite them as Catalan classics, as examples of the few poetic texts in the theatre repertory. Many readers and theatregoers do not expect Shakespeare to sound like a contemporary. At the same time, there has been increasing consciousness of the losses in subordinating meaning to versification, mainly as a result of Oliva's pronouncements on his task as a translator. Whilst his concerns have filtered through to directors and critics, and he is often invited to advise on linguistic questions in the productions which use his translations, his versions are generally admired for being correct rather than inspiring. The lack of consolidation of his position on the Catalan stage might perhaps explain recent publication of new editions of his translations, in volumes of three with introductions by Northrop Frye and Oliva himself, as hardback library classics by the Universitat Pompeu Fabra and Destino. Directors who recognize a problem with the Sagarra texts, particularly for versions of the tragedies or plays that he did not translate, now tend to commission new translations or adapt existing versions. So, Alex Rigola draws on Oliva for *Titus Andronicus*, *Julius Caesar* and *Richard III*, consulting him on dramaturgical matters, but adapting the version to suit his aesthetic vision. Other directors have drawn on new work by Manel Delgado, Eduardo Mendoza and Joan Sellent. Indeed, even Calixto Bieito, who, amidst his considerable Shakespeare output, directed an acclaimed version of *King John* and a more controversial *Macbeth* in translation by

Sagarra, turned to Sellent for his 2004 production of *King Lear*. There have also been numerous adaptations of the plays, and productions using sections from different translators, indicating increasing awareness of the range of translations available in Catalan. This has meant that at times the name of the translator is not given in production details, particularly for amateur stagings, and that this is increasingly replaced with the name of an adapter. At the same time, recent translators show awareness of a tradition of Shakespeare translation into Catalan, often aligning themselves with particular precursors. So, for instance, whilst Oliva pays lip service to the achievement of Carner, he views the liberties the poet takes with the original to be unacceptable in contemporary translation practice. Berating Sagarra for his subordination of meaning to verse form, and reliance on French and Castilian mediating texts, Oliva instead looks to Gabriel Ferrater as his primary influence. This is the tradition in which Sellent places himself, too, acknowledging the influence of Oliva and Ferrater in his approach to prosody. In contrast, Delgado, Mendoza and Moix all express their admiration of Sagarra.

Performance History

Many productions from the 1960s onwards have involved some revision of the Sagarra translations, or an amalgam of Carner and Sagarra, such as that of Jaume Batiste for *Cavall Fort*. There were also 'new' versions, involving rewrites by writers and directors as diverse as Mendoza, Graells and Pep Cruz. These versions were rarely published and again used Sagarra as their main source. Even in productions that involved a variety of Shakespeare texts, Sagarra was for the most part preferred, except for plays which he did not translate, such as *Hamlet*. Then Oliva or Moix were used for the most part, until Homar's production of *Hamlet* in 1999. A divergence from this trend can be found in Parcerisas' anthology of English and North American poetry, where a variety of translators are included, including a couple of sonnets by Oliva and part of Maseras' *Somni*. The policy here may have had something to do with copyright, hence the limited presence of Sagarra, as well as denoting a desire to present the range of approximations to Shakespeare in Catalan. For it is the recuperation of a rich and diverse translation history which is often explicitly used to temper the perceived lacks or failings in Catalan culture. This, together with the constant need to 'return to the great texts', as Terenci Moix would have it, in 'the struggle for communication with the public', opens up the vista of Shakespeare reception and figuration in Catalonia.[79] He is a figure whose classic status can aid artistic communication, whose representations in Catalan can be held as examples of successful literary and linguistic expression and who, transfigured, may become a Catalan figure. So we may begin to understand how and why Moix might write that 'en cualquier literatura normalizada las traducciones de Sagarra deberían ser lectura obligatoria' ('in any normal literature Sagarra's translations would be required reading').[80]

The range and variety of Shakespeare productions since the 1980s is undoubtedly a spin-off of this situation, with Shakespeare increasingly available on the market and, in particular with Sagarra, in such very cheap editions. Versions of the comedies achieved enormous successes in translation by Sagarra, although the tragedies and late plays are often presented as only partial or adequate. Critics in the main complained of a lack of resources, or of trained actors, rather than attacking the quality of the translations or the size of the theatregoing public. However, productions very rarely enjoyed long runs, tending to be put on at festivals, a factor which must have affected the viability of protracted rehearsal periods and large investments. The main exceptions to this rule for Shakespeare have been the plays from the Teatre Lliure tradition, which went on long tours, especially the more recent adaptations by Alex Rigola, who has created a permanent company at the new Lliure. The work of Calixto Bieito has also been instrumental in introducing new approaches to Shakespeare. Beginning with more or less aleatory versions of the comedies, *Els dos cavallers de Verona* and *Somni d'una nit d'estiu*, he achieved a breakthrough with his version of *King John*, which responded to the political corruption of the time in Spain. Increasing recognition of his dramaturgical talents led him to be invited as a director to work internationally, and this led to his infamous *Macbeth*, originally devised as *Macbett* with a German company in Saltzberg, followed by a *Hamlet* with the Birmingham Rep, showcased at the Edinburgh Festival, and most recently the first full production of *King Lear* to tread the Catalan boards.

The end of the millennium saw a number of very successful productions of Shakespeare's tragedies, often in new translations. First of all, Lluís Homar approached Joan Sellent to produce a new translation of *Hamlet* for production in 1999. Admiration of this version led him to be invited to produce a translation of *Coriolanus* for the Teatre Nacional de Catalunya in 2001–2, even though Salvador Oliva is one of the official translators there. Meanwhile, at the Teatre Lliure there have been numerous stagings, including three by Alex Rigola, using revised Oliva translations, a *Romeo and Juliet* by Delgado and a *Troilus and Cressida* by Xavier Albertí and Lluïsa Cunillé. Whilst these most recent productions have often been characterized by iconoclastic direction, most especially in La Fura dels Baus' version of *Macbeth*, which toured as *OBS*, but also in the internationally-acclaimed work of Calixto Bieito and Alex Rigola, in general there has been renewed interest in the importance of Shakespeare's language, with increasing appreciation of clear and contemporary translations for the stage. Significantly, both Bieito and Rigola have been accused by critics of failing to respect the language and smothering it in visual theatrics.

Productions have also been influenced by foreign theatre companies on tour in Spain. Directors often write of the influence of Brook, Bergman and Strehler, as well as the visits of the RSC and Cheek by Jowl in the 1980s and 1990s.[81] In some ways, these companies are seen to represent opposing patterns for Catalan theatre to follow in producing their own Shakespeares: the first only being partially emulated, such grandiose productions being, until recently, beyond the scope of Catalan theatres. However, the second company has been described as a very positive influence on 1990s productions, in particular on two plays at the *Festival Grec* in 1995, versions of Sagarra's translations of *King John* and *Love's Labours Lost*. A further influence on Catalan versions were the stagings in Castilian that reached Barcelona, although until the 1980s they mainly inspired the sense of a need for Catalan productions, and were not considered particularly innovative. It was to be landmarks like Pasqual's *Julius Caesar* for the Centro Dramático Nacional (1988), which toured to the Grec in Barcelona, that made Castilian versions became a significant point of reference. Appreciation was also shown for the Basque director Helena Pimienta's versions of Shakespeare with Ur Teatro, especially *Un sueño de una noche de verano* and *Trabajos de amor*

Constructing a History of Shakespeare Translation in Catalonia 49

perdidos, performed in Barcelona in 1993 and 1998 respectively. Shakespeare productions certainly peaked in number in those years, and after a lull in 1997 and 1999, this trend has largely continued, responding in part to the spate of international films, and the influence of Branagh and Luhrman, in particular. However, whilst for a time the paradigm was such that anything English was perhaps over-respected, or treated with awe, as for instance Tamzin Townsend's production of *Macbeth* in the *Festival Grec* in 1996, the last years of the twentieth century began to see a move towards more transgressive representations, as we have seen. In fact one director, Calixto Bieito, even directed an English *Hamlet* at the Edinburgh Festival.

The New Paradigm

The appearance of new translators from the late 1990s onwards has begun to dislodge Sagarra in the theatre, leading to his translations being sold off cheaply at the Diputació bookshop in Barcelona. However, they are still widely used, in many ways because his translations are available so cheaply. At the same time, versions for children and for schools of popular plays such as *A Midsummer Night's Dream* and *Romeo and Juliet* have contributed to an increase in amateur stagings of the plays. Above all, there has begun to be a shift away from representations of Sagarra as the Catalan Shakespeare, capable of proving Catalan cultural sufficiency and achievement on an international scale to a more language-centred focus on producing equivalent effects in contemporary Catalan, whilst remaining close to the meaning of the original. Both Oliva and Sellent are accomplished linguists familiar with contemporary translation theory. In many ways, they represent what the Instituto Shakespeare–Cátedra venture in Valencia claimed itself to be. Through lectures and metatexts they are able both to defend their practice and influence taste and expectations of what Shakespeare in Catalan should be. Furthermore, there have been a number of erudite and/or academic translators of the sonnets in recent years, from Gerard Vergés and his parallel edition with historical introduction in 1993 to Oliva's triple version, containing the original, a literal and a poetic translation in 2003, but also Joan Jaumà, the professor of English at the Universitat Autònoma de Barcelona, and Nicolau

Dols, a translation theory specialist at the Universitat de les Illes Balears. In the world of theatre, this shift in paradigm has made its presence felt, too, either through intervention to correct Sagarra's mores or through the commissioning of new translations. So, for instance, Lluís Homar cites Núria Espert's advice – 'Es molt important qui et faci la versió' ('It's very important who does the version') – in his decision to ask Joan Sellent to produce a new translation of Hamlet. And Calixto Bieito, once renowned and/or reviled for his subordination of language to visual effect in his dramaturgical revisionings of Shakespeare's plays, indicated new commitment to the importance of the play text in his choice of Sellent for the new version of *King Lear*.[82]

This is far from the whole story, however. In many ways, the trends identified at the beginning of the twentieth century continue. Comedies, and in particular the metatheatrical comedies continue to be the most popular choices for performance. One of the most successful Shakespeare's of the past decade was, in fact, Àngel Llàcer's production of *Un somni d'una nit d'estiu* in 2002-3, and the 2006 edition of the Santa Susanna Shakespeare Festival focuses on readings of *A Midsummer Night's Dream*. However, their prevalence is perhaps more marginal than in the 1960s, 1970s and 1980s. This is not because there are less *Somnis* – on the contrary, *A Midsummer Night's Dream* is now easily the most popular play and, apparently, the most ripe for domestication – but because there has been an explosion in versions of the tragedies since the late 1990s. It is the directors most associated with this shift towards the tragedies who might be held most responsible for a paradigm shift in performance terms. The dramaturgical originality of Calixto Bieito's and Alex Rigola's stagings of *Macbeth, Hamlet* and *King Lear*, and *Titus Andronicus, Julius Caesar* and *Richard III* has gained international recognition and led to numerous invitations and tours beyond the Catalan border. Behind them we find both the influence of non-Catalan productions, and the experimentation of Fabià Puigserver and Lluís Pasqual, as well as Xavier Albertí's adaptations in the 1990s (of *Othello, Hamlet* and *Macbeth*), and director's workshops at the Institut del Teatre. Taken alongside renewed attention to the language of the texts, to their speakability, whether through domestication or not, it is possible to perceive a shift in relationship to Shakespeare in the Catalan theatre.

Whereas at the beginning of the twentieth century and under Franco, the ideal of professional productions of Shakespeare's plays was a faraway dream, and for a long period foreign and above all English Shakespeares were approached and received with deference, nowadays there is more cultural confidence in the value, adequacy and even originality of Catalan approximations. Indeed, it is the productions which fail to give material form to their own reading and vision, like Homar's *Hamlet*, like Lavaudant's *Coriolà*, but also Peter Brook's recent *Hamlet*, that are most criticized. The most visible signs of this development are not primarily Bieito's or Rigola's impact on the international stage, for these directors receive their fair share of criticism for what some critics consider to be their flagrant and excessive subordination of language to the visual, but the regular appearance in the Catalan repertoire of plays that would have been unimaginable even in the mid 1990s because of their reliance on strong ensemble casts, such as *Coriolanus* and *King Lear*, as well as the creation of the annual Santa Susanna Shakespeare Festival in the summer of 2003.[83] The first and only Shakespeare festival in Spain, it is solid indication of Catalonia's urge to compete in the arena of European Shakespeares. Catalan is now, then, globally recognized as one of the languages of Shakespeare. However, and paradoxically, this is at a time when Catalonia is undergoing rapid demographic changes, and when there are increasing numbers of amateur Shakespeare plays in Castilian and in English.[84] Furthermore, increasing linguistic conflict in Barcelona, and political wranglings about the shape and direction of culture, have led some of the more emblematic figures of Catalan theatre to distance themselves from the Catalan cultural scene. So it is that Lluís Pasqual's project to stage *The Tempest* and *Hamlet* at the International Forum of Cultures in 2004 was finally realized in 2005, in Castilian, and in the Basque Country (see fig. 5). When he brought the productions to the Festival Grec in the summer of 2006, they were met with high expectations from Catalan cultural world.

Catalan Shakespeares beyond Catalonia

Outside Catalonia there have been fewer translations and productions in Catalan, mainly due to the conditions of Catalan cultural production in the other Catalan-speaking territories. In the Balearic Islands, we find the example of Marià Villangómez, who translated sonnets in the post-war period, as well as a version of *A Midsummer Night's Dream* that was performed in Eivissa in 1989. More recently there have been some co-productions between Catalonia and Mallorca, and *Iguana Teatre* have staged two very successful productions, which toured the Catalan-speaking territories. In Valencia, there have been translations for the school market, such as those published by Editorial 3 i 4, and two translations for specific productions: Sara Mañero's version of *The Comedy of Errors* and a 1991 version of *Macbeth* from within the *Instituto Shakespeare*. Apart from these, some of the bigger productions toured to Valencia, and *Els Joglars* worked with Valencian actors in putting together *Visanteta la Favara*. Many Catalan Shakespeares have gone on successful tours across the rest of Spain and Europe, although some of the more experimental work, such as *La Fura dels Baus' OBs* and La Cubana's *La Tempestat* met with disapproval or hostility. Whilst non-Catalan directors have often been invited to work on Shakespearian projects in Catalonia, such as Helena Pimienta and Georges Lavaudant at the Teatre Nacional de Catalunya, these projects often led to a subordination of language to visual effect. In many ways, then, recent re-evaluation of Shakespeare's language in Catalan is a sign of decolonization and cultural self-sufficiency. At the same time, however, directors are increasingly open to embracing other languages on the Catalan stage, both to reflect the linguistic diversity of the Catalan-speaking regions and to achieve greater recognition on the international stage.

NOTES

[1] This is the name given to the process of linguistic and cultural revival that took place in the Catalan-speaking territories – Catalonia, Valencia, Balearic Islands, Roussillon – during the nineteenth century. Beginning with a few intellectuals who used Catalan or defended or promoted its use, by the 1870s there was clearly a strong movement amongst the elites to recover a supposedly lost or suppressed identity.

[2] Indeed, Maria Delgado suggests that this has hampered reception of more radical work with the Bard in performance, such as Alex

Constructing a History of Shakespeare Translation in Catalonia 53

Rigola's *Ricard 3er* and *European House* (based on *Hamlet*) or Calixto Bieito's *Macbeth* and *King Lear*. See Maria Delgado, 'Journeys of Cultural Transference: Calixto Bieito's Multilingual Shakespeares', *Modern Language Review*, 102 (2006), 106–50.

3   Julià Martínez, *Shakespeare* (1918) and Ricardo Ruppert y Ujaravi, *Shakespeare en España* (Madrid: Revista de Archivos, Bibliotecas y Museos, 1920). Par's five volumes on Shakespeare history in Spain proved invaluable, particularly for the record of nineteenth-century editions of translations, many of which are now difficult to obtain. In preparing this chapter, and the appendices, I had most recourse to Par, *Contribución*, Par, *Shakespeare*, II, and Par, *Representaciones*, II.

4   Serialized in *La Revista*, *Shakespeare a Catalunya* was eventually published as a volume in 1937. *Lectures europees* came out in 1936 (Barcelona: 'La Revista', 1936).

5   Publications consulted include: José Manuel González Fernández de Sevilla (ed.), *Shakespeare en España. Crítica, traducciones y representaciones* (Zaragoza: Pórtico–Universidad de Alicante, 1993); Serrano Ripoll, *Bibliografía* (1983); Xavier Fàbregas, 'Shakespeare a Catalunya', *Estudios escénicos*, 17 (July 1973), 59–64; and Marta Pessarrodona, 'Shakespeare a Catalunya', *Avui*, 170 (9 May 1984), I–II. There is a more complete list in the bibliography under 'Shakespeare Translation Histories, Bibliographies and Chronologies'.

6   Fàbregas, 'Shakespeare', 64.

7   The institutional dominance of the Schlegel-Tieck versions was critiqued in the 1982–3 Grüber production of *Hamlet*, discussed in 'Self-consuming artifact: *Hamlet* in West Berlin', from Johannes Birringer, *Theatre, Theory, Postmodernism* (Bloomington/Indianapolis: Indiana University Press, 1991), pp. 102–12.

8   The works, respectively, are *L'encís de la glòria* (1917) and *La mare de Hamlet* (1931), *Visanteta la favara* (1989) and *Una altra Ofèlia* (2003).

9   According to Xavier Fàbregas, 'El ventall dels esbarjos s'obre àmpliament durant el modernisme, sobretot a Barcelona que, pel seu volum demogràfic, és el lloc on es couen les transformacions i sorgeix la nova imatge del país'. From 'El teatre a tombant de segle (1874–1909)', *L'Avenç*, 22 (December 1979), 18.

10 Eva Maria Tussetschläger, *Shakespeare-Aufführungen im spanischen Theater. Madrid und Barcelona* (unpublished Ph.D. thesis, University of Vienna, 1973). The thesis presents a history of Shakespeare productions in these two major cities, with appendices listing translations and productions. Her list of Catalan translations and productions is often incorrectly dated and contains a large number of gaps, some of them major ones. This is probably due to her reliance for data on second-hand sources, which she occasionally misreads, such as Ramon Esquerra, Alfons Par and Eduardo Juliá Martínez. For instance, she cites a 1919 Catalan translation of *Macbeth* by Magí Morera i Galícia when his translation of *Macbeth* into Catalan was never published, although he did release a Castilian version that

year. The edition, Madrid: Estrella (Colección 'Palma' XII), is listed in Par, *Contribución*, p. 78.
11 Xavier Lamuela and Josep Murgades argue that the diglossic situation in Catalonia was at no point overcome in the twentieth century and, hence, any suggestion that Catalan might be an instrument of oppression for culture in Castilian is rather far-fetched. See *Teoria de la llengua literària segons Fabra* (Barcelona: Quaderns Crema, 1984), pp. 11–78.
12 A medieval literary festival, originally protagonized by *joglars*, that was reinstated in Barcelona in 1859 and Valencia in 1879.
13 See Enric Gallén on theatre in *HLC*, VIII, 1986, pp. 379–448, and IX, pp. 413–62. It should also be noted that a high proportion of Shakespeare translations into Castilian in the nineteenth and early twentieth centuries were published in Barcelona. Par, *Contribución*, and *Shakespeare*, I and II, give exhaustive information on this aspect of production in Catalonia.
14 There are suggestions in *Estudios escénicos*, 17, and Esquerra, *Shakespeare*, that at least one Piquet version was in Catalan. This is probably based on a misreading of Par.
15 Michael Bristol considers the question of why *Othello* might have given rise to so many parodies in his chapter on 'Race and the Comedy of Abjection in *Othello*', in *Big-Time Shakespeare*, pp. 175–202.
16 I have found reference to other Catalan productions of *Otel·lo* where the translator is not specified. Because there is no record of any other translation of the whole play until 1929, and these productions are all amateur and would be unlikely to use anything but short versions, I believe it is safe to assume that either Coma or Codina were the source texts. The only other possibilities would be that Massó i Torrents unpublished version (1906) was used or, rather more probably, that Perpiñà's version was in circulation long before its publication. Par refers to another version, *¡Otello, o il moro de magnesia!*, performed in 1877, however even he was unable to find further information. Par, *Representaciones*, II, p. 111.
17 Only *Les esposalles de la morta* is ever published on its own, although all three plays regularly appear together in editions of Balaguer's *Tragedias* or *Novas Tragedias*, which at times contain versions of the plays in Castilian as well.
18 See Fàbregas' introduction to Víctor Balaguer, *Les esposalles de la morta/ A raig de lluna* (Barcelona: Edicions 62, 1968), p. 9.
19 These are of course the original sources for Shakespeare's three plays, although mediated by French then English versions.
20 For the relationship between the two versions, see Par, *Representaciones*, II, pp. 118–19, 175–7, and, with caution, Xavier Fàbregas' introduction to his edition of the play in 1968. Balaguer, *Les esposalles de la morta* (1968).
21 It was only performed once in the twentieth century in Catalan, in Sagarra's version, although Balaguer's short play was performed in 1936 and a photograph of the production mistakenly encaptioned '*Coriolanus* de William Shakespeare'. More recently, there was a full

production at the Teatre Nacional de Catalunya in the 2001–2 season, directed by Georges Lavaudant.

22 Albert Dubeux, *Traductions françaises de Shakespeare* (Paris: 'Les Belles Lettres', 1928) and Romy Heylen, *Translation, Poetics, and the Stage. Six French Hamlets* (London/New York: Routledge, 1993).

23 See Tussetschläger, *Aufführungen*, and Angel Berenguer, 'Hamlet en España (1772–1900)' in his *Teoría y crítica del teatro* (Alcalá de Henares: Universidad de Alcalá de Henares, 1991), pp. 61–8. Interestingly, Berenguer's narrative identifies *Hamlet* as a play with scanty reception in Spain, considering its importance elsewhere. He even suggests psychological antipathy for the character amongst Spaniards. Elsewhere I have explored how the intensity of the lack/fullness dialectic accompanying Hamlet's reception in Catalonia and Spain might have more to do with the overmediated nature of the play's incorporation. Helena Buffery, 'The Meaning of Shakespeare in Catalan: El parany del ratolí', *JOCS*, 1 (1997). http://www.uoc.edu/jocs/1/translation/translation.html

24 The lecture was published as Ernesto Rossi, *Discorso improvvisato nell' Ateneo di Barcellona – La sera di lunedì 3 de mese di agosto del 1868, sopra il teatro di Shakespeare, e specialmente sopra la tragedia Hamlet, sua interpretazione, sua esecuzione; per Ernesto Rossi, Artista drammatico* (Bilbao: Eduardo Delmas, 1868), with a translation by Oscar Camps y Soler.

25 Joan Maragall, 'Hamlet', in *Obres completes*, vol. XV (Barcelona: Edició definitiva, 1929–55), pp. 131–6.

26 The production is announced in *Teatre Català*, II (17 December 1932), 192, and then reviewed (24 December 1932), 202.

27 'Es Catalunya que, quan pot tornar a parlar en català, a lluitar..., a pensar..., a *ésser*, en una paraula altra volta..., s'incorpora al cos físic del territori per a donar-li l'ànima que li mancava... i vagava per aquests móns de Déu, com l'esperit del pare de Hamlet pel castell d'Elsinor' *La Esquella de la Torratx*, (27 February 1931), 131.

28 Stripped of words, Rigola's production seeks to speak beyond Catalonia, as is indicated in its title. See Maria Delgado's review in *Western European Stages* 18, 1 (2006), 55–64.

29 An invaluable insight into the aesthetic interest and influence of Adrià Gual is presented in his own *Mitja vida de* teatre (Barcelona: Aedos, 1960), as well as the remarkable studies of Carles Batlle i Jordà, *Adrià Gual (1891–1902), per un teatre simbolista* (Barcelona: Publicacions de l'Abadia de Montserrat, 2001) and *Adrià Gual: mitja vida de modernisme* (Barcelona: Ambit, 1992). David George provides a useful introduction to Gual in *Contemporary Catalan Theatre, An Introduction* (Sheffield: The Cromwell Press, 1996), whilst his more recent *Theatre in Madrid and Barcelona 1892–1936* (Cardiff: University of Wales Press, 2002) offers a more expansive account of his influence.

30 The version of *Othello* can be found in manuscript in the Biblioteca

de Catalunya. The version of the *Shrew* was to be that of Farran i Mayoral, later published with the Biblioteca Popular dels Grans Mestres.

[31] Apart from the sixteen published translations to be found in appendix A, there is evidence of other projected translations: *Hamlet* by Miquel de Sants Oliver, *Els dos gentilhomes de Verona* by F. Torres, and *Romeu y Julieta* by Ignasi Iglésias.

[32] See back cover of A. Bulbena i Tosell, *Hamlet* (Barcelona: F. Giró, 1910). A literal translation of *La furiosa domdada de Shakespere* [sic] is described as being in preparation.

[33] It is fair to assume, then, that Carles Capdevila had completed his translation of *Twelfth Night* in 1903, long before its publication as volume V of the Biblioteca Popular dels Grans Mestres.

[34] Translated into Castilian and French, all three manuscripts are available in the Institut del Teatre library in Barcelona.

[35] Carner refers to the play as a 'vote', invoking a series of values to be represented in this election, from poetic language to social decorum in 'Abans que tot', *El somni d'una nit d'estiu*, trans. Josep Carner (Barcelona: Domènech, 1908). For further discussion of the significance, see Helena Buffery, 'Shakespeare and the Cultural Dream in Catalonia', *Tesserae*, 6, 1 (June 2000), 5–18.

[36] Xènius, 'La Donzella curiosa llegeix una traducció d'en Josep Carner', *La Veu de Catalunya* (8 September 1909).

[37] Jordana, Foix, Sagarra and Farran i Mayoral all perceive it as a formative moment. See especially, Cèsar August Jordana, 'Josep Carner, traductor', in *L'obra de Josep Carner* (Barcelona: Selecta, 1959), pp. 194–7.

[38] Presumably in Salvador Vilaregut's translation for volume I of the Biblioteca Popular dels Grans Mestres. See Gual, *Mitja vida de teatre*, p. 276.

[39] The first two plays were to be translated by Josep Farran i Mayoral, *Coriolanus* and *Julius Caesar* by Magí Morera i Galícia and *A Midsummer Night's Dream* by Alfons Maseras.

[40] It is for this reason that Maseras's typescript is available in the Institut del Teatre library and dated as 1923, even though it was not to be published until 1929.

[41] Par was also responsible for versions of part of *Othello* and the *Rape of Lucrece*, in 1904 and 1906 respectively.

[42] Par's work did, however, meet with respect from contemporary English critics. It was praised by the President of the London Shakespeare Society and by Sidney Lee who was quoted as being of the opinion that 'no tiene rival en una lengua neolatina'. Arturo Llopis, 'Un erudito barcelonés de Shakespeare. Alfonso Par Tusquets', *Destino*, 1421 (October 1964), 33.

[43] Eugeni d'Ors, *Gualba, la de mil veus* (Barcelona: Catalònia, 1935), was first serialized in *La Veu de Catalunya* in 1915, and he was later to associate its composition with the collapse of civilization signalled by the First World War.

[44] Many histories follow Palau in incorrectly dating the publication of

Morera i Galícia's *Coriolà* as 1915 or 1916. A. Palau i Dulcet, *Manual del librero hispano-americano* (Barcelona: Antiquaria; London/Paris: Maggs Bros, 1926), VI, p. 512, and *Manual del librero español* (Barcelona: Palau Dulcet; Oxford: Dolphin, 1969), XXI, p. 163. See also Serrano Ripoll, *Bibliografía*, and *Las traducciones de Shakespeare en España* (Valencia: Arcos, 1974). Both are riddled with gaps and mistakes of this type, as is attested by Gerard Vergés in the introduction to his version of the complete sonnets: *Tots els sonets de Shakespeare* (Barcelona: Columna, 1993), pp. xvi–xvii.

45 The Biblioteca Literària was a collection of classic texts for the Editorial Catalana, selected and translated by writers associated with *La Revista* and, thus, the *Noucentisme* programme.

46 At the same time as the Romea production of Morera i Galícia's translation of *The Merchant of Venice*, much excitement was aroused in the theatre magazine *Comèdia* about the 'definite' prospect of Margarita Xirgu and Enric Borràs, two of the most successful and emblematic Catalan actors of the period, performing his version of *Macbeth*. *Comèdia*, 2 (28 February 1925), 17. This would have been a very significant event for Catalan theatre, as both actors now performed primarily in Castilian.

47 Although Ramon Vinyes' *Hamlet, dramaturg* was written in 1944, it is clearly set in the 1930s.

48 Maria Aurèlia Capmany, *Cartes impertinents*, 2nd edn (Palma de Mallorca: Moll, 1980).

49 Key examples include Carme Portaceli's 1994 staging of *The Merry Wives of Windsor*, Tamzin Townsend's 1996 *Macbeth*, and Helena Pimienta's *Comedy of Errors* at the Teatre Nacional de Catalunya in 2000.

50 These terms are drawn from Itamar Even-Zohar, 'The Position of Translated Literature within the Literary Polysystem', in J. S. Holmes and R. van der Broeck (eds), *Literature and Translation* (Leuven: Acco, 1978) and Gideon Toury, *Descriptive Translation Studies – and Beyond* (Amsterdam: John Benjamins, 1995).

51 Ramon Esquerra's welcome of Jordana's venture on the last pages of *Shakespeare*, pp. 193–4, suggests that justice might at last be done to Shakespeare in Catalan. The series in which the new translations are published is christened 'Clàssics del món'.

52 See Joan Givanel i Mas's index of theatre translations in *La Revista*, XXI (January–June 1935), 131–44.

53 Volumes of the Jordana translations continued to be advertised up until the 1970s. Sagarra's translations, although published between 1945 and 1953, are highbrow editions and had small print runs.

54 J. M. de Sagarra, 'Ofelia', in *La Ilustració Catalana*, IX (19 March 1911), 143.

55 For these reasons I have reproduced the pseudo-date in Appendix A. If nothing else, it should remind one of the hardships faced by Catalan culture in the early Franco years. How Franco's policies affected the publishing world has been catalogued in Albert Manent and Joan Crexell, *Bibliografia catalana: cap a la represa (1944–1946)*,

(Barcelona: Publicacions de l'Abadia de Montserrat, 1988), and most exhaustively in Joan Samsó, *La cultura catalana entre la clandestinitat i la represa pública*, 2 vols (Barcelona: Abadia de Montserrat, 1994).

56 Josep Manyé, 'Per què Shakespeare en Català?', *Avui* (18 March 1979), 29.

57 Maurici Serrahima, *Del passat quan era present* (Barcelona: Edicions 62, 1972), p. 267. The anecdote is reproduced in a number of histories of the period, including Lluís Permanyer's, *Sagarra vist pels seus íntims* (Barcelona: La Campana, 1991), p. 150. Permanyer gives 30 August 1945 as the date on which the first volume of Shakespeare translations appeared (p. 166).

58 Manyé, 'Per què Shakespeare en Català?'. The entire text of Sir Henry Thomas' broadcast was reproduced for the first time in this article.

59 Sagarra was, however, to make his fortune from the clandestine editions of some of his translations, a number of which he sold himself for the commission. See Maria Josepa Gallofré i Virgili, *L'edició catalana i la censura franquista (1939–1951)* (Barcelona: Abadia de Montserrat, 1991), pp. 413–14.

60 Lluís Permanyer, *Sagarra vist pels seus íntims* (Barcelona: La Campana, 1991), p. 154.

61 Joan Samsó, 'L'activitat editorial en català entre el 1939 i el 1951', *Afers*, 22 (1995), 559, n. 15.

62 Ramon Vinyes went into exile in Colombia, and is more widely known as the model for 'el sabio catalán' in Gabriel García Márquez's *Cien años de soledad* (Buenos Aires: Ed. Sudamericana, 1967).

63 An account which refers to both productions can be found in Josep Anton Codina, '*Juli Cèsar*', *Estudios escénicos*, 17, 45–86.

64 The following anecdote is recounted by Gonzalo Pérez de Olaguer about Espert's 1960 performance: 'La funció va transcórrer en una contínua divisió d'opinions cada vegada que Espert/Hamlet parlava, amb forts xiulets i també uns forts aplaudiments . . . "Se organizó un escándalo de envergadura porque se aceptó muy mal que una mujer hiciera el personaje", diu l'actriu . . .', *Teatre BCN*, 37 (January 2003), 46.

65 Reasons for a divide in allegiances in the 1950s may be read in Samsó, *La cultura catalana*, I, pp. 123–47, but also, from the pro-Sagarra camp, in articles such as the following: Jaume Vidal i Alcover, 'Josep Maria de Sagarra, traductor', *Estudis escènics*, 23 (June 1983), 69–94, and Josep Palau i Fabre, 'Consideracions sobre el Shakespeare de Josep Maria de Sagarra', *Estudios escénicos*, 17, 65–74.

66 See Joaquim Carbó, *El teatre de 'Cavall Fort'* (Barcelona: Institut del Teatre/Edicions 62, 1975).

67 Dennis Kennedy, *Looking at Shakespeare: a visual history of twentieth-century performance* (Cambridge and New York: Cambridge University Press, 1993).

68 'Durant els últims anys Shakespeare ha parlat ininterrompudament des dels escenaris catalans', Xavier Fàbregas, 'Shakespeare als països catalans', *Avui* (3 December 1977), 25. In the same mini-chronology

of performances, he expresses sentiments suggested earlier in this chapter with respect to Shakespeare's presence during 'els anys més difícils'. For Fàbregas it is as if 'la rica solidesa de la seva obra hagués estat un refugi per a tots els qui es disposaven a lluitar per la represa cultural del nostre poble'.

69   See especially Xavier Fàbregas, 'Tot buscant Shakespeare amb un llumí', *Avui* (3 December 1977), 25. The 'llumí' image is picked up by later writers in assessing the situation.
70   Fàbregas, 'Tot buscant Shakespeare'.
71   Terenci Moix, 'Shakespeare–Sagarra: el regreso de la maestría', *La Vanguardia* (21 November 1979), 47.
72   Rosa Maria Martínez Ascaso, 'Dos catalans i un anglès: Shakespeare', *Avui* (31 March 1979), 24.
73   'Si l'edició representa una inversió, no pas important, el guany que en traurem ens compensarà amb escreix. Haurem fet una petita passa, petita però preciosa, per tal d'esdevenir un país normal', Fàbregas, 'Tot buscant Shakespeare'.
74   Rosa Maria Piñol, 'Salvador Oliva tradueix mantenint el mateix nombre de versos del text original anglès', *La Vanguardia* (17 April 1984), 39. Here Oliva is quoted as translating at a rate of about two acts per month and has at this stage completed *Romeo and Juliet*, *Richard II* and the first act of *As You Like It*.
75   'Vicens Vives inicia la publicació de tot el *corpus* dramàtic de Shakespeare', *La Vanguardia* (17 April 1984), 40.
76   John Beattie, '"Sutil, falso, traidor...". Tres versiones de *Richard III* de Shakespeare', in S. González and F. Lafarga (eds), *Traducció i literatura. Homenatge a Angel Crespo* (Barcelona: Eumo, 1997), pp. 163–72. Much of the essay is, in fact, dedicated to defending Shakespeare's greatness, his popularity being unequalled by any other writer. Hence, Oliva's is considered the best version, for seeking to reproduce the poetry of the original even though it was originally aimed at a popular television audience.
77   A second edition of Oliva's *Hamlet* was brought out in response to the first film and, more recently, the Morera i Galícia version of *Hamlet* in the MOLU edition of four plays has been brought out on its own, with a promotional photograph from the Kenneth Branagh film on the cover.
78   Many theatregoers expect the classics to feel like classics, rather than to be brought up to date. It will be interesting to see whether this proves true of readers, too.
79   Moix, 'Shakespeare–Sagarra'.
80   Moix, 'Shakespeare–Sagarra'. See also, Marta Pessarrodona, 'Shakespeare en catalán', *La Vanguardia* (22 November 1979), 44.
81   Cheek by Jowl performed *A Midsummer Night's Dream* in 1986 and *Measure for Measure* and *As You Like It* at the Mercat de les Flors in 1994; the RSC brought *Much Ado about Nothing* in 1984 and *King Lear* in 2003.
82   Bieito also intervenes in the process of translation, as explored in Calixto Bieito, Maria Delgado and Patricia Parker, 'Resistant

Readings, Multilingualism and Marginality', in Lynette Hunter and Peter Lifhtenfels (eds), *Shakespeare, Language and the Stage: The Fifth Wall* (London: The Arden Shakespeare and Thomson Learning, 2005), pp. 108–37.

[83] Set up by Paco Azorín, one of the most innovative contemporary Catalan set designers, who designed the sets for Pasqual's *Hamlet* and *Tempest* as well as Llàcer's *Dream*, the festival runs for a fortnight in August in the coastal town of Santa Susanna, north of Barcelona. As well as re-staging key Catalan productions from the previous season, the festival organizers normally invite productions and companies from the rest of Spain and Europe, as well as arranging special lectures, film screenings and exhibitions.

[84] As well as visiting companies from Spain and the rest of Europe, there is a noticeable recent trend to stage amateur English versions in Barcelona. Examples include: *Romeo and Juliet* by The Lingua Arts Theatre Co., dir. J. Gordon, Teatre Zona Nord, March 1998; *Twelfth Night* by the International Theatre Club dir. Keith Farmer, El Casinet d'Hostafrancs, May 1998; and *The Tempest* by 12x12 in June 2003 at IES Verdaguer, Parc de la Ciutadella dir. James Stewart.

Chapter 2

Why Shakespeare? Critical Positionings

In *Shakespeare y el folklore español*, Alfons Par called on the Spanish territories to give due consideration to Shakespeare and all things that might lead to his appreciation, referring both to the advantages of 'filiacions nostrades' ('home-grown connections') uncovered by 'nostres investigadors' ('our researchers') and to their universal value in correcting the gaps in knowledge of foreign critics.[1] In this chapter I will trace Catalan contributions to Shakespeare studies and place them within the context of representation and evaluation of the figure of Shakespeare outside Catalonia. Although I have consulted and am indebted to a number of works in tracing this history of Catalan Shakespeare reception, in particular the Shakespeare histories of Alfons Par and Ramon Esquerra, the object of this study is notably different to theirs. To uncover the operation of the term 'Shakespeare' in a cultural system, one cannot assume a universal meaning for that term. Hence, Shakespeare represents cultural value, an author and a body of works; but even the significance of these latter will vary according to context. As Bergnes de las Casas demonstrated in expounding his theory of influence, the operation and scope of these figures can be observed in a number of different fields, each modifying meaning, and are dependent on language, on the metaphors sanctioned by these fields:

> Para calcular con exactitud el influjo económico de los hombres de numen sobre la civilización, sería menester tomar en cuenta, primero la riqueza positiva que pone en circulación la venta de sus obras, en seguida la reproducción de esa riqueza, que duplican y

triplican los imitadores de su numen; el movimiento que imprimen a la sociedad, y las nuevas riquezas creadas por el amor al trabajo y la actividad intelectual que derraman. Es tan dilatado bajo este respecto el poder de un escritor que se puede decir que huye de todos los cálculos. Si tomamos a Shakespeare, por ejemplo, veremos cuánto se extiende este influjo que abraza el horizonte de un inmenso porvenir.[2]

(To calculate with exactitude the economic influence of numinous men on civilization, it would be necessary to take into account firstly the positive riches put into circulation by the sale of their work, followed by the reproduction of those riches, which are doubled and tripled by the imitators of their numen; the movement that they impress on society, and the new riches created by the love of their work and the intellectual activity that they inspire. The power of a writer in this respect is so vast that it can be said to be beyond all calculation. If we take Shakespeare as an example, we will see his example extend so far that it embraces the horizon of an immense future).

What we find represented in Bergnes's words is a 'Shakespeare' who is exemplary within the different fields of cultural influence, but who simultaneously stands as the supreme example of this model of cultural currency. He is, hence, both metonym and metaphor. In this chapter I will be investigating the reproduction of these riches, aiming to distinguish how Shakespeare in Catalan is represented and incorporated as a universal cultural value, but also how part of this representation is inseparable from the figuration of Shakespeare as man and from the 'amor al trabajo y la actividad intelectual que derrama'. In order to highlight the nature of Shakespeare's distant influence, I have reproduced the actual words with which he is constructed and evoked rather than simply translating, glossing or reappropriating them. For it is their relation to Catalan cultural forms and their echoes of Catalan discourse that determine the particular meaning of Shakespeare in Catalonia, reconstructing a 'universal' Shakespeare made up of the remains excavated from other nations and movements. Thus, whilst on the one hand this chapter will uncover the reasons given by Catalan writers for choosing Shakespeare, by drawing from a list of supposedly 'universal' attributes, on the other hand the expression of this choice in Catalan and his translation into the Catalan cultural system creates new riches, and the possibility of detecting new remains.

Previous works tracing the influence of Shakespeare in Catalonia tend to bemoan the lack of extensive critical studies, and this fact has largely been borne out by my study of nineteenth and twentieth-century criticism in Catalan. The majority of references to Shakespeare – and there are many – are brief and therefore generally considered superficial, making use of the name to stand as exemplary authority for an aesthetic, political or moral judgement, an anecdote or an opinion. However, as we have seen in the words of Martínez Ascaso, this does not mean that Shakespeare was not considered an important figure.[3] On the contrary, in many ways his value went unquestioned. This is not entirely self-evident though, and part of the aim of this chapter is to show that the incorporation of Shakespeare as a universal value in Catalan depended on a number of legitimating processes, which ultimately led him to stand for a fluent system of attributes. The most important legitimating processes are moves towards 'llur debuda aportació', where Catalan critics seek to correct certain lacunae in perceptions of Shakespeare outside Catalonia, alongside the very selection of models of reception from other cultural critics and movements (which can in itself be considered an aspect of the first process). The more revisionary move to be detected in the quotation from Par would be the prioritization of a Catalan Shakespeare, which will be explored more fully in Chapter 3.

Before uncovering the system of Shakespeare representation in Catalonia, it remains necessary to determine the importance of the author function in the presentation of this chapter. One cannot fail to be aware of the close scrutiny the author function has undergone since the 1960s, up to and after Barthes 'declaration' of the death of the author, as a development of the critique of the concept of intentionality. This has led to reformulations of the role of the author within cultural systems in terms of a brand name, a symbol of cultural value or a manifestation of symbolic power. Many of the representations of the figure of Shakespeare to be encountered in the course of this chapter are very clearly to be read in this light, as dealing with a symbolic, 'ideal' author function rather than a 'real' flesh-and-blood writer who is intimately, personally and sincerely linked to the words he wrote. Indeed, an instance of this tendency has already been observed in Bergnes' representation of Shakespeare as nineteenth-century cultural capital. Moreover, the very problematization of the author function is clearly present in the invocation to and refiguration of Shakespeare in Catalan. There are attempts to adjudicate (in terms of reproducing biographies in Catalan) and participate in the debate over the face behind the name, the life and mind of a 'real' Shakespeare.[4] At the same time there is insistence on the value of the author function and its revelation in the works, in particular through nostalgic recourse to the 'ideal sincerity' of the lyric poet as evidenced in the *Sonnets*.[5]

However, alongside acceptance of the idea of a 'real' Shakespeare – the ideal man of the theatre, the petit bourgeois come good, the Catholic poet, the bridge between the popular and the high-brow – there is recurrent invocation of the name of Shakespeare to represent an aesthetic, or indeed a series of aesthetic ideals. The extent of this transfiguration is such that we find criticism of the heritage industry constructed around the figure of Shakespeare in Stratford, the questioning of the necessity for a real, original Shakespeare, and ultimately the idealization of a number of aspects of the myth of the man, which makes them part of an aesthetic system relatively autonomous from any posited 'true' biography.[6] It is this aesthetic system and its relationship with and borrowings from other cultures that I will endeavour to reconstruct here, with particular reference to the representation of the artist, the work and the universe of reference of the work of art ideally represented by Shakespeare in Catalan. One of the features of this reconstruction will be the figuration of Shakespeare as a lack in Catalan culture, the representation of his non-representation, and hence the continuing emphasis on the aesthetic importance of creating Shakespeare reception.

The Beginnings of Shakespeare in Catalan

As might be expected given the conditions of Catalan culture in the eighteenth and nineteenth centuries, up until the beginning of the twentieth century, commentary on the importance of Shakespeare tended to be expressed in Castilian. The only exceptions tend to be found in passing references to productions by foreign companies, and these often bemoaned the existence of a Shakespeare 'gap'. Hence we find the commentary of Joan

Sardà in an 1892 edition of *La Vanguardia*: 'Nos figuramos conocerle y no le conocemos, que no es conocerle haber oído más o menos veces, todos muy pocas, dos o tres de sus obras capitales: *Hamlet* u *Othello*. Muchos hay aún que sólo las conocen en ópera' ('We imagine we know him but we do not, for it is not to know him to have heard two or three of his works, like *Hamlet* or *Othello*, however many times. Many still only know the operatic versions').[7] His judgement is supported by other writers and references to Shakespeare, when the Shakespeare connection is remembered at all.

Even Joan Maragall, perhaps the most important Catalan writer of *Modernisme*, spanning the turn of the century, published the majority of his comments about Shakespeare in Castilian. One of his articles draws a comparison between Spain after the 1898 catastrophe and the character of Hamlet, although it is in *Othello* that he sees the synthesis of human life and action.[8] Shakespeare's all-inclusive humanity is a theme which recurs in many of the critical writings to be considered in this and the following chapter, and is often expressed in relation to personal testimony to the depth of emotion experienced through contact with his work. The issue of how far such observations are linked to the neo-Romantic critical predilection for 'sincerity' and how far to a more modernist, humanist sensibility will be explored in the course of this chapter. However, it will become clear that the discourse of romanticism remains current even in writers who profess modernizing tendencies.

Maragall's belief in the deep humanity of Shakespeare is expressed in a number of articles, as is a sense of the importance of Shakespearian psychology. His praise of impartial objectivity in the dramatist's presentation of the world is later coloured by increasing inclination towards the necessary intervention of the writer in society, but in many works we find the kind of affirmations which are to become a hallmark of Shakespeare criticism in Catalan, with their inescapable flavour of the European Romantic movement: 'Dante, Shakespeare no son morales ni inmorales, porque se limitan a intensificar la vida expresándola' ('Dante and Shakespeare are neither moral nor immoral, they simply intensify life through expression') and 'Homero, Esquilo, Dante, Shakespeare, Goethe, ¡cuán diferentes y cuán iguales! Son las cúspides de la cordillera que se van igualando con la distancia' ('Homer, Aeschylus, Dante,

Shakespeare, Goethe. How very different and yet how very similar! They are the peaks of the mountain range which become more equal the greater the distance').[9] Here we find new expression of the swerve against neo-Classical rules which originated the Romantic movements in England and Germany, through the rejection of charges against Shakespeare made by eighteenth-century figures such as Dr Johnson and Voltaire, of his immorality, vulgarity and, for the latter, barbarity. Instead a new mimesis is extolled, created by the intensifying power of immortal genius; and the canon which Maragall proclaims has as its most recent 'intelligence', a Romantic hero, Goethe.[10]

Maragall's love of Shakespeare does not lead him to attempt translations of any of the plays, but he does insist on the importance of the world created by the English playwright in 'Elogi de la Poesia', a world made up of cultural borrowings and translations: 'Shakespeare, refent drames o llegendes d'altri, ha produït les obres de poesia immortal tant o més fortament personals que no haurien estat les de pura invenció de la [seva] fantasia' ('Shakespeare, in rewriting the plays or legends of others, has produced works of immortal poetry at least as intensely personal as if they had been purely the invention of his own imagination').[11] This approval of the creation of fresh poetic worlds based on stories which are already well known is to become central to appreciation of Shakespeare's work, as well as to underscore early twentieth-century defence of the translation programme into Catalan as a way of forging a new language of culture. So Shakespeare's practice becomes a figure that both determines and is determined by the process of translation.

In Maragall, then, we find a Shakespeare whose greatness lies in his impartiality, his reflection of total humanity, his sincerity, even while reworking the words of others. Although these opinions have unmistakable roots in European romanticism and may be seen as a marker of the sentimental, intuitive aesthetic of *Modernisme* – an aesthetic which is later to be rejected overtly by *Noucentisme* – many of these aspects are echoed in later writers, in particular the validation of the sincerity of the artist and the scope of representation. There are also seeds of a more political Shakespeare, relevant to the historical moment, which become more common in subsequent critical positionings.

Alfons Par and Cebrià Montoliu

Perhaps the most important critic in disseminating a model of Shakespeare in Catalonia is Alfons Par, both because of the length of his contributions and the extent of his legacy within the Catalan cultural system. The only book-length study of Shakespeare's influence in Catalan, that of Ramon Esquerra, is heavily indebted to the work of Par. It is also to be noted that many Shakespeare translations in the Biblioteca de Catalunya were donated by the Par family estate, underlining his historical centrality to any study of Shakespeare in Catalonia.[12] The reviews of *Shakespeare en la literatura española* (1935) are indicative of Par's perceived eminence as a critic and literary historian: his learning is considered exhaustive and his erudition is untouchable.[13] It is, then, appropriate that the first extended studies of the cultural significance of Shakespeare written in Catalan are by Par, in the form of lectures given to the Centre Excursionista de Catalunya and the Associació Wagneriana between 1903 and 1906.[14]

Alfons Par's early twentieth-century promotions of Shakespeare in Catalan are accompanied by a translation of a scene from *Othello* in *Catalunya*, a magazine which, notwithstanding its short life, has been identified as an embryonic organ for what would be christened *Noucentisme* in 1906.[15] Hence, although in many ways Par would seem to fit the pattern of the free-floating, disinterested humanist intellectual, giving lectures at assorted amateur organizations and eventually pursuing his Shakespeare specialism in Castilian, he was initially included in the select circle of writers and intellectuals whom Josep Carner seeks to gather around himself, in what has been perceived as a move towards a more systematic cultural programme. This is underlined by the fact that, unlike Cebrià Montoliu for instance, whom he cited as an erudite friend, he continued to have a cordial relationship with *Noucentista* intellectuals notwithstanding his divergent views on issues of linguistic standardization and readings of Shakespeare. One example of his respect for players in the movement can be seen in a dedication in a copy of his 1916 work on the life of Shakespeare to the 'Director de *La Revista*, l'excels poeta J. M. López Picó'. Although he is at times rather disparaging of Catalan approximations to Shakespeare, he does make favourable comments about the mature judgement and artistic sensibility of some of the followers of Eugeni d'Ors. He perceives the main cause for criticism to be the minority status of modern Catalan literature, which he argues has led to an over-exuberant embracement of neo-Romantic impressionism, obscuring or twisting sound judgement.[16] Whilst one of the paradoxes of the *Noucentista* call for a return to classical forms and values (rather than rules) is that it is often expressed in the rhetoric of romanticism, it cannot be said that Par himself would escape some of his own criticisms in this respect.

Par's first published lecture, dedicated to an exposition of Shakespeare's mind and body of works, 'Shakespeare, sa concepció y sa obra', makes an initial approximation to the dramatist by comparison with Wagner.[17] Here Shakespeare is vindicated of the accusations made against him by French writers such as Taine. Par explains away unfavourable French judgements of Shakespeare by referring to the antithesis of the English and French genius (p. 164). Again the English playwright is slotted in to a canon of what are judged to be the greatest authors; with Par's pantheon of dramatists now formed by Greek drama, Shakespeare and Wagner (p. 160). The imagery used to develop the idea of this trinity reflects the organic figures favoured by Romantic writers to express the inherent nature and unity of great works of art, with Shakespeare being the ultimate example of this model of creativity.[18] Furthermore, it is a rhetorical strategy commonly revisited by writers of the *Renaixença* to convey the development of Catalan culture. The tree image used by Par in this case was often employed to reflect the growth of the Catalan language. Par describes three trees 'que be'n podem dir de la Vida, puix d'ells s'esmuny rosada sana y copiosa... fecondant tota la foresta dramatica' ('which we could well call of Life, for from them trickles healthy and plentiful dew... fertilizing the surrounding theatrical forest'). Already the reader is presented with the idea that these trees can spread and fertilize other dramatic output, a metaphor which remains an essential feature of the aesthetic system Shakespeare represents, signalling the status of the work of art. Amongst the trees, 'el shakesperià es més alt que'ls altres, a tots domina' ('the Shakespearian one is higher than the others and towers over all of them'), an affirmation which reminds the reader of Coleridge's 'Shakespeare is the height, and breadth, and depth of genius', a Shakespeare in whom we find 'growth as in a plant' and in whose drama 'there is a vitality which grows and evolves from within'.[19] Compared with the severity and purity of form of Greek drama and the rich, exuberant power of Wagner, Shakespeare's drama stands less harmonious but more natural, according to Par (p. 161).

Much of this early paper presented anecdotal details about Shakespeare's life, drawing on a range of secondary works, from Ben Jonson to Dr Farmer and his theories about Shakespeare's sources. The second part of the essay is concerned with context setting for what Par hopes will be a deeper understanding of Shakespeare, through description of the theatrical conventions of Elizabethan and Jacobean times and discussion of a few plays before going on to analyse the language of Shakespeare. The playwright presented here by Par is one who has a right to be considered alongside Wagner, if not as greater than him, for although he finds 'L'Obra Wagneriana' to be more intense and spiritual than that of Shakespeare it is simultaneously presented as being less complex and less human (p. 174). For Par, Shakespeare is the poet who, in beholding things, was purest of heart and sight (p. 166). His understanding of humanity is described as being the result of his renouncement of preconceived ideas, and of acquired systems of thought, in favour of love (p. 167). Ultimately, for Par, 'L'obra shakesperiana es espontania: nascuda a l'escalf d'ardenta visió resultà ab les desigualtats y defectes que té la meteixa naturalesa' ('Shakespeare's work is spontaneous: born in the heat of his ardent vision, it emerges with the defects and unevenness of nature itself', p. 170). Shakespeare's vision becomes that of the whole of nature.

In effect, what we find foregrounded in Par, alongside attempts to set the historical context for understanding Shakespeare, is appreciation of Shakespeare's 'sincerity', his artistic 'integrity', rather than artistry, once again revealing the 'lejana influencia' of the major English and German Romantic supporters of Shakespeare. Yet, his celebration of Shakespeare goes beyond the tragedies favoured during much of the nineteenth century, to prove that the 'poeta de la dolor, ho es també de la rialla'. ('the poet of pain is also the poet of laughter', p. 180). Par's representation does not concentrate solely on ideal characteristics of Shakespeare, on his humanist love for humanity. Appreciation is shown for his irony, too, and for the moments of exaggerated passion, conveyed in the spontaneity of his work. The vision of Shakespeare presented and handed on to future Shakespeare critics and readers is one of a man who 'cor-net y ull-pur ens ha fet assaborir l'intimitat misteriosa de l'esser humà, goig més trascendental, lliçó més practica, ensenyament més ver que no pas la resolució d'un conflicte particular, puix si no'ns diu com hem de comportar-nos, ens fa veure, en cambi, lo que som' ('Pure of heart and eye he has allowed us to savour the intimate mystery of humanity; a joy more transcendental, a lesson more practical, a teaching more true than would have resulted from the resolution of a particular conflict; for even if he does not tell us how to behave, he does make us see who we are', p. 183).

Organic unity, sincerity, integrity and spontaneity are the attributes chosen to convey the mind and work of the poet and his art. This is no prescriptive Shakespeare, but a truly mimetic artist whose feeling for the being of things prevented him from retouching their essence which he left in its own state, 'perfecte o imperfecte mes brollant directament de l'original viu' ('perfect or imperfect, but sprouting directly from the living original', p. 182). The attitude of the artist to his universe expounded by Par is similar to that represented by Maragall, yet here it is also used to underline the modernity of Shakespeare. This Shakespeare, like the 'representative poet' of Emerson, is the originator of modern society, revealing rather than instructing modern man how to behave, how to be.[20] The Emersonian concept is extended as Par moves to convey what he perceives to be the 'true' value of Shakespeare in the complex character relationships present in his works: '... puix lo etern de dits personatges li fa sentir en sí meteix aquell acte divinal qui'ns infanta y qui, enclós en aquesta crosta imperfecta, obra continuament en nosaltres. [...] En Shakespeare, qui'ns ha desvelat lo que intimament som, ens en ha fet esser' ('... for the eternal essence of these characters makes one feel within oneself that divine act which gives birth to us and that, enclosed within this imperfect shell, continues to operate within us [...] Shakespeare, in revealing to us our most intimate selves, has made us what we are', p. 185).

Once again we are reminded of Emerson, in his claim that Shakespeare 'wrote the text of modern life; the text of manners [...] the man of England and Europe; the father of the man in America; he drew the man, and described the day, and what is done in it: he read the hearts of men and women, their probity, and their second thoughts and wiles [...] he knew the laws of repression which make the police of nature'.[21] Yet it is interesting to note that although Par begins by using the impersonal pronouns 'se' and 'li', he soon falls into the second person plural, previously observed in his works as a mark of identification with the Catalan people.[22] 'La lejana influencia de la inteligencia sobre las inteligencias' would here seem to be that of Shakespeare on the Catalans.

The second Par lecture is a reading of 'The Rape of Lucrece' and is presented both as a rehabilitation of Shakespeare's longer poems which lay obscured by the shadow of his plays, particularly in Spain, and as an opportunity to survey Shakespeare's lyrical imagination at work in a poem somewhat shorter, and hence more immediately accessible than the more famous plays. Much of the lecture deals with recounting the plot and its relationship with a variety of sources, alongside evaluation and description of the poetic devices used by Shakespeare to achieve what Par describes as 'la justesa ab que sap fer-nos sentir una impressió determinada' ('the accuracy with which he is capable of making us feel a particular impression', p. 471). In writing of what he identifies as Shakspearean moments, Par draws attention to the 'grans y llegitims efectes del poeta' ('great and legitimate effects of the poet'), underlining the truth, harmony and sweetness of his words (p. 486). Again he refers to what he considers the sublime moments when the poet personifies human qualities, and the many accidents of nature, but here they are related with figures of Mediterranean mythology, with a world even closer to the Catalans of this period. Furthermore, in considering Shakespeare's unwillingness to be dictated to by poetic forms, his inability to conform to epic decorum but also the inadequacy of the poem to contain his genius, Par links him to Gaudí in the culmination of his celebration of Shakespeare's virtues: 'Shakespeare, si voleu, no es un poeta, com en Gaudí no es un artista: se mouen en una regió superior, no treuen del món la bellesa abstracta, sinó que'ns isolen y fixen a perpetuitat una part completa, bella y lletja de la vida' ('Shakespeare, if you like, is not a poet, just as Gaudí is not an artist: they move in a higher sphere, do not draw abstract beauty from nature but isolate an integral part of life and fix it for all eternity, in all its beauty and ugliness', p. 490).

It is in this lecture, too, that we first find expression of a conflict between serenity and exuberance, later to be expressed as the all-encompassing *joia*. Par writes of the balance of Shakespeare's faculties, of the 'serenitat de son judici malgrat sa exuberant imaginació' ('the serenity of his judgement in spite of his exuberant imagination', p. 491). The relative action of serenity versus *joia* is something that becomes more and more of an issue in the work of later critics. In some ways this reflects the relationship between fancy and imagination formulated by Coleridge, following Schlegel, who was quite insistent on rejecting the kind of 'psychobabble' which presented Shakespeare as an unconscious genius, exhibiting no reflection. However, the increasing urge to set *joia* against serenity is far more reminiscent of Emerson, and takes on a plethora of cultural meanings as *joia* becomes one of the keywords of the *Noucentista* programme.

The interest of Par's critical judgements lies beyond critical insight or historical accuracy. They mark the first specific attempt to assess the prestige of Shakespeare, and the fruits it might bear, in Catalan. These early lectures pre-date the first sustained attempts to translate Shakespeare's works into Catalan. Before them there had only been translations of *Hamlet* and excerpts from a few other works. Thus there is no overt mention of the importance of Catalan Shakespeare translations, a feature which will become central to later approaches to Shakespeare in essays and newspaper and magazine articles as well as prologues and introductions to translations where such comments seem de rigueur. Par does, however, outline a pattern for the reception of Shakespeare in Catalan. The terms in which he expresses the 'universality' of Shakespeare are drawn on by later critics, and the often personal nature of the message, in the use of first person plural, as well as his attitude to language, point to a parallel drive to relativize Shakespeare, to make him a Catalan figure (as well as figure in Catalan). These issues will be dealt with in more detail in the chapters that follow.

The next extended study of Shakespeare, chronologically, is to be found in Cebrià Montoliu's prologue to his own Catalan translation of *Macbeth* in 1907.[23] Before launching into the first part of the study, entitled 'Shakspere Català' he quotes in English from *The Tempest*: 'Nothing of him that doth fade, / But doth suffer a Sea-change / Into something rich and strange' (p. vii).

As an epigraph to a translation these lines would seem to suggest a disregard for literal faithfulness, allowing the 'original' to be transformed. The afterlife of these words, themselves transformed on Shelley's tombstone, return us to Romantic stress on the transcendent, spiritual dimension of art and to the mystery of divine inspiration. This is a tradition which remains perceptible decades later in the letters of Carles Riba, as he takes up the above lines to explain the sense of inspiration in the third 'Elegia de Bierville', but they are also used in the context of advising one of his translators on how to proceed.[24] The 'Sea-change' in the context of Montoliu's introduction to his translation of the play would seem to refer to Shakespeare, and the mutations (but not necessarily mutability) of his reception.[25] Shakespeare, it is suggested, does not only provide a revolutionary pattern of thought for the modern age but is in fact a son of the modern age. In answering the question of whether Shakespeare was for his contemporaries what he is for 'nosaltres' ('us', p. xiv), Montoliu conjectures that even Ben Jonson could not have guessed the high pedestal given to his contemporary by 'nosaltres', referring both to the 'nosaltres moderns' and the 'nosaltres catalans'. 'Shakspere' [sic] like Christ, is described as having lived twice and as being the son of two eras: the material son of Elizabethan England and the spiritual son of the revolution. Montoliu presents him as the king of the modern Parnassus '... on regna devingut per fi, una realitat viventa com el sol, carn pastada amb la nostra sang i halenada amb la nostra ànima, miracle de la nostra fe incommovible en un ideal d'expressió artística més ampla' ('... where he reigns, having finally become a living reality like the sun; flesh formed of our blood and brought to life with the breath of our soul; a miracle of our unwavering faith in a broader ideal of artistic expression', p. xvii). As such he becomes the flag for the warriors in the aesthetic revolution, shaping the collective soul of Goethe, Carlyle, Hugo, Zola, Ibsen and Maeterlinck – the *Modernista* canon – and ultimately 'el verb de la societat moderna'. It should perhaps be remembered that Montoliu also translated Emerson, and could hence be reckoned familiar with the works of the American poet–critic.[26]

For Montoliu, Shakespeare is a 'geni de tremp sobirà' ('a genius of sovereign mettle', p. xxix), a great jewel in the human crown (p. xxxviii). The position lent him in Montoliu's canon invests the English playwright with incomparable importance for Catalan literature. From amongst the many virtues which Shakespeare possesses in the eyes of Montoliu, that of great educator is foregrounded (p. vii). With Par, he extols the glory of Shakespeare 'd'oferir-nos una representació de la vida més sana i més cabal, ensems que més fidel i imparcial' ('in offering us a healthier and more solid representation of life, as well as being more faithful and impartial') but then goes on to emphasize the immense didactic function of such a vision of the world: '... cap ensenyança es capaç de suplir l'experiencia que dóna la simple lectura d'aquesta nova biblia d'humanisme actual' ('... no teaching is capable of supplanting the experience afforded by simply reading this new bible of present day humanism', p. vii). Finally, the modern Catalan Shakespeare is anticipated by Montoliu's assertion that had Catalan theatre continued to flourish during the Renaissance, then Catalonia would have produced plays like those of Elizabethan England and the national dramatic genius would have resembled Shakespeare (p. x). The indisputable nature of this genius is then reaffirmed in a similar philosophical turn to that of Par and, of course, Emerson: 'Shakespere ns ha fet a nosaltres: la nostra vida espiritual, que es la real, es obra seva' ('Shakespeare has made us: our spiritual life, which is the real life, is his work', p. xi).

Both Par and Montoliu can be seen to be very much a product, in their aesthetic comments rather than their critical analysis of Shakespeare's works, of the *Modernista* ideology of the turn of the century. Montoliu, in particular, with his canonization of Shakespeare as a new humanist bible, reflects a trend in which the artist is less responsible for holding up a mirror to God's nature than he is for creating a means of understanding the world through the unity of the work of art. The move to 'humanize', in a different way, is perhaps reflected in the increasing production of popular editions of the classics of world literature in this period, modelled on similar enterprises in England and France. An example is the Biblioteca Popular dels Grans Mestres, dedicated to the publication of translations of Shakespeare plays by a number of authors, many of them playwrights themselves. Amongst the list of translators, Raventós, Vilaregut, Ruiz, Capdevila and Puig i Ferreter all participate in some way in the Catalan theatre world, whilst Carner and Farran i Mayoral are to become central figures in the *Noucentista* movement, the former arguably the most important Catalan poet. Few of the plays have critical introductions but they do lead to more frequent reference to Shakespeare in the Catalan press. So, for example, news of the publication of the first volume, *Julius César* is greeted with enthusiasm.[27] This attitude is mirrored in other theatre journals of the period, and increasingly, when mentioned, Shakespeare's name is accompanied by tags such as 'immortal', 'genius', 'the great tragedian'; he becomes a benchmark, along with the Greek tragedies, against which to measure the artistry of other dramatists. Lectures such as that of Ramon Vinyes on the geniuses of world theatre place Shakespeare alongside Aeschylus, Sophocles, Euripides, Racine, Corneille and finally Schiller, discussing the principal works and immortal characters created by them, as well as a small number of productions.[28] However, the main body of Shakespeare criticism of the next four years is occasioned by Josep Carner's translations of *A Midsummer Night's Dream* (1908), *The Merry Wives of Windsor* (1909) and *The Tempest* (1910), and productions of the first two.[29]

From Josep Carner to Magí Morera i Galícia

The first of the Carner translations, *El somni d'una nit d'estiu*, has an introduction entitled 'Abans que tot'.[30] It contains a disclaimer as to its value as a critical study of Shakespeare, but notwithstanding its own denial of a critical positionality, it presents an interesting vision of Shakespeare. The spectre of 'Will' is represented as 'agradós y bellament humà' ('amiable and beautiful in its humanity') in contrast with the cloudier face of Ibsen (p. 8). Hence Shakespeare is endowed with a further note of benevolence, in seeking to make a space for him in Catalan. The source of this position can be found in Carner's 1907 essay on 'Del Shakespeare en llengua catalana' which will be discussed later.[31] Shakespeare's place within the 'universal' canon is, for Carner, only rivalled by that of Aristophanes, for the *Somni* is 'la comedia més deliciosament alada que s'ha escrit d'Aristofani ençà' ('the most deliciously winged comedy since Aristophanes', p. 8).

Carner also provided a short prologue for his version of *Les alegres comares*, but this, along with reviews of the *Somni*, has more bearing on the politics of storytelling in Catalan than on critical positionalities with respect to the figure of Shakespeare himself.[32] A review of Carner's translation work in the *Revista Catalana* in 1909 does lead to meditation upon the exemplary plasticity of Shakespeare, to be expanded in a later article on Schiller by the listing of Shakespeare's plays as one of the great emancipating influences on the German spirit, freeing it from French moulds and returning it to nature and the sentiments.[33] According to Raventós, Schiller's drama neither achieves the serenity of Lessing nor the grandeur of Shakespeare, the Shakespeare whom he later describes in December of the same year as helping him to a state of 'vaga somnolencia' ('vague dreaminess') when he was suffering from insomnia in a strange bed. The continuing importance of *somni* in creation, drawing on the Romantic tradition of calling on the fantastic and phantasmagorical aspect of the creative imagination, takes some impetus from the reception of Carner's *Somni*; however, it also represents a more specific dream of Catalan cultural growth. Both meanings coexist in Carner's own description of the process of translating *A Midsummer Night's Dream* and in the popularity of *somni* poems in the early years of the twentieth century in Catalan.

In 1912 Alfons Par produces another work which identifies itself as serious Shakespeare criticism in a volume containing his own translation of *King Lear*. Some of the linguistic questions raised by the translation itself will be discussed later but amongst the three hundred pages of notes there are interesting elements to add to the Shakespearian collage accumulated thus far. The benevolent Shakespeare has by now become more problematic, notwithstanding Par's love of him: 'mon cor ha bategat fortament al llegir lo dramaturc anglès, no hagis dupte que jo verament l'am' ('my heart has beaten strongly on reading the English dramatist, do not doubt that I truly love him').[34] Such emotive language, a feature of much 'personal' testimony to the imaginative and psychological influence of Shakespeare, is close to Carner's tone in his preface to *El somni d'una nit d'estiu*. As something which sets a clear pattern for the imaginative, personal, properly Catalan reception of Shakespeare, it will be dealt with at more length in the next chapter. Now there is deeper recognition of Shakespeare's difficulty: 'no hi ha ningun anglès qui pugui capirlo bé séns un complert y curós glossari. Molt menys, doncs, un estranger' ('no Englishman could understand him fully without a complete and accurate glossary, let alone a foreigner').

In comparison with earlier works of criticism, Par's study of Shakespeare here shows a decided urge towards scientific identification of the facts, as far as they are known, about the

Bard's biography, historical context and textual authenticity. The bibliography bears little evidence of Romantic studies of the Shakespearian texts. In fact, of the nineteen critical works cited only two are published before 1905, although the classic texts of Hazlitt and Coleridge both make an appearance.[35] Yet in his discussion he draws on many of his previous judgements of the English dramatist with only some subtle changes. So for instance he writes of a Shakespeare who 'nos fa percebre sentiments tan pregons com indefinits' ('makes us perceive feelings both profound and indefinite'), of the Bard's deeply profound and universal sentences and of 'enlairades y sublims esclamacions' ('elevated and sublime exclamations') rather than balanced judgments (p. 425). As a classic, Par believes Shakespeare merits the kind of erudite study and presentation he can offer, with references to a variety of source texts and critics. However, by now Shakespeare is presented as something more than just a classic. He figures as something more alive, thus reflecting on Par's erudition in a more spontaneous, human way (p. 424).

Another major Catalan translator of Shakespeare began to publish his translations of the poems in this period. Whilst few of Magí Morera i Galícia's versions of poems and plays have introductions or prologues, he did deliver a number of lectures on Shakespeare. Morera i Galícia's first study of Shakespeare in Catalan is a preamble to his translation of the sonnets.[36] Much of it concentrates on different critical approaches to the sonnet cycle and his criteria for the selection of those sonnets he believes to be most poetic. However, it is also situated within Catalan attempts to canonize Shakespeare, as references to the sonnets as jewels and Shakespeare as the most human of all geniuses would seem to show. Morera i Galícia also seems to invest more credence in the legend of Shakespeare's paltry education than the critics discussed thus far. He writes of the envy and disdain of Shakespeare's contemporaries with regard to 'aquell ingeni camperol, que sens passar per les aules se'ls plantava mestre' ('that country genius, who without having ever set foot in a classroom, stood out as their master', p. 24). Similar sentiments are expressed over twenty years later in a republican magazine, with a whole page being given over to the narrative of Ben Jonson's burning jealousy of the gentle, generous Shakespeare.[37] Whilst commentary of this type might at first appear to be little more than anecdotal, such choices are never entirely neutral and present clues to the cultural values of their time. Increasing personal sympathy for Shakespeare is undoubtedly a by-product of the close engagement with his work undertaken by these translators, and might equally be viewed as a rhetorical trope necessary to convince of the legitimacy of their translations.[38]

Shakespeare's reputation as a life-affirmer is upheld in no uncertain terms, borrowing the intellectual prestige of a quotation from Coleridge about Shakespeare's morality:

> Si Shakespeare en sa obra gran, com en sos sonets parla i pinta sovint amb realisme gens porucs o incontinents, no hi hà ni un sol tret pecaminós que'n reveli delectació morosa [...] 'No pinta adulteris ignocents ni vicis virtuosos' segons justa observació d'En Coleridge

> (If Shakespeare in his great works [...] speaks and paints with a realism that shows neither fear nor lack of restraint, there is not a single sinful trait that might reveal morbid enjoyment. "He paints neither innocent adulteries nor virtuous vices", as Coleridge rightly observes, p. 25).

The 'healthy' life force portrayed here is underlined by recourse to the image of the tree, already to be found in Par's first Shakespeare study. Life for Shakespeare is described as 'una visió integral que baixa pel tronc rugós des del cimall florit, fins a les mateixes arrels i fins a l'*humus* que les volta i les nodreix, les que semblen tares del pintor se veu que són tares del model humà' ('an integral vision that descends from the flowery canopy via the rough trunk to the very roots and even the humus that surrounds and nourishes them; what appear to be the defects of the painter are in fact defects in the human model', p. 25). Thus, with the advance of the *Noucentisme* movement, more emphasis is placed on a Shakespeare whose flaws are less to do with his own being than with the world that is seen through him. The responsibility to produce art which will transform society, present in the *Noucentista* concept of *arbitrarietat* is something which remains confused in Morera i Galícia's study. On the one hand we have a Shakespeare whose sonnets represent his own life history, on the other a Shakespeare whose own flaws do not pass into his work. Equally juxtaposed is the vision of a poet who stands as a mirror to the whole of nature, presenting life and the life force as it is, alongside the poet who makes moral choices, not totally ruled by his unconscious urge to create, as first refined by Coleridge.

Noucentisme

The works of Morera i Galícia, as well as growing numbers of translations from other literatures of the ensuing years, provoke increasing critical interest in the press. Many translations are published with prologues by respected authors, and this is the case with Morera i Galícia's version of *Venus and Adonis*, introduced by Josep Carner.[39] The essay is mainly of interest because of Carner's analysis of the poetic possibilities of Shakespeare in Catalan. However, it reproduces now standard reference to Shakespeare's poetic sovereignty, as well as approval of a quotation from Coleridge, suggesting that 'Shakespeare escriu en aquest poema com si fos d'un altre planeta' ('Shakespeare writes in this poem as if he were from another planet'), referring to a perceived ability to 'fer que la divinitat canviant sigui sentida en el riu, el lleó i la fauna; veu's aquí el que és la vera imaginació' ('allow changing divinity to be felt in the river, the lion and the animal kingdom; see what true imagination is'). The 'true imagination' of this 'English genius' is a feature of the representation of Shakespeare in Catalan which has by this time become quite common, particularly after the partial success of productions of *Somni d'una nit d'estiu* and the lyrical reviews which accompanied it.

By far the majority of Shakespeare criticism and commentary during the period from 1915 onwards is to be found in the magazine *La Revista*, with its interest in promoting the cultural growth of Catalan and the Catalan territories. It is worth remembering how unambiguously this is expressed from its inception. Rovira i Virgili defends its creation, referring to 'La preponderància dins la nostra pàtria, del periòdic i del llibre castellans, ens converteix espiritualment en una colònia' ('The preponderance in our nation of Castilian-language newspapers and books converts us spiritually into a colony') and calls for action to achieve 'aquella *plenitut d'imperi* que per al nostre idioma demanava Prat de la Riba' ('that *fullness of empire* that Prat de la Riba demanded for our language').[40] In *La Revista*, Shakespeare figures in subjects as diverse as his attention to detail and the political importance of a Shakespearian vision for the rise of Catalunya. In the words of Josep Maria López-Picó in his regular column of 'Moralitats i Pretextos', 'En aquest concepte shakespearià de la realitat tenim l'arrel de la nostra poixança' ('In this Shakespearian conception of reality we find the roots of our new strength').[41] Extended studies of Shakespeare as a dramatist are published in the theatre sections of the magazine. Most notably Farran i Mayoral, who is the most regular contributor on theatre in this period, produces a number of essays which consider to differing degrees the nature of Shakespeare's genius, and are later collected in a series of volumes of his essays. One of his earliest and most representative essays is published in 1916. In the same issue which reproduces an excerpt from Morera i Galícia's soon to be published translation of *Venus and Adonis*, Farran i Mayoral contributes an article on 'El sobirà joiós'.[42] Written to mark the tricentenary of Shakespeare's death, it takes as its point of departure Emerson's approaches to Shakespeare, also favoured by Montoliu. Here the keywords to be borrowed in the figuration of Shakespeare are quoted in English: 'His name suggests joy and emancipation to the heart of men'. Farran i Mayoral goes on to emphasize Shakespeare's sovereign nature in Catalan: 'Shakespeare, en mig el món immortal que ell creava fou sobirà, el més alt sobirà que hagi pogut existir' ('Shakespeare, amidst the immortal world that he created, was the sovereign, the greatest sovereign who has ever existed', p. 16).

The joy and emancipation of Emerson's analysis of Shakespeare is reflected in the 'pols de la vida' ('life pulse') which Farran i Mayoral finds throbbing in the plays, and which can be breathed 'lliurement, i amb amplitut joiosa' ('freely and with joyous amplitude'), making him comparable with Rabelais and Michelangelo in Farran i Mayoral's canon. Indeed, the word *joia* becomes central to this study: Shakespeare's verse and prose sing words of joy, his images leap into life, his metaphors twist in dance, all forming part of a powerful enthusiasm – the mark of poetic objectivity – which informs and inspires his ideas (p. 17). The Catalan critic even finds this joy in the tragedies 'on tota joia humana semblaria impossible' ('where all human joy might seem impossible'), going on to write of 'l'abisme de joia que hi havia en el cor del sobirà poeta' ('the abyss of joy at the heart of the sovereign poet', p. 18). Gradually it becomes clear that *joia* expresses Shakespeare's standpoint with respect to creation, the objective celebration of all creation rather than the moralistic filtering of more subjectively perceived poetics. The all-embracing nature of this *joia* in Farran i Mayoral's account, obviously beholden to Keats's notions of negative capability, even produces anxiety in the critic about the dangers for the weaker mortal who reads this 'Ancient God'. For him, only Shakespeare has played so joyfully with absolute evil (p. 21) whilst still being able to maintain a 'serene joy'. Not so the Romantics who sought to emulate Shakespeare: 'Les joioses i verídiques paraules shakesperianes s'han tornat en els romàntics terrabastall de mots i escàndol de frases buides i la majestat del poderós sobirà és en ells desmesura de gest o vanitat de burgesia pretenciosa' ('The joyous and true words of Shakespeare have become in the Romantics an uproarious din of words and empty phrases and the majesty of the powerful sovereign in them is excessive gesture or pretentious bourgeois vanity', p. 22). Although he implies that he is in touch with the serenity of Shakespeare behind the 'terrible jòc' ('terrible game'), he fears for the effects of Shakespeare on readers and theatregoers, who must decide whether they can accept the terrible game, 'si son capaços, per damunt de tot altre interès, de crear joia, joia, sempre joia [...] guardant una serenitat puríssima en força d'ésser cruel' ('whether they are capable, above all, to create joy, joy, always joy [...] maintaining a serene purity through all the cruelty', p. 23). The antidote to the heady drugs and spices of Shakespeare, to the burning cheeks and pounding heart of the Shakespearian feast is the wine of Sophocles, the serene poet, the pure wine approved by Nietzsche, according to Farran i Mayoral. Part of the blame for Shakespeare's excesses is attributed to nineteenth-century readings in a later article, in which the critic goes on to suggest that twentieth-century approximations to Shakespeare were becoming increasingly perceptive.[43] His own, however eccentric, provide an important pattern for the figuration of Shakespeare in Catalan, as well as for the role of the artist in general. For instance, the poet–critic Carles Riba borrows Farran i Mayoral's formulations of *joia*, and even the description of Shakespeare as 'joiós sobirà'. In a review of *Venus i Adonis* by Riba, Shakespeare again figures as 'tota una consciència: l'humanisme [...] esdevingut humà' ('a complete consciousness: humanism [...] become human'), returning once more to his 'infantament d'èpoques noves' ('generation of new eras').[44] Another Riba essay, on Keats, underlines his perception of the moral value of Shakespeare for he suggests that if Keats had been capable of distinguishing a moral action, English poetry would have gained a second Shakespeare.[45]

Whether Catalan can gain a hold on Shakespeare begins to be a greater concern, thrown into relief by the disappointment of scanty coverage in the centenary year of his death. In *La Revista* in 1917, López-Picó reviews Par's contributions to Shakespeare studies, seeing his publication of 'Life of Shakespeare' as signalling the incorporation of a great man – *tot un home* – into Catalan.[46] Recognizing with enthusiasm the role of Shakespeare criticism in Catalan, in translating a 'universal' figure into something that is one of 'nostres homes', López-Picó shows this new familiarity in his reference to the great 'William' rather than 'Shakespeare'. Such use of first name terms previously tended only to appear in the theatre magazines disdained by many *Noucentista* writers, and by some translators in their prologues, perhaps as a mark of affection.[47] Nicolau d'Olwer, in writing of 'El centenari Shakespeare–Cervantes' writes of Par's lectures on Shakespeare's life at the Ateneu as freeing Catalan from 'un mancament imperdonable' ('an unforgiveable ommission').[48]

Mentions of Shakespeare in subsequent years continue, with recourse to 'joia', 'sobirà' and other common critical evaluations. Farran i Mayoral's leanings towards what he perceives as the greater serenity of the classics has him describing Shakespeare as 'un barbre' (a barbarian) compared to Sophocles and even Euripides.[49] However, the *joia* foregrounded in a review of Joaquim Folguera's *Poema espars*, listing Shakespeare amidst Michelangelo and Beethoven as one of the great 'joiosos' wins through once more in Farran i Mayoral's considerations of the Bard in his *Lletres a una amiga estrangera*.[50] In writing of Chesterton's study of Dickens (1906), he refers to an idea of happiness as a passive idea rather than the 'joia activa, creadora i a l'ensems espectacular, independent i contradictòria' ('the active, creative and at the same time spectacular, independent and contradictory joy') of Shakespeare. Likewise Emerson's characterization of Shakespeare's 'sovereign tone' as 'cheerful' ('alegre' is the translation given) is corrected to 'joyous' by Farran i Mayoral.[51]

Following the publication of Magí Morera i Galícia's version of *Coriolanus* in 1918 there is a wide variety of critical commentary, as well as a few additions to the picture of Shakespeare painted so far. Josep Lleonart writes of Shakespeare as a 'new discoverer of humanity' as a 'recreator in everything' who was able to forge a language from the 'cabal popular' ('popular lifespring') that 'sospira, gesticula, percuteix, insinua com un múltiple ser vivent' ('breathes, gestures, percusses and insinuates itself like a multiple living being'), a development on the tree imagery used by Par and Morera i Galícia. Furthermore, the defence of Shakespeare's humanism is presented in terms of familiarity rare in descriptions of other 'classic' authors: 'Als dinou anys vareix conèixer Shakespeare, i sé que és un autor que llegim i rellegim i no hi trobem mai eixuta la virtut confortanta. I és, que llegir-lo és viure' ('At nineteen I discovered Shakespeare, and I know that he is an author who we read and reread and in whom we never fail to find comfort. For to read him is to live').[52] The same sort of personal testimony is presented by writers as diverse as Par, Eugeni d'Ors, Carner and later Cèsar August Jordana and Josep Maria de Sagarra, both of whom were to attempt to translate Shakespeare's complete works.

Once more, Farran i Mayoral is moved to write of Shakespeare by the publication of *Coriolà*. In his *Lletres a una amiga estrangera* he writes of how his spirit burns only on saying the name of Shakespeare and of a 'joia ubriaga' ('heady joy') somewhat tempered in this play by 'la serenor d'un seny en maduresa' ('the serenity of a mature mind', p. 106). The mastery of *joia* of which he so approves in Shakespeare is perhaps not reflected in the same restraint by Farran i Mayoral. The term is used six times in a four-page article, and complemented by the repetition of words such as 'ubriag', 'passions', 'intensa', 'viva', all forming part of Farran i Mayoral's Shakespearian recipe. Somewhat more restraint is shown by Carles Riba in his 'Elogi del poeta traductor', although he too uses the shorthand for Shakespeare of 'joiosa sensualitat'.[53] There are references to foreign writing on Shakespeare throughout this period in *La Revista*, showing a desire to communicate and connect with other cultures, through the optimistic openness associated with *joia*. Shakespeare is the canonical author most fully associated with this attitude in this intense period of cultural growth in Catalonia.

1920s and 1930s

In the 1920s references to Shakespeare become more muted. He is no longer presented as the salvation of Catalan theatre, for productions of the plays did not increase during the heavier propaganda of the 'militant' *Noucentista* years, although this must surely be attributed to the cultural repression of Primo de Rivera's dictatorship. Shakespeare does, however, continue to be represented as a source of influence, as a literary pattern far preferable to the 'decadence' of modern prose theatre, as Esclasans holds in a review of Ferran Soldevila's *Matilde d'Anglaterra*.[54] The article goes on to present a picture of Shakespeare burning with the passions bestowed on him by earlier critics, culminating in a 'voluptuous orgy of attitudes' and a 'conflagration of passions' which can only be resolved in silence 'per manca de potència en el verb' ('due to the powerlessness of words', p. 111).

The seeds sown by his predecessors are reaped once more by López-Picó in his 'Moralitats i Pretextos' in 1924.[55] A tree was once planted by Shakespeare, 'Simplement i sense festa de l'arbre com, potser, per celestial polidesa, hauria fet Tomàs Moore' ('Simply and without celebrating the tree, as perhaps Thomas Moore might have done, through heavenly politeness'). This 'well-planted' tree was to be distinguished by the words of the best poets of the 'gloriosa companyia'. In López-Picó's canon we find Byron, Wordsworth, Burns, Coleridge, Shelley, Browning, Tennyson, Keats, Rossetti, Patmore, Swinburne and Yeats, who are each moved to express their thoughts about Shakespeare's tree. Yeats finally asks himself, 'Què calla l'arbre?' ('What does the tree hide?'), reminding of the mystery of Shakespeare's personality, as well as his enveloping influence over the English poetic tradition. Only one poet in the list does not ask a question in response to Shakespeare's 'affirmative act of planting the tree'. In a note at the end, López-Picó imagines Browning's reaction – 'Jo vull aquest arbre' ('I want that tree') – to express the desire at the heart of immortality, presenting a curious counterpoint to the Catalan desire for Shakespeare. Rather than questioning his influence, this anecdote presents the need to transplant his legacy, and all that it stands for.

The nature of Shakespeare's tree continues to raise questions and inspire commentary in Catalan, but these are increasingly related to his expression in translations or to appreciation of particular plays. On the whole, this is the case with Josep Maria de Sagarra's articles for *La Publicitat*, although in 1923 he pauses to meditate on how Shakespeare figures in his imagination: 'a mida que passen els anys, cada vegada que m'aboco a contemplar la retòrica de Shakespeare, hi veig més ulls que em miren, més llavis que riuen i gemeguen, més paisatges assolellats amb arbres d'una gràcia eterna que es mouen sempre' ('with the passing of the years, every time that I contemplate the rhetoric of Shakespeare, I see more eyes that look, more lips that laugh and groan, more sunny landscapes with eternally graceful trees that are in constant movement').[56] His love of Shakespeare is reinforced by an article the following month describing him as 'l'home de teatre més formidable que hi ha hagut al món' ('the most formidable man of the theatre there has ever been').[57] Sagarra's scorn for approaches to Shakespeare, the 'semi-Déu', which attempt to impose formal rules on the plays also figures in a later article on Hamlet in which he asserts that 'mai em penso que a les branques d'aquest arbre shakespearià hi vagin a fer niu les teories' ('I doubt that theories will ever nest in the branches of this Shakespearian tree').[58]

A more extended consideration of the limits of applying formal, classical rules to Shakespeare is to be found in an article by Joan Crexells in 1925.[59] The question of Shakespeare's good or bad taste is raised following a production of *El marxant de Venècia* at the Romea theatre, in which one critic found the merchant's sharpening of his knife on the sole of his shoe rather vulgar. Crexells quotes Voltaire's criticism of Shakespeare's 'detestable' taste but goes on to deny the value of judging the plays in these terms. As far as he is concerned, 'Shakespeare és un d'aquells casos on totes les regles formals fallen. Es el geni que imposa a la producció les seves pròpies lleis, les quals no són aplicables a cap altra producció' ('Shakespeare is one of those cases where all formal rules fail. Genius imposes its own set of laws on production, which are not applicable to any other production'). Crexells refers to such considerations as 'petiteses' compared with the 'grandesa' and 'autenticitat' of the psychological depiction of character in Shakespeare's oeuvre. The influence of Farran i Mayoral's, and hence Emerson's Shakespeare is apparent here, as Crexells goes on to write: 'La grandesa de Shakespeare està en què els sentiments amb què ell juga joiosament, són els sentiments sota el domini dels quals viu la Humanitat' ('Shakespeare's greatness lies in the fact that the feelings with which he plays joyfully, are the feelings that dominate humanity').

More Shakespeare criticism comes with a series of reflections on the preceding thirty years of cultural activity in Catalan, in the late 1920s and 1930s. This period is also marked by the appearance of new translations and translators of Shakespeare, such as Carme Montoriol and C. A. Jordana. The latter produces two small volumes cataloguing a 'universal' canon of literature for the growing reading public in Catalonia. The first, *Què cal llegir?* lists 'classic' and contemporary works of interest to an educated reader.[60] The second is entitled *Resum de literatura anglesa* and contains a section on the Age of Shakespeare, in which Shakespeare figures as one of two 'genis de gran magnitud' who illuminate the Elizabethan period. The Age of Shakespeare is represented as the most fruitful period in English literature, he himself being the greatest of English poets.[61] The confusion over Shakespeare's life is considered, something that is later reflected upon fictionally by Joan Perucho and Jordi Mata.[62] This is followed by an historical overview of Shakespeare's four main periods of writing, from the history plays described as an attempt to mirror the traits of the England of his time in that of the Plantagenets, the comedies in which the dominant note is 'un interès i una simpatia còsmics que el fan jove eternament' ('a cosmic interest and attraction that make him eternally young'), to the tragedies and the late plays. Of Jonson, Jordana writes that 'les seves frases no tenen ni la gràcia ni l'esplendor de Shakespeare' ('his words have neither the grace nor the splendour of Shakespeare').[63] Carme Montoriol's prologues to her versions of *Cymbeline* and *Twelfth Night* are of interest because of the foreign critics she chooses to quote and her profound interest in Shakespeare's female characters, a position unusual in the critical studies cited up to this point. She also foregrounds the comedies, writing of 'aquella frescor i vivacitat que són la més alta valor de la comèdia shakespeariana' ('that freshness and vivacity that are the highest value in Shakespearian comedy').[64]

The final Shakespeare critic to publish studies of Shakespeare before the censorship of the post-war period is Ramon Esquerra. His contribution to the growing figure of Shakespeare consists of two essays in *Lectures Europees* and the study of influence, *Shakespeare a Catalunya*.[65] The 'Dues notes Shakespearianes' consist of brief studies of *Troilus i Cressida* and *Timó d'Atenes*. In the first, Esquerra expounds a theory of there being two ways to read the classics, 'l'una tenint en compte que ho són; l'altra, prescendint de tot prejudici històric' ('one that takes their classic status into account, the other without any historical prejudgement'). He goes on to maintain that Shakespeare can be read according to modern criteria, referring to his experience of reading C. A. Jordana's translations. Esquerra concludes that of all the classics Shakespeare is 'el més actual, i està molt més prop de la nostra sensibilitat que molts que actualment escriuen' ('the most contemporary, and he is closer to our sensibility than many of those writing today').[66] This prepares for the evangelical thrust of his historical study of *Shakespeare a Catalunya*, discussed earlier in this chapter. Notwithstanding the recognition in his introductory note to the work that: 'El camí a fer és encara molt llarg, fins a arribar a una assimilació dels valors immutables de l'obra shakesperiana' ('There is still a lot to do before achieving full assimilation of the unchanging values of Shakespeare's works', p. 8), he ends his volume with hope in the projected C. A. Jordana version of Shakespeare's complete works: 'Tindrem llavors l'edició catalana de Shakespeare que ens cal. Completa, prou erudita per a satisfer les necessitats del llegidor mitjà i alhora amb la necessària dignitat literària . . .' ('We will then have the Catalan edition of Shakespeare that we need. Complete, both erudite enough for the needs of the average reader and with the necessary literary dignity . . .', p. 194).

His dreams are not fulfilled. The Spanish Civil War puts an end to the 'Clàssics del món' translation project, and Jordana is killed. There are few critical studies of Shakespeare in post-war Catalonia, as Rosa Maria Martínez Ascaso's 1984 essay in the *Cuadernos de traducción e interpretación* will testify. The studies that exist tend to accompany translations, in particular those of Sagarra who gains the legendary status of being 'better than the original'. Sagarra's own prologues to editions of his translations in the 1950s pay lip service to the poet who he was obliged to translate in secret in the years immediately following the Civil War. In the prologue to the *Tragèdies Romanes* volume, there is a synthesis of pre-war recreations of the figure of Shakespeare:

> En l'estremidor volum que és l'obra de Shakespeare, i en el qual, allò que el Dant anomena *i movimenti umani*, és dut a una selecció arquetípica i a una temperatura exhaustiva, ens sorprèn la intuïció terrible del poeta creador, anticipant-se profèticament, i diríem voluntàriament, a les realitats històriques. Shakespeare, situat en el balbuceig de l'Imperi britànic, inclou en el seu teatre, d'una manera gairebé despòtica i al mateix temps ineluctable, la veritat d'aquell imperi dintre la nostra cultura occidental. Shakespeare

[...] situa [...] ja en els llocs definitius, la musculatura, el cor i el pensament d'aquesta edat moderna i d'aquesta cultura occidental que és la nostra.[67]

(In the thrilling volume that is the work of Shakespeare, in which that which Dante calls *i movimenti umani* is taken to a level of archetypal selection and to an exhaustive temperature, we are amazed by the terrifying intuition of the poet creator, who anticipates historical realities prophetically, and we would say intentionally . Shakespeare, located at the beginnings of the British Empire, includes in his theatre, in an almost despotic but at the same time ineluctable manner, the truth of that empire in Western culture. Shakespeare [...] locates [...] definitively, the musculature, the heart and the mind of this our modern age and this our Western culture).

The Post-War Period

The lack of new figurations of Shakespeare in the decades following the war is caused at first by the censorship of Catalan culture by the Franco administration. By the early 1950s there begin to be public productions and the end of that decade brings wider distribution of translations. Articles on Shakespeare's influence, such as the operas inspired by his works, appear in the newly-formed *Serra d'Or* in the 1960s and there are essays published by Catalan intellectuals in *Destino* to celebrate the quatercentenary of Shakespeare's birth.[68] However, even as reference to Shakespeare begins to increase once more, contributions concentrate on specific characteristics of his output, his contribution to the theatre and the quality of Catalan translations. The one great exception is the work of Josep Palau i Fabre in *El mirall embruixat* and *La tragèdia o el llenguatge de la llibertat* in which he focuses mainly on Shakespeare's significance for the theatrical canon, but these were not as widely accessible as criticism produced before the Civil War.[69] In part, the lack of new figurations of Shakespeare's universal currency are due to a sense of there being no question of Shakespeare's status as classic, and so the only points for discussion become rival interpretations of the plays rather than rival interpretations of 'Shakespeare'. Shakespeare continues to be present in Castilian in plays and dubbed films; he never quite disappears from the cultural economy. Yet there seems to be little new to be said about Shakespeare except for his constant 'newness', his ability to generate new theatrical discourses in every production. This perception does not differ from formulations before the War; in fact, the only changes in the universal figure of Shakespeare come in the disappearance of some of the more culturally-rooted keywords, such as *joia*. The Bard continues to be invoked in Catalan for his objectivity, his inclusivity, his poetry, contemporaneity and his generosity, values which conveniently justify the continuation of attempts to translate and perform his work in new versions. There are, of course, other implications in this discovery, of what some critics view as a 'lack' of adequate approximations to Shakespeare. That is, Shakespeare had already been determined in Catalan, by the 1930s, and that future invocations of his name draw with them the discursive strategies and implications that surrounded his early figurations, through the containment of that discourse in the translations. In this, Sagarra forms an important bridge between the two periods, for he is formed in the shadow of the early twentieth-century translations and productions, the cultural debates and ideas about theatre of the period, and it is largely he who determines how Shakespeare will figure in Catalan in the post-war period. It is, then, now necessary to consider what kind of figure Shakespeare cuts in Catalan, how he achieves meaning in Catalan rather than just the meaning, prestige or 'value' he gives Catalan culture.

Coda: Filling the Shakespeare Gap

Before moving on to the Catalan Shakespeare, discussion will centre briefly on why modern critics might focus on a 'lack' of approximations to Shakespeare.[70] It is due to continual concern about the question of how far there has been contribution towards increasing scientific knowledge of Shakespeare, rather than strategic recreation of Shakespeare as a – if not *the* – 'universal' figure of cultural legitimacy.[71] In tracing this history of the construction of Shakespeare in Catalan, I have not been much concerned with the accuracy or inaccuracy of interpretations of the texts, reproduction of Shakespeare's bibliography and the history of Elizabethan theatre, because my interest lies with issues of cultural reappropriation, in which it is more the claim of authenticity that counts than the revelation of ignorance of recent textual and historical evidence. The call for more accurate apparatus (the revelation of 'true' origins) is also part and parcel of a kind of cultural imperialism which continues to have currency today; the idea that only English critics, as well as a large body of Anglo-Americans, can achieve full knowledge of Shakespeare, and contribute to the question of what Shakespeare really means. Not only does this view persist in debates about the place of Shakespeare in the current British education system, where the decision to make certain passages from the complete works compulsory in the National Curriculum in the early 1990s was defended because it was felt they would teach children what it meant to be British, but equally in moves to suppress Shakespeare studies because of his English imperialism.

Although many Catalan editors, theatre reviewers and translators in the post-Civil War and post-Franco years increasingly look to England for the lead in seeking to understand Shakespeare, there is a strong tradition which seeks to break with this yoke, evidenced as early as Sagarra's 1923 article, and Morera i Galícia's decision to ignore textual authority – and also Par, incidentally – in his interpretation of 'To be or not to be' and his acceptance of Arthur Acheson's theories about the sonnets. In accounting for Par's exploration of Shakespeare's fortunes in Spain, one cannot help but be aware that Spanish and Catalan representations of the Bard are ultimately judged against aesthetic criteria implemented by German and English critics, and in terms of textual knowledge it is the advances in the anglophone world which are all important. For Par there is a science, a Shakespearology, which can be added to by working within the kind of textual and biographical studies undertaken in Britain, as part of the increasing professionalization of literary studies. So, it becomes clear that his own work, as a Shakespeare specialist, becomes a benchmark for criticism and its value; his the only translation which reproduces erudite notes based on different editions of the English versions of Lear, his the only respectable version of Shakespeare's life, a monument which is used to blame Morera i Galícia and Jordana for their inaccuracies. In some ways, then, the status of Shakespeare studies for Par is only set right by the appointment of a new professor at the University of Barcelona, Joan Mascaró, to teach English literature in the Facultad de Filosofía y Letras. A graduate of Cambridge, and having taught for a while in India, he has the imperialist credentials to teach a true course on Shakespeare. The lectures, although still perhaps a little too impressionistic for Par's taste, are seen to serve a disseminatory function, to teach his listeners to love Shakespeare.[72] The situation bemoaned by Par continues well into the twentieth century, with the reintroduction of a Faculty of English in Catalonia only occurring in 1979. It is a situation in Shakespeare studies which critics such as Pessarrodona only see being righted by the institution of translation enterprises like that of the *Instituto Shakespeare* in Valencia:

> No hi ha dubte que un traductor actual de Shakespeare té unes versions que no tenia fa cinquanta anys, perquè la massa d'estudis sobre cada obra determinada li pot alleugerir considerablement la seva tasca. Shakespeare va morir el 1616, però els estudis shakespeareans han pres una proporció fabulosa del romanticisme ençà, sinó que ho preguntin als estudiosos de l'Institut Shakespeare de València, una iniciativa i un treball continuat que, ai las!, no tenim.[73]

> (There is no doubt that the modern translator of Shakespeare has versions that were unavailable fifty years ago, so that the mass of studies on each work can alleviate his/her task considerably. Shakespeare died in 1616, but Shakespeare studies have taken on fantastical proportions since the Romantic period. Just ask the experts at the Institut Shakespeare in Valencia, a continuous project and initiative which, sadly, we do not have).

This, in itself, is perhaps another sign of Shakespeare's contemporaneity, his full identification with the advances of the scientific and technological age.

Since 1979 and the *Dies de Shakespeare a Barcelona* there have been a number of attempts to do justice to Shakespeare in Catalan, although in the main these have been through the endeavour to produce adequate productions and respectful translations of the plays. Readings of Shakespeare have been inspired by new generations of critics and directors, from Brecht and Kott and Strehler in the 1960s and 1970s to Brook and Bloom in the 1980s and 1990s.[74] Translations have been underpinned by recourse to new critical editions, and it is these that often contribute the analyses of Shakespeare present in any critical apparatus accompanying new Catalan texts. On the one hand, the figure of Salvador Oliva stands out for his work in raising awareness of the language of Shakespeare, simultaneously making Shakespeare accessible to new generations of readers and theatregoers, and taking a critical perspective on previous attempts to represent Shakespeare in Catalan.[75] Whilst, in the prologue to his 1986 translation of *Hamlet,* Oliva despairs of the 'mar tan immens d'interpretacions' ('immense sea of interpretations') of the play,[76] calling for containment to deal with the weight of critical incontinence, by 2000 he is confidently able to celebrate his own approach to the truth of the works: 'Resumint: la millor manera d'aproximar-se al teatre de Shakespeare és entrar-hi sense prejudicis i, amb l'ajut de les paraules, anar reconstruint el món que se'ns proposa reconstruir' ('To summarize: the best way of approaching the theatre of Shakespeare is to enter without bias, and, with the help of words, to set about reconstructing the world which we are given to reconstruct').[77] On the other hand, there is the Santa Susanna Shakespeare Festival, which seeks to embrace diverse approaches to Shakespeare's meaning, including recovery of the Catalan tradition of Shakespeare reception.[78] It represents a framework in which the true variety of Shakespeare can be viewed by Catalan theatregoers, as in other nations.

In some ways, the Shakespeares represented by these enterprises are embodied in two productions of *The Tempest* in the post-war period. A play often taken as Shakespeare's last will and testament, with Prospero as an alter ego for the ailing playwright, Nuria Espert and Jorge Lavelli (1983) clearly frame the play in such terms, indicating the increasing dramaturgical and paratextual sophistication of productions after the death of Franco, but also rooting their version in the readings of the Romantic movement, with numerous illustrations from works by William Blake. Their Prospero is visualized as a magician, playing with light reflections to produce the illusion of Ariel, within a magic box of theatre that allows only a little television-style window on to the world beyond the island. Thus, his theatre is able to contain all thought, nature, humanity even. Bieito's production in 1997 presents us with a philosophical Prospero, also playing with his resemblance to Shakespeare both in the production and in promotional material (see fig. 6). Once again, his Prospero–Shakespeare appears to be removed from political considerations, for the most part remaining as an observer of the dark actions of the shipwreck survivors. Here it is his everyday humanity that is emphasized; in fact, he appears rather like a school master, reminding us of the many lessons to be learned from Shakespeare as presented by Bieito's precursors. However in the context of a play which uses Catalan and Castilian, the teacher's imposition of Catalan on Caliban presents more problematic readings.[79] Finally, in his recent staging of *Richard III* (2005), Alex Rigola embodies the influence of Shakespeare on the stage, showing a number of Shakespeare clones encircling Richard, in order to signify Shakespeare's misrepresentation of the crimes of the Lancastrian king as politically motivated (see fig. 7). In this, Rigola both presents a creative and transgressive version of the play and begins to explore the nature of Shakespeare's authority, with recourse to a wide range of cultural narratives.

NOTES

1. Par, *Shakespeare y el folklore*, 3. Cited in introduction.
2. 'Influjo que ha ejercido y está ejerciendo Walter Scott en la riqueza, la moralidad y la dicha de la sociedad moderna', *Museo*, I (1838), 355. Bergnes qualified this view in an article in 1839 in which he identified the main sphere of Shakespeare's influence to be in England, but even here there is recognition not only that 'separado de la tierra nativa, no pierde sin embargo todo su poder' but that 'ningún hombre que se precie de literato puede abrirle [Shakespeare] sin encontrar en él mil cosas que no se olvidan jamás, pues en medio de aquel exceso de pujanza, de aquella expresión harto subida que da a menudo a sus caracteres, brillan rasgos de tal naturaleza que hacen olvidar todos sus defectos'. From 'Shakespeare', *Museo*, II (1839), 387.
3. Martínez Ascaso, 'Diàriament', 139. Quoted in introduction.
4. Apart from the introductions to Shakespeare in early lectures, *Lo rei Lear* and his later influence studies in Castilian, Alfons Par produces numerous versions of the life of Shakespeare, beginning with two short sketches in the *Butlletí de l'Ateneu Barcelonès*, I (1915–17), 225 and 287, which were linked to three lectures given at the Ateneu in 1916. See also, Par, *Shakespeare*, II, p. 219. A longer volume appears in the tricentenary year (1916) on the *Vida de Guillem Shakespeare*. The controversy over the real identity of Shakespeare, whether he was a Catholic, or really Bacon or Marlowe, makes regular appearances in different strands of the Barcelona press. See, for instance, 'Qui fou l'autor de *Hamlet*?', *Meridià*, 33 (26 August 1938), 1–2.
5. Morera i Galícia, for instance, insists that the sonnets are the one

work which allows the reader to see Shakespeare's soul. See his 'Proemi' to the *Selecta de sonets de Shakespeare* (Vilanova i la Geltrú: Oliva, 1913), also reproduced in *Catalunya*, 7 (10 January 1914), 23–6.

6   One of the most amusing instances of this catachrestic move was a long anecdote on a trip to Stratford by a friend ('X') of one of the theatre correspondents for a Barcelona magazine. In it we find critique of the 'exploitation' of Shakespeare's name – 'fins el vaig llegir en un *garaje* d'automovils' – and of the myths developed around that name for the benefit of tourists. This visitor was not about to swallow any stories about Shakespeare's birthplace, or death mask or tomb because 'de Shakespeare no se'n sab quasi res de cert y ... per tant, cal pendre ab recel tot quant d'ell te diguin'. He is amused by the way in which the sacred uncut text of *Hamlet* is recited like a prayer by all at a five-hour production, seeing such a practice as 'inútil, pesada i antiestética'. However, he does in the end find the 'true' spirit of Shakespeare 'en els camps que volten Stratford'. Thus we find an alternative spiritual myth of the Bard presented in place of the material vulgarity 'X' found at Stratford. See Loge, 'Qui espera desespera. – L'amich X. que ve de Stratford. – No hi vagis, noy! Shakespeare explotat. – In extenso!', *De tots colors*, IV (1 September 1911), 546–8.

7   This passing reference to Shakespeare comes in an article on the Italian actor, Novelli, and can be found in Joan Sardà, *Obras escogidas. Serie Castellana* (Barcelona: F. Puig y Alfonso, 1914), 117–18. In addition, some performances of Shakespeare's plays in the early twentieth century are announced by their operatic equivalent. So *The Merry Wives of Windsor* becomes *Falstaff* in some magazines, and *Romeo and Juliet*, *Julieta y* (or *i*) *Romeo*.

8   See Joan Maragall, 'Hamlet' and 'La Bella Victoria', in *Obres Completes*, 25 vols (Barcelona: Edició definitiva, 1929–55), XV, pp. 131–6, and VII, pp. 192–6, respectively.

9   Joan Maragall, *Obras completas. Serie Castellana*, 6 vols (Barcelona: Gustau Gili, 1912–13), III, p. 130, and IV, p. 110, respectively. Both assertions are also quoted in Esquerra, *Shakespeare* ..., pp. 113–14.

10 Goethe, Ibsen and, especially, Maeterlinck are considered to be the inheritors of Shakespeare by the *Modernista* movement.

11 Joan Maragall, *Elogi de la paraula i altres assaigs* (Barcelona: Edicions 62/'La Caixa', 1978 (MOLC 1)), p. 61. In a work from the same period, Maragall seals his approval of Shakespeare's value: 'Per embocar la vida de ple en ple en el teatre cal un autor de la raça de Shakespeare o Lope'. 'Angel Guimerà' (1909), p. 151.

12 Even more recent studies of approaches to Shakespeare in Spain admit their reliance on Par's work. See, for instance, González Fernández de Sevilla (ed.), *Shakespeare en España*.

13 As Manuel de Montoliu writes 'Fa temps que la ciència literària no hagi produït entre nosaltres una obra de tal envergadura' (*La Veu de Catalunya*, 18 May 1935). Cited alongside other reviews on the back cover of Par, *Shakespeare*.

14 The *Butlletí del Centre Excursionista de Catalunya*, 19 (April 1903), 118, contains details of two lectures given by Par on the 6 and 27 March of the same year, sketching Shakespeare's place in the history of English theatre, with detailed consideration of *Othello* and its sources and influences. The figure of Shakespeare is studied in more detail in 'Shakespeare; sa concepció y sa obra', *XXV Conferencies dades en la Associació Wagneriana* (Barcelona: Verdaguer, 1908), pp. 158–91. The lecture is dated as 16 May 1904. Also contained in this volume is a twenty-page study of *The Rape of Lucrece*, 'El forçament de Lucreça', pp. 470–92, delivered on 25 June 1906.

15 This translation relates to excerpts used for the second lecture given by Par at the *Centre Excursionista*. '*Othello. Quart acte*', *Catalunya* (May 1904), 5–15. *Catalunya* begins as a fortnightly literary review in 1903, changing to monthly in 1904. Although the final edition comes in 1905 and this might seem to suggest it was of limited interest, subsequent critics and literary historians have stressed the importance of its role in Catalan cultural life for a number of reasons. Most importantly, it was the brainchild of the youthful Josep Carner, soon to become one of the most respected modern Catalan poets. Jordi Castellanos, for instance, cites Carner as one of the key players in the professionalization of intellectual life in Catalonia, in his article 'El Noucentisme: una proposta de cultura', *L'Avenç*, 194 (July–August 1995), 20: 'Carner és, inicialment, el personatge clau: és ell qui modela, qui articula, sobretot des de la revista Catalunya [. . .] unes propostes culturals en les quals es compagina una determinada "modernitat" [. . .] amb actituds més aviat conservadores, sempre, però, amb un objectiu: la configuració d'un corrent cultural que primi la responsabilitat de l'intel·lectual, la seva preparació, la seva competivitat.' This view is supported by Albert Manent in *Josep Carner i el noucentisme* (Barcelona: Edicions 62, 1969) and *Escriptors i Editors del Nou-cents* (Barcelona: Curial, 1984), Jaume Aulet in his *Josep Carner i els orígens del noucentisme* (Barcelona: Edicions 62, 1993) and, in relation to the extension of this professionalization to a systematic programme of translation, Lluís Cabré and Marcel Ortin in 'Aproximació a Josep Carner, traductor (Els anys de l'Editorial Catalana: 1918–1921)', *Els Marges*, 31 (May 1984), 114–25, the philosophy and early basis of which is further developed in a paper given by Ortin at the first *Jornades d'Estudis Catalans* at Manchester in 1993.

16 'La búsqueda de una frase gráfica y que llame en gran manera la atención del lector impulsa, en general, a los críticos catalanes [. . .] a emplear un estilo atormentado, incisivo, lleno de galicismos y de paradojas.' Par, *Shakespeare*. . ., II, p. 218.

17 The page references for this lecture and the subsequent one on *The Rape of Lucrece* refer to the volume of lectures *XXV Conferencies* . . ., pp. 158–91 and 470–92, respectively.

18 The influence of thinkers such as Schlegel and Coleridge, drawing on Herder to prioritize organic models of creation as opposed to mechanical ones, with Shakespeare emerging as the supreme genius,

has been explored with mastery in M. H. Abrams, *The Mirror and the Lamp. Romantic Theory and the Critical tradition* (Oxford: Oxford University Press, 1953). See especially the section on 'Coleridge's Mechanical Fancy and Organic Imagination', pp. 167–77; Chapter VII 'The Psychology of Literary Invention: Mechanical and Organic Theories' and Chapter VIII 'The Psychology of Literary Invention: Unconscious Genius and Organic Growth', in particular part iii, 'German Theories of Vegetable Genius' pp. 201–13.

[19] Quoted on pp. 171 and 176 of *The Mirror and the Lamp*. Exposition of Coleridge's apotheosis of Shakespeare, setting him beyond Sophocles in that the latter's completeness is countered by the former's promise of progression and hence growth, evolution and rebirth, can be found in the section on 'Coleridge and the Aesthetics of Organism' in Abrams, pp. 218–25.

[20] With the dominance of Shakespeare in the English and German Romantic canon, it is hardly surprising that critics increasingly looked to his mind and work as the source of their being, as the supreme father of modern aesthetics. Carlyle, too, could be identified as a source for this generative and regenerative perception of Shakespeare. However, it is surely Emerson in his *Representative Men* who offers the pattern for Shakespeare reception reproduced here. Ralph Waldo Emerson, *Representative Men: Seven Lectures*, in *The Complete Works of Ralph Waldo Emerson: Centenary Edition*, 12 vols (New York: AMS Press, 1968).

[21] Quoted in Bristol, *Shakespeare's America*, p. 125.

[22] This will be explored further in subsequent chapters, drawing on longer excerpts from the same Par essay.

[23] 'Pròleg' to Shakspere, *La Tragedia de Macbeth, Traducció amb pròleg i notes per Cebrià Montoliu* (Barcelona: L'Avenç, 1907), pp. vii–xxxix. Specific page references will be given in the text.

[24] Letter 307 'A Joan Gili', 3 February 1940, collected in *Cartes de Carles Riba II (1939–1952)*, C. J. Guardiola (ed.) (Barcelona: La Magrana, 1991), pp. 97–8.

[25] Alberto Mira has identified this polymorphousness of Shakespeare to be the key to his 'canonicity', although his argument tells us little more really than that Shakespeare is canonical because so many people have read and translated him, that he remains more than the sum of these parts and the more parts the better, as it were. 'La tradición, la traducción, el tiempo: versiones del canon (el ejemplo de *Hamlet*)', *Donaire*, 8 (June 1997), 43–8.

[26] R. W. Emerson, *La confiança en sí mateix. L'amistat. Traducció de l'inglés, amb una introducció, per Cebriá Montoliu* (Barcelona: Biblioteca Popular de 'L'Avenç', 1904).

[27] One example of the many positive reactions in the Catalan press, can be found in *La Escena Catalana*, 36 (8 June 1907), 7.

[28] *La Escena Catalana*, 113 (28 November 1911). The lecture, 'De la tragedia', published by *Revista Teatralia*, 3 (1908), is also reviewed by Par in his *Shakespeare...*, II, pp. 223–4, to highlight the impressionistic character of early Catalan Shakespeare criticism.

29 There is also reference to Italian and Castilian productions and arrangements of Shakespeare plays, in particular the 1912 translation of *Hamlet* by Pompeu Gener.
30 *El somni d'una nit d'estiu* (Barcelona: Domènech, 1908), pp. 7–13. Also reproduced as '*El somni d'una nit d'estiu* de W. Shakespeare' in *El reialme de la poesia de Josep Carner*, N. Nardí and I. Pelegrí (eds) (Barcelona: Edicions 62, 1986), pp. 100–3.
31 Josep Carner, 'Del Shakespeare en llengua catalana', *La Veu de Catalunya* (14 August 1907). Written in response to the appearance of the Biblioteca Popular dels Grans Mestres, this article can also be consulted in *El reialme de la poesia* . . ., pp. 56–7.
32 'Per començar', *Les alegres comares de Windsor* (Barcelona: Domènech, 1909), pp. ii–iv.
33 J. Oller, 'D'En Carner y les seves darreres traduccions', *Catalana*, 2 (21 October 1909), 28–9, and M. Raventós, 'Sobre Schiller en el 150 aniversari de son natalici', *Catalana* 7 (25 November 1909), 102, respectively.
34 A. Par, *Lo rei Lear*, p. ix. Further page references will be given in the text.
35 The list includes Sidney Lee's *Shakespeare and the Modern Stage* (London: Constable & Co, 1907) and *The Chronicle History of King Leir* (London: Chatto & Windus, 1909); R. R. Buckley, *The Shakespeare Revival and the Stratford Movement* (London: Allen, 1911); C. W. Wallace, 'New Shakespeare Discoveries', *Harper's Magazine* (March 1910), and A. C. Bradley, *Shakespearean Tragedy* (London: MacMillan, 1905).
36 Morera, 'Proemi', *Catalunya*, 7, 23–6.
37 *Catalans* (30 September 1938), 12.
38 Carner, for instance, justifies his audacity in publishing a rather free version of *A Midsummer Night's Dream* by referring to the benevolence of Shakespeare. Carner, 'Abans que tot', p. 7.
39 Magí Morera i Galícia, López-Picó, *Venus i Adonis* (Barcelona: 'La Revista', 1917), pp. 9–12. Also see *El reialme de la poesia* . . ., pp. 140–2.
40 Rovira i Virgili, *La Revista*, 1 (15 May 1915), 1–2.
41 López-Picó, 'Temps i Espai', *La Revista*, 13 (15 April 1916), 13, and 8 (30 January 1916), 6.
42 *La Revista*, 14 (30 April 1916), 1–3. The essay is later published with the series of articles on 'La Renovació del teatre' and another essay on Sophocles, 'El poeta serè'. J. Farran i Mayoral, *La Renovació del teatre* (Barcelona: 'La Revista', 1917). Page references in the text are to this volume.
43 'Les humanitats i la nostra candidesa', *La Revista*, 36 (1 April 1917), 129. Collected in *Labor Dispersa* (Barcelona: 'La Revista', 1928), pp. 26–7.
44 Originally published in *La Revista*, 61 (1 June 1917). See Carles Riba, *Obres completes*, 2, I, E. Sullà (ed.), (Barcelona: Edicions 62, 1985), p. 178.
45 'Al marge de *Sonets i Odes*, de Keats, traducció de Marià Manent', *Obres completes*, 2, I, p. 149–50.

46   Josep Maria López-Picó, 'Dietari espiritual', *La Revista*, 31 (16 January 1917), 60.
47   Even in 1969, we find Joan Sagarra, in his introduction to a new edition of his father's translation of *Richard III*, referring to 'el gran Bill' (Barcelona: Selecta). Most Hispanists will also remember the reference in *Luces de Bohemia* to 'el gran William'.
48   *La Revista*, 34 (1 March 1917), 102–4.
49   'Les humanitats . . .', *La Revista*, 36, 129–32.
50   Jordi March (Carles Riba) review of *El poema espars* in *La Revista*, 58 (16 March 1918), 90–2. The *Lletres a una amiga estrangera* are first published in *La Revista* then collected into one volume, (Barcelona: 'La Revista', 1920). All subsequent references will refer to the 1920 volume.
51   '(Remarquem també com Emerson en parlar del *to sobirà* de Shakespeare el califica d'*alegre* . . . no de *joiós* com nosaltres)'. Farran i Mayoral, *Lletres* . . ., p. 44.
52   *La Revista*, 77 (1 December 1918), 419. Lleonart's later review of Magí Morera i Galícia's *Hamlet* is of more interest for the attitude to Shakespearian language shown, rather than any innovations in the representation of the figure of Shakespeare.
53   Riba, *Obres completes*, 2, I, pp. 85–7.
54   A. Esclasans review of Ferran Soldevila's *Matilde d'Anglaterra* in *La Revista*, 185–6 (1–16 June 1923), 110–11.
55   *La Revista*, 199–204 (January–March 1924), 3.
56   Safarra, 'Zacconi-Otel·lo', *La Publicitat* (28 January 1923).
57   Safarra, 'Hamlet a l'escena', *La Publicitat* (8 February 1923).
58   Safarra, 'Shakespeare, Zacconi', *La Publicitat* (7 February 1923).
59   Grexells, 'Shakespeare i el bon gust', *La Publicitat*, (2 April 1925).
60   C. A. Jordana, *Què cal llegir?* (Barcelona: Llibreria Catalonia, 1928).
61   C. A. Jordana, *Resum de literatura anglesa* (Barcelona: Barcino, 1934), pp. 18, 24.
62   Perucho's story 'Sheyton Barrett, el fantasme de Shakespeare' can be found in Castilian in *Destino*, 1421 (October 1964), 53, and in Catalan in his *Obres completes 3. Narracions* (Barcelona: Edicions 62, 1987), pp. 30–4. Jordi Mata's *La segona mort de Shakespeare* (Barcelona: Columna, 1999) plays with the idea that Shakespeare was, in fact, Marlowe.
63   Jordana, *Resum*, p. 34.
64   Introduction to *Nit de Reis* (Barcelona: 'La Revista', 1935).
65   Ramon Esquerra, *Lectures Europees* (Barcelona: Publicacions de 'La Revista', 1936), and *Shakespeare* . . .. Page references from the latter will be cited in the text.
66   Esquerra, *Lectures*, p. 66.
67   Josep Maria de Sagarra, *Shakespeare. Tragèdies Romanes* (Barcelona: Alpha, 1958), p. 7.
68   The latter are obviously in Castilian.
69   Josep Palau i Fabre, *La tragèdia o el llenguatge de la llibertat* (Barcelona: Rafael Dalmau editor, 1961) and *El mirall embruixat* (Palma de Mallorca: Moll, 1962).

70 Pessarrodona, 'Shakespeare a Catalunya' and González Fernández de Sevilla, *Shakespeare en España*.
71 In many ways, this seems to be far more of an anxiety in the rest of Spain, notwithstanding the comments of Rafael Portillo and Manuel Gómez-Lara, to the effect that 'In the case of regional communities like Catalonia or Galicia, Shakespeare is used to fill certain gaps in their own "national" literature, and so the use of their own native language is more important than any specific messages that may be drawn from the plays'. From 'Shakespeare in the New Spain: Or What You Will' in M. Hattaway *et al.* (eds), *Shakespeare in the New Europe* (Sheffield: Sheffield University Press, 1994), p. 219.
72 Par, *Shakespeare...*, II, pp. 239–41.
73 Pessarrodona, 'Shakespeare a Catalunya', I.
74 In particular, Jordi Coca uses every opportunity to review a Shakespeare production in order to offer the 'correct', historicist reading of the play. He is, for instance, critical of the failure of Georges Lavaudant and Calixto Bieito to understand that their respective productions of *Coriolanus* and *Macbeth* ought really to focus on questions of legitimacy. Jordi Coca 'Com que no hi ha rei', *Avui* (11 February 2002) and 'Macbeth, rei humà', *Avui* (4 March 2002). Both reviews may be consulted via http://www.teatrenacional.com
75 His introductions to his translations of the plays, both in the TV3–Vicens Vives and Proa editions offer invaluable insights into his personal understanding of Shakespeare, as well as his personal canon of Shakespeare critics. But most of all, it is his *Introducció a Shakespeare* (Barcelona: Empúries, 2000) which offers the most detailed study of the work of Shakespeare penned by a Catalan author.
76 Salvador Oliva, 'Pròleg', *Hamlet* (Barcelona: Vicens Vives–TV3, 1986), p. 5.
77 Oliva, *Introducció*, p. 60.
78 So far, the festival has incorporated a wide range of interpretations of Shakespeare's work, from musical versions to lectures on contemporary film adaptations; dance theatre to translation studies; opera to theatre history.
79 Helena Buffery, 'Navigating the Tempest: Translation and the configuration of identity in Catalonia', in Bermúdez, Cortijo Ocaña and McGovern (eds), *From Stateless Nations to Postcolonial Spain/De Naciones sin estado a la España Postnacional*, (Boulder: Society of Spanish and Spanish-American Studies, 2002), 63–79.

Chapter 3

The Catalan Shakespeare

Los genios se encuentran porque no toman
residencia fija en una sola nación.[1]

The previous chapter attempted to identify a rather slippery character, that is the kind of Shakespeare chosen by Catalans to shore up their own cultural productions. Why this may be perceived as problematic should by now have become clear in the representation of critical approaches to and descriptions of the playwright in Catalonia. One of the key methodologies to isolate and describe translation policy and its effects on the development of national and international poetics, as well as trends in cultural history, has been to identify choice. This approach continues to be valued by cultural historians and practitioners of translation studies, particularly when analysing the interplay of different fields and discourses in minority cultures, that is, societies in which 'culture' is not so much of a 'given' accepted tradition as that perceived in modern industrial nation states. Polysystems theorists have argued that developing cultures, and cultures in crisis, are far more likely to turn to translation to fill gaps or provide new models for literary production. The work of Foucault, meanwhile, has encouraged scrutiny of such cultural 'givens', showing how many characteristics of modern society which are supposed to be essential are in fact historical constructs rather than unchanging truths. Indeed, the history of Shakespeare reception itself has provided a number of interesting cultural genealogies, in the work of Anglo-American New Historicists and British exploders of the 'Shakemyth' and 'bardolatry'.[2]

Whilst reading patterns into the lists of works and authors chosen can reveal aesthetic trends at a given moment in time, whether in translation or in the drawing up of 'universal' canons, it is also clear that the act of choosing 'Shakespeare' can mean a number of different things. Choosing *Hamlet* as the supreme example of world theatre may not, for instance, be thought to be particularly significant in tracing the aesthetic leanings of a particular culture in the nineteenth and twentieth centuries, whereas the decision to translate a large body of Shakespearian comedies within a cultural context where most attention and prestige has been reserved for the tragedies, might be perceived to be more meaningful.³ Hence the Biblioteca Popular dels Grans Mestres collection of Shakespeare translations, in which of the sixteen volumes published there are ten comedies and two histories, has been identified as a means of popularizing a comic Shakespeare in Catalonia, unprecedented in the peninsula, and the rather spurious evidence of increased Shakespeare translation and interest from 1909 onwards explained as a 'civilized' attempt to counteract the barbarism of the *Setmana Tràgica*. Whilst the welcome given by critics to the advent of the Biblioteca Popular dels Grans Mestres is unanimous in its praise of an incomparable enterprise, to overstate its political intention and impact, although tempting, is rather problematic. Many of the translations were not, for instance, commissioned, but reflected the interests of individual writers; indeed, a few were originally conceived for theatrical production. It is not the kind of uniform project that might be perceived in other translations of the complete works, such as those of Jordana, Sagarra and more recently Oliva into Catalan. Assumpta Camps' vision of an almost institutional turn to Shakespeare and theatre translation after the *Setmana Tràgica*, ignores the fact that interest in Shakespeare was already growing before this event, and that there is no evidence of there being a larger number of Shakespeare translations and commentaries in the years 1910–15.⁴

Just as Shakespeare's 'Englishness' has made him a staple of the heritage industry in England as well as a didactic tool for inculcating national pride in the National Curriculum, in Catalan he can at times be observed to represent the characteristics of English imperialism. The increasing domination of Anglo-American criticism in seeking to reveal the true Shakespeare, in terms of biography, language and textual authenticity, manifest in the works of Alfons Par, as well as in subsequent identification of its supreme authority in analyses of contributions to Shakespeare criticism in Spain, has had immense influence in determining the available meanings of Shakespeare. Presiding over the comparative trend to bemoan the lack of adequate approximations to Shakespeare in the Hispanic world, discussed in the previous chapter, is the inescapable enormity of the Shakespeare industry in the English-speaking world.[5]

Part of the problem in ascribing cultural significance may be traced to the over-evangelism and, at times, downright imperialism of canon criticism. A Western canon composed of mainly white, middle-class gentlemen, may indeed be oppressive but surely more so when the meaning of these gentlemen, what they represent, is fixed by those critiquing them. A Shakespeare who fully represents English colonial greatness is a rather exclusive, marginalizing force, particularly when he is simultaneously used to represent a universal picture of mankind. Yet persistence in upholding the ideal of the exclusive Englishness of Shakespeare (or even attacking Shakespeare for embodying this ideal), even after the now long tradition of postcolonial, feminist, gay, foreign and intercultural readings, is just a way of avoiding the issue of what a 'universal' canon can mean, however reductive the list. The drawing up of canons is arbitrary, and nowhere more so than when it is presented as a 'universal' canon or Bloom's 'Western Canon'.[6] It is arbitrary in the exercise of personal preference, or even knowledge or ignorance, as is now the common acceptance of the term. Canons depend on the accessibility of texts, and access to texts depends on canons. However, the more Nietzschean side of this arbitrariness, a side which Bloom surprisingly did not draw on to defend his transumptive list of North American will-to-power, points to the interventionist aspect of canon-formation, the urge to create a culture in one's own shape.[7] To continue with Bloom, the central place given to Shakespeare, after the Old Testament and Dante, cannot be read in isolation from his own theories of poetic influence and all-inclusiveness, and hence his own anxiety of influence.[8] Long has been his claim, rather sphinx-like, that Shakespeare pre-empts and contains all post-Shakespearean poetry, thought, psychology, humanity even. This is not just a Shakespeare who is 'all things to all men' but one who *is* – because he contains – all things and all men. Shakespeare is, then, as much the authority behind Bloom's 'Western Canon' as he is a part of it. He is the ultimate figure of origins in Bloom's account of modern tradition.

In many ways, the Bloomian model of influence offers some insight into the difficulties of pinning down the meaning of Shakespeare as a cultural symbol. After the re-evaluation of Shakespeare in the Romantic Age, the pattern of the Bard's apotheosis seemed to have been established. Bloom himself does not escape this; in particular he is indebted to Emerson's recreation of Shakespeare to represent the modern age, in line with some of the Catalan commentary we have already seen. However, the previous chapter demonstrated how this is very much based on a nineteenth-century paradigm, one which continued to require some defence in the Catalonia of the turn of the century. So, parallel with clear appropriation of Shakespeare as universal cultural achievement, there is a strong sense of the arbitrariness of his position. Counter-moves to the universalizing tendency can be observed in decisions to choose certain aspects of his 'greatness' over others and to continue the debate (or at least to reproduce the debate, also present in Bloom) over where Shakespeare's strengths and weaknesses lie.

What was presented in its simplest terms in the previous chapter, as recuperating a figure (or figures) of Shakespeare from amidst a list of universal attributes borrowed from other cultural criticism and aesthetic tracts, should now be seen to be far more complex. These choices do not produce a Shakespeare who is wholly different, wholly foreign, even when compared with the Shakespeare of English wartime productions of *Henry V*, or the Shakespeare of the Tory party in the 1980s and 1990s, not to mention Goethe's Shakespeare, Coleridge's Shakespeare, Emerson's Shakespeare, even Bloom's Shakespeare. Yet they do reveal arbitrary urges to create a culture in a particular shape, right down to the most obvious level, the desire to communicate with, and be on a par with other world cultures. There is, then, evidence of the choice of Shakespeare's revealing an aspect of a new aesthetic paradigm in Catalonia, relatively autonomous from other social fields. The identification of this paradigm in Shakespeare, as something which represents a universal value but also a particular, English one – as something that is part of the heritage of all cultures, product of a wide movement, yet is increasingly perceived to be best served by Anglo-American criticism – reveals a tension. How can choice, will-to-power, desire to recreate and pay homage to Shakespeare be sanctioned when there is a true Shakespeare to be recovered behind the tropes? This tension underlies the critical positionings of the previous chapter; the urge to let Shakespeare shine in Catalan as he had in other cultures giving way to criticism of the inadequacy of approximations. In many ways, this is the double bind perceived by alterity theorists, where translation of the other is condemned to reproduce a different other by at the same time seeking to make it the same.[9]

Shakespeare, in his omniscient position, is both insider and outsider, contains and cannot be contained, and this is nowhere more plain than in the initial quotation from Ernesto Rossi's 1868 lecture on *Hamlet* in Barcelona. Shakespeare's residence in every nation does not simply hide or overcome difference but reproduces it, and can be arbitrarily employed to represent the universal and the particular. Catalan refigurations of Shakespeare show signs of embracing this paradox from the very earliest critical formulations and translations. Shakespeare's all-inclusive mirror up to nature and humanity, also contains Catalan and Catalonia. His prefiguration of the modern age can also show the way forward for a modern Catalonia; his theatrical prowess can reflect on Catalan theatre; his use of language can offer a model for the recuperation of the Catalan language. Part of this ubiquity may indeed be traced to the supreme arbitrariness with which Bloom endows Shakespeare himself, as the playwright who drew on a plethora of sources but without anxiety, shaping his own world. As has been shown, the Catalan reshaping of Shakespeare cannot fully escape the history of his global reception. Here, though, Shakespeare will be explored in his Catalan manifestation, in terms of his 'residence' – although never quite 'fixed' – in one particular nation.

It could well be argued that there are as many different meanings of Shakespeare in Catalan as there are translations; as there are readings of those translations, in fact. However, what will be discussed here is how and what Shakespeare means in Catalonia, whether it be through selective recontextualization of the attributes presented in the previous chapter or in the rhetorical urge to convince of specifically Catalan patterns for Shakespeare's figuration. There are a number of different fields in which the meaning of Shakespeare experiences a Catalan shift, is used to sanction, legitimate or anticipate specifically Catalan cultural concerns. On an institutional level, Shakespeare, together with or within select lists of world artists, is drawn upon by different cultural and political agents to defend a pattern for the cultural and political development of Catalonia. This process can be explored in the specific positioning of Shakespeare within an exemplary canon, as evidenced in the chapter on critical positionings, or in calls or nods towards Shakespeare and his texts to underpin political keywords or cultural values. In the previous chapter we witnessed Shakespeare's association with *joia* and the values of the 'modern age', but Shakespeare is, of course, additionally chosen by successive critics to offer a model for the renewal of Catalan theatre, or at least to participate in the debate over how to create a new paradigm for theatrical production. The recuperation of a successful theatrical tradition is also linked to other cultural and political advances in Catalonia, and Shakespeare becomes a figure who can legitimize – as well as be legitimized by – institutional keywords and decisions.

What is more, even in seemingly autonomous considerations of the value of Shakespeare, recourse to the same list of keywords and desired attributes used in other fields, contributes to position the Bard within specific movements or cultural and political ideals.[10] The translations themselves, as shall be seen in chapter 5, are positioned linguistically, whether through conscious or unconscious translation choice, within the interplay of the different cultural fields that inform their moment. Alongside the emerging picture of an institutional Shakespeare, there is strong evidence of a personal Shakespeare, the smiling impartial humanist who influences a succession of writers, according to their own testimony, in their chosen path. This Shakespeare, who is a father to original Catalan writing, however far removed from his stories, reveals to us and underpins another Catalan Shakespeare. It is with the latter Shakespeare that this chapter will end: the Shakespeare who is born of Catalan conception, who can be traced, in that supreme revisionary move, to something Catalan.

The central text for uncovering the figure of Shakespeare in Catalan is Josep Carner's essay 'Del Shakespeare en llengua catalana', which stands as the first sustained attempt to analyse what and how Shakespeare can come to mean in Catalan.[11] Here, it will be considered in relation to other 'anostraments de

Shakespeare'.[12] Why Carner's article may be perceived to hold such significance for the pattern of Shakespeare reception in Catalonia might at first appear to be little more than a cultural accident. Coming in 1907, it can be linked with ease to the origins of *Noucentisme*, although specifically it represents one amongst many positive responses to the Biblioteca Popular dels Grans Mestres collection of Shakespeare translations which began to be published that year. Other writers had drawn attention to the cultural possibilities in translating and appropriating Shakespeare, but Carner's tract builds a bridge between individual testimonies to the greatness of Shakespeare and the more institutional bent of *La Veu de Catalunya*, particularly in the years following Prat de la Riba's exposition of the aims of Catalan nationalism.

Carner's importance to the cultural development of the *Noucentisme* ideal has been recognized by many modern critics, however here he takes on a more specific role as promoter of Shakespeare in Catalan. How influential his essay was in this promotion remains unclear. Praise of the Biblioteca is not uncommon in the periodicals of the period, whatever their ideological tendencies. However, Carner's participation within the collection itself, in translating three plays, two of which were performed in the years that followed, the third programmed for production, left marks of deep and lasting influence. Apart from the debate his translations and the productions raised at the time, subsequent writers and translators have testified to it being a formative moment, in terms of presenting a new vision for the future of Shakespeare and of poetic drama in Catalan (see fig. 8). Farran i Mayoral, for instance, sees the *Somni* as the 'primer pas seriós vers el nostre gran teatre' ('the first serious step towards our own great theatre').[13] Carner's consideration of the meaning of Shakespeare in and for Catalan hence brings together a number of discourses at what has been perceived as a crisis or turning point for Catalan culture. Traces of *Modernista* and Romantic influence blend with the keywords used to define a new cultural programme. Its grounding in a particular cultural moment is further expanded by the links it lays down with subsequent discourse on the value of translation in Catalonia. Before moving to discuss the positions taken in Carner's article and their echoes in other writers of the period it is important to map out briefly the discursive field in which they are inscribed, in order to understand the place Shakespeare held within it.

The importance of the *Noucentista* movement in helping to create, sanction and support a number of model institutions for the promotion and expansion of Catalan culture is widely recognized, notwithstanding some criticism of its conservative nature. Aspects of its legacy that in some way underpin modern Catalan society include the institution of the Mancomunitat, Pompeu Fabra's work on grammar and orthography and the foundation of the Institució de la Llengua, the creation of the Institut d'Estudis Catalans and the reform of the university and public libraries. This was also a period of great social upheaval, punctuated by workers protests and the *Setmana Tràgica*, the economic growth and then slump experienced during the First World War, and increasing censorship leading up to Primo de Rivera's dictatorship. Whatever the landmarks of periodization chosen by critics, the first decade of the twentieth century is recognized as signalling a shift in cultural paradigm, from *Modernisme* to *Noucentisme*. This paradigm shift is visible through a shift in discourse, in particular that used to persuade of the necessary direction of Catalan culture. Central to the development of the Catalan language and culture before the Civil War, and its subsequent interpretation in the postwar and, particularly, post-Franco period, were certain ideological keywords. These were framed in the process of aesthetic and political normalization (the promotion of Catalan in the social sphere) and 'normativization' (the production of agreed standards for written language), and their bearing on the translation of the nationalist ideal.

The publication of Prat de la Riba's *La Nacionalitat Catalana* in 1906 heralded a new sense of purpose in the social and political acculturation of the Catalan territories, with increasing emphasis on the creation of a 'cosmopolitan' centre in Barcelona.[14] It was followed by the identification of many intellectuals of the period with *Noucentisme* and its accompanying baggage of aestheto-political terms. Even writers who questioned or rejected the normativism of the movement would participate in some way in the dialogues and debates produced by its discursive field. Chapter IX of Prat de la Riba's seminal work deals with 'L'Imperialisme', represented as 'el període triomfal d'un nacionalisme: del nacionalisme d'un gran poble' ('the triumphal period of a nationalism: of the nationalism of a great people'). Drawing on Romantic metaphors, the *Lliga* politician represents imperialism as being born of the moment following the fullness of interior life, when the accumulated internal force of nationality moves outwards, emerges from the mother to fill and bring fertility to the surrounding plains: 'Imperialisme és força de civilització, que vessa d'un poble, de vida nacional intensa, sobre els altres' ('Imperialism is a force of civilization, that pours forth from a people, of intense national life, onto others', p. 111).

Here is expressed a perception of the primordial nature of intervention to the thinkers of the period, set against or between the nineteenth-century ethics of revolution and/or evolution.[15] It was accompanied, and underpinned, by renewed interest in the humanist legacy of the Classical world, part of the Mediterranean mythology we have seen underlined by Alfons Par and Cebrià Montoliu.[16] The effects of this attraction can be detected in the proliferation of references to Greek literature in magazines such as *La Revista* and the later programme of translation and re-translation of Greek and Roman writers, culminating in the work of the Fundació Bernat Metge.[17] Eugeni d'Ors, writing as Xènius, reclaimed Classicism as an antidote to Romanticism throughout his *Glosari*, in affirmations such as the following: 'Som imperialistes els altres, i defensem una tradició humana, enriquida de matisos diversos, però fonamentalment única, és a dir, derivada de la cultura greco-llatina...' ('We, however, are imperialists, and we defend a human tradition, which though enriched by many different shades, is fundamentally one, that is, the tradition derived from Graeco-Roman culture...').[18]

Although this prioritization of Classical models, in politics as well as in art, sometimes led to criticism of Shakespeare's natural exuberance, his rare attainment of the serenity of Sophocles, it is important to note that the English tradition was not one which was held to be wholly at odds with this Mediterranean focus.[19] The importance of England as a model, present in official discourse, can also be found in private writings of younger writers such as Marià Manent. His diary entry for 24 July 1919 reads 'Sempre petits nuclis han estat les grans fonts de civilització, perquè les grans extensions territorials són inhumanes. Vegi's quina influència no han exercit en el món el petit tros de península balcànica que s'anomena Grècia, [...] la reduïda Anglaterra al temps d'Isabel i de Shakespeare: foren pobles petits, *però intensos*' ('It has always been small nuclei that have been the main sources of civilization, for the great territorial expanses are inhuman. Consider for instance the influence exercised on the world by the little plot of Balkan peninsula known as Greece, [...] the modest England of the time of Elizabeth and of Shakespeare: they were small lands, but intense ones').[20] In Prat de la Riba, we find:

> Sigues tu mateix. No imitis, no cerquis en els altres, cerca dintre teu. No t'emmotllis als altres, fes que els altres s'emmotllin a tu. Sigues llei i senyor de tu mateix. Allà on tu ets, és l'eix de la terra; així pensaven els qui van fer la Grècia, els qui han fet *l'Anglaterra*. Pensa que tu ets el centre de les coses, que totes les coses són per a tu; que la veritat que tu trobes dintre del teu cor és la veritat per a tothom; que les fórmules de civilització que tu adoptes són les que tot el món ha de seguir i adoptar. Es a dir: sigues tu mateix i per a tu mateix, i seran tributaris del teu jo els qui no són ells ni són per a ells.

> (Be yourself. Do not imitate, do not seek things in others, but in yourself. Do not mould yourself on others, make others mould themselves on you. Wherever you are, there is the centre of the earth; that is how those who made Greece thought, and those who made *England*. Think that you are the centre of all things, that all things are yours; that the truth that you find in your heart is the truth for everyone; that the rules of civilization that you adopt are those that the whole world should follow and adopt. In other words, be yourself and for yourself, and all those who are not themselves nor for themselves will pay tribute to you, p. 109, emphasis added).

The 'imperialism' valued here is clearly advocated as an antidote to colonialism, a call to reject outside influence, particularly that of Spain. The desire to achieve Catalan 'imperialism', then, accompanies the reformulation of nationalism as a process, as something which must go beyond the Romantic recognition of essential difference, a concept which is not enough to guarantee cultural survival. Hence, as well as identifying the necessity of organized intervention rather than simply allowing organic growth to take place, value is placed on the Nietzschean concepts of arbitrariness and voluntarism, on choosing to change the shape of things, whether in politics or linguistic norms or cultural policy. This kind of discourse may indeed produce discomfort today – as it did for many writers then – with its fascist overtones. Many of the conflicting sentiments occasioned by modern nationalisms seem to be contained within these right-wing formulations. Yet there is also a sense in which they exemplify, often consciously, the paradoxes present in all cultural and aesthetic movements: the creation of autonomy being always already dependent on the *other*, the outside, occasioning the constant necessity to shift conceptual and hence metaphorical boundaries. So for instance, England was perceived to have 'exalçat, amb l'exemple tant com en la paraula encesa dels seus grans homes, quelcom que la veu contemporània ha batejat d'imperialisme' ('extolled, both in the stirring words and in the deeds of her great men, something that contemporary wisdom has baptised as imperialism', p. 107). Amongst her 'great men', it was Shakespeare who was to be granted a central role in the adoption of these precepts. As Farran i Mayoral later comments in retrospect: 'si havem de parlar de sincers, Shakespeare ho era tot per a nosaltres en aquells anys d'adolescència' ('to be sincere, Shakespeare was everything to us in the years of our youth').[21]

Why this might have been so can be apprehended in the attributes of Shakespeare underlined in the previous chapter. Shakespeare's figuration as a creator of whole worlds, through reappropriation of the Classics, his blend of serenity and *joia*, his avoidance of imposition in exercising his supreme artistic will, come together to make him a potent figure of imperialism, above and beyond his representation of a peculiarly English genius. Even so, an aspect of English imperialism was also to be criticized, most vocally in its employment against Ireland. There is clear identification with the plight of Ireland, along with that of other minority cultures and states, in periodicals of the period, ranging from commentary on political events to the translation of minority literatures to the fanciful representation of Irish resistance, in the original Catalan play *Jordi Erin*. Furthermore, the 1914–1918 war led to soul-searching over the appropriate frame for intervention, imperialism and arbitrariness, in the problematization of Nietzsche as well as the question of whether to identify with either or neither of the imperialist urges of England or Germany.[22]

The fact that translation – and it was soon to be institutionalized translation, as exemplified in the work of Josep Carner with the Editorial Catalana from 1918 to 1921 – played a central part in the *Noucentista* programme of cultural and linguistic reform, may also seem paradoxical, particularly when set against Prat de la Riba's above advocation of originality and autonomy. *Noucentista* writers encouraged such a programme, at times over and above 'original' creation, as was the case in their attitude towards Catalan theatre, yet it was a policy that provoked debate up to and beyond the Spanish Civil War. Here, a very particular role was postulated for Shakespeare in Catalan, as an example of the virtues of borrowing plots from other writers. Farran i Mayoral, for instance, advised budding dramatists to remember that both Racine and Shakespeare were often inspired adapters.[23] Recourse to Shakespeare thus became a way of overcoming the paradox, for Shakespeare himself was presented as having been able to reconcile creative genius with translation, and with attention to the surrounding marketplace. The radical nature of this paradigm shift becomes clear when one considers the status of '*refundición*' in nineteenth-century Spain. It was not in any way considered a creative exercise.

Translations from other languages of what were perceived to be the 'Classics' of the world literary canon, were identified as an essential tool in the forging of a poetic language in Catalan, with the 'poet' marked out in his role as moral and aesthetic educator. Within this movement Shakespeare was identified – as we have seen – by many writers as the 'Joiós sobirà', the joyous sovereign, underlining his weight as cultural currency in the new age Catalonia. *Joia* became one of the key concepts in aesthetic criticism of the period, as a counterbalance to the perceived decadence of the *fin de siècle*. It has been suggested that the concept is drawn from Keats's 'A thing of beauty is a joy forever', but this is only part of the story. As an intertext which figures the rampant creativity of Shakespeare, mediated by the English and German Romantics and Emerson, *joia* comes to represent the primordial nature of cultural intervention, the individual originality to be obtained from universal communion sensed in readings of the 'Sea-change' quotation from *The Tempest*. Its link to the regenerative tradition of Coleridge, Emerson and Nietzsche took particular meaning in the Catalan cultural climate, as part of an urge towards unflinching humanism, and renewed enthusiasm in sustained cultural revival. Indeed, Prat de la Riba's very chapter on imperialism draws on Emerson to identify individual liberty with national awakening, rewriting the liberalist American address to the individual as an address to the 'poble' or nation. The participation of the individual, active intellectual was in many ways more of a priority than the activation of the masses, although it should be noted that many of these intellectuals were able to lay the foundations of more lasting institutions. The kind of treasure that could be produced by Shakespeare's figuration in Catalan is often considered but perhaps never as concisely or suggestively as in the words of Marià Manent. He writes of Magí Morera i Galícia's renderings of Shakespeare's sonnets as: 'una tasca subtil d'orfebreria catalana amb els diamants i l'or puríssim de Shakespeare' ('a subtle work of Catalan filigree with the diamonds and purest gold of Shakespeare').[24]

In his 1907 'Del Shakespeare en llengua catalana' Josep Carner offers a more explicit picture of the perceived cultural needs in the reworking of Shakespeare:[25]

> Perquè el català esdevingui abundós, complexe, elàstic, elegant, és necessari que els mestres de totes les èpoques i tots els països siguin honorats amb versions a la nostra llengua [...] Perquè la literatura catalana es faci completa, essencial, il·lustre, cal que el nostre esperit s'enriqueixi amb totes les creacions fonamentals. Com podria ésser sumptuós un palau, sense els hostes!
>
> (So that Catalan might become abundant, complex, elastic and elegant, it is necessary that the masters of all the ages and all the nations should be honoured with versions in our language [...] So that Catalan literature might be made complete, essential and illustrious, it is necessary that our spirit be enriched with all the essential creations. How could the palace be sumptuous without its guests! p. 56).

The passage opens with clear recognition of the utility of incorporating 'universal' cultural treasures into Catalan. However, the issue of the nature of their influence is carefully balanced, and it is useful here to observe the transitivity of the passage. These masters of all ages are to be honoured in Catalan, hence Catalan is given the active role in producing the required benefits. Furthermore, it is made plain that it is not the foreign works themselves that will produce 'essential' Catalan literature; they will merely aid in enriching the collective spirit that will achieve such creations. Such a formulation is important in shedding light on the kind of cultural imperialism embraced by Prat de la Riba and his followers. Catalonia is to provide the framework, the palace to contain such treasured guests. There is less of a sense of Catalan culture finding its sustenance in Shakespeare – let alone the cultural anthropophagy prescribed for creative translation in Brazil – than inviting him to eat at the Catalan table. The imagery used by Carner blends a biblical, parabolic feel, which harks back to the evangelical tone of much *Renaixença* glorification of the Catalan language.

The key roles of translators and translations in furthering the Catalan imperialist ideal is also expressed in Carles Riba's 1918 essay 'Elogi del poeta traductor'.[26] He writes of the equivalence of translation to close critical reading, underlining the need for translation in order to form an infallible tradition of cultural heritage, with the treasures of different times and places renewed in Catalan. He goes on to write that 'en ells trobem els catalans una plenitud d'història de l'esperit que, ultra compensar-nos dels segles de silenci, pot fer-nos obirar un nostre futur imperi de cultura' ('in them we Catalans find a fullness of spiritual history that not only makes up for centuries of silence, but might help us create our own future cultural empire'). So we see how what begins as a filling of gaps in cultural production, as a necessary precondition for further creativity, begins to figure the step towards originality more immediately. The treasures become figures of imperialism, understood as endlessly displaced desire for plenitude rather than the oppression of one culture by another.

It would, then, be too simple to see the imperialism advocated by politicians and intellectuals as a mark of respect for the 'English' Empire and all her territories. It is more the expression of a desired step towards cultural normality by universalizing the tastes of Catalan readers and writers. The controlling intellectuals are portrayed as 'imperialist' fighters raiding the hoards of world culture in order to eventually attain universality for the autochthonous literature resulting from this process of acculturation. So the main function of the metaphor may in fact be seen to persuade of the necessity of intellectual intervention, of the primordial function of artists and intellectuals in Catalan culture. It is, perhaps, unsurprising that Shakespeare would represent an ideal model for certain aspects of this will-to-power, and such voluntarism is patent in a wide range of reviews of the BPGM translations. Consideration of Carner's *Somni*, for instance, leads to the following statement of future intent. 'Si algú queda descontent del resultat, paciencia; quan se fa lo que's pot es senyal gairebé infalible de que un temps se farà lo que's voldrà en sentit de perfecció y demés' ('If anybody is dissatisfied with the result, have patience; when one is able to do what one can it is almost a sure sign that the time will come when one will be able to do what one wants, both in terms of perfection and in other senses').[27] Another review has the following messianic presentation of the wondrous event: 'la fé y la voluntat aturen muntanyes: o les redressen, que en ocasions ve a ser la mateixa cosa' ('faith and will stop mountains: or they restore them, which on occasions comes to mean the same thing').[28]

The necessity to look and strive beyond the frontiers of Catalanism is reaffirmed in the second paragraph of Carner's essay, gesturing towards another of Eugeni d'Ors' and Prat de la Riba's keywords, 'universalism':

> I certament mai allò que sigui absolut autoctonisme – i per lo tant parcial humanitat – pot senyorejar l'univers [...] Per fortificar-se un, i viure esplèndidament, necessita quelcom semblant a acaparar la riquesa de la sang agena, convertint-la en estrènua saba personal, multiplicant sempre els esforços per intensificar aqueix exclusivisme heroic i genial de fer afluir a la pròpia essència totes les deus inestroncables de la vida.
>
> (And there is no doubt that nothing that is absolutely autochthonous – and hence of partial humanity – can rule the universe [...] To strengthen oneself, and live in splendour, one needs to be able to collect and store the riches of foreign blood, converting it into a courageous personal sap, and to always multiply one's efforts to intensify the heroic and inspired exclusivism that is to make all the irrepressible springs of life flow into one's personal essence, p. 56).

The pattern for imperialistic growth described here is both indebted to the organic aesthetic of Romanticism and shows the more overtly Catalan twist perceived in *La Nacionalitat Catalana*. By strengthening the centre, the *jo* can produce its own sap, by shaping outside fluids for itself, for its own ends. Such a rejection of absolute autonomy reflects criticism of Spain's separation from European culture in this period, and is counteracted by the universalizing opposite to 'partial humanity' that is the aspiration to greatness. Interestingly, Shakespeare in the same essay fully represents this opposite – 'és el més magnífic compendi de la nissaga humana' ('the most magnificent compendium of the human race') – and hence we may see how a specific cultural value can be transformed into the supreme 'universal' cultural legitimator. The translation of Shakespeare becomes a way of overcoming domination and developing a distinct cultural identity, but also a way of justifying a change in the power relations between different cultures. Indeed, it is arguments such as these that underlie the pan-Catalanism of many Catalan politicians and intellectuals of the early decades of the twentieth century. In their view, recognition and acceptance of the gifts of Catalan culture would help to transform Spain.

The Catalan need for 'universals', as a way to universalize Catalan culture, is underlined in the paragraph which follows, blending imperialism and *joia*, to signify the Catalan process of acculturation, the fight for a cultural empire: 'Es per això que jo veig amb un esguard de joia i entusiasme aqueixos imperialistes de la llengua i la literatura que ens duen o volen dur-nos els tresors que, posseïts per la gent normal de tots els països del món, romanien encara soterrats per a nosaltres' ('It is for this reason that I look with joy and enthusiasm upon those imperialists of the language and literature who bring or wish to bring to us the treasures that, though available to normal people in all the nations of the earth, still remained buried for us', p. 57). Such an urge continued to be a preoccupation throughout the period leading up to the Civil War. Debate over translation policy in the 1920s and 1930s called for more focus on the classics, rather than pandering to the short-term popular market.[29] Notwithstanding perception of the increasing normality of Catalan cultural production in the 1930s, there was still felt to be strong need for the translation of 'Clàssics del món' as well as to enter into a dialogue with contemporary literature and criticism throughout Europe.[30] Claims for the re-energizing effects of such enterprises became less apocalyptic than in the first two decades of the twentieth century, but there was a strong push for the process of translation to continue. Even after Jordana's supposedly definitive translations of Shakespeare in the early 1930s, there was a return to Shakespeare, through Sagarra, in the years following the Civil War.[31] Distaste was shown for the discourse of imperialism of the earlier period, but Shakespeare continued to intervene in debates about cultural power and influence, although his politics were increasingly a politics of resistance.[32] It must not, then, be forgotten that the origins of Shakespeare's purposiveness in Catalan are very much linked to the origins of *Imperialisme* and that his figuration carries this history in Catalan. However, he was employed and configured in other more specific fields and discourses, such as the debate over language, authorship and genius, which add to the scope of his meaning and show that he was not just a tool of the establishment.

Where Shakespeare's centrality is felt most strongly, right up to the present day, is in the debate over Catalan theatre. Many early twentieth-century critics express the way forward for a Catalan theatre in crisis to be the coming of 'their own Shakespeare', and this motif was taken up post-Sagarra, in the identification of the Catalan playwright as the supreme translator of Shakespeare. Palau i Fabre reflects the gist of much positive evaluation of Sagarra's Shakespeare when he writes that the translations 'ens restitueixen l'obra de Shakespeare tan a vora de l'original, un privilegi que potser cap o ben poques cultures deuen tenir' ('they restore to us the works of Shakespeare so close to the original, a privilege enjoyed by no other culture, or by very few of them at least').[33] Other writers who were to deliver such positive evaluation of Sagarra include Serrahima, Fàbregas, Coca and Codina; in fact, many of the key figures in Catalan theatre from the 1970s to the 1990s would attest to the deserved classic status of Sagarra's translations. Above all, it is the defenders of textual theatre who turn to the 'authentic' Shakespeare, and hence the 'authenticity' of Sagarra, whilst the performance groups most associated with the revival of Catalan theatre in the 1970s and 1980s opt for more playful re-visions of the Bard.[34] However, actors and directors also attest to the classic status of Sagarra's Shakespeare.[35]

In the same article in which Palau i Fabre affirms the universal importance of this Catalan Shakespeare, he goes on to outline a particular significance for Sagarra's feat: ' . . . com que Catalunya no posseeix un autèntic repertori, intentem de substituir-lo o suplantar-lo amb el del més gran geni teatral que ha existit del Renaixement encà, per tal que es vagi creant el clima d'on surten autors, actors, directors etc.' (' . . . as Catalonia does not possess an authentic repertoire, let us try to substitute it or supplant it with that of the greatest theatrical genius who has existed since the Renaissance, so that we can begin to create the climate for authors, actors, directors etc. to appear').[36] This statement may be compared to Fàbregas' later 'Muntar un Shakespeare és arreu del món una empresa arriscada; les referències, les comparacions sorgeixen de manera inevitable. Muntar-lo aquí, on manquem d'una tradició adequada, i muntar-lo en unes poques setmanes i amb uns actors vinguts d'ací d'allà, resulta una temeritat' ('To stage Shakespeare is a risky business all over the world; comparisons and reference to other works are almost inevitable. Yet to stage him here, where we lack an adequate tradition, and to stage him in a few weeks and with actors drawn from here and there, is nothing short of rash').[37] Perception of a crisis in Catalan theatre dates back to the turn of the century, and it is attributed to a number of factors, ranging from the lack of a strong Catalan theatre tradition, to the poor discernment of theatregoers; lack of funds, lack of genius, as well as the relative dominance of Castilian theatre in Barcelona. However, there is a strong sense that theatre is fundamental to cultural revival, that theatre 'és l'art que més transcendeix el poble' ('is the art that speaks most to the people').[38] It is not only, then, the actors, directors, playwrights and empresarios who participate in the debate over the way forward for Catalan theatre, but a wide range of cultural commentators, ranging from the satirical papers of the period to *Noucentista* intellectuals, a group which has tended to be identified with an interest in poetry rather than in theatre (see fig. 9).

The main objectives of the debate are to recreate a tradition for Catalan theatre, either by re-evaluating playwrights of the nineteenth century, encouraging the translation of contemporary foreign plays, producing versions of the classics of world theatre, or concentrating on original production. Rossend Llúria, writing in *De tots colors*, for instance, questioned the value of reading Shakespeare for theatrical inspiration, preferring to advise young authors to look within themselves, to reproduce their own nature, that of Catalonia.[39] Such a view may superficially seem closer to the model of imperialism proposed by Prat de la Riba, but it is not reflected in many writers associated with *Noucentisme*. The latter are famed (and reviled at times) for their intervention in the theatrical debate to try to raise the tone of Catalan theatrical production by encouraging selective translation of the classics. Adrià Gual's production of *El somni d'una nit d'estiu* in October 1908 was greeted as a dream-like impression of what Catalan theatre could be, and leads to an expansion of the debate over the value of translations in the theatre, as well as whether

Catalonia might be capable of doing justice to Shakespeare. Many critics would have identified with the position outlined by Morera i Galícia in his 1917 lecture on 'Consideracions sobre les interpretacions de Shakespeare': 'Jo crec que si els nostres actors logren, entre altres coses, proporcionar al teatre català una adequada interpretació de les obres de Shakespeare, li hauran aportat un valuós tribut' ('I believe that if our actors succeed, amongst other things, in providing Catalan theatre with an adequate interpretation of the works of Shakespeare, they will have endowed it with an invaluable gift').[40]

Calls for the professionalization of Catalan theatre, beginning with Adrià Gual, were also underlined by recourse to Shakespeare, right up to present day appreciation of the professionalism of the Royal Shakespeare Company. Furthermore, in many ways the use of translations helped to keep the issue of the future of theatre from slipping to the back of people's minds. Josep Canals i Gordó's reminiscences about the years from 1917 to 1932 reflect exactly the activity in newspapers and magazines of the period: ' . . . cada vegada que havia pujat a l'escenari una traducció o una adaptació de teatre estranger havia motivat suggeriments, consells, protestes i censures' (' . . . every time a translation or adaptation of foreign theatre had been presented on stage, it had given rise to suggestions, advice, protests and censure').[41] The kinds of critiques, suggestions and dreams aroused by translations and particularly those perceived to be as influential as the Shakespeare productions and adaptations of the period, reveal that attitudes to Shakespeare were often dependent on each individual or group's position on theatre, translation, politics and language. Yet it is also clear that these ideological positions were as likely to be affected, or even determined by personal preference for Shakespeare or any other author. Satirical papers such as *La Esquella de la Torratxa* and *Cu-Cut*, as well as listings in theatre magazines, show the extent of the divide between the ideal and the reality. Appreciation of Shakespeare was de rigueur for most self-respecting cultural critics and tended to go hand in hand with disgust at the poor public appreciation of such artistic treasures. Meanwhile, certain of Shakespeare's stories found continuing popular support, appearing far more frequently than the kind of artistic soirées produced by the *Teatre Català*. Examples include amateur productions of *Othello* and various parodies of the play, continuing performances of Balaguer's *Les esposalles de la morta*, and the popularity of a three-act arrangement of *The Taming of the Shrew*. How far and what Shakespeare meant outside of a largely bourgeois cultural field remains unclear, however, and even within that field, there was enough fun-poking at ignorance of the name of Shakespeare, to suggest that his levels of meaning, and of artistic significance, varied greatly.

The popular press generally reacted positively to productions of Shakespeare in 1904 and 1908, whilst underlining the uncertain status of the Bard amongst Catalans in facetious wordplay such as the following: 'Tothom se desfeya en alabansas del autor, que és un tal Shakespeare – o Sach-y-peras que deya una senyora del meu costat – en el qual poden posar-se molt fundades esperansas' ('Everyone outdid themselves in their praise of the author, a chap called Shakespeare – or Sack-y-pears as one lady sitting by my side called him – in whom we might ground our hopes for the future').[42]

Such anecdotes reflect problems in the theatrical environment, the lack of an educated public (let alone a home-grown genius), but also demonstrate a tendency to associate Shakespeare, and what he represents – poetic theatre, artistic integrity, the ability to dream – with the ideals of *Noucentisme*. Adrià Gual, too, has one of his creations speak of Shakespeare as 'imperialista com era i com jo ho soc encara' ('imperialist as I was and still am'), reflecting the *Noucentista* fashion.[43] Later critics and reviewers also display the tendency to link Shakespeare with the production of a more identifiably Catalan genius. After Vilaregut's recasting of two Shakespeare plays in Catalan history and society, a reviewer looks forward to the attendance of Shakespeare, a promising new writer, at a banquet in his honour.[44] Similarly, Sagarra's literary development is subsumed into a higher, ideal process, which is the true rendering of Shakespeare, often identified as one of the greatest twentieth-century services to Catalan theatre.

The misspelling of Shakespeare, as well as reflecting a long line of meaningful gaffs, such as the identification of Shilock (*sic*) with Sherlock Holmes or the categorization of *The Merchant of Venice* as a tragedy, also points to moves to Catalanize the very name of Shakespeare. Some theatrical magazines recast the name in Catalan as Xespir, within a period when the debate over the 'true' spelling of Shakespeare's name was filtering through to articles in Catalan. On the one hand this is part and parcel of increasing use of Shakespeare as a Catalan trope – 'teatre shakesperià', 'valors shakespearians' and other such formulations – but there is also a sense in which it represents part of a revisionary move to hide the existence of an original figure of Shakespeare. Manuel de Montoliu, writing in 1908, rejects the wrangling over who wrote Shakespeare's works as irrelevant: 'Poden discutir furiosament els erudits durant segles sencers sobre si Homer, Troya, Ossiàn, Shakespeare o la Beatriu del Dant han existit o no; deixem-los discutir en plena indiferència [. . .] Hi hà una realitat superior a-n aquella qu'acostumen anomenar realitat' ('Intellectuals may argue for whole centuries whether Homer, Troy, Ossian, Shakespeare or Dante's Beatrice have ever existed; let us leave them to their arguments in all indifference[. . .] There is a superior reality to that which they tend to call reality').[45] Instead, the mirror held up by Shakespeare's works to reality is felt to be all-important, the fact that for many writers Shakespeare is the most contemporary of all the classics and 'molt més prop de la nostra sensibilitat' ('much closer to our own sensibilities').[46]

Perceptions of such a role for Shakespeare range from López-Picó's 'En aquest concepte shakespearià de la realitat tenim l'arrel de la nostra poixança' ('In this Shakespearian concept of reality we find the root of our strength'), to the 'enchanted mirror' of Palau i Fabre which underlines the supreme metatheatrical value of Shakespeare's theatre.[47] In terms of practice, there are constant calls on Shakespeare to arbitrate on practical matters relating to Catalan theatre. This does constitute a distinct model in that the Shakespeare that is recruited on different sides of the debate about theatre is treated as a practical authority rather than a universal cultural value to be translated and/or appropriated. Issues which call for Shakespeare's participation begin with conferences on the history of the theatre, showing the link between social conventions and theatrical tradition. Shakespeare is hence held up as an example, for theatregoers and dramatists, that theatre can appeal to the masses without compromising artistic integrity. Shakespeare's legendary status as a man of the theatre, although not necessarily a good actor, surfaces on different sides in the debate to advocate the involvement of playwrights in the theatre world, particularly those who translate, or to defend the authority of 'men of the theatre' over other cultural commentators, often critics of the *Teatre Català*. Hamlet's advice to the players is reproduced regularly (particularly in the first decade or so of the twentieth century) as advice to Catalan actors (see fig. 10), and his producing only his own plays with his own company used to defend similar monopolies.[48] There are various attempts to create schools of declamation and acting based on the institutions which surround the Shakespeare industry in the rest of Europe, as well as advice to directors to base their choice of plays on the actors at their disposal, using Shakespeare's creation of characters with the strengths and weaknesses of his company in mind as an example of the success of this method. Furthermore Shakespeare's prestige as a man of the theatre is used to elevate his Catalan 'equivalents', ranging from Guimerà to Maragall to Gual to Sagarra. This is, perhaps, most overtly achieved with the latter.

> El temps, però, el coneixement més profund de Shakespeare, especialment després del llibre de Jan Kott, ens ha fet veure que, més enllà de la fidelitat del poeta català al fons i a les formes del poeta anglès, hi ha la semblança de dos enamorats de la vida i del teatre. Això ens ha dut al fet que, cada vegada més, quan Shakespeare puja als escenaris catalans ho fa de la mà de Josep Maria de Sagarra.[49]

> (Time, however, and a deeper understanding of Shakespeare, in particular after the publication of Jan Kott's book, has led us to see that, beyond the Catalan poet's faithfulness to the form and content of the English poet, there are the similarities between two lovers of life and of the theatre. This recognition has led to the fact that, increasingly, whenever Shakespeare treads the Catalan boards he does so by the hand of Sagarra').

Jordi Coca's defence of the Sagarra translations is based on something beyond fidelity to the form and content of the plays. It is his closeness to Shakespeare in terms of love for life and the theatre that makes the translations work on stage. Although other translations have been used, or his versions adapted, for a long time Sagarra would remain the official stage Shakespeare, because like his source he was a man of the theatre.

Whether Catalonia could or can produce its own Shakespeare is approached from a very different perspective by Fàbregas:

> Considerem unes dades objectives: una societat amb una història immediata asumida com a passat nacional, una economia en expansió, la crisi d'unes formes polítiques antiquades que l'auge mateix de l'economia fa evolucionar, un marge raonable de llibertat d'expressió, unes institucions encara no prou

encarcarades per a ofegar la iniciativa individual [...] i una possibilitat d'oci per tal que els rics puguin organitzar festes sumptuoses i coincidir, en el teatre, amb els estrats populars decidits a divertir-se. Si un cop tenim tots aquests ingredients, i els disposem i els dosifiquem al nostre gust, esperem que ens sorgeixi la figura de Shakespeare, és que som ingenus incorregibles i no mereixem perdó.

Malgrat tot, però, subsisteix un fet: que Shakespeare va néixer enmig d'aquest cúmul de circunstàncies. I un altre: que Shakespeare no fou una excepció, un cas d'il·luminació personal, sinó l'exemple màxim d'una dramatúrgia generada sota els supòsits enumerats: Marlowe, Jonson, Ford, Beaumont, Fletcher, i un llarg etcètera, el rodegen per totes bandes.[50]

(Let us consider some objective facts: a society with an immediate past that has been taken on board as national history, an expanding economy, a crisis in outdated political forms that is exacerbated by this economic growth, a reasonable margin for freedom of speech, the existence of institutions that are not yet fossilized enough to stifle individual initiative [...] and a scope for leisure that allows the rich to organize sumptuous parties but at the same time frequent the same theatres as the popular strata, intent on enjoying themselves. If once we have all these ingredients, and we dispose of them and manage them as we wish, we think that a figure like Shakespeare might appear, then we are impossibly naive and cannot be excused.

A fact remains, all the same: that Shakespeare was born amidst this pile of circumstances. Another is that Shakespeare was not the exception, a case of personal illumination, but the greatest example of a dramaturgy generated under the hypotheses described: Marlowe, Jonson, Beaumont, Fletcher etc. etc., surround him on all sides).

Perhaps the most important issues which occasioned recourse to Shakespeare were the debates over the necessity or not of a home-grown genius for Catalan theatre to develop, and the related question of the need for originality. The first question was very much a chicken-and-egg situation. The fact that certain cultures had theatrical geniuses that sustained the theatrical tradition, such as Spain and Lope de Vega or England and Shakespeare, was used to defend the need for Catalonia to produce its own Shakespeare. The enlightened participation of Gual was felt to be a step towards this. However, there were also critics who questioned Gual's position, arguing that it was important to create the tradition first in order to produce the right environment for genius to occur, and that in any case, the presence of a 'genius' of the stature of Shakespeare was unnecessary in Catalonia to ensure the health and survival of Catalan theatre. Both positions showed inner divergence over the role of translations and adaptations in the development of a Catalan theatre. Whilst some writers felt that translations could produce a model of taste and artistry to inspire Catalan playwrights, others felt that the Catalan genius must come from within. There was also concern about the seeming lack of discrimination in the translation of plays. In *La Esquella de la Torratxa* for instance one critic observed that to translate indiscriminately was more harmful than not translating at all.[51] This was not an unusual position, even in the 1930s. J. R. Masoliver's 'Què cal traduir?' calls for attention to the 'specific weight' of a text in selecting translations.[52] There were even some critics who felt translation was harmful.

More optimistically, perhaps the supreme Shakespearian defence of cultural borrowing and translation comes in Carles Capdevila's 1931 article on 'El mite de l'originalitat'.[53] He begins by observing that: 'La importància de l'originalitat dels temes en una literatura, i sobretot en el teatre, està en raó inversa de la dosi d'humanitat, és a dir, de la bona qualitat literària' ('The importance of thematic originality in a literature, and above all in the theatre, is in inverse proportion to the dose of humanity, that is to say, of good literary quality'). His defence of such a position depends on the fact that both Elizabethan and Golden Age dramatists showed no scruples in borrowing stories, rather than inventing their own. But the clinching argument is based on Shakespeare's practice: '... com Shakespeare, per motius de competència mercantil, posava la grapa del seu geni en les obres dels contemporanis, en els antecessors més obscurs o en la llegenda' ('... just as Shakespeare, to be able to compete in the market, placed the stamp of his genius on the works of his contemporaries, on that of his more obscure predecessors or on legend'). This argument would, of course, have been decisive given a theatrical situation like that of Catalonia, dependent on a diverse public and mainly private funding. However, he extends his argument to use such practice to criticize the fickle nature of modern theatre, the fetishization of originality brought about by realist and living-room drama: 'Jutjar una obra per la novetat del tema és tancar els ulls als valors literaris i humans que l'obra pugui tenir. El tema pot ésser una preferència del gust o de la moda d'una època, però allò que és susceptible d'eternitzar-se no és l'argument, sinó la part de personalitat que hi ha adherit a l'autor' ('To judge a play by the novelty of its subject is to close one's eyes to the literary and human values that a work might hold. The subject might be the preference of the taste or fashion of an age, but that which is susceptible to being eternalized is not the argument, but the part of the author's personality that is found there').[54] Once again, Shakespeare is presented as a universalizing force, as providing the basis on which to look beyond the immediate realities of a cultural climate, as an example of the ability to rise above day to day reality to the 'realitat superior' advocated by Montoliu above.

Shakespeare's containment of both the urge and the necessity to translate increases the importance of translation of his works and multiplies his cultural currency; and it is this which leads Fàbregas in 1974 to affirm his lasting influence. In a private letter he writes, 'Shakespeare és contemporani perquè hom l'escorcolla una vegada i una altra' ('Shakespeare is our contemporary because we scrutinize him over and over again').[55] This statement reflects the extent of twentieth-century interest in Shakespeare, the level of productions, translations and borrowings world wide, but the terms in which it is expressed lead to a realization of why Shakespeare might have been so close to, almost synonymous with the 'imperialism' envisioned by the *Noucentisme* movement. His universality is something which can be shaped, by arbitrary choice of the elements which best reflect a given moment, in the same way that his universality is also attributed by Bloom and others to his own arbitrariness, his lack of anxiety of influence. This is further legitimated by constant figuration of Shakespeare's generosity. He is a 'smiling humanist', as we have seen in the critical positionings of the previous chapter, who is patient with all who approach him. The prologue to Carner's translation of *El somni d'una nit d'estiu*, for instance, defends his audacity in 'dreaming the dream' through reference to the company of writers who have tried their hand at Shakespeare.[56] This particular thread of Shakespeare's figuration, which presents him as far more approachable than any other classic notwithstanding his greatness, can be traced throughout reception of Shakespeare in Catalonia. It is particularly common in theatre reviews which, even when critical of productions, suggest that Shakespeare's magnanimity often allows directors and actors to get away with it.

The *Noucentista* position in this debate tended to involve recourse to the keyword 'creació', which appears in many contemporary considerations of Shakespeare. The Bard is respected for his disregard of the Classical unities, for his ability to break away from rules and laws of theatrical conduct. We have already seen how Crexells (1925) marks out Shakespeare's rewriting of the rule books and Farran i Mayoral (1920) writes of a *Coriolanus* who is not contained ('qui no es conté') within the grave form of Roman grandeur. Shakespeare's recreation as the model man of culture, in defence of the cultural intervention of the intellectual, is further tempered by a sense of his moral responsibility. Set against his creative freedom is the duty of the poet and translator to his nation and culture, although expressed in terms of a future utopia, a collective dream to be compared with Shakespeare's 'Midsummer Night's Dream'. The esoteric comments of Farran i Mayoral in 1920 may be placed in this tradition: 'Jo vull dir aquella eterna societat dels esperits sota normes sempre iguals i sempre diverses que establiria llaços de comprensió mútua en un banquet on s'asseguessin Sòfocles i Shakespeare, Dant i Molière. [. . .] aquesta socialització ideal i per tant difícil d'assolir, és la universalització de la Intuïció' ('I mean to say that eternal society of souls that resides under norms that are always the same and yet always diverse, that would establish ties of mutual comprehension at a banquet at which Sophocles and Shakespeare, Dante and Molière might sit. [. . .] this ideal socialization, so difficult to achieve, is the universalization of Intuition').[57]

Farran i Mayoral is perhaps one of the most extreme adherents to *Noucentisme* ideals of an aristocracy of intellectuals to create a pattern for a new society, and his constant recourse to Emerson is perhaps evidence of this.[58] Yet there is reference to Shakespeare's role in the creation of an ideal Catalonia by most of the writers of the period, whether it be expressed as a dream or a utopia. It is important to note that such an ideal is often expressed using a janus-faced trope, linking future greatness to a particular, arbitrarily chosen, cultural tradition. An example can be found in Carner's 'Del Shakespeare en llengua catalana' where utopian nostalgia, looking back to Renaissance humanism and the cultural greatness of Greece and Rome, is linked to the enterprise of appropriating Shakespeare.

> Una labor formidable s'ha imposat en aquest ordre la 'Biblioteca dels Grans Mestres', que debutà pel Shakespeare i dins del Shakespeare per 'Juli Cèsar', on en Salvador Vilaregut s'ha trobat amb un incomparable motiu de crear una concisa i enèrgica plasmació de l'idioma pairal, com en recercament d'aquella noble severitat supremacial dels grans temps del llatí.

> (The Biblioteca Popular dels Grans Mestres has taken a formidable task upon itself, beginning with Shakespeare and within Shakespeare with Julius Caesar, in which Salvador Vilaregut has discovered an incomparable excuse to create a concise and energetic representation of our ancestral language, as if in search of that noble severity and supremacy of the great age of Latin, p. 57).

The Classicism expressed here is further underlined by a description of what such a 'gegantina empresa' ('gigantic enterprise') – Shakespeare in Catalan – means in political, didactic and aesthetic terms for the Catalans.

> Shakespeare en català és la naturalització a casa nostra de la sublimitat pels polítics, de la grandiloqüència pels oradors, de l'ample sentit humà pels artistes, de la fantasia pels infants. Shakespeare és un mestre absolut, integral i omnipresent.

> (Shakespeare in Catalan is the naturalization in our land of the sublime for politicians, of grandiloquence for orators, of a broad humanity for artists, of fantasy for children. Shakespeare is an absolute, integral and omnipresent master, p. 57).

Shakespeare's particular figuration of 'creació' is something which can be applied in a number of areas, not just in the realms of art. The epic nature of this collective voyage (of immigration and emigration, as can be drawn from the use of 'naturalització') is expressed in praise of the new translators of Shakespeare; their resolve is described as 'epic and transcendental' as they embark on 'incredible adventures'. The sense of pulling together in this epic struggle is expressed further on in Carles Riba's 'Elogi del poeta traductor', in his perception that when translation is creation, it is not a cry for help but a victory for the collaboration which is the empire.[59] The concurrent idea of the naturalization of Shakespeare, suggesting the existence of a specifically Catalan

Shakespeare, also recurs in a number of articles considering his influence. So, for example, Carner writes of *Venus i Adonis* that 'En Morera naturalitza en l'alt catalanesc el geni anglès' ('Morera naturalizes the English genius in high Catalan').[60] This can be compared with Cebrià Montoliu's citing of Shakespeare's 'dolços i prudents oracles' ('sweet and prudent oracles') in the introduction to his translation of *Macbeth*, which for a Catalan 'semblaran a ta orella com un fill teu, fins al punt de fer-te oblidar a estones el pregon mancament de ton tràgic passat' ('they will sound to your ear like your own son, so much so that at times they will make you forget the deep lack of your tragic past').[61]

The above representation of Shakespeare as a kind of saviour for Catalan culture is reinforced in 'Del Shakespeare en llengua catalana' by recourse to the biblical terms, so often associated with the promotion of the 'Verb català': 'la naixent Biblioteca anuncia els noms dels traductors; tots ells són joves, són ells qui breguen i malden amb fe hebraica per la glòria d'una llengua ara per ara tan plena de bàtecs prodigiosos i estupendes adivinacions com d'inseguritats i desordres' ('the new Biblioteca (Library) announces the names of its translators; all of them are young, it is they who toil and struggle with biblical faith for the glory of a language now so full of prodigious strokes and stupendous intuition as with insecurities and confusion', p. 57). And the article ends with a celebration of the moral implications of the Shakespeare translation venture, as representing an 'elevació de l'esperit':

> I encert impecable als traductors que hauran de fer tots una mica la lluita gloriosa de Jacob amb l'àngel. I a la gent, a l'honrada gent catalana, li desitjo frenesí de llegir, magnanimitat excepcional per aquesta obra intrèpida de cultura, amor sempre creixent pel fill d'un marxant i una pagesa que assolí totes les elevacions de l'esperit i ha pesat en la meitat dels somnis que la humanitat ha fet després d'ell.

> (And I wish impeccable success to the translators who will all have to in a way reproduce the glorious struggle of Jacob with the angel. And to the people, to the honest Catalan people, I wish a furious desire to read, exceptional magnanimity for this intrepid cultural enterprise, ever-increasing love for the son of a merchant and a countrywoman who attained all the elevations of the soul and has weighed on half the dreams that humanity has dreamed since him, p. 57).

A year later Carner continues to push his vision of the relevance of Shakespeare to political concerns, to the desired transformation of Catalonia. In the introduction to his *Somni d'una nit d'estiu* he draws explicit parallels between the cultural enterprise that is the Biblioteca Popular dels Grans Mestres and democracy. Amongst the many changes which the enterprise may potentially engender are 'que'ls nostres grans senyors siguin, com Teseu, polids, enamorats, de paraula florida, y somrients al mateix temps que heroes' ('that our great gentlemen might be, like Theseus, polite, enamoured, rhetorically gifted, and amiable as well as heroic') and 'que les nostres dònes gentils, siguin com Hermia y Helena, agils, discrets, boniques en el dir com en la cara, y templadoses en amor al mateix temps que honestes' ('that our gentlewomen might be like Hermia and Helena, agile, discreet, beautiful, and temperate in love as well as chaste').[62] The description of the early Biblioteca Popular dels Grans Mestres Shakespeare translation programme in terms of a heroic struggle is taken up by other writers and intellectuals as the translation machine – the 'gran empresa' – grows in strength and support in the *Noucentista* period. Time after time, Shakespeare is described, Shakespeare in Catalan defended in terms of the keywords which appear in Carner's article, as in the political manifestos of the period.

There is also a moral utopia to be taken into account, and Shakespeare becomes pregnant with moral meaning in Catalan. In the above words from Carner's translation prologue Shakespeare is described as a pattern for moral behaviour, and is earlier found to be 'agradós i bellament humà' in contrast with other more severe writers. For Esclasans, in 1925, Shakespeare is the pattern of the objective–subjective poet, uniting the virtues of Homer and Dante. Morera i Galícia describes his 'fort humanisme' before reaffirming his own faith in Catalan civilization and its humanism. Carles Riba, on the latter's *Venus i Adonis* translation, writes that he is an entire consciousness: 'humanism become human'.

The didactic possibilities of a Catalan Shakespeare are also fully recognized by Farran i Mayoral in a number of articles. In 'L'educació política del poble', he writes of reflections in Shakespeare of the problems of the masses which might have modern day implications, and his essay on *Coriolà* in *Lletres a una amiga estrangera* refers to the play as an incomparable pattern for true political passion, urging the reader to a 'tensió aspiradora d'heroisme' ('a tension that aspires to heroism').[63] He explicitly refers to the play as a means of educating the people, even advocating its performance on the eve of elections.[64] This view is later to be illustrated by events in Paris surrounding the production of *Coriolanus* in 1934. It is a situation which arouses great interest in the Catalan press, in that it demonstrates the social impact of theatre, placing it within national and international moves to redefine the status of the genre.

Political readings of Shakespeare plays become even more common in commentary after the 1940s, largely due to observation of international representations of Shakespeare mediated by Brecht, Kott, Brook and a variety of other influential critics and directors. Prefaces to translations embrace these new readings, defiantly signalling Shakespeare's modernity, whilst at the same time pointing to Catalan culture's participation in that modernity. References to productions, too, reveal the temptation to politicize Shakespeare in affirming his importance for 'l'home d'avui' ('the man of today').[65] However, increasing awareness of the need to defend recourse to Shakespeare in original terms has also led to denial of political influence in seeking to reproduce the true Shakespeare. So for instance the director of a 1996 production of *Macbeth* in Catalan translation sought to downplay the political significance of the play, foregrounding instead the personal, psychological struggles within it. Interestingly, much of the excitement caused by the play was due to the fact the director was English and could hence perhaps reveal the true way of representing Shakespeare. In this sense, politics, the politics of appropriating Shakespeare, of who can be granted the authority and the legitimacy to do so, were very much present.[66]

The more prescriptive, didactic side to the role of poet and intellectual in *Noucentista* Catalonia presents a more imperious side to Catalan 'Imperialisme'. When it is considered how some of the more institutionalized sections of the programme of acculturation sought to control the list of authors translated and how judgement would be sometimes passed on 'less valuable' authors based on their perceived moral failings, a quite different light is thrown on Josep Carner's call for 'la dignitat literària', and the kind of barn-storming treatises produced in the discourse of some of his contemporaries.[67] Shakespeare's value as a teacher of language, of humanity, history and politics, leads him to be recommended reading outside the theatre, yet from the beginning there is awareness that his message needs to be mediated, that his even-handed treatment of good and evil requires explanation. Such a feature of his reception cannot fail to be heard in the works of Farran i Mayoral, but it remains a feature of Shakespeare criticism (and Shakespeare is set against Molière in this respect), especially in versions of his works for children.[68] As such 'necessary' mediation can also be used as an argument for the responsible intervention of the translator, it is perhaps not surprising that Riba was to write of the poet's moral gains in embarking on the adventure of translation.[69] But, as well as the humility advised as part of the process, Morera i Galícia's urge to stay true to the author's intention, to the profound sincerity of the English genius, as Farran i Mayoral would have it, perceived Catalan attributes are not to be lost along the way. All the poet–critics encourage a sense of pride in the translation enterprise. Carles Riba writes of 'l'orgull de l'adaptament' ('the pride of adaptation') in his 'Elogi al poeta traductor', going on to describe Morera i Galícia's collaboration with Shakespeare as 'la tragèdia de la passió d'orgull traduint-se en acció' ('the tragedy of the passion of pride translated into action'). Looking to the 1930s and C. A. Jordana's translation precepts in *L'Art de Traduir* where he suggests that an inventory of translations into Catalan would show in the novice Catalan culture a desire to enrich itself by looking beyond its borders, a desire which other cultures full of pride could envy, it becomes clear how the ways in which Shakespeare is made to speak in Catalan, alongside other writers, might indeed provide assurance of the continued fortunes of Catalan poetry and culture. And it is perhaps for this reason that Shakespeare in Catalan is blessed with the culturally-specific attribute of 'seny'.[70]

The figure of Shakespeare in Catalan comes to represent personal as well as institutional struggles and positionings. Many writers, as has been seen in chapter 2, feel the need to add to the wealth of discourse about Shakespeare in writing that ranges from philosophical tracts to jokey anecdotes, specific biographies to diaries, studies of influence or of theatrical tradition to literary works. Once again, this may be attributed to nothing more than a desire to show learning, to add a mark of cultural legitimacy to a particular text. However, it is clear that for many, Shakespeare represents rather more than that. Notwithstanding the signs of despair often shown by Catalan critics when reflecting on the lack of genius in Catalan theatre, the apparent lack of influence on original work of approximations to Shakespearean texts, many writers identify Shakespeare as an early influence on their work.[71] This is particularly the case with writers who gain in stature in the first few decades of the twentieth century up to the Civil War, but can also be detected in memoirs and biographies written after this period. Adrià Gual, perceived to be perhaps the most important figure in pre-war theatre in Catalonia, time and again turns to Shakespeare when drawing up listings for each theatre season. The plays announced more often than not go unperformed, but there are strong signs here of a personal commitment to the bard from Stratford which go beyond debates about the way forward for Catalan drama. This more personal formulation of the fruitful influence of the Bard shows forth in *Les alegres comediantes*, featuring a character whose love of Shakespeare leads to a fanciful adventure.

The presence of Shakespeare on school curricula is evidenced in personal testimonies, usually only to underline the truer inspiration of personal encounters with his works. The list of writers who claim fruitful encounters with Shakespeare in their youth range from Alfons Par and Cebrià Montoliu to Puig y Ferreter, Gual and Carner, Eugeni d'Ors, López-Picó and Farran i Mayoral, Joan Crexells, Riba, Manuel de Montoliu, and Palau i Fabre, Sagarra and Marià Manent. Many of these testimonies come as responses to questionnaires, interviews or obituaries, mapping out the intensity of influence felt by Shakespeare in general terms. So, for instance, we find Montoliu's memory of 'la conmoció espiritual que em van causar les tragèdies de Shakespeare, llegides als claustres de Poblet' ('the spiritual upheaval produced in me by Shakespeare's tragedies, which I read in the cloisters of Poblet'), Raventós' passionate discovery of Shakespeare in his grandparents' house, López-Picó's experience of Shakespeare as an adolescent, an experience which he hopes to share with the younger generations of his family and Guansé's claim not to remember 'cap altra impressió com la d'aquesta lectura, ni tampoc de res que deixés una emprenta més fonda en el meu esperit' ('no other impression like that of this reading, nor anything else that left a deeper mark on my soul').[72] Yet there is also evidence that goes beyond these testimonies, of writers whose first literary production was influenced by Shakespeare, or who had been awakened to the possibilities of writing in Catalan by witnessing a performance of Shakespeare. An example of the former is, rather fittingly, Josep Maria de Sagarra who wrote his first poem, on Ophelia, at fifteen, whereas the latter may be recognized in Cèsar August Jordana, who ended up attempting to translate Shakespeare's complete works. Palau i Fabre, in a 1986 article, responding to questions about the roots of his theatre, signals a lack of models presented by Catalan theatrical tradition, tracing his influences to Shakespeare 'en una primera lectura feta quan tenia tretze anys' ('in a first reading when I was thirteen').[73] In fact, some of his works may be seen as tracts exploring the kinds of Catalan Shakespeares in existence. His *Avui, Romeo i Julieta* in particular focuses on the Shakespeares conjured in the minds of the Catalan spectators at a production of *Romeo and Juliet*.[74] Indeed, it is in 'original' rewritings of this type that culturally-bound readings of Shakespeare become clearest, although usually this is with reference to specific plays. Writers as diverse as Dídac Ruiz, Salvador Vilaregut, Adrià Gual, Ignasi Iglésias, Millàs-Raurell, Ramon Vinyes and Xavier Albertí have all presented their own Catalan versions of Shakespeare.

What these names represent may be that Shakespeare in Catalonia is little more than the 'universalization' of 'personal' intuition, as formulated by Farran i Mayoral. In other words, their perception (and this writer's) of the extent of Shakespeare's influence on Catalonia, and the existence of a Catalan Shakespeare may be little more than wishful thinking, produced by the model of intellectual action proposed by *Noucentisme*. Certainly, complaints of the lack of approximations to Shakespeare have been a critical constant. The number of successful productions of Shakespeare before the Civil War is very small, but after the Civil War, notwithstanding Tussetschläger's rather barren list, performances have been on the increase. What is more, the thrust of evidence in this chapter shows that Shakespeare had a strong part to play in underpinning, and in some ways embodying, the cultural discourse of the twentieth century in Catalonia, part of this indeed being the presentation of lack, the sense that Catalonia still had a lot of catching up to do. The divide between lack and plenitude in configurations of Shakespeare may in fact have been exacerbated by the simultaneous desire to have Shakespeare represent 'universality' and Englishness, especially given the multinational status he has achieved in Anglo-American formulations. Yet, against the great Shakespeare industry can stand the common sense ('seny') of Catalan approximations, of Catalan Shakespeares, such as Loge's antidote to 'Shakespeare's exploitation' in Stratford or Ferrater's demystification of debates over the existence of Shakespeare. Referring to the authorship detectives, he writes:

> Están locos, desde luego. Y como la locura es lo más vacío que hay en el mundo, matan de aburrimiento. Para un escritor, de todos modos, son útiles, por aquello de que un clavo saca a otro clavo. Cuando nos fatigan hasta lo indecible nuestros compañeros de gremio, y pensamos que la literatura debía en seguida apartarse de los escritores tal y como a los padres irresponsables se les aleja de sus hijos, basta mirar a los autores de teorías fantásticas sobre Shakespeare para darnos cuenta de que, a pesar de todo, nuestra experiencia algo vale, y que tal vez la literatura prospere mejor entre nosotros que entre los demás, los que no saben lo que se hace con ella, los que deslizan por carriles de ideas y no ven ningún paisaje.[75]

> (They are mad, of course. And as madness is the most vacuous thing in the world, they bore one to death. For a writer, however, they have their uses, if only because you need a nail to remove another nail. When we are bored to tears by our colleagues in the profession, and think that literature ought to be separated from writers in the same way that one separates irresponsible parents from their children, it is enough to look at the authors of fantastical theories about Shakespeare to realize that, in spite of everything, our experience counts for something, and that perhaps literature is better off with us than with the others, those who have no idea what to do with literature, and slip along carriages of ideas without looking at the landscape).

Although Ferrater is defending writers in general here against critics in particular, his words are a fitting end to a chapter in which it is partly Shakespeare's perceived escape from all the moulds, his intuitive embracement of experience, that has led him to represent so much for Catalan writers, and for at least an imagined Catalonia. How he came to express these ideals in Catalan is something that will be further explored in the chapter which follows. This will be followed by more specific consideration of the origination and creation of meaning in Shakespeare, in tracing Shakespeare's influence through specific plays and the discourse within and surrounding them, in the continuing search for Rossi's 'genio' – Shakespeare in Catalan.

NOTES

1 From Ernesto Rossi, *Discorso Improvvisato*, p. 29.
2 Crucial to our understanding of the configuration of Shakespeare as 'National Poet' is Michael Dobson, *The Making of the National Poet. Shakespeare, Adaptation and Authorship, 1660–1769* (Oxford: Clarendon Press, 1992).
3 Historically, *Hamlet* has often been the first Shakespeare play to be translated into other languages, and although other plays enjoyed more popularity in the Romantic period, the play returned to favour in the second half of the nineteenth century. It was, for instance, the most frequently performed Shakespeare play in Barcelona, although largely in Italian. Tussetschläger's appendices provide the clearest representation of available data for numerical comparison in *Aufführungen*, pp. xix and xxiii–xxv.
4 'La incidència dels gèneres en la traducció en català', *Revista de Catalunya*, 95 (April 1995), 109–17. See also appendix A.
5 Hugh Grady in *The Modernist Shakespeare*, explores Shakespeare's underpinning of the Literary Academy in the twentieth century.
6 Harold Bloom, *The Western Canon. The Books and School of the Ages* (London: Macmillan, 1995).
7 It is Bloom's vision of tradition as an agonistic struggle persuasively to figure origins and hence convince of originality that contributed to renewed polemic about canon-formation in the 1980s and 1990s. See Judith Still and Michael Worton (eds), *Intertextuality: Theories and Practices* (Manchester: Manchester University Press, 1990), pp. 27–8.
8 Bloom, *The Western Canon*. One of a number of chapters which refer to Shakespeare is entitled 'Shakespeare, Center of the Canon', pp. 45–75. The extent of Bloom's theories about Shakespeare's escape from anxiety to become the supreme influence on Western culture is most unequivocally expressed in *Ruin the Sacred Truths*. He revisits many of these ideas in *Shakespeare. The Invention of the Human* (New York: Riverhead Books, 1998), a book to which Salvador Oliva's more recent study in Catalan, *Introducció a Shakespeare* (Barcelona: Editorial Empúries, 2000), is indebted.
9 Gayatri Spivak attempts to counter this in her exploration of a Derridean understanding of difference to negotiate cultural relations. Unsurprisingly, she roundly condemns translation practice in a postcolonial context which seeks to renationalize foreign works, incorporate and assimilate them. She reserves even stronger criticism for deliberate exoticism, where representation of the foreign becomes a controlling aesthetic. Her solution, apart from for people

to learn more languages, sounds very much like the translation practice recommended by Walter Benjamin (1923). See especially 'The Politics of Translation', *Outside in the Teaching Machine* (London/New York: Routledge, 1993), pp. 178–200.

10 By autonomous here I refer to the representation of Shakespeare found in diaries or letters not necessarily intended for publication, as well as to formulations which claim their freedom from any official programme. But perhaps more importantly to the apparent autonomy of discourse about Shakespeare, the kind of 'universal' attributes explored in the previous chapter are also historically fixed, taking on some specific significance in Catalonia at different times.

11 Originally published in *La Veu de Catalunya*, it can be consulted in *El reialme de la poesia . . .*, pp. 56–7.

12 Literally the 'ouring' of Shakespeare, this can be translated into English as appropriation or naturalization. As we have seen, both Par and Montoliu write of Shakespeare using first person plural forms of verbs, pronouns and possessive adjectives, but it is also a feature of later Catalan figurations of Shakespeare. See, for instance, Xavier Fàbregas' brief plotting of 'l'anostrament de Shakespeare' before going on to discuss particular translations in his 'Notes introductòries a les traduccions catalanes de Shakespeare', in *Estudis de Llengua i Literatura I* (Barcelona: Curial, 1979), pp. 181–204.

13 See 'El teatre i els poetes' in *La Revista*, 9 (15 February 1916), 7.

14 Enric Prat de la Riba, *La Nacionalitat Catalana* (1906), revised edition, (Barcelona: Edicions 62, 1978). Page references given in text.

15 'Evolució' continues to be the keyword in the Catalan writings of Alfons Par and his ideas about the development of the Catalan language and literature. I am indebted to Josep Murgades' introduction to Noucentisme in *HLC* IX, pp. 9–72, for a general presentation of the scope of *Noucentisme*.

16 See Par, 'El forçament de Lucreça' and *Shakespeare y el folklore*. Par himself would have been loth to align himself with all the aesthetic tendencies of *Noucentisme* or *Modernisme*, but there is a clear move towards re-evaluation of Classical and Mediterranean antecedents in the whole spectrum of turn of the century Catalan cultural production. Further exploration of the classicizing tendencies of the *Noucentisme* movement, although they are perhaps clearest in plastic art rather than literature, can be found in J. Vallcorba, *Noucentisme, Mediterraneisme i Classicisme. Apunts per a la història d'una estètica* (Barcelona: Quaderns Crema, 1994), although there are reservations to be made over the true extent of its paradigmatic influence on the cultural programme and Vallcorba concentrates mainly on French influence, foregrounding Maurras and Moréas. Also of great service are: C. Miralles, 'Clàssics i no entre Modernisme i Noucentisme a Catalunya', *Eulàlia. Estudis i Notes de Literatura Catalana* (Barcelona: Edicions del Mall, 1986); N. Bilbeny, *Eugeni d'Ors i la ideologia del Noucentisme* (Barcelona: La Magrana, 1988), and Carles Garriga, *La Restauració Clàssica d'Eugeni d'Ors* (Barcelona: Curial, 1981).

17 The extensive collection of translations, considered one of the great

pre-Civil War 'obres de cultura', are published from 1924 onwards, under the direction of Carles Riba.
18   Eugeni d'Ors, *Obra catalana completa* (Barcelona: Selecta, 1950), p. 1481. Along with similar statements, this is commonly quoted in studies of the ideology of *Noucentisme*.
19   Farran i Mayoral, in particular, points to Shakespeare's failings in this respect. See especially *Labor dispersa* and the 'Reflexions i Sentiments' in *La Revista*, 1920.
20   *Dietari dispers (1918–1984)*, J. Muñoz Millanes (ed.), (Barcelona: Edicions 62, 1995), p. 30.
21   'El nostre Ibsen', *La Veu de Catalunya* (20 March 1928), later collected in *Homes, Coses, Polèmiques* (Mataró: 'Diari de Mataró', 1931).
22   *La Revista* for instance published a regular questionnaire on the views of Catalan intellectuals on the 'Gran Guerra' from 1915 onwards. The Nietzsche problem was resolved, rather arbitrarily, by the affirmation that Catalonia, unlike Germany, had taken the good things in Nietzsche. Once again, we are reminded of the difficulty of ascribing meaning to translation choices.
23   'El teatre i els poetes', *La Revista*, 9 (15 February 1916), 7.
24   Marià Manent's dedication to Morera i Galícia precedes his own translation of John Keats, *Sonets i Odes* (Barcelona: 'La Revista', 1919).
25   Page references given in the text are from *El reialme de la poesia*.
26   *Obres completes*, 2, I, pp. 85–7.
27   *Empori* (December 1908), 207.
28   *La Veu de Catalunya* (17 October 1908).
29   One example is Farran i Mayoral's article, 'Mesura, responsabilitat i... traduccions directes', *La Veu de Catalunya* (29–30 August 1928): 'sempre la mateixa manca de mesura: quan encara tenim per traduir la major partida de les obres mestres qui són el fons comú de la cultura humana'. Similar sentiments are expressed in a wide range of magazines and periodicals, not just the right-wing petit bourgeois organs. The debate also feeds into the question of what constitutes originality, and whether it is always a good thing, discussed later in this chapter.
30   Analysis of the importance of the Editorial Barcino in the decade preceding the Spanish Civil War, including the 'Clàssics del món' series can be found in A. Manent, *Escriptors i editors del Nou-cents*, pp. 159–75. C. A. Jordana was propelled into the position of official Shakespeare translator through his collaboration with the popular and successful enterprise. Having published a version of *Macbeth* for the Col·lecció Popular Barcino in 1928, he goes on to publish four volumes of Shakespeare translations with the company in the 1930s. The selfless, collaborative cultural outlook of Barcino, underwritten at great personal expense by Ramon Casacuberta, leads it to rally a number of important writers of the period. C. A. Jordana's own celebration of the Col·lecció Popular from the editorial of *La Nova Revista* should be seen in this light rather than as self-advancement. However, it also follows that claims for the quality of Jordana's

translation should be read in the context of the wider aims and promotion of Barcino.

31 Esquerra, *Shakespeare*..., p. 193: 'En C. A. Jordana ha trobat Shakespeare el traductor definitiu'; and p. 194: 'Cal esperar que es publiquin successivament els volums restants fins a tenir la traducció completa de les obres shakesperianes. Tindrem llavors l'edició catalana de Shakespeare que ens cal. Completa, prou erudita per a satisfer les necessitats del llegidor mitjà i alhora amb la necessària dignitat literària, que no desmereixi de la fidelitat de la versió'. Sagarra begins to translate Shakespeare in the early 1940s, barely ten years after the publication of Jordana's translations.

32 This development will be explored in more depth in the final chapter on readings of *Coriolanus*. Whilst many cultural historians have identified the role of translation of canonical texts in countering the hegemony of the Franco period, it was generally in versions of classical texts that oblique political commentary on the state of Spain was to be found. In Catalonia, the very act of translation became an act of resistance, because of the 1939 ban on the use of Catalan in the public sphere.

33 Palau i Fabre, 'Consideracions', p. 71.

34 Examples include Els Joglars' *Visanteta la Favara* (1989) and La Cubana's *Tempestat* (1986).

35 The emblematic Catalan actors Rosa Novell and Lluís Soler both spoke of the difficult pleasure of speaking Sagarra's lines, clearly identifying his Shakespeare as the epitome of Catalan poetic theatre in a seminar at the University of Barcelona in 1997.

36 Palau i Fabre, 'Consideracions', p. 73.

37 M. Badiou (ed.), *Teatre en viu (1969–1972)*, (Barcelona: Institut del Teatre/Edicions 62, 1987), p. 208. The comments were occasioned by a production of *Les alegres comares de Windsor* in December 1972.

38 *El Nostre Teatre*, 1 (8 February 1919), 4. The same magazine advertised a competition, organized by the Escola Catalana d'Art Dramàtic, for original plays in Catalan. The jury was to comprise Magí Morera i Galícia, Gabriel Alomar and Adrià Gual, which might be held as emblematic of the 'meeting of minds' from a number of different political and aesthetic backgrounds in the fight for a theatre (9–10).

39 Rossend Llúria, 'Del amor al art del teatre', *De tots colors*, V (15 March 1912), 165–6.

40 Morera i Galícia, *Consideracions sobre els personatges de Shakespeare* (Barcelona: Escola Catalana d'Art Dramàtic, 1921), p. 10.

41 Quoted from the diaries of Canals i Gordó in R. Batlle i Gordó, *Quinze anys de teatre català. Els teatres Romea i Novetats de 1917 a 1932* (Barcelona: Institut del teatre/Edicions 62, 1984).

42 *Cu-Cut*, 106 (7 January 1904), 42, on the forthcoming production of *Twelfth Night* by the Teatre Intim. Press coverage elsewhere is critical of the 'silly story' but praises Shakespeare's supremacy in drawing types. Significantly, *The Taming of the Shrew* is considered a better play. See, for instance, *La Esquella de l Torratxa*, 1307 (22 January 1904), 59.

A review of *El somni d'una nit d'estiu* four years later, replays the name joke as follows: 'apúntisel a la memoria aquet nom, que es el d'un dels noucentistes que prometen més. Si'l troben difícil de recordar, usin el meu procediment mnemotèchnich y diguin Sakiperes. Es cosa que no falla.' *Cu-Cut* (22 October 1908), 680.

43 *Les alegres comediantes*, 1913.

44 '... sembla que degut a l'èxit que ha tingut el jove escriptor Guillem Shakespeare amb motiu de la seva obra de costums barcelonins, "Com més petita és la nou", hi ha el propòsit de retre-li un homenatge que consistirà en un banquet popular'. *Mirador*, 1 (31 January 1929), 5.

45 From 'Beatriu – Assaig de crítica dantesca' *Empori*, 8 (February 1908), 48.

46 Esquerra, *Lectures Europees*, p. 66.

47 *La Revista*, 8 (30 January 1916), 6, and Palau i Fabre, *El mirall embruixat*.

48 Artur Balot seeks to defend his own practice from criticism by citing Shakespeare in 'El Teatre Català no morirà, mentre jo visqui', *La Escena Catalana*, 221 (28 December 1910): '¿Que'm poden dir que jo mateix imposo les meves obres? També en Xespir a n'els seus comediants no'ls feya fer més que l'*Otelo*, l'*Hamlet*, *El Mercader de Venecia*, *Romeo i Julieta*, en fi, tot comedies seves; ves si era... *dalló.*'

49 Jordi Coca's *Qüestions del Teatre* (Barcelona: Institut del Teatre/Edicions 62, 1985), p. 125. Also on p. 126: 'Cada nova estrena (Codina, Ventura Pons, Meselles, Espert-Lavelli, Pasqual...), ha servit per a demostrar que la gent del teatre prefereix Sagarra a l'hora d'estrenar Shakespeare.'

50 'Com es fa un dramaturg', from *El teatre o la vida* (Barcelona: Galba, 1976), pp. 39–41.

51 Wifret, 'Crònica. De Teatro Català. Traduccions i Traductors', *La Esquella de la Torratxa*, XXXI (19 March 1909), 178–80: 'Jo no soch pas enemich de les traduccions. Crech, pel contrari, que s'ha d'anar traduint al català lo bó y millor del teatro de fora casa' (178). 'Pocas traduccions, pero bonas y ben fetas, y combinadas convenientment. Que traduheixi qui en sàpiga. Y que à certs traductors els siguin lligades les mans' (180).

52 *Mirador*, V (27 April 1933), 6.

53 *Mirador*, III (5 February 1931), 7.

54 We find similar arguments rehearsed with respect to cultural education and discernment, too. C. A. Jordana's *Què cal llegir?* is one example of a work designed to refine reading tastes, written in response to demand by readers of *La Nova Revista*.

55 From a letter to Feliu Formosa dated 9 September 1974, reproduced in *El teatre o la vida*, p. 159. Calderón, in contrast cannot be considered our contemporary 'perquè hom el treu sempre de l'armari amb sentor de naftalina'.

56 *El somni d'una nit d'estiu*, p. 8.

57 'Reflexions i sentiments', *La Revista*, 109 (1 April 1920), 73.

58 As well as constant references to and echoes of Emerson in his works

in Catalan, Farran i Mayoral translates the key Emersonian work containing reference to Shakespeare's ideal poetic status, *Representative Men*. The translation into Castilian is published long after the Civil War, but contains a prologue written during the war which refers to the great influence Emerson had on the intellectuals of the first twenty years of the twentieth century. *Hombres representativos* (Barcelona: Iberia, 1960).

59 *Obres completes*, 2, I, p. 86.
60 *El reialme de la poesia* . . ., p. 141.
61 *La tragedia de Macbeth*, p. x.
62 *El somni d'una nit d'estiu*, pp. 12–13
63 'L'educació política del poble', *Un enemic del poble* (5 August 1917). Later collected in *Labor dispersa*, pp. 53–7.
64 *Lletres* . . ., p. 168.
65 See for instance J. A. Codina's account of his 1968 production of Sagarra's translation of *Juli Cèsar* in L'Hospitalet de Llobregat.
66 The production of *Macbeth* took place at the Pati Manning during the Teatre del Grec Festival in the summer of 1996. It was directed by Tamzin Townsend.
67 'La dignitat literària', in *La Veu de Catalunya*, 2 June 1913. Later collected in *El reialme de la poesia* . . ., pp. 122–32.
68 C. A. Jordana's children's version of *Macbeth* is transformed into a story of Scotland's loss of independence, and hence the dangers of individual ambition untempered by consideration for the health of the nation. The Teatre Joc d'Equip version of *The Taming of the Shrew* and *The Merchant of Venice* resort to overt glosses on Shakespeare's 'message' in these plays. The latter, for instance, is presented not as an anti-semitic play, but as one which shows how prejudice can create havoc.
69 Riba, 'Al marge de *Sonets i Odes* . . . ' and 'La nostra expansió literària', in *Obres completes*, 2, I, pp. 149–50 and pp. 125–6.
70 See for example Farran i Mayoral's description in *Lletres* . . ., p. 166, of the Shakespeare who wrote Coriolanus, possessing 'la serenor d'un seny en maduresa'. Also the liberal use of 'seny' in the plays to translate anything from reason to good sense to fellow feeling can sometimes produce resistant readings of certain plays. This will be explored further in chapter 5, on *Coriolanus*.
71 Note that a review of Par's translation of *King Lear* in *La Esquella de la Torratxa* (2 August 1912), 503, refers to 'Els fervents devots de Shakespeare, que són molts a Catalunya'.
72 M. de Montoliu, *Mirador* (7 July 1932), 6; M. Raventós 'La casa dels avis', *Revista Catalana*, 11 (23 December 1909), 170; López-Picó's memories of his adolescent discovery of Shakespeare, *Mirador* (16 June 1932), 6 and comments in the 'Moralitats i Pretextos' sections of *La Revista*; and D. Guansé *Mirador* (28 July 1932), 6.
73 'Josep Palau i Fabre', Special Feature and Interview in *Serra d'Or* (November 1986), p. 27. Palau i Fabre, better known for his works on Picasso, has also published a number of works on twentieth-century

metatheatre as well as plays which recast traditional theatrical figures and stories, such as Don Juan, Romeo and Juliet, Hamlet, Antony and Cleopatra.

[74] J. Palau i Fabre, *Avui, Romeo i Julieta* (Barcelona: Institut del Teatre/Mall, 1986).

[75] G. Ferrater, 'El enigma de la personalidad de Shakespeare', *Destino*, 1421 (October 1964), 14.

Chapter 4

Shakespeare and the Catalan Language – 'La llengua més shakespeariana del món'

The previous two chapters have been concerned primarily with tracing the ways in which 'Shakespeare' comes to mean as a term in Catalan. As has been shown, the scope of his signification ranges from a posited universal, transcultural level to a series of particular, Catalan meanings. A dictionary entry on Shakespeare in Catalan would have to include an etymological entry, tracking down the origins of his significance to external authorities: the German Romantics, Coleridge, Emerson, Carlyle and the shadow of French neo-Classical reception, as well as more contemporary critical discourse and theatrical representations. The list of definitions would include universal excellence, spontaneity, natural genius, organic growth, creativity and contemporary humanity, alongside a number of Catalan glosses: political and cultural imperialism, a pattern for acting and the future of theatre in Catalonia, personal inspiration, the dream, *joia*, and an originality which allows for borrowings from other cultures. The entry would have to include a range of variant spellings and pronunciations, underlining the fact that Shakespeare means differently and has different, sometimes contradictory meanings in Catalan. However, Shakespeare does not just exist as a term or a series of tropes in Catalan. He is also an *oeuvre*, whether considered complete and authentic or otherwise, the variant composition of which works to expand his meaning, his status as a signifier. This 'other' Shakespeare, the plays, reveals a series of different origins for his influence, and for his rhetorical scope in Catalonia. Certain specific plays, such as *Hamlet* and *Romeo and Juliet*, lay claims to originating meaning for Shakespeare in Catalan, or at least seem to herald changes in the Shakespeare paradigm and its place within Catalan culture.

The urge to pin down a unitary Shakespeare, to trace some kind of univalent chronological history of the development of his significance and transcendence in Catalan is once again confounded. A reason for this may be the problematic status of the original Shakespeare, not only in deciding what we mean by 'Shakespeare' but also the chaotic state of the texts which constitute his legacy, the language which presents them and is re-presented in translation. However, it may also bear witness to the paradoxes of cultural growth set against the accompanying signals of lack and weakness manifested in the bumpy history of Catalan culture in the twentieth century. In order to uncover the nature of the relationship between Shakespeare, translation and Catalan culture, it is essential to address the question of language. When expression of *catalanitat*, the strength or health of Catalan culture, is so intimately bound up with the Catalan language, it becomes necessary to explore where Shakespeare figures in this equation.

The *Noucentisme* project, which effectively underpins the representation of Shakespeare in Catalan, as well as the institution and consolidation of the translation enterprise, has itself been perceived by critics to have made little mark, in terms of a coherent (unitary) aesthetic, on the subsequent cultural development of Catalonia.[1] In terms of the production of 'original' literature that transcends its time, the tradition of 'strong poets' so valued by Bloom, few names from the *Noucentisme* movement are chosen to regale the halls of cultural glory. Furthermore, concentration on such names might produce a fragmentary, partial and in some ways erroneous vision of the period itself. The movement's importance in programmatic terms lies in the creation of a certain ambiance for literary production, a climate which permeates many different fields of cultural activity. In some ways, the case of Shakespeare reflects this, as does the model of influence usually associated with translation. Translation does not tend to be valued for its originality but as an aid in the production of a normalized situation for subsequent creative activity. Although we have seen how Shakespeare is often cited as an inspiration for original production, thus giving rise to original readings – not least the prioritization of originality – and to 'original' recastings of 'his' stories, there is also a more institutional, programmatic side to his figuration. Hence, a historical study of Shakespeare in Catalan which sought to identify 'transcendent' moments, in terms of attaining the peaks of literary achievement, would not be representative of the extent of his influence. With Shakespeare, too, the exact nature and extent of influence on successive generations is unclear, or at least never fully transparent.

Much translation criticism has tended to support the view that translations are historically bound, the accepted commonplace that each generation needs its own translation. New attempts and approximations usually seek to devalue, ignore or hide earlier attempts and influences. A different model of history – of Shakespeare's story – needs to be embraced, one that recognizes linguistic interaction with previous models, even if simply to reject them, right down to the level of reading about Shakespeare or the plays. To clarify, at the most basic level, when a Catalan reader reads an article on Shakespeare – in Catalan on his role in Catalonia, or in Castilian – it is unlikely to be the Shakespeare read by any English reader, nor even by the Catalan critic but the transplanted Shakespeare.[2] When a Catalan translator produces a version of a Shakespeare play, he creates an intertext which has at least as many links with texts in Catalan as it does with a possible English source text. It is of utmost importance, then, to consider the linguistic attributes given to Shakespeare in Catalan, how the Catalan language is expected to represent him, and the linguistic gains to be made from this figuration. This linguistic contextualization is crucial to an understanding of the relationship between Shakespeare and Catalan culture, the areas in which he was called upon to participate, the discourse surrounding him and to the creation of which he (a very Catalan Shakespeare, as has been seen in the previous chapter) contributes. It is in considering the words Shakespeare comes to speak in Catalan translation and adaptation, and how they interact with historical debates over the post-*Renaixença* development of the Catalan language, that one may discern how and why Catalan might come to be represented as 'la llengua més shakespeariana del món'.[3]

There are a number of related issues at stake in the presentation of this chapter. The first is the status of language in Catalonia, and the different critical, linguistic and political positions on its relationship to the nationalist ideal, and more importantly its representation of *catalanitat*. Throughout Catalonia's history, Catalan has been perceived to be a defining 'difference' with respect to the other communities which came to form the modern Spanish state.[4] Indeed, the status and health of the Catalan linguistic tradition was the primary concern of writers and intellectuals throughout the nineteenth and twentieth centuries. Although spoken Catalan has an unbroken – although at times extremely troubled – history, the level of 'literary' language, the language of culture sought by many, left rather more to be desired. There was increasing interest in reviving the tradition of written Catalan in the latter half of the nineteenth century, and for this reason the period was viewed as one of cultural rebirth, known as the *Renaixença*. Language became linked organically to the spirit and health of the nation and, as such, its cultivation (again as something organic) was approved. Also, *catalanisme* was often defined in relation to *españolismo*, so the relationship of the language with Spanish, of Catalan culture with that of the rest of Spain (but especially Castile) was of central importance in renewing Catalan. The perception of the invasion and imposition of Castilian was an example of oppressive imperialism to be rejected, and the purification of Catalan became very much linked to expressive (political and creative) freedom. Although this is often perceived as an imaginary, retrograde anxiety nowadays, it is important to reiterate that the situation was not one of attempted eradication of Castilian through the imposition of an alternative linguistic norm. Some writers were very much against the imposition of a specific dialect, whereas *antinormistes*, against norms in general, bought wholeheartedly into the concept of organic growth, seeing the Catalan language as liberating in its variety. Pompeu Fabra, in drawing up his Catalan grammar, was careful to make it flexible enough to be acceptable to all the different dialects of the geographical areas where Catalan continued to be spoken.[5]

Perhaps the most important document in evaluating different positions on language in the early twentieth century, showing the unquestioned link of language to 'Catalanness' or *catalanitat*, is the proceedings of the *Primer Congrés Internacional de la Llengua*

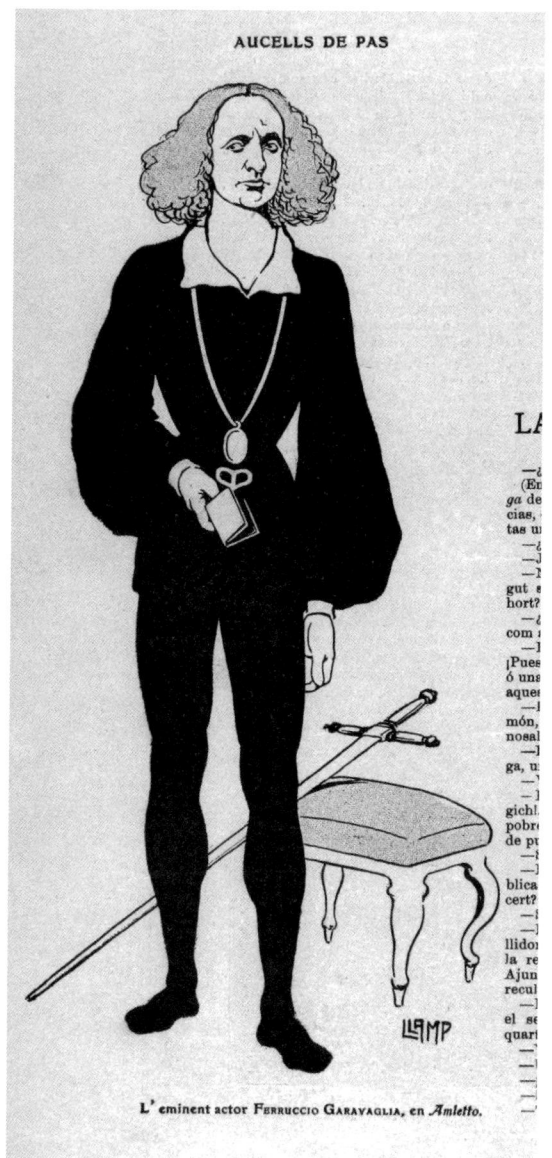

Fig. 1. Garavaglia cartoon in *L'Esquella de la Torratxa*, 1909. Reproduced with the permission of the Biblioteca de Catalienya.

Fig. 2. Adrià Gual's sketch for his production of *A Midsummer Night's Dream*, 1908. From the on-line visual archive in Barcelona's Institut del Teatre.

Fig. 3. Scene from *Titus Andrònic*, directed by Fabià Puigserver at the Thatre Lliure in Gràcia, 1977. © Ros Ribas 1977.

Fig. 4. Scene from *Titus Andrònic*, directed by Fabià Puigserver. © Ros Ribas 1977.

Fig. 5. Francesc Orella as Prospero in Lluís Pasqual's 2005 production of *La tempestad*. © Ros Ribas 2005.

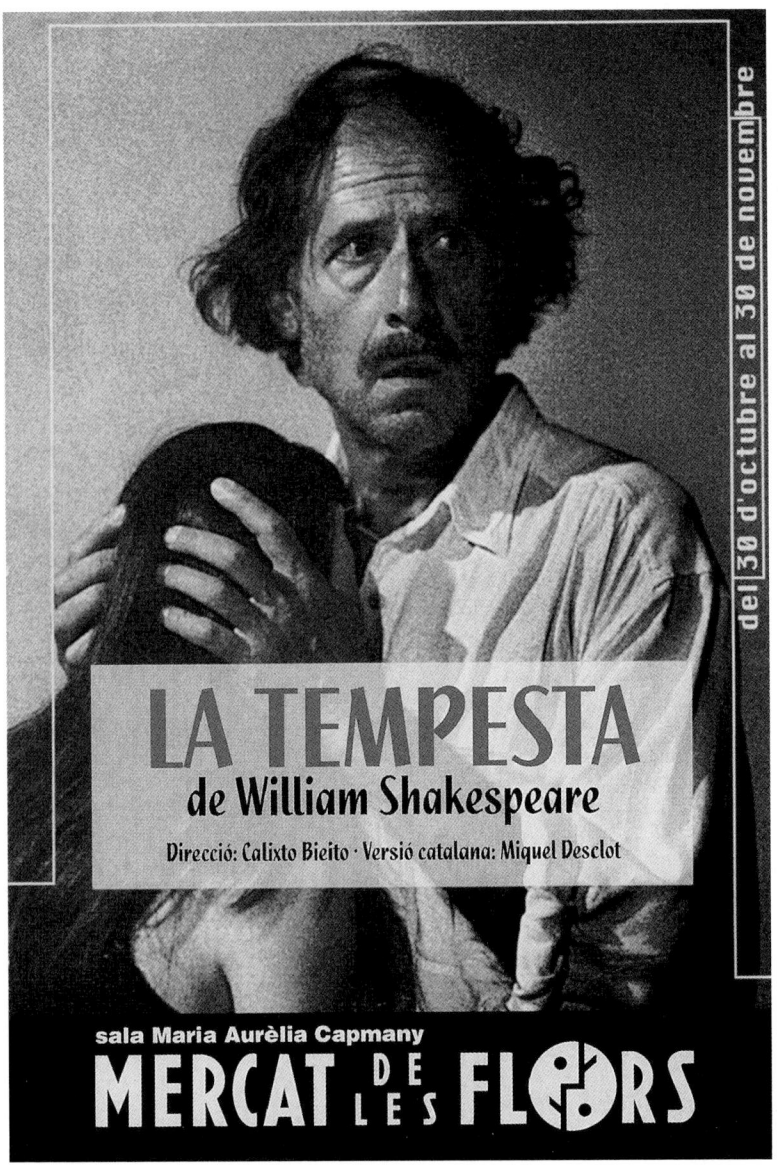

Fig. 6. Free promotional postcard for Calixto Bieito's 1997 production of *La Tempesta*.

Fig. 7. One of the 'ghosts' of Shakespeare haunting Alex Rigola's *Richard III*. © Ros Ribas 2005.

Fig. 8. Actresses in costumes for Adrià Gual's production of *El somni d'una nit d'estiu*, as reproduced in the women's magazine *Feminal*, 1909. Reproduced with the permission of the Biblioteca de Catalunya.

Fig. 12. Anna Lizaran's decidedly earthy representation of Ariel in Lluís Pasqual's production of *La Tempestad*. © Ros Ribas 2004.

Fig. 11. Eduard Fernàndez's Hamlet gives advice to Anna Lizaran's player who is wearing a badge calling for freedom of speech in Basque. From Lluís Pasqual's production of *Hamlet*. © Ros Ribas 2004.

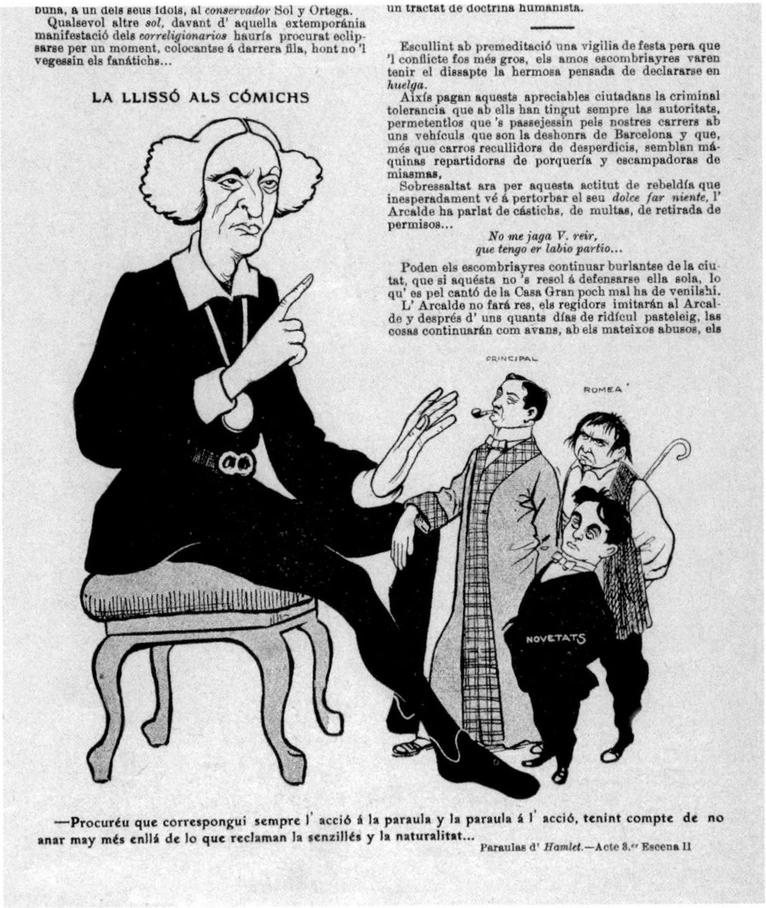

duna, á un dels seus ídols, al *conservador* Sol y Ortega.

Qualsevol altre *sol*, davant d' aquella extemporánia manifestació dels *correligionarios* hauría procurat eclipsarse per un moment, colocantse á darrera fila, hont no 'l vegessin els fanátichs...

un tractat de doctrina humanista.

Escullint ab premeditació una vigilia de festa pera que 'l conflicte fos més gros, els amos escombriayres varen tenir el dissapte la hermosa pensada de declararse en *huelga*.

Axís pagan aquests apreciables ciutadans la criminal tolerancia que ab ells han tingut sempre las autoritats, permetentlos que 's passejessin pels nostres carrers ab uns vehículs que son la deshonra de Barcelona y que, més que carros recullidors de desperdicis, semblan máquinas repartidoras de porquería y escampadoras de miasmas,

Sobressaltat ara per aquesta actitut de rebeldía que inesperadament vé á pertorbar el seu *dolce far niente*, l' Arcalde ha parlat de cástichs, de multas, de retirada de permisos...

No me jaga V. reir,
que tengo er labio partío...

Poden els escombriayres continuar burlantse de la ciutat, que si aquésta no 's resol á defensarse ella sola, lo qu' es pel cantó de la Casa Gran poch mal ha de venilshi.

L' Arcalde no fará res, els regidors imitarán al Arcalde y després d' uns quants días de ridícul pasteleig, las cosas continuarán com avans, ab els mateixos abusos, els

LA LLISSÓ ALS CÓMICHS

—Procuréu que correspongui sempre l' acció á la paraula y la paraula á l' acció, tenint compte de no anar may més enllá de lo que reclaman la senzillés y la naturalitat...

Paraulas d' *Hamlet*.—Acte 8.er Escena II

Fig. 10. Garavaglia's Hamlet presents his advice to the key players in Catalan Theatre, *L'Esquella de la Torratxa*, 1909, 356. Reproduced with the permission of the Biblioteca de Catalunya.

Fig. 9. A cartoon representation of the 'crusade' for Catalan Theatre, in *L'Esquella de la Torratxa*, 1909, 480. Reproduced with the permission of the Biblioteca de Catalunya.

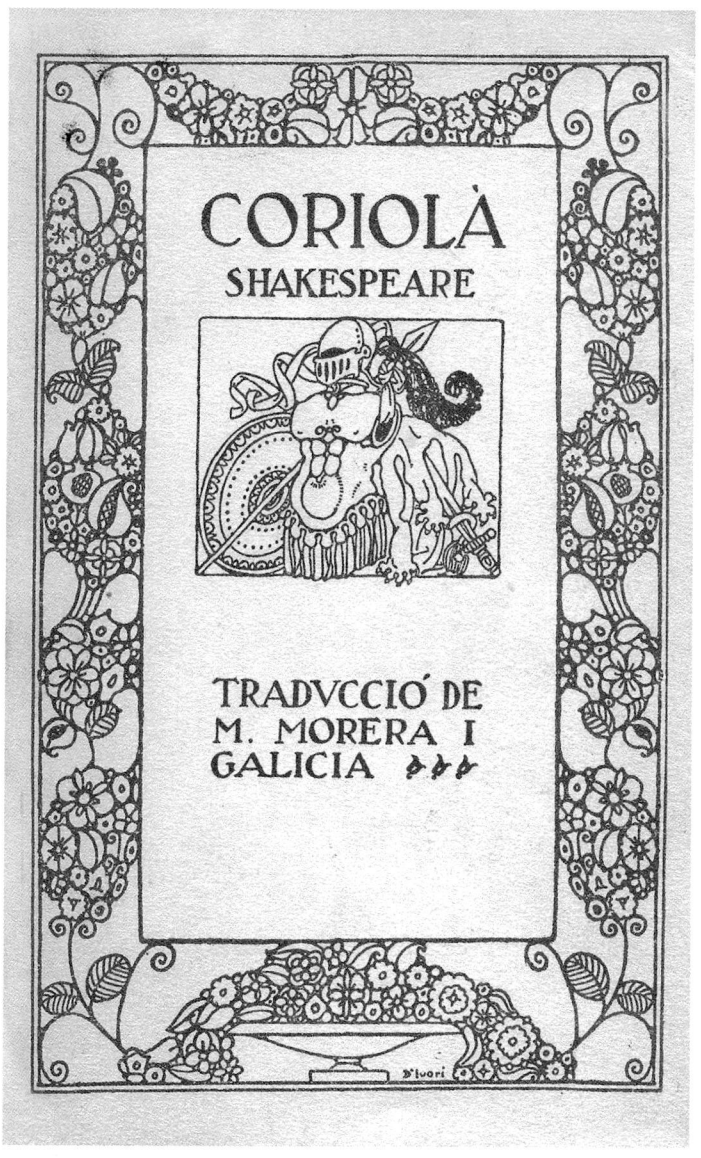

Fig. 13. Frontispiece of Magí Morera i Galícia's 1918 translation of *Coriolanus* for the Editorial Catalana.

Fig. 14. The women in the 1977 production of *Coriolà* at the Teatre Casal Catòlic de Sant Andreu. Reproduced with the permission of the Institut del Teatre.

Fig. 15. Section of promotional poster for Georges Lavaudant's 2002 production of *Coriolà* at the Teatre Nacional de Catalunya with Lluís Homar as Coriolanus.

Fig. 16. The Macbeths according to Calixto Bieito. © Ros Ribas 2002.

Catalana (First International Conference on the Catalan Language) held in October 1906 and published in 1908. Enric Prat de la Riba's contribution, immediately before the close of the conference, was entitled 'Importancia de la llengua dins del concepte de la nacionalitat'.[6] Language here is perceived as a unifying force; and Prat de la Riba gives priority to Hebrew versions of the Bible in order to prove his point, returning to the Babel myth to explore the relationship between nation and language.[7] The main thrust of his paper is to show that whatever arguments are followed, whichever philosopher believed, the crucial point is that language and identity are inextricably linked: 'La força unitiva, aglutinant de l'idioma ha estat vista sempre' ('The unitive, cohesive force of language has always been recognized', p. 665). Prat de la Riba begins, then, with a pragmatic argument, based on historical observation, which develops (or is naturalized) into and alternates with an ontological argument by which 'true' origins can be recovered.

> Tant els súbdits dels grans imperis orientals com els ciutadans dels petits estats municipals o tribals, tant els homes de les civilisacions semítiques com els de les races arianes, tots han vist més o menys perfectament en la llengua un gran principi d'associació, sempre en la gradació de les societats han fet esment de l'unitat llingüística.

> (Both the subjects of the great eastern empires and the citizens of the small city or tribal states, both the men of semitic civilizations and those of the arian race, all of them have recognized more or less perfectly in language a great principle of association, in the grading of societies they have always mentioned linguistic unity, p. 665).

> Verb y idea, intel·ligencia y llenguatge s'uneixen y compenetren en lligam íntim y indisoluble, lligam d'un rastre inesborrable, per més unions eventuals que contregui després l'intel·ligencia ab altres idiomes.

> (Word and idea, intelligence and language are united and intermingle in an intimate and indissoluble link, a link with an ineffaceable trace, however many future unions intelligence may later enter into with other languages, p. 667).

> ... totes les escoles qui s'han ocupat de la nacionalitat en un sentit realista y positiu [han] atribuit a l'unitat de la llengua un valor considerable.
>
> (... all the schools that have concerned themselves with nationality in a realist and positive sense have attributed considerable value to linguistic unity, p. 668).

In the sections cited above, we find sandwiched between the two common-sense observations on 'general' attitudes to language, a third that essentializes the relationship between language and identity. This is what strengthens rhetorically the value judgement about what constitute useful and realistic approaches to language and nation. Unsurprisingly, the boundaries between the 'real' and the metaphorical are blurred in the essay.

Affirmations like those above should be seen as distinct moves to support first the importance of Catalan to Catalan identity, and subsequently the need for its unification and consolidation to achieve the same with Catalan society. The arguments used are both based on supposedly 'natural' divisions and on social necessities, such as the use of language to stand against invading nations, the case of England and Ireland being given as an example of how the destruction of a native language can aid domination, and Hungary as an example of how adherence to the native language can lead to salvation: 'La llengua es la mateixa nacionalitat, deien els patriotes húngars' ('Our language is our very nationality, so said the Hungarian patriots', p. 667).

Such arguments have obvious relevance to the relationship between Catalonia and Spain, although this is never made fully explicit, an example of how the fixing of meaning is not necessarily 'transparent', but depends on intertexuality. The supreme authority of Prat de la Riba's argument, however, resides in his reading of the Bible, and in conflicting translations of the Babel episode, itself a symbol often used for the problem of translation: 'El text hebrèu [. . .] se diferencia de la traducció de la Vulgata en un punt que té per nosaltres una gran importancia...' ('The Hebrew text [. . .] differs from the Vulgate in one point of great significance to us', footnote to p. 665). Whereas the Vulgate translation suggests that the tower and city were built to perpetuate the name of the people before scattering across the earth, the Hebrew text has it that 'la torre y la ciutat té per objecte cohesionar, reunir en una sola unitat social tots els homes d'aleshores *per evitar que sien dispersos damunt la terra*' ('the tower and the city have the object of creating cohesion, of uniting in one social unit all the men of that time to prevent them from being scattered across the face of the earth'). Furthermore, Prat de la Riba appeals to a different etymological version of 'ciutat', that is *civitas*, meaning state not city: 'De manera que en el relat bíblich edificar una ciutat i una torra vol dir fundar un Estat, y construir per aquesta unitat–Estat, la urbs corresponent' ('So that in the biblical tale the construction of a city and a tower means the foundation of a state, and the construction for this unitary state, of the city that corresponds to it'). Of course, this is a narrative which translates far better the relationship between language, state and city, desired for Catalonia. Once more it becomes apparent how the refiguration of a story can be used for purposes of idealization or transfiguration.

The importance of Prat de la Riba's speech, in seeking to draw together different positions on language, is something that is often held to be reflected in the post-conference ambience of consensus with respect to Pompeu Fabra's creation of grammatical norms for Catalan, although there were many dissenters, and the debate over language continued. However, this speech is of particular interest to the presentation of this chapter because of its dependence on translation, on the choice of a version of a story which can have purpose in the target system. Because this choice is based on a central text in the representation of language and relation, in terms of relating the origins of language and the power of translation, in itself it becomes a narrative of what is meant by translation and how changes in translation poetics can point to changes in attitude to language. In the specific case here, translation is both authoritative and false, both a means of cohesion and of differentiation. When read in relation to the rest of the essay, it becomes clear that all the meanings are necessary: the difference between languages and the internal cohesion of language, the sharing of stories (about language, identity, origins) and the rejection of particular versions. Perhaps ultimately the rhetorical persuasion of ideal cohesion is the only 'essential' possibility.

Although historically translation has tended to be defined and valued in terms of supposedly essential values, such as fidelity to a source text, whether to the words or the concepts contained by those words, or textual equivalence, there has been increasing scepticism as to the utility of such an approach both in evaluating translations and tracing translation poetics. The reasons for this are patent in arguments about the perceived cultural contribution of translation in the previous chapter. The great burst of translation which takes place at the end of the first decade of the twentieth century in Catalonia, and continues up to the Civil War, was indeed presented as a way of enriching Catalan culture by importing universal values, other world currencies.[8] Yet, the state of affairs was not as simple as filling the gaps left by the lack of original literary production with somebody else's words, although such a view would not be uncommon in the English-speaking world today where literary translation forms a small percentage of the total published works, and is an activity which tends to be undervalued.[9] Polysystems theory has led to perception of the relativization of translation, of how it means different things and involves different activities, depending on the interplay of cultural fields or 'systems' within a given culture. At the same time, it has been demonstrated that translation plays a much larger role in minority literatures than in the linguistic cultures of the multinationals, where economic power seems to go hand in hand with editorial power. However, it would be too simple to see such a state of affairs as a relationship of imperialism and colonialism. This model, if it ever did hold true, has been undermined by postcolonial revisions of supposedly 'universal', canonical texts.

What is clear is that translation provides a field of encounter between cultures, in which choices are made and boundaries drawn, depending on the relative status of the source and target language and text, but also on the purpose of translation. Significance may be found in the choice of authors, the prioritization of a particular genre or movement, or indeed there may be an urge to fill gaps in cultural production, as would seem to be the case in self-representations of early twentieth-century Catalonia. The scope of such enterprises, whether isolated or institutional, can be observed in the presence and extent of metatexts, defending particular positions and approaches to translation, and in the differential relationships between the translations themselves. Boundaries and choices vary according – mainly – to the perception of the relative importance of different linguistic attributes, whether the emphasis is on literary language, common expression or popular language; on expanding the range of registers, or on developing that elusive 'language of culture'. Yet even where certain metanarratives or norms are chosen over others, this does not guarantee their afterlives nor those of the texts or textual practices they describe. Unanticipated outcomes are almost bound to appear, depending on the dialectical relationship between language and history, between ideal (metaphor) and reality (history). It is this which will determine whether we see Catalonia as a translating imperialism, or focus on Catalan translations of 'imperialism' – meaning Shakespeare, perhaps – either into or out of the dialectic of colonialism. It is the history of what is meant by meaning.

Many cultural critics have identified the importance of translation in the development of the Catalan language and culture. Joaquim Molas in his dictionary of Catalan literature writes that translations were very influential in the fixing of the language and thus in the cultural developments of the period; that they 'encetaren un període brillant i coherent, que es proposà de fixar la llengua literària i, alhora, obrir la cultura catalana als grans corrents clàssics i moderns' ('they began a brilliant and coherent period, whose aim was to fix the literary language and, at the same time, open up Catalan culture to the great classical and modern currents').[10] His retrospective validation of the role of translation in twentieth-century Catalan culture is not simply a vision of past achievements now completed, consolidated and ready to be read as history. Translation continues to be perceived as a necessity for cultural survival today. In fact, discourse surrounding translation throughout the twentieth century in Catalonia, continuously treads the line between past and future, between rewriting and creating a history of translation. So, on the death of Magí Morera i Galícia in 1927, we find his contribution to Catalan culture already written into history: 'Sabeu ben bé el servei que ens ha fet aquest home en incorporar *Hàmlet, Coriolà* [. . .] al nostre Renaixement?' ('Do you know the great service this man has done us in incorporating *Hamlet, Coriolanus* [. . .] into our Renaissance?').[11] More recently, in 1989, C. A. Jordana's essay on 'L'Art de Traduir' was used as a pretext to discuss the contemporary needs of translation.[12] Within the Catalan cultural economy, translation history now seems to share equal importance with translation practice, so much so that the two are at times conflated.

The role of Shakespeare in this expansive enterprise of Catalan cultural development has already been seen to be lauded by Josep Carner, in 'Del Shakespeare en llengua catalana', who underlines the importance of translation, both of works and of their authors, in order to ensure and underpin the future of Catalanism.[13] But it is not only writers who can be fully identified with *Noucentisme* ideals who perceive some value in such cultural borrowings. The approach and philosophy of institutional translation programmes, such as those set up under the auspices of the *Noucentisme* project and the projected complete works of Jordana, Sagarra and Oliva, often differ in presentation from those of individual translators in the same periods. Even within groups with a coherent policy and direction, the participation of individual translators can produce versions which seem to defend or suggest a different set of choices or criteria. So for instance, Víctor Balaguer's reworkings of stories used by Shakespeare were identified as being an attempt to introduce serious drama in Catalan to the nineteenth-century Barcelona stage, Bulbena i Tosell made much of targeting the language of his *Hamlet* to the requirements of the theatre and its actors, and Barallat's translation sought to demonstrate the superiority of Catalan for translation of Shakespeare over Moratín's version.[14] Yet Balaguer's versions were rarely performed outside popular or provincial theatres, Bulbena i Tosell's version is hopelessly clumsy and prosaic and Barallat's clearly indebted to Moratín.

In the early decades of the twentieth century, it is the diversity in translation practice which stands out amidst the narratives of cultural cohesion. Carner's *somni* was to incorporate a dream of poetic language in Catalan; Morera i Galícia was held up as the lyrical version of 'Shakespeare' as against C. A. Jordana's prosaic accuracy; whilst Alfons Par sought to recuperate a medieval linguistic flavour in his translation of *King Lear*.[15] In the post-war decades we range from a target-orientated Sagarra, reproducing the popular richness of Catalan, to Oliva's modern Catalan Shakespeare, objectively seeking to reproduce the effect Shakespeare had amongst his Elizabethan and Jacobean contemporaries in the Catalonia of the 1980s and 1990s, whilst at the same time admitting his reliance on inspiration. More recently, we have witnessed a conflict on the Catalan stage between the attempt to reproduce a language that is representative of contemporary urban trends in speech, thus incorporating Castilian turns of phrase and bilingual conversations, such as in the productions based on translations by Desclot and Mendoza, amongst others, and the work of Sellent to produce speakable versions in a more normative Catalan. What this chapter will show is that the range in approaches to translation does not just reveal changes in attitude to translation, increasing professionalism perhaps or more satisfactory knowledge of the relationships between English and Catalan, but changes in the figuration of Shakespeare, in understandings of what constitutes good Catalan and in perception of language in general.

The history of the Catalan language in the twentieth century has been punctuated by periods of debate over the value of instituting norms as against allowing 'natural' linguistic growth. Whereas intellectuals of the *Noucentista* movement tended to identify with the *normativisme* represented by Fabra, there were also *antinormativistes* who questioned the imposition of 'artificial' standards of grammar and orthography. After 1913, there was general acceptance of the rules introduced by Pompeu Fabra, and divergent positions were less vocal.[16] None the less, there were still translations which ignored or deliberately flouted Fabrian developments after this date and, in particular with Shakespeare, debate continued over the kind of language which he would sanction, and consequently the language most appropriate for translating him. As we shall see subsequently, Alfons Par rejected modern Catalan as a vehicle for Shakespeare, Perpiñà did not follow the Fabrian norms and Farran i Mayoral, although generally compliant, insisted on his own idiosyncratic usage of the relative pronoun 'qui' ('who'). In many ways, there is far more scope for divergence today, even with the widespread success of language planning, the so-called normalization programme, to implant a standard in education and in the public and official use of Catalan. The Franco regime displaced and sought to destroy the newly-regained normality of Catalan, leading to almost forty years of enforced diglossia. This has led to increasing self-perception of the gap between standard Catalan and spoken, street Catalan. Furthermore, politically-motivated attacks on Catalan 'hegemony' in more recent years have resulted in a sense of a need to recognize and represent the presence of Castilian in Catalan culture, and even the legitimacy of Catalan cultural production in Castilian. Yet, as can be seen most clearly in the Catalan-speaking communities of Valencia and the Balearic Islands, such developments rarely lead to more linguistic harmony and understanding, let alone to the achievement of a sense of cultural normality. Instead, they are usually about seeking a return to the acceptance of Castilian as the main language of culture, and the rejection of Catalan as anything more than a 'regional' language, limited to familiar and colloquial domains.

One of the most interesting manifestations of the debate over the ideal development of Catalan can be perceived in recourse to the language used by Prat de la Riba to define and fix the operation of Catalan nationalism. The role of imperialism will be discussed later, but here we will hark back to his comments on the duty of people involved in the Catalan political and cultural enterprise. The need to escape the imposition of external patterns of culture, politics and language is something we have seen in quotations from *La Nacionalitat Catalana*, in the prioritization of an 'imperial' model rather than a colonial model. Thus, we find recourse to Prat de la Riba's words in relation to linguistic analysis: 'Lo imposat no sol durar . . .' ('That which is imposed tends not to last'), ' . . . tota imposició crida a la rebel·lió' (' . . . all imposition calls for rebellion').[17] The meaning of such statements produces equivocation in its application to the language situation. In general terms, it involves an operation to dislodge the centrality of Castilian, presented as the model of an imposed language. This is achieved by downplaying the formal possibilities of Castilian and stressing the foundational nature of Catalan, as the originating moment which underpins Catalanism. So, we see Shakespeare used to embarrass Castilian, in references to inadequate translations and adaptations of plays. Reviews of a production of *Cleopatra* in Madrid hold that Spanish is now only capable of the *género chico*, and is certainly not up to the tragic grandeur of Shakespeare. There is biting criticism of Castilian adaptations of Shakespeare's stories such as *Lear* and *Hamlet*. Also, whilst the Castilian literary genius is respected – there are for instance more events dedicated to Cervantes than to Shakespeare in Catalonia in their shared tricentenary year – Castilian is at times presented as inadequate to contain that genius. On *Don Quixote*, for instance: ' . . . ja la llengua castellana fou petita per a encloure l'obra del geni, y les famoses aventures del més enamorat dels paldins es traduiren a la llengua de Shakespeare y de Rabelais' (' . . . the Castilian language was already too limited to contain the work of this genius, and the famous adventures of the most enamoured of paladins were translated into the language of Shakespeare and of Rabelais').[18] Furthermore, the *Quixote* was translated into Catalan (by Bulbena i Tosell), notwithstanding some criticism of such enterprises. This kind of activity and representation of the relationship between Catalan and Castilian offers the possibility of an arbitrary reading of Farran i Mayoral's response to Unamuno and his anti-regionalism: 'Nosaltres, senyor Unamuno, quan defensem la nostra llengua, defensem un *pa de l'esperit* tan necessari com la llibertat de pensament. Perxò, de la nostra llengua, i del nostre pensament, en fem qüestió previa' ('When we, honoured friend Unamuno, defend our language, we defend a *bread of the soul* as necessary as freedom of thought. That is why we make of our language, and of our thought, a primary principle).[9]

The identification of the Catalan language as an essential concern for the Catalans is here clearly and unashamedly presented as a rhetorical act, as a necessary figuration of origins. The same sort of process can be recognized in the representation of Shakespeare, particularly in relation to his expression in Catalan, as for instance in the rhetorical prioritization of Sagarra's translations of Shakespeare: 'podem congratular-nos de posseir en llengua catalana una de les millors traduccions de Shakespeare que existeixen al món' ('we may congratulate ourselves on possessing in Catalan one of the best translations of Shakespeare in the world').[20]

The link of language to the genius of a people is a process that shows attachment to Romantic ideas about the spirit of a nation. So we find regular recourse to the translation of European thinkers to defend the prioritization of the Catalan question. Arguments for natural organic growth, such as that of T. Davis, 'la llengua no és un diccionari, és una ànima' ('language is not a dictionary, it is a soul'), are found alongside reference to good government, to the artificial administration of language: 'Aconsella el bon govern l'ús oficial de les llengües regionals' ('Good government recommends the official use of the regional languages').[21] Whilst leftwing writers such as Alomar hold that 'el catalanisme és una de les accions més fortes de cultura popular que mai s'hagin exercit' ('Catalanism is one of the strongest actions of popular culture to have ever been carried out'), others reclaim the necessity for a literary language, presented in the kind of aristocratic language used to refer to the need for translation of Shakespeare and other classics in the previous chapter.[22] Elsewhere we find expression of the importance of variety but also of 'direcció superior', of intellectuals taking responsibility in developing the language.[23]

This state of affairs also provides a different slant on the question of the scope of imposition. Many writers and cultural commentators view the introduction of grammar rules and norms by Fabra, and its acceptance by *Noucentista* intellectuals, as an attempt to impose an unnatural shape on Catalan. The extent of duality of argumentation, due perhaps to attempts to reconcile wholly Romantic ideals with a drive towards modernity (often presented as a rejection of romanticism), can be viewed in quotations such as the following from Prat de la Riba, underlining the importance of the 'herencia del passat':

> Crear una llengua literària és l'obra cabdal d'un poble.
>
> Les llengües surten de l'anarquia dialectal que porta a la descomposició i a la mort, per cultiu literari, per la força intensa de la raça que fa sentir a tots els homes que la formen la identitat fonamental, la continuitat de la vida col·lectiva, i els empenya a *traduir* aquesta unitat de sentiment, de voluntat, de vida col·lectiva, en institucions i costums i lleis i llengua . . .[24]
>
> (To create a literary language is the supreme work of a people).
>
> (Languages emerge from the dialectal anarchy that leads to breakdown and death, through literary cultivation, through the intense force of the race that makes all the men who are part of it feel their essential identity, the continuity of collective existence, and pushes them to *translate* this unity of feeling, of will, of collective existence, into institutions and customs and laws and language . . .).

The 'obra cabdal' to which he refers here is underpinned, as we have seen, by the incorporation of chosen cultural values to enrich the spirit of Catalanism. It is a work of art to be created by a people, a nation, whilst at the same time *for* a nation. This ambiguity underlines the nature of argumentation about the necessary development of the Catalan language. Many argue for the continued diversity of Catalan, and against the imposition of a central standard, whereas here we see this variety presented as 'anarchy', an extremely significant judgement given the political conflicts of the period. The need for agents to translate – or even transfigure – the raw spirit of the nation into something more refined, transcendent and perhaps 'universal' is foregrounded. This may explain the rather utopian, baroque feel of much *Noucentista* writing, notwithstanding *Noucentisme*'s famed embracement of Classicism. Many writers seem to identify this transcendent urge in the production of writing as far from the spoken norm as possible. Such a paradox is often underlined in satirical papers of the period, and we see that even those who are satisfied with the necessity of Fabrian norms, are sceptical about their immediate value in improving the standard of Catalan. So for instance we find the following joke cartoon in *La Esquella de la Torratxa*: 'Ja tinc l'ortografía! . . . Ara sols em manca saber escriure! . . .' ('I've got my orthography! . . . Now all I need to know is how to write! . . '.).[25] Once again the insoluble question of what should be made the 'qüestió previa' (first principle) is raised: language or nation, writing or speech, creativity or rules, individual or collective, translation or original.

Fabra himself shows awareness of the necessity of individual production when he says: 'Aneu fent, els gramàtics enregistrem' ('You keep writing, and we grammaticians will record it').[26] Yet suspicion about contrasting positions on language are rife, and continues to be present in later consideration of Catalan, and what Shakespeare in Catalan should be. On the one hand Shakespeare represents extreme diversity and linguistic freedom; on the other, the imposition of individual genius on collective culture. Shakespeare's language in and for Catalan is a model both to be revered and feared. Indeed, sometimes both positions are held simultaneously. Why this is so takes us back to an earlier 'qüestió previa', that of translatability: the question of what exact mode of relation between languages is present in translation, or even perhaps in a particular text. More simply, how far is translation limited by the source or the target language. In the case of the particular translation relationships between English and Catalan, relevant here, there is a fascinating insight into the question by Carles Riba.

In a letter to Joan Gili, advising him on the translation of *Les Elegies de Bierville*, Riba admits that:

> L'anglès és la llengua en la qual més m'hauria plagut d'escriure els meus versos – si hagués estat la meva; i us diré que de vegades, sense adonar-me'n, una mica, per sota el català, penso en anglès, i llavors el català és sotmés a una tortura de sintetització que el pobre no mereix.[27]
>
> (English is the language in which I would have most liked to write my poetry – if it had been my own language; and I'll admit to you that at times, without realising it, and just a little, beneath the Catalan, I'm thinking in English, and then my Catalan undergoes a torture of synthesization that the poor thing does not deserve).

Although on one level, these words may exemplify little more than the anglophilia of many writers of Riba's generation, they are also important in drawing attention to the simultaneous attraction and incompatibility of languages in the translation equation. Shakespeare's words from *The Tempest* are presented as originators of the poem which Joan Gili is attempting to translate, as the idea that traverses and connects the whole poem, which he carries everywhere in his memory. But such 'thinking in English' is also presented as something destructive to Catalan, as 'una tortura de sintetització'. These contrasting pulls in the relationship of the languages of translation are a strong presence in evaluation of translations of Shakespeare into Catalan. Although Catalan is often presented as a language more appropriate for translating the rhythms of English than others of the Romance family, it is also maintained that 'el geni d'una llengua no es pot contradir' ('the genius of a language may not be contradicted').[28] In fact, if we were to consider praise of Sagarra's translations, we would note that his versions were valued both for their remarkable and exemplary 'faithfulness' to the original, attributed to anything from his own literary and theatrical background to his affinities with Shakespeare, and for their inescapable *catalanitat*, to the extent that detractors coined the verb *sagarrejar* to account for his consistent 'betrayals' of his source. Once again, it is arguable that such apparent contradictions are sanctioned by representations of Shakespeare's genius, his figuration of the authority of the creative agent to break with the norm, and his patience and generosity in the figure of 'l'ingeni camperol' ('the country genius').[29]

Models of Shakespeare's interaction with the Catalan language are dependent on three different factors: his own linguistic position in English, particular translation poetics, and attitudes to the Catalan language. Often, links between the two languages, Shakespeare's and Catalan are made fully explicit, such as comparisons made between the problematic orthography of Shakespeare's name and the orthographical state of Catalan.[30] At other times, it is the difference in development between Shakespeare's English and modern Catalan which is foregrounded. To uncover the different positionalities which are revealed, one must first look at how Shakespeare's linguistic distinctness can stand as a model for Catalan, before moving on to consider the practical outcomes of such a model.

Alfons Par's words on the matter, in his first essay on Shakespeare for the Associació Wagneriana, draw the following relationship between the two languages involved in this study:

> Davallant ara a la materialitat del llenguatge restareu sorpresos davant de sa riquesa. Es, en efecte, En Shakespeare'l pare de la llengua anglesa; son vocabulari es verament immens, cal tan sols cercar les autoritats dels diccionaris moderns: ell apadrina la majoria dels mots. Emperò no's cregui que'l llenguatge d'En Shakespeare sigui actualment molt castiç. Y el perquè es ben clar pels catalans. El llenguatge del més castiç de nostres poetes no ho resultarà pas dins d'un segle, quan la llengua catalana hagi assolida, no mitjançant academies, ni diccionaris ni gramatiques oficials, sinó lliurement y espontania, com correspon a una parla viva, sa unitat y perfecció.[31]

> (Turning now to the substance of the language you will be surprised by its richness. Shakespeare is, in effect, the father of the English language; his vocabulary is truly immense, you have only to seek the authority of modern dictionaries: he is the godfather of the majority of words. However, do not think that the language of Shakespeare is particularly pure. And the reason for this is clear for the Catalans. The language of the purest of our poets will not be so in less than a century, when the language has attained, not through academies or dictionaries or official grammars, but freely and spontaneously, as corresponds to a living language, its unity and perfection).

The interest of this passage lies in Par's identification of the fluid lexical boundaries in Shakespeare's work, something which he feels reflects, and can perhaps be best reflected by, the linguistic situation in Catalonia. In many ways, Shakespeare here is presented as an organic agent for the natural development of the

English language, and can perhaps extend such a role in Catalan. Such a position is exemplified in reliance on popular, spoken forms – the tradition called upon by translators of the nineteenth century, as well as by Par, Perpiñà and certainly in theory by Montoliu. Yet recourse to such a 'natural' pre-normative richness is clearer in orthography than anything else, and this is what sets it apart from the writers who fully accepted Fabra's 'normes'.[32] However, the linguistic picture is not quite so simple. *Noucentistes* and *Neo-Noucentistes*, too, value the richness of Shakespeare's vocabulary, and, particularly in lexis, call on recourse to a wide range of regional and dialectal forms. Josep Carner, for instance, cites widespread appreciation for Morera i Galícia's 'lleidatà'.[33] Only *barbarismes* were to be avoided, referring to words or phrases borrowed from Castilian. Shakespeare was also used as an authority for neologisms, for the shaping of words, which Fabra seems to sanction. This aspect can be witnessed in the work of Carner, who single-handedly – and through translation – introduced enough new usages to merit a volume on his contribution to Catalan lexis.[34] Many modern writers look back wistfully to the times when Catalan allowed Carner's invention. However, critics were vigilant against perceived 'Gallicisms' and foreign forms, and it is once again Carner who comes in for most criticism, as his Shakespeare translations were felt to be too reliant on French lexis and prosody.[35]

Par was later, to some extent, to reject the parallelisms between the language of Shakespeare and modern Catalan drawn in the above passage. By 1912, with his own translation of *King Lear*, and after witnessing a number of more popular translations into Catalan, he felt that modern Catalan was not adequate for the translation of Shakespeare. Full understanding and transference of Shakespeare's works could only be achieved in an approximation to medieval Catalan, to the language of a time when he felt the two languages were etymologically, conceptually and historically closest. This new leaning seems to be driven by an urge for erudition, to present a study of Shakespeare comparable to the kind of annotated texts found elsewhere in the Western world. However, there is an aspect of Par's visionary ideal which has strong bearing on the representation of the Catalan language. Rather than being a poor reflection of Shakespeare's language, in some ways the focus is now placed on a Catalan tradition. The title page describes the play as being 'fidelment arromansada en l'estil de catalana prosa' ('faithfully rendered into romance in the style of Catalan prose'). The use of 'arromansada' places it very much within the target tradition. Par suggests recourse to medieval Catalan can provide solutions to problems of meaning which would be beyond modern speakers of English. Hence, in some ways, this represents another early claim for Catalan to be considered a most 'Shakespearian' of languages.

Alfons Par cannot really be placed within the linguistic normalization drive which finds its expression in the Institut d'Estudis Catalans and the work of Pompeu Fabra. In fact his *Lo Rei Lear*, although welcomed by many critics, is generally presented as something of an anomaly up to 1939; as more of a source-orientated participation in Shakespeare studies rather than a target-orientated attempt to share in Shakespeare as a representative of 'universal' culture. Later translators and critics, such as Xavier Fàbregas and Salvador Oliva, critique Par's attempts in terms of their artificiality, both in defence of more pragmatic, target (and stage) orientated translation practice, and in questioning the logic of Par's equation of Shakespearian English with medieval Catalan. However, his promotion of Shakespeare as father of the English language provides a role for his translators, for himself in Catalan, and for the other Catalan 'bards', as surrogate fathers for the new-born baby that was Catalan culture post-*Renaixença*. This gives an intriguing angle on the title quotation for the chapter, and other similar though not so blatant comments from the period. Could Catalan be seen as the most Shakespearian of languages because, if not born of Shakespeare, at least brought up by him? To reveal the exact nature of Shakespeare's desired relationship with the Catalan language, Shakespeare's Catalan, it will be necessary to consider the kind of linguistic values Catalan writers hoped he would instil, or perceived to be figured through him.

The perception of Catalan as an ideal vehicle for the works of Shakespeare is expressed in many more ways than Farran i Mayoral's assertion that Catalan is the most Shakespearian language in the world. Carner considers the aptitude of Catalan for the translation of Shakespeare to be a result of Catalan's closeness to fourteenth-century Italian. This follows reasoning to the effect that were Shakespeare not to have written in Elizabethan English, the language in which we could most easily imagine him expressing himself would be the Italian of the

Renaissance. The 'virtues' which recommend Catalan are described as follows: 'La nostra poesia té avui una frescor, una plasticitat, jovenívola, no minvades per cap retòrica (per cap s'entén, que li sigui pròpia), que recorden tant l'italià trescentista' ('Our poetry today has a youthful freshness and plasticity, undiminished by any rhetoric (that is by none that is its own), that recall fourteenth-century Italian').[36] Likewise, Gabriel Alomar describes Carner's versions of the *Somni* and St. Francis 'com unint en la gràcia d'una sola mà la versió de dues maneres en apariencia divergentes del meteix vital italianisme' ('as if they united in the grace of a single hand in two apparently divergent ways the version of the same vital Italianism').[37]

This optimism about Shakespeare in the Catalan language is not reflected as easily in Montoliu or Par. Par's 1905 assertion of the similarities between the status of Elizabethan English and post-Renaixença Catalan is supplanted when he comes to translate *King Lear* by a feeling that modern Catalan did not have the expressive capacity to transmit a Shakespeare play. His choice of an approximation to medieval Catalan is supported by earlier meditations on the similarity of some expressions in the language of *Tirant lo Blanc* and that of Shakespeare: 'Molt després d'haver-se escrita aquesta conferencia, he anat descobrint en nostres classics, frases y comparances usats per Shakespeare, qui actualment ja no viuen ni en la literatura anglesa, ni en la catalana. Es açò una prova de ma opinió que no's pot trelladar be un escritor antic forà en el català actual, tan anemic y maldeixat pel jou castellà' ('Long after having written this paper, I have been able to discover in our classics, phrases and comparisons used by Shakespeare, which do not now live on either in English or Catalan literature. This confirms my opinion that a foreign writer from the past cannot be translated properly into modern Catalan, so drained and damaged by the Castilian yoke').[38] Montoliu, in contrast, despairs of the task of translation because of the advanced status of Elizabethan English compared to a Catalan which had not yet been fixed. Fàbregas' later consideration of both arguments in his 'Notes introductòries' leads him to the conclusion that: 'Par [. . .] creu innecessari mirar endavant, o sigui, intentar el desenvolupament d'un idioma literari endegat a partir de la parla quotidiana, perquè, pensa que té la solució a l'abast de la mà en el tresor lingüístic dels nostres clàssics' ('Par [. . .] thinks it is unnecessary to be forward looking, in other words, to develop a literary language drawn from everyday speech, because he thinks he has the solution to hand in the linguistic treasure of our classics').[39] He is far more approving of the work of Montoliu in this respect.

Shakespeare's language, which Sagarra describes in his introduction to *Romeo i Julieta* as 'que permetia tota mena d'excentrismes i era el contrari del llenguatge de la prudència i de la mediocritat' ('which permitted every sort of eccentricity and was the opposite to the language of prudence and of mediocrity'),[40] was often linked to the intensity and economy of expression of Catalan. So Farran i Mayoral writes that: 'La catalana, essencialment, és una llengua intensa, com l'anglès de Shakespeare, l'italià de Dant, el grec de Sòfocles. Intensa, és a dir que els seus mots poden fer sentir la força més forta i la delicadesa més delicada. Una llengua festosa, digna de les més belles festes de la paraula' ('The Catalan language is essentially an intense language, like the English of Shakespeare, the Italian of Dante, the Greek of Sophocles. Intense, that is to say that its words can make one feel the most forceful of forces and the most delicate of delicacies. A festive language, worthy of the most beautiful festivals of the word').[41] In contrast the works of Shakespeare are described here and by other writers as losing intensity in French and Spanish. They can only be 'conceived' successfully in Catalan. So, for instance, Ramon Esquerra writes of C. A. Jordana's versions of Shakespeare in 1936, as if 'm'ha semblat estar llegint una obra escrita fa uns quants mesos tan sols' ('it seemed to me as if I were reading a work written only a few months ago').[42] Shakespeare, thus, both 'fathers' Catalan and is naturalized by the language. A complete expression of this duality can be found, again, in Carner's introduction to *Venus i Adonis:* 'La gran, la formosa realitat és, d'una banda, que Shakespeare és ENDEVINAT – tot simplement – en català; i, d'altra banda, que un dels fruits més daurats del Renaixement ha servit per ENDEVINAR el to de la llengua literària catalana' ('The great, the beautiful reality is, on the one hand, that Shakespeare is – simply – DIVINED in Catalan; and, on the other hand, that one of the most golden fruits of the Renaissance has served to DIVINE the tone of the Catalan literary language').[43]

Translation here is presented as a far more instinctual process than later calls for 'scientific' translation, grounded in linguistic study and textual analysis, would seem to allow. Even translators such as Moix and Oliva who ground their efforts in the mountain of Shakespeare studies and annotated texts now readily available in the global marketplace, confess their debt to instinct and inspiration, something which is not really accounted for in the many narratives of the Shakespeare gap referred to earlier. The rhetorical imperative of Shakespeare's incorporation could not here be more marked. Shakespeare is both divined in Catalan, brought into imaginative existence, and serves as a figure for the divination of the Catalan language. On both sides of this representation, the Catalan language is prioritized.

The main areas in which Shakespeare's linguistic potential was identified in Catalan were as follows: poetic language, a language of the theatre, language for the novel, popular language, as well as the 'llengua de cultura' most cited as the aim of the translation drive.[44] The poetic values which could be brought to Catalan by Shakespeare translation seem in the late nineteenth century to have been subordinated to interest in particular stories, the incorporation of the great Shakespearian myths such as *Romeo and Juliet*, *Hamlet* and *Macbeth*. This situation begins to be countered with Par's revelation of the lyrical value of Shakespeare in his lecture on *Lucrece*, but it is Carner's translation of *A Midsummer Night's Dream* which leads to most 'divination' of the poetic possibilities Shakespeare could bring. Raventós writes in response that such an enterprise could contribute to the 'depuración de nuestra lengua, moldeándola en las necesidades de una vida noble y refinada, la consagración definitiva de una métrica moderna' ('purification of our language, moulding it to the necessities of a noble and refined existence, the definitive consecration of a modern metre').[45] Magí Morera i Galícia, too, is valued for his lyrical approximations to Shakespeare, and continues to be so by more recent translators such as Terenci Moix and Gerard Vergés, although they also imply such translations are no longer viable.[46] The question is how Shakespeare's poetry should be translated, without the meaning becoming a slave to prosody. This debate has been a constant in responses to Catalan Shakespeare translations, ranging from questions of the appropriateness of Carner's alexandrines to Oliva's attacks on the 'false' poetry of translators who attempt to transplant unproblematically the iambic pentameter to a Catalan decasyllabic line.[47]

Whilst, on the whole, prosody is not one of the most important or 'meaningful' factors in translation of Shakespeare into Catalan, except insofar as the range of poetic translations contrasts with largely prose renderings in Castilian, it is worth considering the main positions taken by translators. Oliva criticizes Sagarra, and even Ferrater, because the fixing of a verse form means that the meaning and stress of the original become subordinate to the line. He also considers the association of the iambic pentameter with the Catalan decasyllable to be a false friend. Whilst Catalan prosody is based on syllable counting and accents, Shakespeare's iambic pentameter is more dependent on rhythm and stress patterns. This issue is something which is clearly not of interest to Carner in his translation of the *Somni*, and he is defended in his choice of alexandrines by Albert Torrellas as follows: 'Shakespeare no era un estilista, Shakespeare era un pensador; de conseqüent, podriem criticar, y fins compadir, al traductor que's proposés millorar els seus pensaments, però no al que's proposés millorar la forma en la qual aquets son exposats, o que la millorés sense proposarho' ('Shakespeare was not a stylist, Shakespeare was a thinker; in consequence, we can criticize, and even pity, the translator who attempts to improve his thoughts, but not the one who attempts to improve the form in which these are expressed').[48] Carner's translation of Shakespeare offers a highly target-orientated transfiguration of the original and this may explain why it has not been re-published since, notwithstanding the favourable comments of critics ranging from C. A. Jordana to Oliva. Carner's interest in the cultivation of new verse forms, and especially the recuperation of the alexandrine, can be observed in the range of examples from Carner used by Oliva in his *Introducció a la mètrica*. As for the decasyllabic line, with or without caesura, it is a common metre in Catalan, and hence offers a satisfactory equivalent to the iambic pentameter in terms of usage. However, notwithstanding claims that Catalan is the closest romance language to English because of its high proportion of monosyllables and masculine stresses, it remains difficult to keep the same number of lines in Catalan. Oliva's own response is to combine different syllable lengths, focusing more on the stress patterns in the original, but he was also constrained by having to keep to exactly the same number of lines as the original to facilitate dubbing and subtitling.

The range of positions taken also reflects the alternative leanings towards seeing the translation of Shakespeare's poetry as something which could expand the poetic possibility of Catalan or towards insistence on serving the meaning of the original, without bending the rules of prosody. How far the gamut of positions is a question of historical taste is a moot point here. Early criticisms of Morera i Galícia's translations often focus on aspects which would be perceived to be a feature of the original. For instance, in his version of *Romeo and Juliet* 'va xocar, sí, una mica la cruesa del llenguatge' ('the crudeness of the language was, indeed, a bit shocking').[49] Oliva's position, meanwhile, reflects a more communicative approach to language, based on notions of competence drawn from Chomsky (and hence absolutes of performance). His criticism of other translators draws attention to the low 'speakability' of some of the lines, as they try to adhere to the decasyllabic line.[50] Furthermore, his chapter on 'L'elocució dels versos' in his introduction to Catalan versification makes it quite plain that elocution for him is a political issue of some urgency.[51]

Translations which had some pretence towards theatrical performance were presented from very early on as original endeavours, relatively unique and of extreme utility to Catalan culture. So for instance Masriera places great importance on this aspect. Shakespeare becomes key in the debate over what kind of language is appropriate to the theatre. Carner and Morera i Galícia, for example, are considered by some to be too 'poetic' to appeal to a theatregoing public; Vilaregut is valued for his ability to bring Shakespeare closer to a Catalan audience; and Sagarra, Moix and Oliva are careful to present their credentials in terms of achieving this desired end. Sellent even admits to incorporating the suggestions of actors and directors of his versions into his final translations. Supporters of Sagarra, in particular, hold his 'popular' translations of Shakespeare's plays to be one of the most important events in Catalan theatre after the Civil War, his theatrical ability being presented ad nauseam.[52]

The debate over 'theatre language' also holds the distinction – as we have seen to some extent in the previous chapter – of drawing in the figure of Shakespeare to defend different linguistic ideals. *Hamlet* is cited abundantly in early *Teatre Català* periodicals and in more recent critical formulations, as exemplary in teaching the kind of language appropriate to the theatre.[53] The pertinent section, Hamlet's advice to the players, alongside reference to Pere Codony (Peter Quince) and his merry band of mechanicals, is also used to denounce the flawed declamation of many actors, in particular amateurs, and to underpin calls for schools of speech and drama.[54] Shakespeare's language hence becomes something that can train Catalan actors to speak appropriately, so we see Shakespeare serves equally in defence of a 'tradició culta' (high tradition) and a more popular aspect, of written, literary language and of speech. Often there is a divide between calls for the cultured and the popular in theatre translation. *Noucentista* participation in the debate is firmly associated with attempts to intervene to raise the artistic standard of Catalan theatre: 'Cal en el teatre...el triomf de *la paraula intel·ligent*' (What is necessary in theatre is the triumph of *the intelligent word*').[55] Attention to reviews and recollections suggest that audiences could not understand, and this may well be a clue to the popularity of Sagarra's translations with what Fàbregas describes as their lexical richness and precision.[56]

From early twentieth-century criticism and prologues to translations it is clear that the different linguistic values which Shakespeare can represent give rise to very divergent positions with respect to language and approaches to translation. The question of what makes a translation 'bona' (good) brings divergent answers, usually reflecting the variety of ways in which the question is posed. Sagarra's consecration has been based on reasons ranging from his perceived political and poetical engagement to the numbers of lines he uses. Ferrater's translation of *Coriolà* is a classic for the initiated, because of his 'recreative spirit', his lack of conformity to closeness, to fidelity to the original, a reflection perhaps of the mythical status of nonconformist which he has been given. Carner's translation of the *Somni* comes in for praise and criticism because of its prioritization of poetic language. There is some concern that it is not, indeed, a poetry based on the language of Shakespeare – instead imposing a particular symbolist reading related to poetic topoi of the time, but more importantly questions are raised over the success of such an attempt at theatre translation. Some blame Carner, others the lack of a tradition for such a language, which means that actors and public do not assimilate or understand it. For many though, the poetic translation remains the ideal, and this would appear to be very much a feature of the *Noucentista* model of Shakespearian language, and Shakespeare translation. In the case of Morera i Galícia, some criticism is based on a knowledge of English – i.e. comparative – but much of it on the perceived success of a lyrical feel. Although in the 1930s there appears to be increasing prioritization of clarity and homogeneity in translation, followed by Oliva in the 1980s, Shakespeare's language continues to be presented as something beyond technique.[57] The major anomaly would appear to be Sagarra, whose translations are felt to be on the popular side, notwithstanding his aristocratic background, neither classical nor poetic (except in terms of versification). But in some ways his equivalence is drawn with Shakespeare because of the chaotic status of his work. All these values become ways of showing Catalan to be a language favoured by Shakespeare, but also one which favours his expression.

The role of the Catalan poet-translator in creating or forging a literary language, a 'llengua de cultura' as Carles Riba expresses it, is emphasized as Shakespeare is given meaning in Catalan. Josep Carner describes Morera i Galícia's rendering of some of the more problematic lines in *Venus and Adonis* as singing in Catalan with such familiarity as if it were the language in which they were first conceived. He describes his own translation of *A Midsummer Night's Dream* as an attempt to say 'd'una faisó catalana les belles coses del Somni' ('in a Catalan manner the beautiful things of the Dream') for the good of the Catalan people. The desired end of such a rendering is expressed in the 'vote' that his *Somni* represents, a hope that 'per l'enaltiment del nostre idioma, se tradueixin al català tots els poetes que han parlat de l'amor' ('for the elevation of our language, all the poets who have spoken of love will be translated into Catalan').[58]

Josep Lleonart expresses the hope that in following and translating Shakespeare, Catalan writers will draw on the riches of 'dialectal' Catalan: 'Remembrem com el mateix Shakespeare, i tantes figures fonamentals [...] en èpoques, justament apassionades d'humanitats, acolliren i volgueren el caliu del seu geni lo dialectal, el llenguatge pur que no era immediatament en els llibres, i com bufant-hi el llur esperit, crearen meravelles' ('Let us remember how Shakespeare himself, and so many essential figures [...] in times that were passionate in the humanities, embraced and wished to keep in the hearth of their genius the essence of the dialectal, the pure language that was not immediately accessible in books, and as if breathing their spirit into it, they created marvels').[59] There is even a suggestion in *Bibliofília* that Magí Morera i Galícia's versions of the sonnets would produce 'major fruïció' ('greater fruition') in Catalan than in English for an English reader, and so Morera's *Sonets* 'semblen concebuts en català' ('seem to have been conceived in Catalan').[60]

What becomes increasingly important is the kind of Catalan in which Shakespeare is expressed, and this both limits the afterlives of certain translations to extremely short periods, and becomes a controlling imperative for new editions of 'old classics'. To clarify, it is not just a question of choosing whether to render Shakespeare in a deliberately archaic language or dialect, in order to approximate Elizabethan speech patterns in Catalan, or bring Shakespeare up to date for a modern reader, aiming for equivalence of effect, as Oliva would express such a practice. Inextricably linked to this 'choice' is the question of the path Catalan should take, as well as the 'choice' of what Shakespeare should represent.

As this chapter has attempted to show, the relationship between Shakespeare and Catalan that figures in Catalan culture is far more complicated than the quotation from Carner's introduction to *Venus i Adonis* would suggest. Shakespeare's 'tone' depends on more than just a literary language, his personal figuration on more than just perceived 'universals'. By considering and contrasting some translations of Shakespeare's works undertaken in this period, I will approach and further analyse the discursive strategies which surround and are attributed to his cultural transference and their relationship to other social forms. This will lead to a fuller description of the changing figure of Shakespeare in Catalan culture, a Shakespeare which we believe we recognize and are encouraged to recognize as 'universal', but who is made up of other less abstract referents, as are his stories when retold in Catalan. In fact, the relationship of the Catalan language to Shakespeare, in the struggle to figure origins, is one which makes the materialization of Shakespeare's language (its figuration) something as necessary as its dematerialization, its poeticization or transfiguration. It is a way to emulate the naturalization of Shakespeare performed by other cultures, such as Volkof in Russia:

> No era més que un imitador dels models francesos; a Shakespeare el coneixia per les traduccions alemanyes; els subjectes de les seves obres eren invariablement estrangers. No es preocupava de l'originalitat; la seva única preocupació era escriure en rus; el seu objecte principal [. . .] era la nacionalització del llenguatge.[61]

(He was nothing more than an imitator of French models; he knew Shakespeare through the German translations; the subjects of his works were invariably foreign. He was not worried about originality; his only preoccupation was writing in Russian; his principal object [. . .] was the nationalization of the language').

And here we might perceive a parallel representation in the figure of Sagarra, where his 'paraula' ('word') and, hence, that of Shakespeare 'té cos, tres dimensions' ('is embodied, has three dimensions').[62] Yet it is also necessary for this fixing to have a more imaginary, desired afterlife, something sensed in representations of Shakespeare's language in reviews of the Hollywood film version of *A Midsummer Night's Dream*: 'en l'obra de Shakespeare, el verb passa davant de tot' ('in the plays of Shakespeare, the word comes before everything') and 'té un 'potencial poètic' que no necessita [. . .] totes les materialitzacions' ('has a poetic potential that does not need to be materialized in all its forms').[63]

Coda: Words and Dreams

It is in contemporary productions of *Hamlet* and, especially, *A Midsummer Night's Dream* that we continue to find most reflection on the relationship between language and culture in Catalonia. Dance adaptations of Shakespeare's plays, such as Ramon Ollé's *Romeo i Julieta* and Cia Senza Tempo's *El jardí inexistent* are defended through expression of their embodiment of the metaphors of the original. Likewise the subplot of the mechanicals in the *Dream* is used as a counterpoint to comment on the material conditions of Catalan theatre, and the relationship between the poetry of the star-crossed love stories at the centre of the play and the prosaic everyday life of the artisans. Indeed, it is the rehearsals of Peter Quince and his merry band, alongside other comic episodes in the plays, especially *The Merry Wives of Windsor*, that have led to most instances of domestication in Catalan translations of Shakespeare in performance. From Helena Pimienta's Spanish language version (1992–3), in which the mechanicals represent the stereotypes of post-transition Spain to Angel Llàcer's employment of a band of municipal musicians, these elements never fail to charm local audiences. Yet Llàcer's *Dream* deliberately associates itself with an amateur tradition of

Shakespeare representation, by invoking a prior staging, five years previously as part of an Institut del Teatre workshop, and by using the following quotation from the play as a handwritten calling card for his version:

> Si us avorrim, ho fem perquè volem
> que no us penseu que us venim a avorrir
> només per poca traça. Ens presentem,
> i això ja és el principi de la fi.
> Preneu-vos-ho com cal. Inútilment
> no hem pas vingut. Per destorbar a tothom,
> no som aquí. Per fer a tothom content,
> tots els actors tenim a punt l'aplom.
> Per que ells us mostraran, perfectament
> sabreu que passa, i quin es l'argument.

Using the words of the mechanicals to apologize in advance for the Catalan group's failings prepares the audience for the lack of magic in this version. Young and dynamic, it is a deferent staging, which focuses more on correct elocution than on imaginative flight, receiving advice from the translator, Salvador Oliva, on poetic diction. Whilst the audiences loved it, and many critics preferred it to the more daring readings of Bieito and Rigola, others were critical of its pedestrianism. For instance, whilst Pablo Ley recognizes the indisputable classic status of Shakespeare, as presented in chapter 2 – 'su condición de clásico es tan monolítica que sólo cabe discutir, en todo caso, el valor de la interpretación que de él se haga' ('his status as a classic is so monolithic that the only thing open to discussion is the value of the interpretation made of him') – in Llàcer, he critiques the 'gélida distancia que lo impregna todo, una distancia que es como una máscara con la que [...] lanza una cortina de humo que sustituye lo que debería ser una lectura personal [...] Lo que falta es [...] riesgo, voluntad de saltar del oficio (que sin duda domina) al arte (con peligro de descolabrarse)' ('icy distance that impregnates everything, a distance that is like a mask with which [...] he throws a smokescreen that stands in for a personal reading [...] What is lacking is [...] risk, the willingness to leap beyond his craft (in which there is no doubt of his expertise) to art (with the danger of slipping up)').[64]

Such criticism indicates that the problems identified in the early twentieth-century because of the lack of material conditions in which to do justice to Shakespeare on the Catalan stage have largely been overcome; indeed, that perhaps there is now too much focus on materialism and not enough on *dreams* in Catalan culture. This is the reason given by Lluís Pasqual for his decision to withdraw his projected production of *Hamlet* from the International Forum of Cultures in 2004. The funding he was promised was cut, and this was partly because of his decision to stage the version in Castilian. Seeking alternative funding, Pasqual eventually rehearsed and staged *Hamlet* alongside a version of *The Tempest* in the Basque Country in 2005, returning to showcase it in Catalonia during the Festival Grec of 2006. Whilst there is a long tradition of Hamlet in Catalan being used to give advice to Catalan actors and theatre, in Pasqual's version his players wear badges calling for freedom of speech (see figs. 11–12). This both responds to the local rehearsal conditions of Pasqual's *Hamlet* in Bilbao, but also presents a new lesson to be learned from Shakespeare's language. Above all it is a reminder, just a few years after the Russian actress Demidova's presentation of the lessons of Pasternak's *Hamlet* that there is more to theatre than words: 'Es gesticulació, emoció, sentiment [. . .] L'espectador té ulls per mirar, cor per sentir i cervell per pensar!" ('It is gesture, emotion, sentiment [. . .] The spectator has eyes to see, a heart to feel and a brain to think!)'.

NOTES

[1] '. . . el Noucentisme [. . .] com a corrent aproximadament homogeni resulta especialment o precisament interessant des d'una perspectiva sincrònica, no per la seva projecció en el temps, ja que difícilment es pot demostrar la vigència d'unes característiques formals o ideològiques pròpies de la formulació noucentista projectades més enllà de la seva existència cronològica real'. From Joan Minguet i Batllori, 'Els altres noucentistes. Ramon Rucabado', in *Estudis de llengua i literatura catalanes XIX. Miscel·lània Joan Bastardas*, 2 (Barcelona: Abadia de Montserrat, 1989), p. 235.

[2] Even in the period before Catalan translation of the plays, a reader's contact with Shakespeare was unlikely to be through the English but through French or Spanish translations. What was more often the case was that knowledge of Shakespeare came mediated through Italian or French theatrical productions or operatic versions of the tragedies and *Falstaff*.

[3] Farran i Mayoral, *Lletres . . .*, p. 169. Although this quotation may be linked to some of the more extreme eccentricities of *Noucentisme*,

particularly in its source, the very conservative figure of Farran i Mayoral, it is not so very far from other representations of Shakespeare and the Catalan language as to be considered an exception or distortion of twentieth-century Catalan approximations to the Bard.

4   For formulations of this 'difference' common in the early decades of the twentieth century it is useful to consult *Antoni Rovira i Virgili i la qüestió nacional: Textos polítics (1913–1947)*, Josep-Lluís Carod Rovira (ed.) (Barcelona: Generalitat de Catalunya, 1995), especially the section on 'La llengua catalana i els seus drets', and the article 'Espanyolisme i Catalanisme', pp. 295–7.

5   See Lamuela and Murgades, *Teoria de la llengua literària*.

6   *Primer Congrés Internacional de la Llengua Catalana* (Barcelona: Joaquim Horta, 1908), pp. 665–9. Page references for quotations from this lecture will be given in the text.

7   The Tower of Babel story is the classic myth of the origins of linguistic diversity. It has also become central to accounts of translation in the twentieth century, as a metaphor for the relationships – or lack of them – between languages. See George Steiner, *After Babel* (Oxford: Oxford University Press, 1975); Benjamin, 'The Task of the Translator'; Jacques Derrida, *The Ear of the Other* (Lincoln/London: University of Nebraska Press, 1988); and John Graham (ed.), *Difference in Translation* (Ithaca: Cornell University Press, 1985).

8   It was identified as such in the *Primer Congrés* itself. See especially Manuel de Montoliu's contribution: 'Moviment assimilista de la literatura catalana', pp. 569–73. There was also to be a contribution by Dr Eberarth Vogel from Aachen on the 'Conveniencia de formar les traduccions de les llengues del Nort a Catalunya', although there is no sign of his actual participation in the conference.

9   In fact, according to Laurence Venuti, the most important attribute of a translator in the twentieth century tended to be his or her invisibility. See *The Translator's Invisibility*, chapter 1, especially pp. 1–17.

10 Molas, *Diccionari de la literatura catalana*, p. 712.

11 Soldevila, 'En la mort de Magí Morera i Galícia', *D'Ací D'Allà*, 114 (June 1927), 165. An article on translation in *Mirador* (11 August 1932), 6, stresses its 'funció – evidentment decisiva – en la nostra Renaixença', presenting *La Revista*, in particular, as an 'empresa exemplar'.

12 Fontcuberta i Gel, 'Als cinquanta anys', cited in the introduction.

13 *El reialme de la poesia* . . ., pp. 56–7.

14 These cases have been described and dated in chapter 1. See also Buffery, 'The Meaning of Shakespeare in Catalan' for more detailed information on the versions of *Hamlet*.

15 As we have seen in chapter 4, the coincidence between abbreviation of translations of *A Midsummer Night's Dream* to *Somni* and more culturally-specific *somnis* is a feature of the play's figuration in Catalan. See also Buffery, 'Shakespeare and the Cultural Dream'. Magí Morera i Galícia translated four plays as well as some of the

sonnets and longer poems, such as *Venus and Adonis*. Jordana's enterprise to translate the complete works of Shakespeare into prose should be seen in parallel with that of his contemporary, Astrana Marín's work in Castilian. As for Par's pseudo-medieval Lear, this has been perceived as an anomaly by subsequent critics.

16 A. M. Badia i Margarit presents a picture of widespread acceptance of Fabra's norms after 1913 and identifies the *Primer Congrés Internacional de La Llengua Catalana* as being instrumental in achieving this. *Llengua i cultura als països catalans* (Barcelona: Edicions 62, 1966), especially: 'La llengua catalana en l'actualitat', pp. 79–116. He insists in the three further subsections on the 'universalitat i la penetració d'aquestes empreses dins el poble català', p. 105: 'El cinquantenari de les normes ortogràfiques', pp. 79–96, 'El català des de Pompeu Fabra fins a Carles Riba', pp. 97–104, and 'Tres problemes de Català d'avui', pp. 105–16.

17 Quoted in *Catalana*, I (1918), 454. Also present in his speech at the *Primer Congrés de la Llengua Catalana*.

18 *Butlletí de l'Ateneu Barcelonès*, I (1915–17), 129.

19 Josep Farran i Mayoral, 'Dietari espiritual', *La Revista*, 54 (16 December 1917), 444.

20 Codina, '*Juli Cèsar*', 81.

21 Pi i Maragall is reproduced in 'L'ús oficial de la llengua propia', *Anuari dels Catalans*, III (1925), 104 and I (1923), 17, respectively.

22 Gabriel Alomar, 'La llengua catalana, instrument de cultura', *Anuari dels Catalans*, I (1923), 17. Although there is a common perception that the middle classes were the upholders of the future of Catalan, and that the working class were not concerned with their linguistic tradition, labour histories make it plain that union debates and speeches took place in Catalan. There is propaganda from the 1910s and 1920s, showing the fear of the middle class, that presents a working class led astray from its Catalan roots by rabble-rousers such as Lerroux. See J. M. Huertas Claveria, *Obrers a Catalunya. Manual d'història del moviment obrer 1840–1975* (Barcelona: L'Avenç, 1982), especially chapter 7, 'El primer sindicalisme d'empenta (1911–1923)', pp. 148–64, and chapter 8, 'Anys d'esperança, anys de violència (1912–1923)', pp. 175–92.

23 *Catalana*, I (1918), 70.

24 Prat de la Riba, reproduced in *Anuari dels catalans*, IV (1926), 203.

25 *Esquella de la Torratxa*, (7 February 1913), 112.

26 Reproduced in J. V. Foix, *Catalans de 1918* (Barcelona: Edicions 62, 1986), p. 39. The observation is dated at 30 April 1920.

27 Letter to Joan Gili, 3 February 1940, *Cartes...*, II, p. 97. The subsequent quotations are from p. 98.

28 Palau i Fabre, 'Consideracions', 70–1.

29 This particular figuration of Shakespeare is used by Morera i Galícia, himself from the agricultural province of Lleida, in his 'Proemi', *Catalunya*, I (10 January 1914), 24.

30 R. E. Bassegoda, 'Crónica General', *La Ilustració Catalana*, II (30

August 1881), 338, compares problems over the spelling of Shakespeare with those of Catalan orthography.
31 'Shakespeare, sa concepció y sa obra', *XXV Conferencies* . . ., p. 190.
32 Cebrià Montoliu ends up translating Shakespeare into Castilian instead of continuing his translations into Catalan. His political differences with the *Noucentista* politicians and intellectuals lead him to emigrate to the United States, where he dies.
33 J. Carner, 'Les persones fines i llur mig català', *Mirador* (16 August 1934), 6: 'si les nostres pobres vocals àtones han d'ésser considerades com forçosament plebees per les persones fines, no hem de fer sinó parlar en català de Lleida. L'enyorat Magí Morera bé en treia efectes de majestat i tot. I àdhuc em recordo d'haver-li sentit que Lleida teni el punt dolç del parlar català, per semblances d'altitud, per ell assíduament anotades, amb d'altres zones on cristal·litzaren il·lustres llengües literàries d'Europa'.
34 Loreto Busquets (ed.), *Aportació lèxica de Josep Carner a la llengua literària catalana* (Barcelona: Rafael Dalmau, 1977).
35 With reference to a 1911 production of *The Merry Wives of Windsor*, we find the following comments: 'Shakespeare s'indignà de que li profanessin *Les alegres comares* . . . En Carner, que es un excelent poeta, pero en coses de teatre no hi entén futil·la, feu un arranjament ab una riquesa de llenguatge gran, pero tan ple de formes arcaiques y de galocismes que'l bon publich no hi entenia gota'. *Joventut Teatral*, III (16 February 1911), 479.
36 J. Carner prologue to *Venus i Adonis* (1917), reproduced in *El reialme de la poesia* . . ., p. 141.
37 *Esquella de la Torratxa* (5 November 1909), 720. Furthermore, both Morera i Galícia and Sagarra try their hands at Dante and Shakespeare.
38 Par, 'El forçament de Lucreça', *XXV Conferencies* . . ., pp. 472-3.
39 'Notes introductòries . . .', p. 185.
40 Josep Maria de Sagarra, 'Prefaci', *Romeo i Julieta. Otel·lo. Macbeth* (Barcelona: Alpha, 1959), p. 10.
41 Farran i Mayoral, *Lletres* . . ., p. 169
42 Esquerra, 'Dues notes shakespearianes', p. 68.
43 Carner, *El reialme de la poesia* . . ., p. 142.
44 The surprising inclusion of 'language for the novel' here is drawn from a thread in Catalan discourse on Shakespeare which presents him as the precursor of the psychological novel. Hence, he is an inspiration for the prose writing of Puig i Ferreter, and Maseras is presented as almost Shakespearian in his novel writing. J. Puig i Ferreter, *Diari d'un escriptor. Ressonàncies 1942-1952* (Barcelona: Edicions 62, 1975). See, for instance, p. 835: (1948) 'Fa temps que em treballa el pensament de mesclar en la novel·la la prosa i la poesia, com Shakespeare barreja prosa i vers en el seu teatre'. In *Meridià*, 32 (19 August 1938), 6, it is suggested that through Maseras's 'arbre del Bé i del Mal' there blows at times 'un buf de Shakespeare, que només he trobat en tres autors contemporanis'.
45 *La Cataluña*, 18 (1 February 1908), 70.

46 Moix draws attention to this in explaining his reasons for not translating *Hamlet* into verse. See also Vergés, *Tots els sonnets* . . ., pp. xiv–xv.
47 Salvador Oliva, 'Shakespeare en catalán: problemas y soluciones', in González Fernández de Sevilla (ed.), *Shakespeare en España* . . ., pp. 193–217.
48 'Donchs', *Teatralia*, 7 (15 December 1908), 199.
49 *Esquella de la Torratxa* (20 February 1920), 280, on the production of *Julieta i Romeo* by the Escola Catalana d'Art Dramàtic.
50 Oliva, 'Shakespeare en catalán'.
51 *Introducció a la mètrica* (Barcelona: Quaderns Crema, 1986), pp. 97–101. For consideration of the necessity of producing 'performable' theatre translations, see Susan Bassnett, 'The Problems of Translating Theatre Texts', *Theatre Quarterly*, 40 (1981), 37–49.
52 Palau i Fabre, 'Consideracions', 65: 'Cal que la paraula sigui pensada en relació amb algú que la dirà'.
53 Codina's article on his production of '*Juli Cèsar*' quotes incessantly from Shakespeare's plays to support his views of theatre. The quotation from *Hamlet* is to draw attention to the importance for the actor of 'movent amb naturalitat la llengua', 79.
54 It is even at one point used as a more positive analogy for amateur theatre groups in Catalonia. C. Capdevila, 'Punts de vista. (El teatre d'aficionats)', *Mirador* (25 January 1934), 5: 'Aquella colla de fadrins menestrals del segle XVI podrien ésser un antecedent de les nostres companyies d'aficionats'.
55 Josep Farran i Mayoral, 'El teatre i la llengua', *Revista de la 'Nostra Parla'*, 6 (November 1918), 129. His ultimate aim in this is for the 'major glòria i diffusió de la nostra llengua sobirana'.
56 Xavier Fàbregas, in a review of '*Les alegres casades de Windsor*' (1972), *Teatre en viu (1969–1972)* (Barcelona: Institut del Teatre/Edicions 62, 1987), p. 208. Further comments on the value of Sagarra can be found in *El teatre o la vida*, p. 29: 'va posar la seva portentosa facilitat al servei d'una de les obres més considerables de la cultura occidental' 'un filó de possibilitats que el nostre teatre té encara, en gran part, per explotar'. Joan Fuster in *Breu Història del teatre català* (Barcelona: Bruguera, 1967), p. 91, sees Sagarra's versions as adaptations rather than translations, written in a 'català popular' which 'arribava al seu públic i feia de les representacions un èxit popular i econòmic'.
57 Puig i Ferreter's early translation of *The Merchant* is praised in *La Esquella de la Torratxa* (16 April 1909), 246, for its 'sobrietat del llenguatge y . . . discreció'. Many articles on translation in *Mirador* in the 1930s also call for sobriety and homogeneity. See the criticism of Farran i Mayoral's baroque style in *Mirador*, I (21 March 1929), 3 and the translation of M. Brion, 'Etica de la traducció', IV (11 August 1932), calling for more scientific models. However, other writers in *Mirador* point to the ineffable nature of Shakespeare's language. See

58 the review of the 1935 film of *A Midsummer Night's Dream*, cited below. Both Oliva and Moix admit their ultimate reliance on inspiration.
See *El reialme de la poesia*..., p. 141 and 'Abans que tot', *El somni d'una nit d'estiu*, pp. 11 and 13.
59 Lleonart review of *Hamlet* in *La Revista*, 110 (16 April 1920), 96.
60 '... semblen els sonets, concebuts ja en català pel mateix Shakespeare, car dubtem que als compatricis del gran tràgic els sia permesa una major fruició estètica que la que a nosaltres catalans ens pot produhir una traducció tan gentil y arrodonida', *Bibliofilia*, I (1911–14), 404.
61 Sarni, 'La formació del llenguatge rus modern', *D'Ací D'Allà*, 3 (March 1921), on Volkof version of *Hamlet*.
62 Palau i Fabre, *El mirall embruixat*, p. 41.
63 Although many reviews of the 1935 film of *A Midsummer Night's Dream*, with Mickey Rooney as Puck and James Cagney as Bottom, see it as an admirable materialization of Shakespeare's vision, Just Cabot, quoted above, sees it as a betrayal both of Shakespeare and of cinema. 'Una veu discordant – Parlem d'El somni', *Mirador* (16 January 1936): 'I tot plegat, teatre fotografiat, terriblement teatre.' He suggests that only Walt Disney films would be anywhere near capable of transposing 'tota la poesia i la faderia (vull dir féerie) de la natura imaginada pel somni del poeta'.
64 Pablo Ley , 'Jugando con Shakespeare', *El País*, (21 October 2002), 46.

Chapter 5

The Politics of Storytelling: the Case of *Coriolanus/Coriolà*

> The text about translation is itself a translation and the untranslatability which it mentions about itself inhabits its own texture and will inhabit anybody who in his turn will try to translate it, as I am now trying and failing, to do. The text is untranslatable for the translators who tried to do it, it is untranslatable for the commentators who talk about it, it is an example of what it states, it is a *mise en abyme* in the technical sense, a story within the story of what is its own statement.[1]

This passage, taken from Paul de Man's discussion of Walter Benjamin's *The Task of the Translator* and its English and French translators, provides a cautionary note for the text of the chapter which follows. This chapter, like the book as a whole, was originally conceived in hermeneutic terms, as a pursuit of meaning or meanings. First to be considered was the meaning of Shakespeare (as man and body of texts) in Catalan, and second the significance of translation in and into Catalan, how and what a given translation – here *The Tragedy of Coriolanus* and its particular 'Body Politicke' – comes to mean in Catalan culture. In attempting this, the task becomes comparable to that described by Paul de Man above, a never-ending fragmentation of an already fragmentary text about political-through-identity fragmentation.

The problems presented by this apprehension are inescapable, yet the task in isolating the various politics or ideologies of storytelling within these texts is less an attempt to unite the diverse fragments (including the traditionally perceived 'original', Shakespeare's *Coriolanus*) into some recognizable whole, than to show the political and poetical process of storytelling, the process by which a diversity of voices present themselves, represent a story, through delegation, collaboration, translation, symbolic nation and narration, in relation to other voices, other discourses, and in particular the dominant discourse, story, delegate, however it be presented. In order to do this, the chapter is divided into three sections. The first deals with the question of why *Coriolanus* might be taken as a paradigmatic text or translation in the tracing of a history of Catalan Shakespeares; and the second will show how its dominance, containing that of Shakespeare, is played out, commented on and narrated, within the textual staging of a particular version of the Coriolanus story, Magí Morera i Galícia's *Coriolà*. The third part of the chapter will explore how the political and cultural rhetoric of the Coriolanus story can be traced in subsequent versions, to begin to uncover the politics of the positioning of the translator in Catalan.

Superficial consideration of the list of Shakespeare translations into Catalan would not in any way suggest that particular significance be attributed to *Coriolanus*. It is not the first play to be translated, nor the most frequent. As shown in previous chapters, *Hamlet* and *Romeo and Juliet* have clearer claims to being the originators of Shakespeare's Catalan meanings, the former in particular proving the most fruitful generator of discourse about origination and originality.[2] In terms of numbers of translations, as might be expected, *Hamlet* again gives rise to perhaps the widest range of rewritings, rivalled only by *Macbeth* and the sonnets (although there are fewer complete versions of the sonnet cycle). The comedies too lay claim to a more expansive space in the different fields of Catalan culture, something to be observed in the numbers and relevance of productions on the Catalan stage. *Coriolanus*, in contrast, has only been performed twice in Catalan, in an amateur production in 1977 and more recently in 2002, directed by Georges Lavaudant.[3] Nevertheless it has produced some of the most interesting commentary on the political and cultural possibilities of Shakespeare in performance, partly in response to the publication of Magí Morera i Galícia's translation in 1918, partly in the debate unleashed by the infamous 1934 Comédie Française production in Paris.[4]

The Politics of Storytelling: the Case of Coriolanus/Coriolà   181

Coriolanus has been perceived by some to be the source of one of the earliest Shakespeare translations into Catalan, in that Víctor Balaguer produced a one-act play on the Roman warrior's conversion from scourge of Rome to bringer of peace at his mother's request.[5] However, not only does Balaguer himself neglect to attribute the source for his play to Shakespeare, but the aspects which the two plays share can be clearly traced to Plutarch.[6] It should be remembered that the Coriolanus story had inspired a number of other writers in Spain and elsewhere.[7] The episode chosen by Balaguer is one of the ones in which Shakespeare adheres most closely to Plutarch's version, as Perpiñà observes in the notes to his translation of the play.[8] Above all, it is where Balaguer diverges from Shakespeare, such as in the complete absence of Tullus Aufidius and the preparatory suing of Titus Larcius rather than Menenius, that we must observe the unlikelihood of his version's constituting a variation on that of the English playwright.[9] The most important difference is the non-tragic ending to Balaguer's rewriting of the Coriolanus story, as follows.

> Volumnia, Coriolá.
> (*Quan Volumnia ha vist partir á Lavinius y s'ha convensut de la certesa de l'órde se precipita vers Marcius ab un arranch d'entusiasme y ab los brassos oberts.*)
> Volumnia.
> ¡He recobrat mon fill! –¡Gracias, oh Roma!
> Coriolá. (*Abrassantse ab sa mare.*)
> No es Roma, ets tú qui m'ha vensut, ¡oh mare!
> *Cau lo teló.*
>
> [(*When Volumnia sees Lavinius leave and is convinced of the truth of the order she rushes open-armed to Marcius in excitement.*) / *Volumnia:* I have recovered my son! Thanks, oh Rome!/ *Coriolanus* (*Embracing his mother.*) It is not Rome but you who has vanquished me, oh mother!/ *The curtain falls*].[10]

After Balaguer's version of the 1880s, there are no new Catalan versions of *Coriolanus* published until 1917, although Cebrià Montoliu produces a Castilian version in 1908.[11] The first published Catalan translation is in fact that of Joan Perpiñà, notwithstanding the many bibliographies that place the publication of Magí Morera i Galícia's in 1915.[12] In fact, the Morera translation appeared in 1918 {see fig. 13), within a year of

Perpiñà's *La Tragedia de Coriolanus*, thus creating intriguing focus on a single text as the only Shakespeare play apart from Alfons Par's *Lo rei Lear* and Bulbena i Tosell's *Hamlet* to be published whole between 1910 and 1920.[13] After Morera's version there were no more translations of the play until the 1940s and Josep Maria de Sagarra's seminal translations of twenty-eight of the complete works. First published in the second volume of the bibliophile Calíope editions of the complete works between 1946 and 1953, these versions were re-published with the other Roman tragedies in 1958 and in a number of subsequent editions right up until the present day.[14] The twentieth century saw only one other full translation to compete with Sagarra's *Coriolà*, that of Salvador Oliva in 1989, although Gabriel Ferrater translated two acts between 1970 and 1971, for a projected performance.[15] More recently, Joan Sellent was invited to provide the translation for Georges Lavaudant's production at the Teatre Nacional de Catalunya in 2002, and participated in readings and rehearsals.[16] As can be seen, only five full versions of the play have been translated, all but that of Perpiñà being readily available to the contemporary reader or performer. No conclusions as to the particular importance of the Coriolanus story can be drawn from these details.

The source and scope of *Coriolanus*'s importance must instead be traced to a number of apparently external and coincidental factors in cultural and historical criticism. In studies of Shakespearian influence in the Catalan territories, although *Coriolanus* is rarely identified as a text of central importance, one of its earliest translators is. Magí Morera i Galícia, a middle-aged writer, lawyer and politician from Lleida, made the decision to write in Catalan quite late in life, and part of his evangelical drive was diverted into the translation of the works of Shakespeare. There are many accounts of his conversion and its import. Josep Lleonart, for instance, writes the following parable:

> Ell [...] és dels homes exemplars qui són entre nosaltres per a donar testimoni de la joventut perenne d'un ideal. [...ha] romput a rimar en llengua catalana en l'hora de la vida madura i més susceptible d'estancament, després de rebudes diverses aures d'honors i vistos diversos camins, demostrant-se així flexible al foc d'un ideal, per vergonya dels que es descarreguen sobre l'ànonim [*sic*] personatge *edat*, de les culpes del seu propi empedreïment.[17]

(He is one of those exemplary men who walk amongst us to bear witness to the perennial youthfulness of an idea [...] he has broken into verse in Catalan in the mature stage of life when one is more susceptible to staleness, after receiving various honours and exploring many paths, thus showing flexibility in the flame of an ideal, to the shame of those who lay the blame on the anonymous personage of age for their own stubbornness).

Whilst Carles Riba sets his language switch in the context of a heroic struggle for Catalan culture: 'Com en Costa, com l'Alcover, també en Morera i Galícia és un desenganyat del bilingüisme, un noble repatriat de la poesia castellana' ('Like Costa, like Alcover, Morera i Galícia, too, has awoken to the truth of bilingualism, and has been nobly repatriated from Castilian poetry').[18]

Morera's abandonment of his career as a lawyer in 1912 is often represented as coinciding exactly with his dedication to Shakespeare studies, perhaps under the influence of Josep Carner, who is credited by figures such as Rovira i Virgili as being the one who introduced Morera i Galícia to Barcelona's cultural circles and invited him to a literary session at the Joventut Nacionalista, introducing the older poet as follows: 'Se pot dir sense paradoxa, que la traducció de Shakespeare per en Morera es una de les més pures originalitats del renaxement literari català' ('One can say without paradox that the translation of Shakespeare by Morera is one of the purest and most original achievements of the Catalan literary renaissance').[19] In reviews of his works and his contribution to Catalan culture, these two central aspects of his production in Catalan become almost synonymous. It is as if his belief in the Catalan language and his passion for Shakespeare could not be separated. Hence we find that in the period between the earliest completion date of his *Coriolà* and its publication in 1918, Morera i Galícia was actively involved, as a *Lliga Regionalista* politician, in seeking co-official status for the Catalan language.[20]

Coriolà was not Morera i Galícia's first translation of Shakespeare. He had already translated a number of the sonnets and published a translation of *Venus and Adonis* the year before the version of the Coriolanus story appeared. His studies of Shakespeare led him to give a number of lectures in the period, and he collaborated with Adrià Gual on conferences, productions and competitions at the *Escola Catalana d'Art Dramàtic*.[21] The perceived calibre of his translations led to renewed interest in the value of translating Shakespeare as well as other classics of world literature. As Ramon Esquerra writes: 'Les traduccions de Morera i Galícia provocaren un seguit de comentaris shakespearians. Catalunya acabava de descobrir el veritable Shakespeare...' ('Morera i Galícia's translations provoked an array of commentaries on Shakespeare. For Catalonia had just discovered the real Shakespeare ..').[22] Not only does Esquerra link a change in attitude and appreciation of Shakespeare to the appearance of the Magí Morera i Galícia translations but within his overview of Shakespeare reception he underlines their exemplarity. They are 'la causa pròxima d'algunes de les millors crítiques shakespearianes que s'hagin fet a Catalunya' ('the immediate cause of some of the best Shakespearian criticism written in Catalonia').[23] Esquerra's observation is supported by that of other writers, particularly in reminders of Morera's importance during the 1920s and 1930s. Certain of the great 'crítiques' are collected in editions of the critical essays of some of the most important figures in twentieth-century Catalan literature, such as Carles Riba and Josep Carner. In contrast, it should be noted that Perpiñà's translation, although published during the same period, does not awaken much critical interest. It is only later rehabilitated by Par and Esquerra in their histories as a sign of the increasing sophistication of Shakespeare translation in Catalonia.

The reasons why Morera i Galícia may have chosen to open his Catalan translations of Shakespeare's plays with *Coriolà* are more difficult to ascertain. Part of the reason may be traced to the influence of Adrià Gual who, after the experience of producing *Twelfth Night*, his own variation on the theme of *The Merry Wives of Windsor*, the influential staging of *A Midsummer Night's Dream* and Carner's translation of *The Merry Wives*, continued to show interest in Shakespeare in performance during the 1910s. Indeed, there is evidence that *Coriolà* was planned for production in the 1917–18 season, but by the autumn of 1917 there was to be no more mention of the play.[24] Alternatively, the decade is notable for its revival of interest in Classicism, as an overt counteraction to the perceived excesses of romanticism; hence Morera i Galícia's choice of one of the Roman plays might be linked to such moves given his increasing acceptance in *Noucentista* institutions.

Although the Catalan penchant for Classicism tended to identify its cultural origins in Greece, it has already been observed how the Greek and the English empire were often interchangeable models in political, if not always cultural discourse. We also find certain

The Politics of Storytelling: the Case of Coriolanus/Coriolà 185

translations of Classical culture, Amyot's of Plutarch and hence perhaps Shakespeare's by extension, prioritized for praise amidst the many betrayals in the history of translation. Farran i Mayoral cites Amyot as one of three beautiful exceptions to the general rule that translations from the Greek are dry and artificial rather than 'living' like their originals.[25] This attitude can also, unsurprisingly, be traced to earlier observations such as that of Francesc Torres y Ferrer in his notes to *Antonius y Cleopatra*, grouping the play together with '*Coriolan*':

> ... aital traducció [that of North] no fou extreta del texte grec [Plutarch], sinó de la versió francesa d'Amyot, poguent tenir *l'orgull*, els francesos, de dir que'ls fonaments de que va servirse Shakespeare per á bastir el séu monument, foren els treballs de llur compatriota. Tant escrupulosa es l'exactitut ab que Shakespeare reprodueix a Amyot que'n molts y molts passatges lo mateix té traduir l'un que l'altre (my emphasis).[26]
>
> (... this translation was not extracted from the Greek, but from the French version by Amyot, thus the French may take *pride* in saying that the foundations on which Shakespeare built his monument were laid by their compatriot. So scrupulously exact is Shakespeare's reproduction of Amyot that in very many passages it is the same to translate one as the other).

This passage points, once again, to why there might be confusion about the source of Balaguer's translation. It also represents an example of the positive metacommentary characteristic of a culture-building process so dependent on translation, drawing attention to how the metacommentary often interacts with the very text of the translation. Reference to pride ('orgull') in translation may be desirable in shoring up national cultural revival but when linked to the pride of Coriolà we see identified as central in later criticism it becomes rather more problematic. Here, too, Shakespeare's 'monument' cannot help but remind us of the monuments Caesar evokes after the death of Cleopatra but also, in certain Catalan versions, of the monument Tullus Aufidius proposes to build for Coriolanus.

Comparison of the Catalan translations of the closing words to the play reveal very different re-presentations of the duty and process involved in the creation of such a cultural monument. Shakespeare's original has an open ending as follows: 'Yet he shall have a noble memory. / Assist'.²⁷ This is translated by Perpiñà as: '... no per axò ens li resta de sa vida / menys noble la memoria! Ara ajudèume!' referring back to the preceding catalogue of the horrors Coriolanus visited on Corioli, a version whose focus on one aspect of the word 'memory' is mirrored by that of Oliva in 1989 and Sellent in 2002, who both refer to a '*record noble*' ('noble memory'). In contrast, Morera i Galícia, presents a far more active, physical role for the Corioli in bearing witness to their enemy's achievements: '... hem d'aixecar-li/ un noble monument. Amics: aideu-me!' This translation both refers more clearly to the history chronicled in Plutarch, in which the Corioli build a noble tomb to Coriolanus whereas in Rome a temple is built to the ladies who sued for peace, and it may be taken to stand for the kind of cultural monument sought in collaborative translation by critics of the period. Sagarra uses '*monument*', too, but his version dwells less on the collective duty to produce it: '... tindrà un noble monument. / Ajudeu'. Once more a metaphor for translation which suggests the positive remembrance of tradition belies undertones of revisionism, betrayal and destruction. The monument is dependent on the death of that which it marks and, in the case of Tullus Aufidius and Coriolanus, the murder of the hero (the original) by the rememberer (the translator).

Whilst the play would certainly have appealed to aesthetic and cultural sensibilities, it is its political resonance which may well have contributed to its absence from the stage in the period. On the other hand, it is tempting to link Morera i Galícia's very choice of *Coriolà* to the cultural and political climate of the time. The second half of the 1910s saw extreme unrest and unease due to increasing economic difficulties during the First World War, notwithstanding Spain's neutrality, and the problems arising from the central government's policies towards Barcelona and the Catalan language.²⁸ The date of completion given by Morera, for instance, coincides with deep-rooted social unrest about the food supply, and more specifically, bread prices in Spain, an external crisis which reflects struggles internal to the play. However, other sources cite 1917 as the year in which he produced the final version of the play, and this would sit more easily with evidence that points to the influence of Adrià Gual.²⁹ Reviews of Magí Morera i Galícia's translation reflect some of these fields of discourse, and even the circumstances of its bumpy ride towards performance and publication play a marginal part in the political turmoil. The main source for this observation is an anecdote recounted in *La Esquella de la Torratxa* in August 1917 and entitled 'Se non è vero'.[30] It is set within an atmosphere of political disruption, during which there was a high level of censorship of the popular press, and particularly of satirical papers. The article itself followed on from coverage of the failed 19 July Assembly, organized in response to the king's failure to summon the *Cortes*, the imposition of martial law in Barcelona and Prat de la Riba's plans for federal reform. All coverage of the events, apart from the title, had been censored in July as had the original reference to Morera i Galícia's experiences.

Morera was travelling by train with a packet of documents which fascinated an army colonel in the same carriage. As a *Lliga* politician, Morera might have been assumed to be carrying important political documents, perhaps even relating to the meeting of the Assembly, or numerous other more clandestine meetings that were suspected. Furthermore, Morera did nothing to quell the suspicions of his travelling companion, who tried all sorts of gambits to find out about the papers, and by the end of the journey was quite beside himself with excitement. On arrival in Barcelona, when the military representative's curiosity had become almost unbearable, Morera i Galícia finally allowed him access to his 'very important' documents, in fact the original and a copy of his translation of *Coriolanus*, presumably to deliver to Adrià Gual for the forthcoming season. The anecdote may seem unimportant, except for the evidence it gives for dating Morera's version and confirmation that a production of the play was planned. However, because the original version of the article was censored, along with calls for *seny* in response to the unprecedented events of that month, perhaps to save the embarrassment of the government, it offers an interesting counterpoint to the political possibilities and implications of the publication and performance of this translation. Its link to *seny*, both in the high usage of the word within the play and in the circumstances which surround its publication, make it a poignant symbol of rational cultural intervention. Yet as a recommended tool for 'l'educació política del poble' it is nothing if not double edged.[31]

The subject matter of the play, to be described later by Sagarra as: '*Coriolà* és l'exaltació d'un estrepitós trontoll militar, en el qual una Roma llegendària basteix les columnes de la seva dignitat'

('*Coriolanus* is the celebration of a resounding military blunder, on which a mythical Rome constructs the columns of its dignity'),[32] cannot help but have resonance in a region faced with martial law during a period of European war. Later links drawn between the central character and 'la moral del «Führer-Duce» d'inspiració feixista' ('the morality of the "Führer-Duce, of fascist inspiration'), perhaps with Brecht's and Jan Kott's readings of Shakespeare in mind, should alert any critic to the political and social volatility of the story.[33] Yet, this perception may be little more than an anecdote to underscore the great myth of Shakespeare, the miracle described by Sagarra of 'la gran deformació shakespeariana' ('the great Shakesperian deformation'), how history retold by him enlarges and intensifies the anecdotes until they are 'arquetípics monuments de consistència eterna' ('archetypal monuments of eternal consistency').[34] As Puig i Ferreter observes in a conference on the cultural relevance and possibilities of theatre:

> Un dia, conversant amb el poeta Maragall, li vaig sentir parlar dels drames que Shakespeare féu de l'època romana: els romans de Shakespeare són tan veritat perquè el poeta era un essencial creador d'homes, i com els romans foren sobretot tan homes [. . .] la conclusió és natural; els romans de Shakespeare ho són per l'ànima no per la vestimenta, ni per la farda d'erudició històrica, com els de tants altres escriptors.[35]
>
> (One day, in conversation with the poet Maragall, I heard him speak of the plays that Shakespeare wrote about the Roman age: Shakespeare's Romans are so real because the poet was an essential creator of men, and as the Romans were above all men [. . .]. the conclusion is obvious; Shakespeare's Romans are Roman in their soul rather than in their clothing, or the cloak of historical erudition, as is the case with other writers).

Another writer sees the key feature of Shakespeare's Romans to be their Englishness, their containment of the spirit of England,[36] yet on the whole this is read as a 'universal' value, drawing on the appraisal of English 'civilization' we have seen in chapter 3. Maragall's celebration of personal intuition rather than historical erudition stands poles apart from calls for scientific approximations to Shakespeare. A strong feature of Shakespeare criticism, as argued earlier, has been to leave unquestioned his cultural universality, his containment of all humanity, implying that humanity is unchanging, whilst simultaneously showing individual readings to be reductive. As will be seen, Catalan readings of the Coriolanus story do appear to lay emphasis on certain specific aspects of the text, whether through misreadings, lexical or syntactic constraints, critical influences or otherwise. However, it does not necessarily mean that the meanings of these readings themselves are fixed; indeed, the ways in which they mean depend largely on their readers and the environment in which they were translated.

Turning specifically to the Morera i Galícia version, its publication within a period of debate over competing representations of imperialism identifies it as a text at the crossroads of cultural, political and linguistic discourse about the state and future of Catalonia, a fact that is underlined by reviews of the work. The shifting allegiances of Catalan intellectuals during the First World War, the attitude of the Spanish central government to the growth in independent political action of Catalonia under the *Lliga*, the calls for cultural imperialism represented by the newly inaugurated Catalan cultural institutions including the Editorial Catalana by which Morera i Galícia's translation was eventually published, are set against the mass action and anarchy symbolized by the *Setmana Tràgica* and later strikes – fearful events for the Catalan ruling classes and especially the bourgeoisie. Before going on to see what kind of Romans appear in Magí Morera i Galícia's version of the story, and whether they are the traditionally perceived impartial moulds for common humanity so often associated with Shakespeare's genius, we will first look at the kind of critical discourse generated by the Coriolanus story at the time of its first publication in Catalan and in response to the French riots of the 1930s, to see how far the ideal treatment of Shakespeare as an autonomous cultural entity is erroneous at least in this case, if not in all cases.

Perhaps the most overt political greeting to Magí Morera i Galícia's *Coriolà* is that of Carles Riba, in his essay 'Elogi del poeta traductor'.[37] Together with Carner's 'Del Shakespeare en llengua catalana' the 'Elogi' represents one of the most explicit texts on the perception of the value of translation and sustained cultural action in Catalan, with Shakespeare as a supreme cultural signifier. Prefiguring Ramon Esquerra's representation of Magí Morera i Galícia as a key translator, much of the essay is, however, dedicated to underlining the importance of translation to Catalonia's cultural future: 'Fermança segura de la venturosa continuïtat de la nostra poesia és aquesta aurora de grans traduccions que avui lluu damunt la renaixença catalana' ('A surefire guarantee of the future fortunes of our poetry is in this dawning of great translations that shines upon the Catalan renaissance', p. 85). Now to be noted is that it is less the biblical adventure outlined by Carner in 1907 than a classical enterprise, marked by the sign of Ulysses. This perception of the epic nature of the translation enterprise is specifically contrasted with the lyrical emphasis of contemporary Catalan cultural production, a perception which has become a commonplace in readings of the *Noucentista* aesthetic but which also has more specific significance given Morera i Galícia's own poetic background and career.[38] As we have seen, Morera found literary fame as a lyrical poet who had converted to writing in Catalan quite late in his career; and, as a translator, the version of *Coriolà* is his first non-lyrical translation. Central to this new enterprise is the need to 'airejar el resclosiment del monòleg líric . . .' ('air the fustiness of the lyrical monologue') and 'exercitar la valentia dins l'aventura, i l'orgull dins l'adaptament; prevenir cautament, l'estrangulació per febre lírica . . .' ('to show valour in adventure, and pride in adaptation; to prevent suffocation by lyrical fever . . .', pp. 85–6).

The embracement of a wider tradition than the lyrical, the exploration of new literary landscapes, is repeatedly associated by Riba with an imperialist ideal throughout the first half of the article. Once again cultural growth is expressed through the figures of geographical discovery and conquest, a discourse which is often used to criticize the perceived cultural atrophy of the rest of Spain and specifically Castile. As has been perceived in earlier chapters, focus remains on individual contributions to a wider cultural ideal, but the ideal is a community of like-minded actors (hence the emphasis on collaboration and perhaps translation) rather than a personal pattern imposed by the solitary, 'strangled' individual.[39] The imperialist desire is: 'més que fer una pàtria per a diverses gents, fòrmula jurídica, fer una pàtria de diverses gents, fórmula d'incorporació cultural, és a dir, de traducció' ('more than to construct a nation for diverse peoples, through the legal formula, to construct a nation of diverse peoples, through a formula of cultural incorporation, that is, through translation', p. 86). Pride, again, is instrumental in this process of adaptation and translation, but within the context it is not the personal pride of Coriolà, or so one might hope, but the collective, national pride of the ideal poet–translator.

It is only after such an introduction that Riba places Morera and his *Coriolanus* within this imperial, nation-building context, as a move away from the lyrical to wider community cultural action: 'Després dels poemes de la passió d'amor resolent-se en consiració intel·ligent [...] avui la tragèdia de la passió d'orgull traduint-se en acció' ('After the poems about the passion of love resolving itself in intelligent reflexion [...] today we have the tragedy of the passion of love translating itself into action', p. 86). Coriolanus is presented as containing the seeds of an arbitrator, someone who holds the future of his country and his people in his hands, and his problem reduced to that of reconciling pride with tenderness; indeed, he and his mother are described as being marked by an inexorable battle between the two emotions. Significantly, this is to set the tenor of readings of *Coriolanus* on the issue of the power and operation of pride, a focus which is not uncommon in critical readings of the play but has wider implications in Catalan given the role of *orgull* as a *Noucentista* translation keyword. Furthermore, such readings are supported by the translation choices made by Morera i Galícia in his version.[40] In particular, there is a fundamental shift in meaning early in the play, where the citizens discuss the virtues and vices of Coriolanus.

> First Citizen: I say unto you, what he hath done famously, he did it to that end: though soft-conscienced men can be content to say it was for his country, he did it to please his mother, and to be partly proud, which he is, even to the altitude of his virtue.
>
> Second Citizen: What he cannot help in his nature, you account a vice in him. You must in no way say he is covetous.
>
> First Citizen: If I must not, I need not be barren of accusations. He hath faults, with surplus, to tire in repetition.
>
> Ciutadà Primer: Doncs, vos ho dic: ço que ha fet de famós, per això ho ha fet. Encar que els de conciència flonja poden acontentar-se dient que fou per son país, ell sols ha obrat per tal de complaure a sa mare i per a satisfer son orgull, que li arriba ben né a la alçada de son coratge.
>
> Ciutadà segon: Ço que ell no pot treure's, perquè ho té a la sang, vós l'hi compteu com un vici. I avar no direu pas que ho sigui.

> Ciutadà Primer: Si no ho puc dir, puc en canvi fer-li molts més càrrecs.[41]

There are a number of aspects in Morera i Galícia's version which, although they might seem unimportant in the context of the first act discussion, create the opportunity for other meanings or encourage specific readings when traced in relation to the rest of the play and metacommentary on the translation. The rendering of 'to be partly proud' – 'per a satisfer son orgull' – places this apparently secondary aim in the original on equal footing with the desire to please Volumnia. Furthermore, in the Catalan there is focus on Coriolà's courage rather than his virtue, which corresponds with a reluctance to recount his vices. In Morera's version there are no 'faults, with surplus, to tire in repetition'; the sentence is omitted, perhaps rather fittingly given that his *Coriolà* is a repetition, a retelling of Shakespeare's original.[42] Most important for the 'tragèdia d'orgull' though is the perceived source of this pride in Morera's Catalan. Whereas in English it is in his 'nature', in Catalan 'ho té a la sang' ('it is in his blood'), placing emphasis on him having inherited it from his mother. Later, of course, she will deny this, as she does in the English.[43]

> M'apena ton orgull, mes a ta mare
> no li causa cap por ço que esdevingui:
> car jo em ric de la mort amb un cor ample,
> tant com el teu. Ja pots obrar com vulguis.
> Ton coratge em pertany: de mi el xuclares;
> l'orgull tu te l'has fet.

> . . . let
> Thy mother rather feel thy pride than fear
> Thy dangerous stoutness, for I mock at death
> With a big heart as thou. Do as thou list,
> Thy valiantness was mine, thou suck'st it from me,
> But owe thy pride thyself.

Volumnia denies responsibility for her son's pride, yet her 'orgull' is more insistently marked in the Catalan version. The difference is that it is consistently tempered with the 'tendresa' Carles Riba observes, and with the 'traça' and 'seny' that Menenius recommends to her son during the third act. This is a significant nuance in comparing the 'orgull' of Coriolà with the pride desirable in the act of translation. Coriolanus' personal pride must bow to the collective 'orgull' in the *pàtria* – hence the link to the culturally-specific Catalan *seny* –, to the kind of pride which desires and strives to create a 'pàtria de diverses gents, fórmula d'incorporació cultural', as cited by Riba (p. 85).

Farran i Mayoral, too, was to draw attention to the pride of Coriolà in tracing the significance of Shakespeare's play. For him the play is one of the highest examples of politics transformed into art, a critical position which both supports the tradition of Shakespeare's genius lying in his ability to transform the anecdotal into the universal and transcendental, but also gives further legitimacy to the very enterprise of translation.

> Exemple massa alt, vora les pobres temptatives modernes en el llibre i en el teatre per a dur-hi la política; la tesi en Shakespeare és, i així ha d'ésser en l'obra bella, tornada una festa de passions. Un torrent de sang joiosa circula dels uns personatges als altres. Un Coriolà qui no es conté dins la forma greu de la grandesa romana, shakespearià, és a dir, violent, ubriag d'orgull i de fortalesa, formidablement lúcid en ses paraules; sarcàstic, apostrofador, qui sent la joia, tan shakespeariana, dels mots qui insulten i maleeixen.[44]

> (An overwhelming example, when set alongside modern attempts to bring politics into both books and theatre; the thesis in Shakespeare is, as it should be in a beautiful work, transformed into a festival of the passions. A torrent of joyous blood circulates from one set of characters to another. A Coriolanus who cannot be contained in the grave form of Roman greatness; a Shakespearian Coriolanus, that is to say, violent, drunk on pride and strength, formidably lucid in his words; sarcastic, apostrophizing, who feels that so very Shakespearian joy of words that insult and curse).

For if Shakespeare can produce a Coriolanus who is not contained within the grave form of Roman greatness, his translators too might participate in this liberating enterprise. As we have seen, a strong feature of Farran i Mayoral's criticism is this focus on *joia* which implies a celebration of objective embracement of nature through rampant creativity. Here, politics is presented as a passionate endeavour, as 'passió encesa, viva tragèdia' ('burning passion, living tragedy'), fitting in nicely with the 'joia ubriaga' ('drunken joy') of Shakespeare. However, in *Coriolà* this passion is tempered by the 'serenor d'un seny en maduresa' ('serenity of mature common sense'). This is both the 'seny' of Volumnia within the play and the 'seny' of Shakespeare in creating the play, but above all a very Catalan 'seny'. The rhetorical move presented here, then, is very much the *apophrades* of Bloom, tracing the story and, perhaps, Shakespeare's retelling of it to a source in Catalan culture. By presenting political action as something alive and immediate, using the example of Napoleon's legendary words at Austerlitz – 'La política, heu's aquí el gran ressort de la tragèdia moderna' ('Politics, here we have the great influence for modern tragedy') – Farran i Mayoral is able to argue for the contemporary relevance of Shakespeare's play both in general and in specifically Catalan terms: 'Quina patró aquesta obra incomparable, de vera passió política [...] Heu's aquí un mitjà en extrem directe per a l'educació política del nostre poble! ¡Quin experiment a fer, una representació ben popular del "Coriolà" en vetlla d'eleccions' ('What a pattern is this incomparable work, of true political passion [...] Here we find an extremely direct medium for the polticial education of our people! What an experiment for the future it would be to put on a truly popular production of *Coriolanus* on the eve of elections').[45]

The political significance of the piece is presented in terms of message, but also in terms of the significance of translation for the Catalan stage and language: 'Els discursos del *Coriolà* tindrien molts bells ressons en la nostra escena' ('The speeches of Coriolanus would have wonderful resonance on our stage').[46] However, the extent to which Farran i Mayoral's advocation of *Coriolà* as a political pattern reflects the objectivity he often invokes in figurations of Shakespeare's 'joia', and that is commonly invoked in theatrical defences of Shakespeare from the 1960s onwards, is far more problematic to ascertain.[47] For in the earlier essay 'L'educació política del poble', *Coriolanus* is used as an example in arguments for the political education of the masses. Beginning by separating his understanding of politics from 'electoral propaganda', he calls for courses and lectures about 'true' politics).[48] He moves on to an anecdote about how easily fooled people can be by appeal to their stomachs, citing as immortal examples the cajoling of the people of Rome by the tribunes: 'Aquesta manera de salvar el poble és molt antiga. Shakespeare, millorant Plutarc, n'ha deixat immortals exemples en aquelles multituts ingènues i malicioses de Coriolà i en els ignorants i envejosos tribuns qui les manegen' ('This way of saving the people is very ancient. Shakespeare, improving on Plutarch, has left immortal examples of it in those naive and malicious multitudes in *Coriolanus* and in the ignorant and envious tribunes who manipulate them').[49]

The whole tenor of the essay is to counter populism, to encourage people to be more discerning in their choice of leader, rejecting empty words, technical jargon and bureaucrats.[50] It is a call for patience to allow for durable improvement in social conditions. But it is also a call which clearly separates the *poble* from the men of understanding who should be entrusted with their future. It is not therefore the 'absolutament desinteressada educació política del nostre poble' ('absolutely disinterested political education of our nation') that Farran i Mayoral suggests in his closing words, but something far closer to the 'imperialism' of Noucentisme, figured through a Catalan cultural plot that could have been transplanted from *Coriolanus*.[51]

The political significance of performance as well as the fascist undertones activated in the play in the early twentieth century (after Nietzsche) is borne out by events in France in 1934, themselves identified and debated in a number of Catalan periodicals. According to a review in *Mirador* (1934) a production of *Coriolanus* at the Comédie Française became 'la més eficaç de les propagandes: la de la passió política' ('the most efficacious of propaganda techniques: that of political passion').[52] Arguments seeking to deny the specific political relevance of the production fell on deaf ears, and certain of the more rabble-rousing scenes, the exchanges between Coriolanus and the plebeians, had to be toned down. Yet after the Stavisky affair, even these changes were insufficient to prevent violent reactions: 'El capdill romà, rebel imprecador de la plebs i dels tribuns, tornava a conèixer la fortuna. Si hagués pogut sortir al carrer trotant sobre un cavall blanc segurament hauria empal·lidit els records del boulangisme. Shakespeare era l'autor del dia' ('The Roman captain, rebellious challenger to the plebeians and the tribunes, was coming home to know his fortune. If he had been able to trot out into the streets on the back of a white horse he would surely have subdued people's memories of *Boulangisme*. Shakespeare was the author of the hour'). People's political suspicions had been confirmed by Shakespeare.

The reviewer absolves Shakespeare of any political subversion, instead using the anecdote to underline the importance of artistic liberty. Once again Shakespeare's genius is identified in his ability to transform a prosaic, unoriginal history into a compelling work, and his political leanings played down: 'Nat en una època on el dogma democràtic no tenia cap sentit [...] el dramaturg inseria en *Coriolà* durs retrets pels representants de les masses i per la plebs mateixa en allò que té de cruel, d'ignorant i de primària. Però amb la caiguda del cabdill es subratlla també el just fracàs de la fatuïtat, de la fredor distant i de la feblesa disfressada que fan la fusta dels dictadors' ('Born in an age when democratic dogma had no meaning [...] the dramatist inserted into *Coriolanus* harsh reprimands for the representatives of the masses and for the plebeians themselves, for their cruelty, ignorance and baseness. But with the fall of the captain he underlines the just fall of the fatuity, the distant coldness and disguised weakness that are the making of dictators'). Following the ideas of Coleridge, then, it is Shakespeare's political and philosophical impartiality which is underlined, but this does not deny the particular relevance of the story at a single moment in time, however distasteful the critic may find such a confluence: '... les agitacions promogudes amb Coriolà són ben bé filles d'una coincidència circumstancial dintre el temps [...] Però és el fet anecdòtic directe el que sedueix sempre tots els públics...' ('... the disturbances caused by *Coriolanus* are basically born of chance temporal coincidences [...] However, it is always the direct anecdotal event that seduces audiences...').[53]

Noticeably, the critic does not deny the political potential of the play, but calls for the ability to historicize; to figure Shakespeare as a man of his times, but whose universal relevance lies beyond such concerns. Similar commentary occurs in other newspapers and periodicals, and relevant sections of Morera i Galícia's translation are reprinted in *Teatre* during the same year in order to alert readers to the cultural and political possibilities of the play. It is also an event which occasions almost wistful commentary from Ramon Tasis i Marca in 1938, reflecting on a performance of *The Taming of the Shrew* in a version by Farran i Mayoral, and musing at its significance for Catalan theatre:

> Darrerament ha estat assenyalat moltes vegades l'exemple del drama de Shakespeare *Coriolà*, que ha obtingut a París un èxit d'actualitat, com si es tractés d'una obra escrita ara mateix. L'èxit de *La feréstega* domada [...] demostra que ací també són possibles aquests casos, i que per donar una obra nova i dolenta d'un actor del país és preferible extreure del repertori estranger algun drama o alguna comèdia que poden tenir per al públic el mateix encís de cosa desconeguda i a la vegada han de servir perquè els autors

dramàtics catalans sentin la necessitat de posar llur obra d'acord amb els il·lustres models que li són exhibits des de l'escena oficial.[54]

(Lately there have been many references to the example of Shakespeare's *Coriolanus*, which has achieved contemporary success in France, as if it were a work that had been written here and now. The success of *The Taming of the Shrew* [...] shows that these cases are also possible here, and that instead of staging a bad new work by a local actor it is preferable to take a drama or comedy from the foreign repertoire that might have the same charming unfamiliarity for the public at the same time as serving to remind Catalan dramatists to put their own work in line with the illustrious models displayed before them on the official stage).

As can be observed, the specific, immediate political significance of a version of the play would depend very much on it being performed at a particular moment in time, and *Coriolà* was not performed at this time in Catalonia. However, reviews also underline the linguistic significance of the translation, itself a political issue within the play and in the Catalan cultural climate in which it is translated. In fact the most important aspect identified by Carles Riba in his review of the work is the translator – it is after all an 'Elogi del poeta traductor' – and the act of translation, presented as a fruitful collaboration between Shakespeare and Morera i Galícia. It is the variety of nuances it can bring to the Catalan language that is most minutely catalogued: 'la fuga sonora de l'estil, que va accelerant-se, furient, amb la progressió del drama; [...] el vers articulat i mòbil damunt del ritme inlassable; [...] la llengua conceptual i plàstica, pregona i en certa manera mesurable, precisa i emocionadament esvaïdissa ensems...' ('the sonorous fugue of its style, that accelerates, furiously, with the denouement of the drama; [...] the flexibility and articulacy of each line upon the untiring rhythm; [...] the conceptual and plastic language, both profound and somehow measurable, both precise and emotionally elusive').[55]

The language of the translation is praised by other reviewers, including Josep Lleonart, and it is to be noticed that *Coriolà* and *Hàmlet* gain far superior reviews in this respect than Morera's subsequent translations of *Romeo and Juliet* and *The Merchant of Venice*. This also compares with the silence enveloping Perpiñá's translation which, although quoted as one of the key poetic translations by Esquerra and Par, is, in truth, far clumsier and more prosaic. For Farran i Mayoral consideration of the language leads him to address problems and solutions in translation, before praising the quality of Morera i Galícia's version: 'El vers endecasíl·lab [...] no li és obstacle per a seguir l'ondulació de la paraula shakespeariana, i assolir una literalitat qui arriba sovint a la correspondència numeral de paraules' ('The hendecasyllabic line [...] is no obstacle for him to follow the undulations of Shakespeare's language, and thus to achieve a literalness that often results in the numerical correspondence between words').[56] Morera i Galícia is praised elsewhere as achieving the impossible, the perfect blending of the close and the free in translation: 'Ell ha fet prou perquè no l'oblidem: Si els francesos comptaven a Amyot, traductor de Plutarc, entre els seus grans escriptors, nosaltres comptarem Morera i Galícia, traductor de Shakespeare, entre els patriarques de la nostra literatura' ('He has done enough for us never to forget him. If the French include Amyot, the translator of Plutarch, amongst their great writers, we should count Morera i Galícia, translator of Shakespeare, amongst the patriarchs of our literature').[57]

It is worth remembering that Morera i Galícia and Perpiñà were the first to attempt to translate Shakespeare into a blend of decasyllables and prose. Only Carner had produced a successful poetic version of a Shakespeare play before 1917, and this used alexandrines interspersed with other more popular verse forms. The choice of verse form is not important, except in so far as it denotes a tendency to associate Shakespeare's iambic pentameter with the Catalan decasyllabic line, traditional in medieval poetry. However, the decision to produce poetic translations is more significant as a mark of cultural distinction. The existing Spanish translations were in prose.

Even in *Lletres a una amiga estrangera* the weight of the piece is on the linguistic significance of the translation event, with Farran i Mayoral claiming the reason for Morera's success to be: 'Perquè el català és la llengua més shakespeariana del món' ('For Catalan is the most Shakespearian language in the world'). In this sublimation he most clearly differentiates Catalan from French and Spanish, although in some ways it is also set above German and Italian: 'Concebem l'*Hamlet* escrit originàriament en alemany, el *Romeu i Julieta* en italià [...] Però en català les concebem totes' ('We can conceive of *Hamlet* written originally in

German, and of *Romeo and Juliet* in Italian [. . .] But in Catalan we can conceive of them all').[58] His own urge to translate the complete works of Shakespeare is relinquished in favour of the eminence and superiority of Morera i Galícia, although the article ends with doubt as to whether Catalan actors would be up to scratch speaking the words.[59] How *Coriolanus* can be expressed in Catalan thus becomes inseparable from the question of its ultimate significance, underlined by its own thematic focus on language and storytelling. In tracing an answer to the question of the significance of *Coriolà* and Shakespeare in Catalan it becomes clear that the focus on tongues and voices (a term used interchangeably with votes) in the play gains political impetus in its new linguistic framings. For the relationship of 'llengua' and 'orgull' prominent in the play is omnipresent in the cultural discourse of the time of its publication. 'El dia que cap català distingit deixi d'usar ab orgull la seva llengua, el català serà l'idioma més fi del món' ('The day on which no distinguished Catalan fails to use his language with pride, will be the day that Catalan is the finest language in the world').[60]

The individual tongues of the plebeians, the many-headed hydra, the people who welcome Caius Marcius on his triumphant return from war with the *Volsci*, the unpractised tongue of Coriolanus himself, are all translated as 'llengua' in Catalan, with the additional meanings this carries. The 'tongue our trumpeter' of Act I scene i becomes 'la llengua trompetera', although interestingly in Perpiñà's version, closer to early Renaixença poetics and orthography it is 'la llengua nostra que ens fa d'heraut'. In Act II scene ii of the English, where the citizens of Rome prepare to be rallied by Coriolanus for their votes, the words of the Third Citizen 'every one of us has a single honour, in giving him our voices with our own tongues' become 'a fi que tinguem cadaú, particularment la honor de dir-li, amb *la nostra pròpia llengua*, que li donem el nostre vot' (my emphasis). Thus, their political impetus becomes attached to the ability to express themselves in their own language; here, in Catalan. The Coriolanus texts are formed of a cacophony of voices, every one having something to say about the political situation in which their discourse is embedded. The very language they use, and often a singular rather than plural language in the Morera version as shown above, and whether they are allowed to use it becomes a political issue, one which can be traced in many different forms throughout the play. By exploring how the political fact of language, linguistic difference and differentiation, transfers into performance and presents itself rhetorically, it will be possible to perceive how *Coriolà* might become a trope for the struggle to mean through translation, adding a new valency to the historical figuration of Shakespeare in Catalonia.

It is, then, in positionings on the purposiveness of language that an answer may be found to the Citizen's questioning of Menenius after his Belly tale. 'Mes, què en surt d'aquesta faula?' – 'It was an answer. How apply you this?' These words of the Ciutadà Primer/First Citizen draw attention to the political problems of storytelling, although for significantly different reasons. The First Citizen draws attention to the Belly tale's position within a dialogue, 'It was an answer', before questioning its application, how it is to be used. The Ciutadà's 'Mes, què en surt d'aquesta faula?' is a more direct attack on the story's use-value, evading the narrator's concluding question, 'Què tal el ventre/ respongué?' with another question, an act which in itself places a question mark over this story's ability to generate meaningful communication.

The political positionings of the characters in relation to the different stories which form *Coriolanus/Coriolà* call for detailed analysis, as do those of the more influential readers of the different versions. Looking at the 'belly speech' in Magí Morera i Galícia's version, the moral aims would seem to be more self-sufficient than in the Shakespeare:

> The senators of Rome are this good belly,
> And you the mutinous members: for examine
> Their counsels and their cares, digest things rightly
> Touching the weal o'th'common, you shall find
> No public benefit which you receive
> But it proceeds or comes from them to you.
> And no way from yourselves.

> Que aquell bon ventre és el Senat de Roma,
> i vosaltres els membres motinaires;
> car si esbrineu ses acurades ordes,
> i com les coses dirigeix amb seny
> en tot quant toca als aliments del poble,
> veureu que no hi ha públic benefici
> que d'ell no vingui o que ses mans no endrecin,

sens que en cap ocasió pugueu trobar-lo
per vosaltres mateixos.[61]

The Catalan passage is both descriptive of the generosity and good management of the Senate, as in the English, and prescriptive in the negative imperative use of 'poder' when concluding 'sens que en cap ocasió pugueu trobar-lo/ per vosaltres mateixos'. The attribution of culturally-specific 'seny' to the Senate would seem to inscribe Menenius' speech within the discourse of Catalan nationalism, and his expression of the specific role of the ruling power to oversee 'amb seny/ en tot quant toca als aliments del poble', would seem politically loaded on referring out to the date of composition and completion of *Coriolà*. The overt reference to the people's inability to fend for themselves, to a kind of enforced dependence on the ruling body reflects the position of the *Mancomunitat* and *Lliga Regionalista*, increasingly conservative after the events of the *Setmana Tràgica* in 1909 and again after the strikes of 1917, the death of the more moderate *Lliga* mentor, Prat de la Riba, and the growing power of Francesc Cambó, with his willingness to negotiate with the Spanish state. It might also be taken to reflect the pressure placed by the Spanish central government on Barcelona. The sneering question which follows Menenius' English reaffirmation of the status quo, '... What do you think, / You, the great toe of the assembly?' seems far more playful, far more patronizing in the Catalan, by juxtaposing the more respectful use of 'Què en judiques?' with the almost childish, '–Tu, dic, dit gros del peu de l'assamblea'. There is less sarcasm in the explanation of the 'insult' which follows: 'Perquè essent el més baix, més vil i pobre d'aquesta rebel·lió' as opposed to 'For that being one o'th' lowest, basest, poorest / Of this most wise rebellion'. In fact, the attitude of the senators when speaking before the people is perceptibly more indulgent than that of their 'English' counterparts. Even Caius Marcius shows a little more respect for the plebeians when he appears shortly afterwards, asking an explanation for their behaviour – 'Què voleu?' – rather than remaining aloof in asking 'What's their meaning?'

This foregrounds the role of storytelling, communication and narration within political systems, in *Coriolanus*, with respect to democracy. Brutus and Sicinius are well aware of the story they must tell to achieve their political ends in the play. Referring to

Coriolanus' imminent campaign to be named consul, they formulate the following plan of action:

> *Brutus:*
> Al poble hem de parlar-li del gran odi
> que ell sempre li ha tingut; de què, a poder-ho,
> d'ell en faria cosa igual que bèsties,
> emmudint per a sempre als qui el defensen,
> furtant ses llibertats, i concedint-los,
> per tot albir de ses accions humanes,
> no més ànima i seny per a la vida,
> que en els camells de guerra, que si mengen,
> és sols per a dur pes, i encar se'ls punxa
> si sota el pes flecten genolls i cauen.
>
> *Sicinius:*
> Aquestes coses, a son temps ben dites,
> quan, prenent més volada, sa insolència
> fereixi al poble – i la ocasió és segura
> per poc que ens hi esmercem: cosa tan facil
> com per fer que abordi un ca ramats qui passen, –
> la palla seca d'ells, i aqueix incendi
> l'ennegrirà per sempre. (pp. 59–60)

This exchange follows Coriolà's triumphant return from war with the Volsci in Act II scene i, and is immediately preceded by discussion of the rumours surrounding the soldier's personality and fitness for office. Whereas in the Shakespeare version Brutus and Sicinius speak of 'suggesting' the people: 'We must suggest the people in what hatred/ He still hath held them' and 'This (as you say) suggested / At some time when his soaring insolence / Shall touch the people'; the Catalan-speaking consuls are more open about the story they must tell, and the circumstances in which it must be embedded. So we find Brutus' overt statement of intention: 'Al poble hem de parlar-li del gran odi' and Sicinius' later affirmation, 'Aquestes coses a son temps ben dites', less in the language of conspiracy than that of moral conviction. Hence, Coriolà's evils are represented as far more serious and enduring than in the English. Compare, for instance, 'that to's power he would / Have them made mules, silenc'd their pleaders, and / Dispropertied their freedoms; holding them / ... / Of no more soul nor fitness for the world / Than camels in their war' with 'd'ell en faria cosa igual que bèsties / emmudint per a sempre als qui el defensen / furtant ses llibertats, i concedint-los, / per tot albir de ses accions humanes, / no més ànima i seny per a la vida, / que an els camells de guerra'. Coriolà's sins are here multiplied by the words of perpetuity, and the Catalan listener's sympathy is demanded against him with speculation about his future suppression of the people's (cultural) right to *seny*.

Different representations of Coriolanus the man – or god-like figure, depending on the narrator – shed light on differing attitudes towards storytelling in each version of the story. In Act I scene ii, the women of the play discuss their feelings about Caius Marcius and his role as Rome's champion (see fig. 14). When Virgilia asks how Volumnia would have reacted had her son died in an earlier 'guerra cruel', she replies: 'Que de sa fama n'haguera fet mon fill, i això m'hauria aconsolat' showing a strong perception of the ability of words to create realities. The differing reactions to Valeria's story, later in the same scene, of Caius Marcius' game with the butterfly, further demonstrates the power of stories and storytellers to create and reinforce myths (pp. 21–7).

Thus, at Coriolanus' return from the war at the beginning of Act II, Brutus describes how:

> Totes les llengües parlen d'ell; per veure'l
> els lleganyosos s'han posat ulleres.
> Xerraire mainadera, embadalida,
> deixa que plori el noi i s'enrabii
> mentre ella parla d'ell.

The power of the hero to generate discourse – in all languages (totes les llengües, as could be read above – is central to the story. Coriolà's failure to be accepted by the populace in the third act is attributed to his inability to take part in this process of generation, and perhaps regeneration. In Act III scene i, Menenius explains Coriolà's behaviour to the senators:

> Tingueu present que ell es crià en la guerra
> des que pugué desenveinar una espasa,
> i ha mal-aprés d'empolainar sa llengua,
> que barreja amb descuit segó i farina (p. 104).

This should be compared with Menenius' pragmatically literal approach to language – although again embedded within a certain conversational context, addressing the returning soldiers – in Act II scene i:

> A centes i a milers les benvingudes.
> Ploraria i riuria; em sento àgil
> i feixuc ...

followed by:

> No hi fa res: benvinguts, flor de l'exèrcit.
> Jo a l'herba que fa mal, li dic mal-herba,
> i al fet del neci, necetat (p. 56).

These approaches to speech and rhetoric reflect the language and comments made about the role of the poet in Catalan nationalism. Carles Riba, in his 1924 prologue to the Magí Morera i Galícia volume of *Els poetes d'ara* (Poets of Today), refers to the poet's midlife change from writing in Castilian to Catalan as allowing him innumerable possibilities for virtuosity. The sense of a need to 'empolainar sa llengua' is further reflected in the following lines: 'la retòrica en què creu En Morera, a l'italiana i a l'anglesa, filla d'un esperit de magnificiència, d'una convicció de la gran dignitat i la gran joia de la poesia, d'una pura voluntat d'art, en suma' ('the rhetoric in which Morera i Galícia believes, drawing on the Italian and the English, is born of a spirit of magnificence, and of a conviction of the great dignity and great joy of poetry; in effect, of a pure wish to create art').[62]

The importance placed on adherence to a certain form, to tradition, in retelling a story, is central to Coriolanus/Coriolà's role in both versions of the Coriolanus story. This becomes clear in the events surrounding his 'courtship' of the voters for their support in his campaign to be elected consul. Again, the plain-speaking soldier is given advice as to his expected performance:

> *Sicinius:*
> Senyor, el poble
> té dret al vot; no llevarà una titlla
> de cerimònia a l'acte.
> *Menenius:*
> ... No en feu massa.
> Plegueu-se a aquest costum, vos ho suplico,
> concerteu, com els passats ho feren,
> la forma d'eixa honor amb la honor vostra.
> *Coriolà:*
> És un paper que enrogiré tot fent-lo,
> i que qui sap si desplaurà an el poble (p. 68).

Sicinius' explicit reference to 'l'acte', which is not present in the English version, gives a metatextual edge to the discussion of the importance of form, a feature which is underlined by the repeated use of 'obres/obrar' (as deeds, acts, work) throughout Morera i Galícia's version. Coriolà is, then, urged by Menenius to reconcile himself to collaborating with traditional form, in order that the honour conferred by custom (and hence the honour enjoyed by his predecessors) be added to his own. This may be compared with the English version: 'Take to you, as your predecessors have,/ Your honour with your form' where there is no such sense of honour in collaboration, so central to Catalan discourse about translation. A further reading might focus on Morera's use of poetry, and particularly the decasyllabic verse form, as part of the honour of his rhetorical act. In a similar manner, Volumnia's later advocation that her son should face the people once more 'amb uns mots que et llisquin sobre la llengua' is reminiscent of the urge towards poetic harmony in writing about the creation of a language of culture in the Noucentiste period. Joaquim Molas, in looking back on the period in 1983, writes that: 'La gent noucentista, amb més recursos polítics, i més ben armada culturalment, reduí les dues opcions, la retòrica i la terrorista, a una de sola: la retòrica' ('The people of the Noucentista period, with more political options, and more cultural tools, reduced the two choices, between rhetoric and terrorism, into one: that of rhetoric').[63]

Such themes are perhaps most visible in the central scenes of Act II and Act III where Coriolà first gains then loses the support of the people through constant changes in representation of his character and deeds, these being the very sections reproduced by *Teatre* in response to the events at the Comédie Française in 1934. The citizens themselves attest to the emptiness of their democratic power, as long as Coriolà performs according to custom, in the following exchange:

> Ciutadà primer: Un pic ens demana el vot, no hem de negar-li.
> Ciutadà segon: Però podem, si volem.
> Ciutadà tercer: Clar és que el poder el tenim; més és un poder que no podem usar; puix si ns mostra ses ferides i ens conta ses proeses, la llengua se'ns anirà a llepar-les i a parlar per elles (p. 69).

Furthermore, when Coriolà arrives in humble garb the Ciutadà tercer reaffirms his belief in the duty of 'la llengua': 'Ell ha de dirigir-nos individualment sa requesta, a fi que tinguem cadaú, particularment, la honor de dir-li, amb la nostra pròpia llengua, que li donem el nostre vot' (p. 71). The English version, 'in giving him our own voices with our own tongues', does not carry the same sense of linguistic affirmation. But the link between the exercising of one's democratic right and 'dignified' freedom of expression in Catalan is common in *Noucentista* aesthetic and political discourse. An example can be found in the periodical *Catalunya* of 18 July 1914. In bemoaning the lack of particular 'genius' upon the Catalan stage of the time, J. Morató goes on to advocate the creation of a 'geni col·lectiu' which 'és, en el cas de França, sinònim d'esperit nacional' ('in the case of France synonymous with national spirit').[64] He then refers out to recent elections, supporting his argument with the fact that Barcelona's theatres had been used as polling stations, offended that: 'els mateixos que amb el seu vot havíen fet traició a la terra, fulminéssin maledicions contra la passivitat dels catalanistes davant les traduccions en català relatiu que constituíen el repertori de la temporada' ('the same people who with their vote have betrayed their land, should utter curses against the passivity of Catalanists before the translations into a relative Catalan that constituted the repertoire for the season').[65] In the same way 'vots' and 'veus' become interchangeable as Coriolà calls on the 'dolces veus' of the citizens.[66] It is not surprising that Farran i Mayoral was to write of Morera i Galícia's version in political terms.

The choice of Catalan as the ideal delegate to retell Shakespeare's stories, to retell Coriolà/Coriolanus, raises the whole question of delegation, a problem which is central to the political and narrative positionings within the play. In Act III scene i, Coriolà turns on Brutus and Sicinius:

> ... Quin bestiar el vostre!
> I que hagin d'heure vot, aquells que poden
> donar-lo, i totseguit deixa embustera
> sa llengua pròpia! – Doncs, i el vostre ofici?
> Perquè, si sou sa veu, si sou sa boca,
> no governeu ses dents? – Sereu vosaltres
> qui els mogué d'eixa guisa (p. 86).

Voices, and their possible interpretation, become central. Even Coriolà seems loath to criticize the voices of the citizens, putting himself above their votes but not their voices as in the English: 'Tinc raons de més pes que els seus sufragis' ('... I'll give my reasons/ More worthier than their voices'). Likewise, rather than 'deeds' expressing 'What's like to be' the words of the people, the Catalan version has 'Oïnt-los/ ho sabreu, puix entre ells bé prou s'ho duien'.

Hence it is clear that the problematic nature of the relationship between actions and words becomes central to a reading of the Catalan *Coriolà*, strongly linking it to debate over the shape cultural regeneration should take. Coriolà's awkward position in relation to language and therefore in relation to Catalanism is reflected in critical reference to the significance of the play. Brutus and Sicinius are aware of this yet their machinations bring to the fore problems of the ethical relationship between the two. Does their linguistic persuasion have the best interest of the 'poble' at heart or just their own self-interest? Menenius' controlling and pacifying rhetoric, although in many ways a more positive model for the persuasiveness of language, does not always achieve communication, as we have seen. Sicinius and Brutus suggest that 'Són ses faules/ Són ses faules només'. Whether these 'faules' are the attempts to impose a rather Nietzschean voluntarism or the collective cultural monument achieved by collaboration might then be expected to change according to the political environment which frames them, or the understanding of Shakespeare, the language question and translation of the translator who translates them.

Although attitudes to Shakespeare, to the Catalan language and the shape and purpose of cultural intervention undergo many changes after the 1920s, some having far less to do with choice than with necessity, subsequent cultural activity does not take place in a vacuum. This is nowhere more true than in the case of translation, with metacommentary to argue for the priority of each new version. Where we have perceived that the central political and cultural problem of Coriolanus in Catalan is the question of how to retell the story, who gives the right to speak, noting the strategies used to legitimize particular rhetorical choices, it is understandable that a degree of anxiety of influence may be apparent between the rival translators. To trace the changing role and implications of storytelling it is necessary to analyse the anxieties at work in these translations. Having demonstrated briefly how the struggle for legitimacy and authority underscores the presentation or staging of the versions, it shall be seen how the words themselves, chosen to express *Coriolanus* and which Coriolanus speaks, read as chapters in the Shakespeare translation story.

The versions to be considered, penned by the writers listed earlier in the chapter, date from between 1915 and 2002. The ways in which they are presented make different claims to legitimacy and authority with or without the support of contemporary critics. Each version revises tradition in order to make a claim for its own priority. This can be observed in the staging, each seeking to upstage its precursors; the positioning of the precursors in specific contexts, to sanction the latecomer's claim to be the inheritor of true 'original' meaning; the absorption of meanings, image patterns, devices used by previous translators; as well as swerves and misreadings of previous texts and contexts, questioning their fidelity to the 'original'. The questions posed could be summarized as follows: Who gives the 'original' the freedom to speak in Catalan? Who is the original? Referring to respective poetic or dramatic ability, who is the better writer? And with respect to each writer's power over language ('llengua'), who is the better Catalan? By reading these texts across the boundaries which they set up to mark out their own superiority, these boundaries begin to disintegrate. This is clear in a consideration of parallel extracts from their versions of *Coriolanus/Coriolà* (Act II scene iii). The choice of extract was influenced by Salvador Oliva who gave a talk on the problems of translating Shakespeare at the University of Birmingham in June 1993. He produced a handout with the Shakespeare, Sagarra and Ferrater versions of this passage in order to discuss the relative merits of the two Catalan translations. The English version, included here, is the one he used. The section is also one of the few excerpts included in *Teatre* in 1934, in order to sublimate the cultural-political relevance of the play:

> Nosaltres, al marge de voler entrar en consideracions d'ordre polític, ens toca evocar les paraules que foren escrites en anglès, però que les pròpies passions i defectes dels homes les posen a la

comprensió viva de tots els pobles que hagin abastat en sentit col·lectiu de llibertat i de dignitat humana.[67]

(Without wishing to enter into considerations of a political nature, it falls to us to evoke the words that were written in English, but that the individual passions and defects of men make comprehensible to all the nations they have reached in the collective name of freedom and human dignity).

Furthermore, it was used in promotional flyers and posters for the production at the Teatre Nacional de Catalunya in 2002 (see fig. 15).

Coriolanus:
   Most sweet voices:
   Better it is to die, better to starve,
   Than crave the hire, which first we do deserve.
   Why, in this woolvish toge should I stand here,
   To beg of Hob and Dick, that does appear,
   Their needless vouches: custom calls me to't.
   What custom wills in all things, should we do't?
   The dust of antique time would lie unswept,
   And mountainous error be too highly heap'd,
   For truth to o'er-peer. Rather than fool it so,
   Let the high office and the honour go
   To one that would do thus. I am half through,
   The one part suffer'd, the other will I do.

1. M. Morera i Galícia (1918):

Coriolà:
   O, dolces veus . . . !
   Val més morir, val més morir de gana,
   que emmatllevar a precs ço que guanyàrem.
   Per què romandre amb la rapada toga,
   captant de tots els *tal i qual* que vinguin
   el vot inútil? El costum m'ho ordena.
   Si tot quant manen els costums deu fer-se,
   la pols de l'antigor mai es treuria
   i els munts d'errors, creixent, foren muntanyes
   massa altes, perquè el cap tregués, per dalt,
   la veritat. Ans que seguir tal burla
   siguin honors i oficis pels qui vulguin
   acaçar-los així. — Porto ja feta
   la meitat de la via: anem seguint-la (p. 75).

2. J. Perpiñà (1917):

Coriolanus:
    O les veus dolces! Quànt més preferible
    no es morirse; millor patir miseria
    que no implorar axís aquesta paga
    que tinch, d'avans, de sobres merescuda!
    ¿Y perquè, aquí, cubert d'aquesta toga,
    com llop vestit d'ovella, cal qu'estigui
    per implorar l'inútil testimoni
    d'en Pau y en Pere y del primer que passi?
    M'hi crida la costum; però si en totes
    les coses hem de fer lo qu'exigeixi
    la consuetat, la pols de la velluria
    s'anirà apilotant, may escombrada,
    y encimbrellant l'error en alta cima
    tan amunt pujarà que ni permeti
    qu'un raig de llum de veritat traspongui . . .
    Abans que m'abandoni a tal follia
    que'l Consulat y'ls grans honors se'n vagin
    a qui tot axò fassi per guanyarlos . . .
    Mes tinch mig camí fet y en tinch suferta
    la meytat dels fatichs, sufrimne l'altra (pp. 91–2).

3. J. M. de Sagarra (1940s):

Coriolà:
    Dolcíssims vots!
    Més val morirse i rebentar de fam
    que, del que mereixem, fer-ne el reclam!
    ¿Per què aquí vinc, ensamarrat de pega,
    a demanar a en Mossega i a en Rosega
    un vot inútil? Perquè és el costum.
    Oh, si, en tot, al costum déssim tendrum!
    La no escombrada pols del temps passat
    s'enfilaria sobre del terrat.
    Tan alta la muntanya pujaria
    de l'error, que no la dominaria
    mai més la veritat! Potser més val
    ans de ser tan beneit, deixar el vial
    ben lliure per a aquells que amb tal programa
    van darrera dels càrrecs i la fama.
    Mig camí, ja l'he fet, ja he començat
    a patir; doncs patim-ho tot plegat (p. 77).

4. G. Ferrater (1972):

Coriolà:
    Dolcíssims vots.
    És millor de morir, de passar gana,
    si el sou degut no el rep qui no el demana.
    Qui em posa aquesta roba de ferum
    i em planta aquí captant. Diu que el costum.
    Si seguim el costum en tot dictat,
    no escombrarem la pols del temps passat.
    I el munt de pols d'estupidesa puja
    i ofega, i mai no se l'endú cap pluja
    de decisió fresca. I he d'obeir
    quan els meus diuen que m'he d'envilir
    captant allò que tan poc vull. Ja és
    mig fet. Ho acabaré. Que en vinguin més (p. 289).

5. M. Morera i Galícia (MOLU edition):

Coriolà:
    Oh, dolces veus . . .!
    Val més morir, val més morir de gana,
    que manllevar a precs ço que guanyàrem.
    Per què romandre amb la llobada toga,
    captant de tots els tal i tal que vinguin
    el vot inútil? El costum m'ho ordena.
    Si allò que manen els costums cal fer,
    la pols de l'antigor mai no es trauria
    i els munts d'errors, creixent, foren muntanyes
    massa altes, perquè el cap tragués, per dalt,
    la veritat. Ans que seguir tal burla
    siguin honors i oficis pels qui vulguin
    acaçar-los així. Porto ja feta
    la meitat de la via: anem seguint-la (pp. 449–50).

6. S. Oliva (1989):

Coriolà:
    Ah, dolços vots!
    Val més morir, val més morir de fam,
    que demanar la paga d'allò que mereixem.
    ¿Per què m'he d'estar aquí amb aquesta toga
    semblant a un llop vestit d'ovella,
    per demanar-li a un tal i a un tal
    els seus inútils vots? ¿Que m'hi obliga el costum?

Si en tot seguíssim el costum,
no escombraríem mai la pols del temps passat,
i el munt d'errors s'aniria fent alt,
massa alt perquè la veritat pogués
veure què hi ha al darrere. Abans de fer el beneit així,
val més deixar l'honor i el càrrec
a qui s'avingui a fer-ho. Però ja ho tinc mig fet;
si fins ara he aguantat, arribaré fins al final (pp. 68–9).

7. J. Sellent (2002):

Coriolà:
Oh, dolços vots!
És millor caure mort o passar gana
que no implorar una paga ja guanyada.
Què hi faig, aquí, com un llop disfressat,
pidolant al primer que em surt al pas
uns vots inútils? Obeir el costum?
Si el costum l'obeíssim punt per punt,
no escombraríem mai la pols antiga,
i el gruix dels vells errors amagaria
la veritat. No accepto aquesta farsa;
que els càrrecs i els honors se'ls quedi un altre
que s'hi vulgui prestar. Pro sóc a mig camí;
si he resistit fins ara, vull fer l'altre mig (pp. 127–8).

On a purely lexical level, in Oliva's version there are surprising echoes, considering his claims elsewhere, of more than just Ferrater's voice.[68] The 'llengua' of his Coriolà is made up of that of Morera and Sagarra too, swerving to produce its own meaning. These swerves can be best observed in the different rhetorical attitudes or stationings within the texts. With respect to judgement of value, of personal and textual worth perhaps, as far as Morera i Galícia's Coriolà is concerned he has already won the battle, referring to 'ço que guanyàrem'. Perpiñà's 'd'avans de sobres merescuda' mirrors the question of temporal priority between these two texts. Sagarra's and Oliva's claim only what each deserves. Respectively: 'més val morirse/ que, del que mereixem, fer-ne el reclam!' and 'val més morir,/ que demanar la paga d'allò que mereixem'. Ferrater's text further underlines a disdain for requesting approval: 'Es millor de morir/ si el sou degut no el rep qui no el demana'. Sellent's meanwhile is a patchwork of the others, imitating the formal solutions of Ferrater and Oliva, but with lexical echoes of Morera and Perpiñà.

The toga is treated as a disguise by Sellent, Oliva and Perpiñà, suggesting the mask or masking of translation, as a ritual repetition of custom, of tradition, all using a simile to mark out their role-playing as 'llops vestit d'ovellas' or simply disguised. In this way their agency for another 'llengua' is also underlined. Distaste for this role is presented by Sagarra's Coriolà, as an ugly robe unfitting to and, perhaps, falsifying his station: '¿Per què aquí vinc, ensamarrat de pega', whilst Ferrater's is an abject reaction, concentrating on the stench (*ferum*) of this traditional garb: 'Qui em posa aquesta roba de ferum / i em planta aquí captant. Diu que el costum'. Sellent's use of 'pidolant' stands out for the sense of disdain and pride that it conveys, something that is underlined in the challenge to tradition of his sarcastic question 'Obeir el costum?' and in the representation of such an activity as a farce.

The texts portray varying attitudes towards custom, towards the tradition in which they are voiced. The variety of conditional uses to denote the reaction of each to the piling dust of past tradition, have Morera's Coriolà voicing a more hypothetical condition or problem, thus implying it is not really a problem: 'si tot quant manen els costums deu fer-se, / la pols de l'antigor mai es treuria' and suggesting that his 'veritat' does indeed show through – although some 'pols' at least is removed in the MOLU editorial change from 'treuria' to 'trauria' and 'Si tot quant manen' to 'Si allò que manen'. Joan Perpiñà's Coriolanus speaks of the 'pols de la velluria' ever piling ('s'anirà apilotant'), and ever-increasing ('encimbrellant') error, never to be inverted. Sagarra's concern is to allow 'truth', his truth, to dominate: 'Tan alta muntanya pujaria de l'error que no la dominaria mai més la veritat!' Even more defiantly, Ferrater denounces outright the stupidity of tradition which chokes, calling for fresh decisions to clean it away: 'I el munt de pols d'estupidesa puja i ofega, i mai ho se l'endú cap pluja de decisió fresca.' Hence, he signals an urge to freedom of expression in his version of the Coriolanus story, whereas Oliva's sweeping away of the past is to allow the truth to see what is behind it all, the origins, an explicitly epistemological search: 'i el munt d'errors s'aniria fent alt massa alt perquè la veritat pogués veure què hi ha darrere.' Sellent's version contains echoes of

Morera, Ferrater and Oliva, thus suggesting that his complete rejection of tradition is a rhetorical position only: 'Si el costum l'obeíssim punt per punt, no escombraríem mai la pols antiga, i el gruix dels vells errors amagaria la veritat.' Whilst he refers to the mass of old errors hiding the truth, his use of 'punt per punt' earlier suggests the need to choose wisely in order to make headway.

If acceptance (in translation) depends on following tradition, on sanctioning past errors, then let others who are prepared to do this continue. Here the pull between the pride ('orgull') of Coriolà, the pride of each version, and the humility necessary to follow in tradition (the humility advocated by Catalan treatises on translation, set against the pride of other cultures) is clearly marked. The solutions: Morera's Coriolà, halfway there, opts to continue: 'Porto ja feta / la meitat de la via: anem seguint-la'. Sagarra's will continue to suffer alongside Perpiñà's: 'ja he començat / a patir, doncs patim-ho tot plegat' and 'en tinch suferta / la meitat dels fatichs, sufrimne l'altra'. Ferrater will finish what he has started, ending with an ironic challenge, 'Que en vinguin més'. Whilst Oliva's Coriolà states his intention to arrive ('arribaré'), alone, according to his text, 'fins al final'. This fits in with his metacommentary on the translation which plays down the 'tragèdia de la passió d'orgull' presented in other versions, attributing the tragedy instead to Volumnia's depriving Coriolà of an identity which we (as readers, perhaps) might perceive to be worthwhile. Finally, Sellent's Coriolà falls between the different versions: 'Pro sóc a mig camí'. His struggle is a resistant one, suggesting the strength to withstand the anxiety of influence in translation and negotiate a way between the different versions. The three early translations in contrast all resort to use of the first person plural, so associated with early formulations of the need for translation and of collective identity, in some way underlining a vision of translation as collaboration. The main anxiety of the MOLU text is in relation to what is standard 'llengua', at times changing forms in the Morera text which are standardly accepted, for instance, 'trauria' for 'treuria', perhaps to make the version acceptable in Valencian. This anxiety is reflected, as has been seen, in many critical readings of the Coriolà tradition for as Ferrater writes to Jakobson: 'I am a poet in Catalan, and a Catalan writer cannot fail to be very much language conscious'.[69]

The anxiety of influence, then, is to be seen here in a variety of revisionary moves to hide, or absorb clandestinely, the figuration of origins in the precursors, allowing the later translator to proceed with licence, with authority, thus both avoiding and engaging with the problem as posed by Perpiñà.

> Perquè posar la ma pecadora damunt d'una tragedia de Shakespeare [...] pot resultar una tasca dura, però a la fi gloriosa per un literat de bona fusta, en cambi per un aficionat es una gosadia que dificilment arribarien a perdonarli ni Shakespeare [...] ni tal vegada la matexa llengua catalana, per força, violentada, en la versió del complicadíssim texte original.[70]

> (For to place one's sinful hand upon a Shakespearian tragedy [...] may turn out to be a difficult task, but at the end of the day a glorious one for a writer of solid credentials; however, for an amateur it is an affront that can only be pardoned with difficulty by Shakespeare, but also perhaps by the Catalan language itself, unavoidably manhandled in translating the extremely complicated original text).

Authority can be achieved by placing the weight of such sins on the shoulders of the precursors, by historicizing their contribution. And such a revisionary move is perhaps necessary to continue translating. For if the problem of how to allow the original to speak (let alone identifying it) becomes overwhelming (as Joan Perpiñà suggests in connection with Quixotic denunciations of this feat) then the anxiety becomes a block.[71] So we see how Shakespeare (as a figure of universal culture) and translation (as the figure of the relationship between languages and cultures) can be used to represent particular political or cultural purpose, to persuade of the need for the speech act. Yet at the same time this act is always simultaneously based on a lack, a representation of its rhetoricity, of the lack of real origins, which is made explicit in translation. It is perhaps for this reason that Murgades sees the translation theories of *Noucentisme* as the formulations which offer the clearest picture of how the movement conceived of their cultural future:

> ... unes justificacions teòriques que, fonamentades en part en la mateixa racionalització imperialista del noucentisme, compten entre les més il·lustratives a l'hora d'entendre la dialèctica entre afirmació de la pròpia identitat i recerca irrenunciable de la no menys necessària universalitat.[72]

(... a set of theoretical justifications which, partly based in the very imperialist rationalization of Noucentisme, may be counted amongst the most expressive when it comes to understanding the dialectic between the affirmation of one's identity and the unrenounceable search for a no less necessary universality').

Coda

Curiously, the 'Most sweet voices' speech is used in promotional material for the Georges Lavaudant production in 2002, with Lluís Homar's Coriolà addressing a Catalan audience, both to entice them to come and see the performance at the Teatre Nacional de Catalunya, and, given what we know of Coriolanus's intentions, challenging them to confront tradition with him. In the context of a version staged at the controversial theatrical monument of what many would consider 'patrician' Catalonia, this presents numerous possible readings. The TNC was intended to stand as a centre for cultural normality as envisioned by Convergència i Unió, but was attacked from its inception because of its exclusionary tactics. Even when reclaimed for a different view of tradition, the production of *Coriolà* is viewed as problematic because of the invitation to a French director to direct it, continuing a tendency to throw money at international stars. Once again, we can observe a tendency to subordinate the value of local readings and talent to all that is foreign, particularly French, English and German, suggesting a lack of pride in the Catalan tradition. Furthermore one of the greatest criticisms of the production, notwithstanding praise of Sellent's translation, is perception of the problematic diction, put down to Lavaudant's lack of feeling for a Catalan oral tradition. The production is also compared unfavourably with Bieito's *Macbeth* at the Romea (both by Catalan theatre critics and by Michael Billington), as one that does not produce a compelling reading of the play.

Whilst the paratexts accompanying the performance do not engage with the tradition of translations we have explored, they do draw on key moments in the play for the question of the positioning of tradition: the pull between a desire for local identity and universality, the creation of home-grown genius and the adaptation of foreign cultural values. The programme opens with a fragment from Act V scene ii, in which the relationship and role of Volumnia and her decision to subordinate the welfare of the individual (her son) to the collective is foregrounded, with a reproduction of one of Shakespeare's portraits on the facing page in order to lend authority to this reading. The dramaturg for this version, Daniel Loayza, underlines this reading in identifying the meaning of the play as follows: 'Coriolà és una brillant expressió de la inutilitat de l'heroisme militar quan no té en compte els valors humanístics i de com convèncer, decidir, pactar o comprometre's són virtuts, no necessàriament modèliques, però sí més complexes i civilitzades que lluitar o conquerir' ('Coriolanus is a brilliant illustration of the uselessness of military heroism if it does not take into account humanistic values, and that to convince, decide, agree or commit to something are, if not entirely model virtues, at least more complex and civilized than fighting and conquering').[73] However, whilst the symbology of fascism is present in the promotional material, it is muted in the actual staging of the play, just as any sense of an alternative collective decision-making process is confused and ineffectual. Indeed, the contemporary setting of the play on the margins of a metropolitan skyline at twilight set up a sense of ambiguity and ambivalence, in which the version is neither fully located nor localized. Whilst the intention of Lavaudant was to focus on the contemporary sense of futility and dissatisfaction with politics, enacted as a struggle over metropolitan space,[74] the action is curiously muted, lazy and lethargic, leaving us with the sense that Coriolà is less a warrior than a displaced and confused politician in disguise (Artur Mas, perhaps, in 2002), waiting to inherit what he thinks he deserves, but curiously unable to engage with contemporary discourse. The red earth, stylized battles and silhouette of the city all lend the play a rather expressionist feel, punctuated by the often monotonous recitation of the lines. Only Rosa Novell as Volumnia shines in this version, surrounded by tired, confused and static men.

The representation of the struggle for the city from the margins in some ways mimics the space of the TNC at the edge of the metropolitan centre of Barcelona, in an area redeveloped and rebranded for the International Forum of Cultures in 2004. In many ways it foregrounds what is at stake in the Catalan translation of Shakespeare, if presenting an inadequately realized answer. At its heart is the question of the location of tradition, the relationship to the foreign, and the need to strike a balance between individual action and collaboration. It raises the question of representation, both of who is entitled to speak for whom, and what makes a story acceptable or meaningful, yet tells this story through a figure who according to Loayza 'sent aversió a la paraula, un element ben indicatiu de la importància que Shakespeare atorgava a l'eloqüència' ('feels an aversion for words, an element which is indicative of the importance Shakespeare gave to eloquence').[75] Perhaps the answer is in the posters and on the front cover of the programme, in a call to Catalan audiences to decide, to lend their voices and their votes. 'Què és la ciutat sinó la gent, el poble?' ('What is the city, if not the people, the nation?').

NOTES

1. De Man, *The Resistance to Theory* (1986), p. 86.
2. For further exploration of this issue, see Buffery, 'The Meaning of Shakespeare'.
3. See appendix C for details. There is mention of another performance in Codina, but this probably refers to the 1986 version at the Festival Grec, performed in Castilian. The amateur production was reviewed by X. Fàbregas in *Avui* (23 November 1977). Whilst critical of the production, he suggests that 'La presència de Coriolà a l'escenari [...] és un fet que magnetitza. O que hauria de magnetitzar'. Reproduced in *Teatre en viu (1977–1982)*, ed. Maryse Badiou (Barcelona: Institut del Teatre, 1995), p. 96. The Lavaudant production was also criticized for its lack of dynamism. A further version was staged in theatre workshops at the Institut del Teatre in 1999, directed by Francesc Nel·lo.
4. For extensive information on the Comédie Française version of *Coriolanus*, and the troubles it provoked see 'Shakespeare and and the General Strike', in Hawkes, *Meaning by...*, pp. 42–60 and D. Daniell, *'Coriolanus' in Europe* (London: Athlone Press, 1980), pp. 18–19, 60–4.
5. The introduction to the 1983 edition of the Sagarra version of *Coriolà* cites Balaguer's, rather ambiguously, as a 'modesta aportació al tema'. It also contains a number of other inaccuracies as to the history of Coriolanus translation, the main purpose of the introduction being to convince the reader of Sagarra's superiority. 'Calia posseir en grau superlatiu l'instint del teatre unit a l'instint de la llengua per a aconseguir una traducció de la desimboltura, la frescor i la qualitat literària de la present.' *Coriolà* (Barcelona: Institut del Teatre-Bruguera, 1983), pp. 6–7.
6. In the foreword to the Catalan version in V. Balaguer, *Tragedias*, 3rd

edn (Madrid: Manuel Tello, 1882), p. 22, there is the note that 'El autor ha escrito esta escena según la versión de Plutarco'.

7   Professor Don Cruikshank cites Calderón's *Las armas de la hermosura* (?1652) and the earlier *El privilegio de las mujeres* (pre-1636), written in conjunction with Coello and Pérez de Montalbán, as examples. Yet he classes Balaguer's Spanish version of *Coriolano* (1877) as a free adaptation of Shakespeare's play. From unpublished notes for projected editions of parallel texts of Shakespeare's plays in Spain.

8   'Els parlaments de Coriolanus a Tul·lus Aufidius y de Volumnia a Coriolanus en el quint acte, són poc menys que literalment transcrits per Shakespeare de Plutarch'. J. Perpiñà, *La tragedia de Coriolanus* (Barcelona: La Renaixensa, 1917), p. 242.

9   Instead of Tullus Aufidius, Balaguer introduces a character called Lavinius, which would hold with Plutarch being the main source in that Tullus Aufidius barely merits a mention in the early chronicle. In Shakespeare it is Menenius who is the most important suer for peace. To compare versions, I have made use of North's translation of Plutarch in the Arden edition of *Coriolanus* and Carles Riba's translation of Plutarch, Plutarc, *Vides Paral·leles, I, v. Coriolà i Alcibíades, Demòstenes i Cicerò* (Barcelona: Fundació Bernat Matge, 1928).

10 Balaguer, *Coriolanus*, in *Tragedias*, 1879.

11 The first translator of *Macbeth* into Catalan, as we have seen, he attempts to translate the complete works into Castilian.

12 This is how it appears in Palau's *Manual del librero*, XXI, p. 163, as the only date that appears on the first edition is Morera's date of completion of the version which he gives as 17 August 1915. See Magí Morera i Galícia, *Coriolà* (Barcelona: Editorial Catalana, 1918), p. 191. Perpiñà's translation was, in fact, completed in 1914, long before its eventual publication. See his introduction, p. 6.

13 The earliest reference to the publication is an advertisement in *La Esquella de la Torratxa*, under the heading of *Ultimas Novedades* (23 August 1918), 551.

14 Because it is part of the second Calíope volume, it can be surmised that it was published between 1945 and 1949.

15 The date of Ferrater's translation is given by his brother in Gabriel Ferrater, *Papers, cartes, paraules*, ed. Joan Ferraté, (Barcelona: Quaderns Crema, 1986), p. 12. Xavier Fàbregas is the source of additional information that the translation was commissioned by the Centre de Teatre Independent in 'Un Shakespeare dels afores', *Teatre en viu* (1995), p. 96: 'és una traducció molt personal, molt "ferrateriana", i poc respectuosa amb l'original'.

16 In his 'Nota del traductor', Sellent discusses this process: Joan Sellent (trad.), *William Shakespeare. Coriolà* (Barcelona: Proa, 2002), pp. 39–42.

17 In a review of *Coriolà* in *La Revista*, IV, 77 (1 December 1918), 419.

18 Riba, 'Pròleg', *Els poetes d'ara* . . ., p. 7.

19 Reported in *La Ilustració Catalana*, (1 December 1912), 641.

20 Francesc Ferrer i Gironès, *La persecució política de la llengua catalana*

(Barcelona: Edicions 62, 1986). See especially the title of Morera i Galícia's speech to the *Cortes* on 8 July 1916 'Proposició sobre el lliure ús de la Llengua Catalana en la vida interior de Catalunya', p. 131.

21 The first in 1912 to the *Lliga Regionalista* on 'L'error dels dubtes, respecte la personalitat de Shakespeare', the second to the *Ateneo Barcelonès* in 1917 on Shakespearean characters, the third 'Absurditats relatives a la personalitat de Shakespeare'. Morera i Galícia was also to speak on Shakespeare in introductions to performances of two of his translations, *Romeo i Julieta* in 1920 and *El marxant de Venècia* in 1925. There is record of a further conference on a Shakespearean tragedy in 1922 at the *Centre de Dependents del Comerç i la Indústria*, but it has not been possible to locate the text.

22 Esquerra, Shakespeare ... *Shakespeare*, p. 169.

23 Esquerra, Shakespeare ... *Shakespeare*, p. 169.

24 There are rumours of a production in *Esquella de la Torratxa* (28 June 1917), 493, and it is announced again as late as 21 August 1917, 635. See also *La Ilustració Catalana*, XV (26 August 1917), 598. Herman Bonnin's book, *Adrià Gual i l'Escola Catalana d'Art Dramàtic (1913–1923)*, (Barcelona: Rafael Dalmau, 1974) catalogues the many difficulties faced by the playwright and director in producing plays in this period.

25 Farran i Mayoral, *La renovació del teatre*, p. 126.

26 F. Torres y Ferrer, *Antonius y Cleopatra* (Barcelona: Domenech, 1907).

27 *Coriolanus*, The Arden Shakespeare, p. 311, Act V scene iv.

28 See Ferrer Gironès, *La persecució política ...*, ch. 5, 'La Lluita nacional', pp. 93–151.

29 1917 is the date given by A. Bergós i Massó in his 'Vida i obres de Magí Morera i Galícia' published in *Vida Lleidatana* (Número extraordinari dedicat a Magí Morera i Galícia), II, 28 (15 June 1927), 135–42.

30 *Esquella de la Torratxa* (3 August 1917), 565–6.

31 It was Farran i Mayoral who first recommended *Coriolà* as a play full of political lessons in 'L'educació política del poble', *Labor dispersa*, pp. 53–7. The article first appeared on 5 August 1917, soon after Morera's encounter with the military official.

32 From Sagarra's 1958 introduction to the Shakespearean *Tragèdies romanes*, p. 8.

33 From the introduction to the Institut del Teatre edition of Sagarra's *Coriolà* (Barcelona: Institut del Teatre-Bruguera, 1983), p. 6.

34 From Sagarra's introduction to the 1958 and 1959 editions of the Roman plays and the tragedies, reproduced also in the Institut del Teatre edition of *Coriolà*, p. 6.

35 Reproduced in Joan Puig i Ferreter, *Textos sobre teatre*, ed. G.-J. Graells (Barcelona: Institut del Teatre, 1982), p. 21.

36 V. Solé de Sojo, 'Orientacions perilloses', *Gaseta Catalana d'Art Dramàtic*, 3 (June 1917), 1: 'Els pobles tenen, ademés una personalitat ideològica i sentimental, que es tradueix en l'obra dels seus grans dramaturgs. Aixís els romans de Shakespeare es comporten com a grans anglesos, i l'esperit d'Anglaterra batega

igualment en les obres shakespearianes d'assumpte històric que en les que la faula és característicament nacional'.

37 The essay was originally published in *La Revista* in 1918 before being incorporated into the 1921 volume, *Escolis i altres articles*. Carles Riba, 'Elogi del poeta traductor' (1918), *Obres completes*, II, 1, pp. 85–7.

38 The preferential treatment given by Noucentistes to poetry and the essay is something cited in many general works of Catalan literature. A recent example is George and London (eds), *Contemporary Catalan Theatre*, p. 13.

39 Hamlet is presented as being a more appropriate representation of the latter, although this figuration is subsequently revised in Riba's 1920 meditation on Morera i Galícia's *Hàmlet*, 'Al marge de Hamlet', (1920), *Obres completes*, II, 1, pp.151–2.

40 The other possible operation of pride, the kind of disdain for the masses traced in histories of Modernism in England, is a tantalizing presence behind the disinterested, supposedly progressive, 'orgull' eulogized by Riba. It should be remembered that there were readings of *Coriolanus* which saw it as a reflection of Shakespeare's personal pride. Benedetto Croce criticizes Brandes for suggesting that 'Coriolano, con su desdén por la lisonja, encarna la actitud del propio Shakespeare con respecto al público y la crítica'. In *Shakespeare* (Buenos Aires: Escuela, 1955), p. 21.

41 Reproduced from the Arden edition, I. i. 35–45, and Morera i Galícia, *Coriolà*, p. 7.

42 It should be remembered that throughout the play competing versions of the Coriolanus story are told, from the tales of heroic deeds told by Menenius to the scandalmongering of Brutus and Sicinius to Tullus Aufidius' 'noble memory'.

43 *Coriolà*, p. 111 and *Coriolanus*, III. ii. 125–9, pp. 226–7.

44 Farran i Mayoral, *Lletres*, X, p. 167.

45 Farran i Mayoral, *Lletres*, X, p. 168.

46 Farran i Mayoral, *Lletres*, X, p. 169.

47 The 'political' nature of Shakespeare plays is very rarely presented as 'ideological'. Instead Shakespeare is usually figured as going beyond local politics, history and the like to engage with the problems at the core of our common humanity. 'El nostre autor va més enllà, va al fons del problema. Ell sap que tots els fets i els esdeveniments són obra del pensament i de l'acció de l'home. L'home serà lliure de pensar i de triar el seu camí; una vegada triat aquest, l'engranatge de la història es posarà en marxa amb totes les seves conseqüencies'. Codina, *'Juli César'*, p. 78.

48 Farran i Mayoral, *Labor dispersa . . .*, p. 53.

49 Farran i Mayoral, *Labor dispersa . . .*, p. 54.

50 Farran i Mayoral, *Labor dispersa . . .*, p. 55

51 Farran i Mayoral, *Labor dispersa . . .*, p. 57.

52 A. Junyent, 'De París, estant – Shakespeare, agitador subversiu', *Mirador* (22 February 1934), 5. All the references which follow on the subject of the riots are from this article and page number.

53 Junyent, 'De París, estant', 5.

54 *Revista de Catalunya*, X (June 1938), 331. It should be remembered that theatre was employed as a vehicle for propaganda both by Republican and Nationalist forces during the Spanish Civil War. Through Tasis, however, it is possible to observe the continued focus on Catalan cultural revival during hostilities.
55 Riba, 'Elogi . . .', p. 87.
56 Farran i Mayoral, *Lletres* . . ., p. 169.
57 Carles Soldevila 'En la mort de Magí Morera i Galícia', *D'Ací D'Allà*, 114 (June 1927), 165.
58 Farran i Mayoral, *Lletres* . . ., p. 169.
59 This recalls reviews of the Gual production of Carner's translation of the *Somni*, where the quality of the translation and the possibilities of the enterprise for the stage were often felt to be something detected despite rather than through the quality of enunciation of the actors.
60 *La Ilustració Catalana*, XV (28 October 1917), 766.
61 *Coriolanus*, I. i. 147–53, p. 106, and *Coriolà*, p. 12. Subsequent references to Morera's translation will be given within the text.
62 Riba, *Els poetes d'ara*, p. 4.
63 Joaquim Molas, *La literatura catalana d'Avantguarda* (Barcelona: Bosch, 1983), p. 35.
64 J. Morató, 'Per la nostra escena. El sentit nacional', *Catalunya*, I (18 July 1914), 460.
65 This blurring between the 'real' and the 'metaphorical' continues to be found in later essays about theatre and representation.
66 Note that only Morera and Perpiñà maintain 'veus' in their translation of Coriolanus' 'Most sweet voices'. All more recent translators opt for the disambiguating use of 'vots'.
67 *Teatre*, 5 (April 1934), 68–9.
68 Oliva's critique of other versions is usually based on unsatisfactory prosody. Sagarra he believes allows meaning to become a slave to the verse form, and other attempts to use the decasyllable to translate Shakespeare often result in bad verse because meaning is subordinated to the line length, which makes the plays unplayable in his opinion. However, although he shows Ferrater to have fallen into this trap, he still admits himself to be indebted to the famous poet's versions of the first two acts, signalling evidence of this influence as homage to the poet who, in his opinion, has left us the best example of Shakespeare translation ever produced in Catalan.
69 *Papers, cartes, paraules*, p. 444.
70 Perpiñà, *La tragedia de Coriolanus*, p. 7.
71 'De totes maneres el repte de Cervantes me dexa molt impressionat per nous atreviments d'aquesta mena'. Perpiñà, *La tragedia de Coriolanus*, p. 8.
72 *HLC* IX, p. 72.
73 In Sellent (trans.), *William Shakespeare, Coriolà*, p. 9.
74 See interview with Georges Lavaudant by Carme Tierz in *Teatre BCN*, 27 (Feburary 2002), 18–21.
75 Sellent (trans.), *William Shakespeare, Coriolà*, p. 20.

Conclusions

The history of Shakespeare traced in this book does not end with the *Coriolanus* texts analysed in the final chapter, nor would it had the study ended with the most recent translation or production. Instead of uncovering a seamless narrative of continuous progression from a unified origin, what has been revealed is the non-existence of an original or essential Shakespeare, except through his subsequent rhetorical figuration. It is a history which manifests itself differently in each and every reader of Shakespeare, to be observed in the readings of the translations themselves. If one were to approach the 'common reader' in Catalonia and ask them what was the significance of *Macbeth*, let alone 'What happens in *Hamlet*?', the answer would depend as much on their own personal history, and the context in which they find themselves (including their perception of the questioner's expectations), as on any previous encounters with or knowledge of Shakespeare. It might be perceived as simply a tragic story, or a parable on the horrors of war and ambition, of the need for peaceful collaborative government or even of the hardships of colonialism. It is a play which both calls for judgement and defies it, in its tantalizing blurring of causality. The judgement of the play may indeed be unconscious, or a particular moral or 'virtue' imposed, following Carner's *Dream*. C. A. Jordana's rendering of a children's version of *Macbeth* focuses on the 'seny' of Duncan, and the disaster individual ambition brought to an independent nation, as the lesson to be learned. At the other extreme of readings, Tamzin Townsend's 1996 production of *Macbeth* called for a rejection of political readings, a return to the mental anguish of the Macbeths as mere toys in the three witches' games, whilst La Fura dels Baus (2000) and Calixto Bieito (2002) foreground the violence born of desire and obsession. However, all these positions reflect other discourses, other possibilities, with or without their knowledge.

Tamzin Townsend's production was surrounded by excitement in the press at the prospect of discovering the 'real' Shakespeare, through the eyes of a privileged – because British – director. Yet within the play itself, the only English used was in the incantations of the witches, offering an interesting counterpoint to the spell Townsend sought to cast on her audience. The ending of the play contrived to suggest the witches' spell would be cast once more, on the victors of the fray, simultaneously drawing attention to the repetition of the story, to the existence of other *Macbeth*s beyond Townsend's personal apprehension of the 'truth'. Bieito's staging (see fig 16), like almost all his versions of Shakespeare, draws on contemporary culture to frame his reading of Shakespeare as our contemporary, defending his transgressive reading of the play, in which the Macbeths' victims are dispatched by ever more ingenious means, with recourse to Nick Cave's rendering of 'Death is not the end'. It is Shakespeare's very translatability, his canonicity, that sanctions such a variety of afterlives.

Although directors such as Townsend might wish for a return to the innocent reading of Shakespeare, unburdened by centuries of cultural commentary, it is not possible to turn back the tide of history, in fact they themselves merely represent another wave in the immense sea of interpretations described by Oliva in his consideration of *Hamlet*. Many of the Catalan (trans)figurations of Shakespeare explored in each of the chapters produce a sense of recognition: of figuration as repetition, the mirror up to nature – or at least the mirror up to what the reader conceives to be natural. We see the Shakespeare who is the supreme tragedian, the Shakespeare who offers a pattern for the theatre, the Shakespeare who is an immense lexicon, the Shakespeare who contains contemporary humanity, and ultimately Bloom's figure, the Shakespeare who is all things to all men. However, there is a danger in such recognition, of perceiving little more than one's own desire for recognition, glossing over the differences. There is a danger of forgetting that Shakespeare means nothing, stands for nothing unless figured, translated or transfigured.

The history traced in this book has sought to embrace both sameness and difference, to reveal where Catalan figurations of Shakespeare borrow from cultural discourse outside of Catalonia, but also how that discourse becomes domesticated and transfigured within a new context. This does not mean that the final conclusion is one that points to the inherent inclusiveness of

Shakespeare: his meaning, his figuring everything. Instead this history has shown how even such a representation is culturally constructed, and perhaps underpinned by the little hard information about Shakespeare that remained for posterity. So it is that Shakespeare's figuration may be represented in terms of the 'heroic' mould, where Shakespeare can be fully recovered and be figured 'truthfully' for the glory of a culture, and yet there is also a humbler, 'antiheroic' version produced by the impression that part of Shakespeare's figuration is inevitably wrapped in its impossibility. In terms of Catalan translation of Shakespeare, this has been observed in the pull between 'orgull' and humility as key words in the enterprise of cultural appropriation, and between representations of a history of Catalan achievement in this field, which for many decades held Sagarra at its centre, and anxieties at their inadequacy when compared with the great Anglo-American Shakespeare empire.

Although there is indeed a sense of Shakespeare having multiple meanings, as being always already a site of difference, certain patterns and crossroads have appeared in Catalonia. The plays that prove most interesting are, through no accident, plays which themselves explore the different implications of representation: in terms of translation and communication, theatre and identity, but also cultural understanding and democracy. Each recasting of the story positions itself within the debate over representation, whether overtly, as in Carner's presentation of his *Somni*, or inadvertently, such as perhaps Oliva's call for the triumph of the individual in *Coriolà*, revealing the different cultural and historical pressures surrounding the moment of translation.

In many ways, this history reads as a rhetorical history of *Noucentisme*, as was discussed towards the end of chapter 5. The beginnings of extensive figuration of Shakespeare coincide with the purported origins of that movement. Notwithstanding later rejection of the politics of *Noucentisme*, the rhetoric surrounding Shakespeare's figuration has remained. Many of the writers who welcome the popular editions of Sagarra's translations in the 1980s have recourse to terms such as 'joia', 'empresa' and 'aventura', representing the gains to be made for Catalan culture from successful figuration of Shakespeare. In effect, Shakespeare's transfiguration continues to be represented in terms of cultural conquest.

This final observation brings us to the meaning of 'translating imperialism' within the context of the texts and discourses uncovered in the course of this study. Imperialism can stand for Shakespeare's cultural authority, for his representation of the origins of Empire, for the conquest of literary worlds, myths which can be read in all cultures, as was perceived as early as Víctor Balaguer, in his translation of the Romeo and Juliet story. All these types of 'imperialism' have been translated in the course of Shakespeare's figuration. More specifically, the representation of the translation enterprise during *Noucentisme* might itself be perceived as a 'translating imperialism', both in its desire for cultural conquest and the necessity to impose such conquests on the shape of Catalonia. Most of all, however, it represents the very process of political, rhetorical and representational negotiation involved in the translation of 'culture'.

Appendix A
Catalan Translations of Shakespeare

Year	Work	Translator	Edition
1874	Oth.	A. Coma	*Otello il moro di Valenzia. Paroddia scrita in versi per...*, Barcelona: Barcelonesa.
1878	Rom.	V. Balaguer	*Las esposallas de la morta*, Barcelona: *Revista Catalana de la Literatura, Ciencias y Arts*, 1 (31 October 1878). 2nd edn, Barcelona: La Renaixensa.
1879	Rom.	V. Balaguer	*Las esposallas de la morta*, in *Novas Tragedias*, Barcelona: La Renaixensa, pp. 13–53 (2 editions this year).
1880	Hml.	J. Franquesa i Gomis	'Hamlet y Ofelia', III.i., with introduction by E. Tamaro and folio illustration by José Narváez, *La Ilustració Catalana*, I (30 August 1880), 43–46.
1881	Rom.	J. M. Codolsa	Parody. *Las ventallas de la porta. Sabaterada en dos cuadros escénicos, escrita en vers y en català del que tothom enten per...*, Barcelona: Espanyola.
1882	Rom.	V. Balaguer	*Tragedias*. Also contains *Coriolà* and *La sombra de César*. Versions in Catalan and Castilian. Madrid: Tello (3rd edn).
1884	Oth.	A. Ferrer y Codina	*Otel·lo o il moro di... Parodia en un acto y en prosa itaiana macarrónica*, Barcelona: Peninsular de Mariol y López.
1884	Hml.	O. de Llanza	'Hamlet. Monòlech', *L'Avens*, 32 (15 June), 322.

Year	Work	Translator	Edition
1885	Hml.	A. Bulbena i Tosell	Date of completion.
1890	Hml.	C. Barallat	V.i., in 'Memoria leída en la Real Academia de las Buenas Letras', 1 December.
1890	Rom.	V. Balaguer	*Tragedias.* Madrid: Tello (6th edn).
1891	Rom.	V. Balaguer	*Tragedias,* Barcelona: Tasso.
1893	Rom.	V. Balguer	*Tragedias,* Barcelona: Biblioteca Popular Catalana.
1894	Rom.	V. Balaguer	*Las esposalles de la morta,* Barcelona: 'Lo Teatro Regional.'
1896	Hml.	C. Barallat	V.i., in *Shakespeare y Moratín ante la fosa y traducción catalana de un cuadro de Shakespeare,* Barcelona: Jaime Jepús, pp. 11–23.
1896	Oth.	A. Coma	*Otello il moro di Valenzia,* Barcelona: Biblioteca de 'Lo Teatro Regional'.
1898	Hml.	A. Masriera	*Hamlet. Príncep de Dinamarca. Tragedia de Guillem Shakespeare. Versió catalana de . . . ,* Barcelona: 'L'Atlantida'.
1898	Hml.	G. Soler	*Hamlet-Drama en tres actes y en vers. Original de Shakspeare. Traduhit y arreglat á l'escena católica per G.S. (Angel Guerra),* Barcelona: Altés (Biblioteca de 'La Talia Catalana' 3).
1902	Oth.	A. Coma	As above, Barcelona: F. Badia (3rd edn).
1903	Sonn.	R. Font y Presas	'Sonet. Pentámetres iambichs', *Catalunya,* 12 (30 June), 548. Sonnet XX.
1904	Oth.	A. Par	'Othello–Quart acte', *Catalunya* (May 1904), 5–15.
1903	Tw.	C. Capdevila	*La festa dels reis*: date of completion. Performed January 1904.
1905	Wiv.	A. Gual	*Les alegres comediantes*: original play containing sections translated from *The Merry Wives of Windsor,* first performed. Published 1913.

Year	Work	Translator	Edition
1906	Lucr.	A. Par	*El forçament de Lucreça*. Lecture to Associació Wagneriana, 25 June, with translation of sections of the poem. Published 1908.
1906	Oth.	J. Massó i Torrents	Unpublished. Manuscript copy in Biblioteca de Catalunya (MS. 1700). There is clear evidence that the translation was begun in or after 1901 and continued in 1903–5. It was to be published as Biblioteca Popular de 'L'Avenç' vol. 55. The manuscript shows evidence of later additions and corrections in the 1910s.
1907	JC	S.Vilaregut	*Julius César. Drama en cinc actes*, Barcelona: Domènech (Biblioteca Popular dels Grans Mestres I).
1907	Ant.	F. Torres Ferrer	*Antonius y Cleopatra*, Barcelona: Domènech (Biblioteca Popular dels Grans Mestres II).
1907	H4A	J. Sandaran Bacaria	*Enric IV (Primera Part)*, Barcelona: Domènech (Biblioteca Popular dels Grans Mestres IV).
1907	Tw.	C. Capdevila	*La festa dels reis o lo que vulgueu. Comèdia en cinc actes*, Barcelona: Domènech (Biblioteca Popular dels Grans Mestres V).
1907	Mcb.	C. Montoliu	*La tragedia de Macbeth*. Barcelona: 'L'Avenç'.
1908	Mcb.	C. Montoliu	*La tragedia de Macbeth*. Barcelona: 'L'Avenç' (2nd edn).
1908	Mcb.	C. Montoliu	Barcelona: 'L'Avenç' (Biblioteca Popular de l'Avenç 74), without introduction or notes.
1908	Mcb.	D. Ruiz	Barcelona: Domènech (Biblioteca Popular dels Grans Mestres VI).

Year	Work	Translator	Edition
1908	Lucr.	A. Par	'El forçament de Lucreça', *XXV Conferències dades en La Associació Wagneriana*, Barcelona: Verdaguer, pp. 470–92.
1908	Shr.	J. Farran i Mayoral	*La feréstega domada*, Barcelona: Domènech (Biblioteca Popular dels Grans Mestres VII).
1908	Mids.	J. Carner	*El somni d'una nit d'estiu*, Barcelona: Domènech (Biblioteca Popular dels grans Mestres III).
1908	Mids.	R. Vives i Pastor	'La traducció del Somni', *Teatralia*, 5 (15 November), 132–5. Fragment of V.i. 2 versions, as well as that of Carner. Claims also translated *The Tempest*.
1908	Lr.	A. Albert Torrellas	*El rei Lear. Tragèdia en cinc actes*, Barcelona: Domènech (Biblioteca Popular dels Grans Mestres VIII).
1908	LLL	M. Raventós	*Treball d'amor endebades*, Barcelona: Domènech (Biblioteca Popular dels Grans Mestres IX).
1909	Merch.	J. Puig i Ferreter	*El marxant de Venècia*, Barcelona: Domènech (Biblioteca Popular dels Grans Mestres X).
1909	Wint.	V. Caldes Arús	*Conte d'hivern*, Barcelona: Domènech (Biblioteca Popular dels Grans Mestres XI).
1909	Wiv.	J. Carner	*Les alegres comares de Windsor*, Barcelona: Domènech (Biblioteca Popular dels Grans Mestres XII).
1909	John	J. Martí Sabat	*El Rei Joan*. Barcelona: Domènec (Biblioteca Popular dels Grans Mestres XIII).
1909	Ado	R. Pomés Soler	*Molt soroll per res*, Barcelona: Domènech (Biblioteca Popular dels Grans Mestres XIV).
1909	All's	F. Girbat Jaume	*Tot va bé si acaba bé*, Barcelona: Domènech (Biblioteca Popular dels Grans Mestres XV).

Appendix A

Year	Work	Translator	Edition
1909	Sonn.	C. Riba	Sonnets LXXI, CVI, XXXII, CXXVII, XVII. Undated prose translations, latest possible completion date. Published 1990.
1910	Tp.	J. Carner	*La Tempesta*, Barcelona: Domènech (Biblioteca Popular dels Grans Mestres XVI).
1910	Hml.	A. Bulbena i Tosell	*Guillem Shakespere. Hamlet. Príncep de Dinamarca. Versió en prosa literària, del anglès directament traslladad y per primera volta apropriada a la catalana escena per . . .*, Barcelona: F. Giró.
1910	Hml.	?	Fragment of III.ii., in 'Parla Shakespeare', *De tots colors* (6 May), 274–5.
1911	Hml.	A. Masriera	Fragment of III.ii., in J. Baldrich, 'L'art de representar segons Shakespeare', *Joventut Teatral* (6 April), 535.
1911	Hml.	P. M. de Tirs	Fragments in translated Coleridge essay on '*Hamlet*', *De tots colors* (28 April), 258–63, 274–8.
1911	Rom.	V. Balaguer	*Les esposalles de la morta*, Barcelona: Salvador Bonavia.
1912	Lr.	A. Par	*Lo rei Lear*, Barcelona: F. Giró, 1912.
1912	Sonn.	M. Morera i Galícia	*XXIV Sonets de Shakespeare*, Vilanova i la Geltrú: Oliva.
1912	Sonn.	M. Morera i Galícia	Sonnets LXXIII and LXXIV, *La Ilustració Catalana*, 484 (15 September), 493; Sonnets XXVII, XXX and CXLVI, *La Ilustració Catalana*, 495 (1 December), 641.
1913	Sonn.	M. Morera i Galícia	Sonnets L, LI, *La Ilustració Catalana*, (20 April), 24, and XCVIII (14 December), 606.
1913	Sonn.	M. Morera i Galícia	*Selecta de sonets de Shakespeare.* Vilanova i la Geltrú: Oliva.

Year	Work	Translator	Edition
1913	H4A	J. Farran i Mayoral	'Una escena de *Enric IV* de Shakespeare', *Catalunya*, 278 (8 February).
1913	Wiv.	A. Gual	*Les alegres comediantes* (see above 1905) published. Barcelona: A. Artés.
1914	Misc.	M. Morera i Galícia	Fragments of *Love's Labour's Lost* and *Antony and Cleopatra*, 'Proemi' to *Selecta de Sonets*, reproduced in *Catalunya* (10 January).
1914	Cor.	J. Perpiñà	Completion date.
1915	Hml.	Johannus	Fragment of V.i., *El Teatre Català*, 150 (9 January), 40.
1915	Hml.	Johannus	Fragment of III.ii., in 'Pàgines d'Or', *El Teatre Català*, 181 (14 August), 540–1.
1915	Sonn.	M. Morera i Galícia	Sonnet CXLIII, 'Dels sonets de Shakespeare', *Almanach de la Poesia*, I (June).
1915	Cor.	M. Morera i Galícia	Completion date, 17 August.
1915	Phoen.	M. Morera i Galícia	'El fenix i la tortra', *La Revista*, 5 (10 September), 9–10.
1916	Ven.	M. Morera i Galícia	Fragment in *La Revista*, 14 (19 June), 4.
1917	Cor.	J. Perpiñà	*La Tragedia de Coriolanus*, Barcelona: La Renaixensa.
1917	Ven.	M. Morera i Galícia	*Venus i Adonis*, Barcelona: 'La Revista' (Col·lecció de lírics mundials 1).
1917	Hml.	I. Iglésias	Fragment of III. i., in *L'encís de la glòria*. See *Obres completes d'Ignasi Iglésias*, X, Barcelona: Minerva, 1933, pp. 316–19.
1918	Ven.	M. Morera i Galícia	As above, 2nd edn.
1918	Hml.	M. Morera i Galícia	Fragment of III. iii., *Catalana*, I (1918), 189.
1918	Cor.	M. Morera i Galícia	*Coriolà*, Barcelona: Editorial Catalana (Biblioteca Literària 8).

Appendix A

Year	Work	Translator	Edition
1918	Hml.	A. Bulbena i Tosell	*La novel·la nova*, 48, Barcelona: Imprenta Rafals.
1919	Rom.	Víctor Balaguer	*Les esposalles de la morta (Julieta i Romeu) i El guant del degollat*, in *La Escena Catalana*, 35 (June).
1919	Sonn.	M. Morera i Galícia	Sonnet XVII, *La Revista*, 100–1 (1 December), 346.
1919	Sonn.	M. Morera i Galícia	*XXIV Sonets de Shakespeare*, as above, 2nd edn.
1920	Hml.	M. Morera i Galícia	*Hàmlet*, Barcelona: Editorial Catalana (Biblioteca Literària 25).
1920	Rom.	M. Morera i Galícia	*Romeu i Julieta*. Translation completed for Escola Catalana d'Art Dramàtic.
1921	Sonn.	M. Morera i Galícia	Sonnets III, XX, XXXVII, XXXVIII, LIX, CXXX, *La Revista*, 139 (1 July), 200–2 (from *Nou i vell*).
1921	Sonn. Phoen. Ven.	M. Morera i Galícia	Sonnets III, IX, XVIII, XX, XXXVII, XXXVIII, LV, LIX, LXVIII, LXXXV, CXXVII, CXXX, CXXXI, 'El fènix i la tortra' and 'Venus i Adonis', *Nou i Vell*, Barcelona: Oliva de Vilanova, pp. 69–127.
1923	Rom.	M. Morera i Galícia	*Romeu i Julieta*, Barcelona: Editorial Catalana (Biblioteca Literària 62).
1923	Mids.	A. Maseras	Date of completion on typescript in Institut del Teatre library, 1482–2–3. Intended for production.
1924	Sonn.	M. Morera i Galícia	*Els poetes d'ara. Magí Morera i Galícia*, with prologue by C. Riba, Barcelona: Omega.
1924	Merch.	J. Puig i Ferreter	*El marxant de Venècia*, Barcelona: Garrofé (La comèdia catalana 11), new edition.
1924	Merch.	M. Morera i Galícia	*El marxant de Venècia*, Barcelona: Editorial Catalana (Biblioteca Literària 78).
1925	Ado	J. Lleonart.	*Molta remor i poca saó de Shakespeare*, fragments of II i and IV, *La Revista*, 231 (1 May), 130–5.

Year	Work	Translator	Edition
1925	Merch.	M. Morera i Galícia	Fragment of III, *Comèdia*, 3 (15 March), 13.
1925	Sonn.	M. Morera i Galícia	Sonnet XXX, *Comèdia*, 3 (15 March), 11.
1926	Tp.	J. Farran i Mayoral	*La Tempestat*, notice of near completion in *Theatron*, 1 (October), 7.
1927	JC	M. Morera i Galícia	Date of completion, 10 January, given in letter from Morera to Gual. Unpublished.
1927	Mcb.	M. Morera i Galícia	Fragment of V.i., (manuscript reproduction), in *Vida Lleidatana*, 28 (15 June), 112.
1927	Sonn. Ven.	M. Morera i Galícia	Sonnets XII, XXXVII, LV, LXXV and CXXX, and fragment of *Venus i Adonis*, *Vida Lleidatana*, 28 (15 June), 104–6, 111.
1927	Ven.	M. Morera i Galícia	As above, 1917.
1927	Tp.	R. Negre	'La tempestat', translated from C. Lamb's *Tales of Shakespeare*, *Llegiu-me*, 4 (January), 29–38.
1927	Wint.	R. Negre	'Rondalla hivernenca', as above, *Llegiu-me*, 6 (March), 236–42, 311.
1927	Mcb.	R. Negre?	'Macbeth', as above, *Llegiu-me*, 10 (July), 615–22.
1927	Mids.	R. Negre?	'El somni d'una nit d'estiu', as above, *Llegiu-me*, 13 (October), 883–90.
1927	Sonn. Ven. Rom.	M. Morera i Galícia	Sonnet CXLVI, stanzas 195–199 of 'Venus' and a fragment of V,i,, 'Pàgines antològiques', *La Nova Revista*, 6 (June), 97–102.
1927	Sonn. Phoen. Ven.	M. Morera i Galícia	As above, *Nou i vell*, 1921.
1928	Shr.	M. Duran Tortajada	*La indomable, domada*. Unable to find details.
1928	Sonn.	J. López-Picó	'A l'ànima', gloss of sonnet CXLVI, *La Revista*, XIV (January–June), 37.

Year	Work	Translator	Edition
1928	Sonn.	C. Montoriol Puig	Sonnet CXL, *Joia*, (1 March).
1928	Sonn.	C. Montoriol Puig	*Els sonets de Shakespeare*, Barcelona: Verdaguer.
1928	Mcb.	C. A. Jordana	Barcelona: Barcino (Col·lecció Popular Barcino 35).
1928	Meas.	S. Vilaregut	*La novícia de Sta. Clara*, arrangement, *La Escena Catalana*, 274 (November).
1929	Mids.	A. Maseras	*Somni d'una nit d'estiu*, Barcelona: Barcino (Col·lecció Popular Barcino 50).
1929	Mcb.	C. A. Jordana	*La història de Macbeth. Explicada als infans segons la obra de Shakespeare*, Barcelona: Proa (Biblioteca Grumet 49).
1929	Ado	S. Vilaregut	*¡Com més petita és la nou!*, arrangement, *La Escena Catalana*, 289 (May).
1929	Rom.	R. Llates	'Romeu i Julieta', translated from Bandello's novella, Barcelona: Catalonia (Biblioteca 'Univers' IX).
1929	Oth.	J. Perpiñà	*La Tragedia d'Othel·lo*, Barcelona: La Renaixença.
1930	Caes.	C. A. Jordana	*Julius Cèsar*, Barcelona: Barcino (Els Clàssics del món I, Obres de Shakespeare I), pp. 29–120.
1930	Ant.	C. A. Jordana	*Antoni i Cleopatra. Drama en cinc actes*, Barcelona: Barcino (Clàssics del món I, Obres de Shakespeare I), pp. 121–251.
1930	Cymb.	C. Montoriol Puig	*G. Shakespeare. Cimbelí. Tragèdia en cinc actes*, Barcelona: 'La Revista'.
1930	Cymb.	C. Montoriol Puig	*Cimbelí. Tragèdia en cinc actes*, *La Revista*, XVI (January–June), 17–78.
1930	Shr.	C. A. Jordana	*L'amansiment de la fera*, Barcelona: Barcino (Els Clàssics del món III, Obres de Shakespeare II), pp. 77–168.

Year	Work	Translator	Edition
1930	Tp.	C. A. Jordana	*La Tempestat. Comèdia en cinc actes*, Barcelona: Barcino (Els Clàssics del món 3, Obres completes de Shakespeare II), pp. 8–76.
1930	Gent.	C. A. Jordana	*Els dos cavallers de Verona. Comèdia en cinc actes*, Barcelona: Barcino (Els Clàssics del món, 3 Obres Completes de Shakespeare II), pp. 169–253.
1930	Shr.	E. Giménez Lloberes	*La fera amansida. Versió catalana d'* . . ., first put on in 1930s. Unable to verify details.
1931	Sonn.	M. Morera i Galícia	*Selecta de sonets de Shakespeare*, Vilanova i la Geltrú: Oliva.
1931	Hml.	J. Millàs-Raurell	Fragment of III.iv, based on Morera i Galícia's translation, in *La mare de Hamlet, La Escena Catalana*, 336.
1931	Tp. Troil.	C. A. Jordana	Caliban's song and fragment of Troilus in 'Actualitats de Shakespeare', *D'Ací D'Allà*, XX (December), 450. Signed Arnau de Bellcaire (pseudonym).
1932	Troil.	C. A. Jordana	*Troilus i Cressida. Drama en cinc actes*, Barcelona: Barcino (Els Clàssics del món 6, Obres Completes de Shakespeare III), pp. 5–128.
1932	Tim.	C. A. Jordana	*Timó d'Atenes. Tragèdia en cinc actes*, Barcelona: Barcino (Els Clàssics del món 6, Obres Completes de Shakespeare III), pp. 129–216.
1932	Rom.	C. A. Jordana	*Romeu i Julieta*, Barcelona: Barcino (Els Clàssics del món 7, Obres Completes de Shakespeare IV), pp. 5–165.
1932	Oth.	C. A. Jordana	*Otel·lo. Tragèdia en cinc actes*, Barcelona: Barcino (Els clàssics del món 7, Obres completes de Shakespeare IV), pp. 167–215.
1934	Tw.	C. Montoriol Puig	*La nit de reis o el que vulgueu, La Revista*, XX (July–December), 41–75.

Year	Work	Translator	Edition
1934	Ant.	M. Manent	Fragment of *Antoni i Cleopatra*, V, in *Notes sobre literatura estrangera*, Barcelona: Publicacions de 'La Revista', pp. 47–8.
1934	Cor.	M. Morera i Galícia	Fragments of II and III, 'El *Coriolà* de Shakespeare', *El Teatre*, 5 (April), 68–9.
1935	Tw.	C. Montoriol Puig	*La nit de reis o el que vulgueu. Comèdia en cinc actes*, Barcelona: 'La Revista'.
1935	Misc.	J. M. de Sagarra	Date of publication given on the seven volumes. See below.
1938	Sonn.	C. A. Jordana	Unpublished.
1938	Sonn.	M. Manent	2 poems in *Versions de l'anglès*, Barcelona: Residència d'Estudiants.
1944	Hml.	R. Vinyes	Assorted fragments, *Hamlet, dramaturg*. Unpublished until 1980s.
1944–5	Misc.	J. M. de Sagarra	'Dues cançons de Shakespeare', *Poesia* (1944–5).
1945	Tp. Rom. Tw. Oth.	J. M. de Sagarra	*Teatre: La Tempesta, Romeo i Julieta, Nit de reis, Otel·lo*, I, Barcelona: Edicions Calíope. The only details on all seven volumes are: Barcelona: 1935.
1946–9	Cor. JC Ant. Tit.	J. M. de Sagarra	*Teatre: Coriolà, Juli Cèsar, Antoni i Cleopatra, Titus Andrònic*, II, as above.
1946–9	As Merch. Ado Mcb.	J. M. de Sagarra	*Teatre: Al vostre gust, El mercader de Venècia, Molt soroll per res, Macbeth*, III, as above.
1946–9	Gent. Shr. Wiv. All's	J. M. de Sagarra	*Teatre: Els dos cavallers de Verona, L'amansiment de l'hàrpia, Les alegres casades de Windsor, A bon fi tot li és camí*, IV, as above.
1946–9	Per. Cymb. Mids. Err.	J. M. de Sagarra	*Teatre: Pericles, Cimbelí, Un somni de nit de Sant Joan, La comèdia dels errors*, V, as above.

Year	Work	Translator	Edition
1949–53	Wint. LLL Meas. Tim.	J. M. de Sagarra	*Teatre: Conte d'hivern, Treball d'amor perdut, Mesura per mesura, Timon d'Atenes*, VI, as above.
1946–53	John H4A H4B R3	J. M. de Sagarra	*Teatre: El rei Joan, El rei Enric IV (Primera i Segona Parts), El rei Ricard III*, VII, as above.
1955	Various	M. Manent	Sonnets XVIII, LXXIII, XCVII, XCVIII; and assorted poems and fragments from the plays, *Poesia anglesa i nord-americana*, Barcelona: Alpha (Clàssics de tots els temps).
1958	JC Ant. Cor.	J. M. de Sagarra	*Tragèdies Romanes*, Barcelona: Alpha (Clàssics de tots els temps 6).
1958	Sonn.	J. Triadú	*Els sonets de Shakespeare*, Barcelona: 'Els cinquanta cinc'.
1959	Rom. Oth. Mcb.	J. M. de Sagarra	*Romeo i Julieta. Otel·lo. Macbeth*, Barcelona: Alpha (Clàssics de tots els temps 8).
1959	Merch. Tp. Shr.	J. M. de Sagarra	*El mercader de Venècia. La Tempestat. L'amansiment de l'hàrpia*, Barcelona: Alpha (Clàssics de tots els temps 9).
1962	Ant.	J. M. de Sagarra M. Manent	Versions of 'La barca de Cleopatra', in J. Palau i Fabre, *El mirall embruixat*, Palma de Mallorca: Moll (Raixa 58), pp. 39–40.
1964	Various	M. Morera i Galícia C. Montoriol M. Manent J. Triadú M. Villangómez	Versions of Shakespeare, in *Poemes*, 8 (Autumn).
1964	Hml.	M. Morera i Galícia	*Hàmlet*, with prologue by Joan Triadú, Barcelona: Selecta (Biblioteca Selecta 366, Traduccions XXX).

Year	Work	Translator	Edition
1968	Rom.	V. Balaguer	*Les esposalles de la morta*, X. Fàbregas (ed.), Barcelona: Edicions 62 (Antologia Catalana 38).
1969	R3	J. M. de Sagarra	*Ricard III*, with introduction by J. M. de Sagarra, Barcelona: Selecta (Biblioteca Selecta 425, Traduccions XXXVIII).
1970	Sonn.	J. Triadú	*40 sonets de Shakespeare. Pròleg, selecció i versions de* . . ., Barcelona: Proa (Ossa Menor 66). New edition of 1958 volume with Picasso print of 'Shakespeare'.
1970	Shr.	A. Díaz-Plaja – J. Batiste	*La feréstega domada*, adaptation for children, Barcelona: La Galera (Teatre Joc d'Equip 4).
1972	Cor.	G. Ferrater	*Coriolà*, I–II, typescript in Institut del Teatre library.
1973	John	J. M. de Sagarra	*El rei Joan*, in *Estudios Escénicos*, 17 (July 1973), 95–175.
1973	Merch.	J. Voltas	*El mercader de Venècia de William Shakespeare*, adaptation for children, Barcelona: La Galera (Teatre Joc d'Equip 10).
1975	Mcb.	J. Pujol Cofan	*La tragèdia de Macbeth. Adaptació de* . . ., Girona: Teatre Independent.
1977	Sonn.	M. Villangómez	In *Noves versions de poesia anglesa i francesa*.
1977	Tit.	J. M. de Sagarra	Sections in programme for Puigserver production.
1978	Shr.	A. Díaz Plaja	As above, 1970 (2nd edn).
1978	Hml.	T. Moix	Fragment of III. iv., in *La Vanguardia*, (28 November 1978), 17. In verse.
1978	Hml.	T. Moix	Completed in Maó and performed on TV and in theatre tour 1979–80.
1979	Poems	M. Villangómez	*Noves versions de poesia anglesa i francesa*, Palma de Mallorca: Moll.
1979	Rom.	J. M. de Sagarra	*Romeo i Julieta*, Barcelona: Institut del Teatre–Bruguera (Col·lecció Popular de Teatre Clàssic Universal 1).

Year	Work	Translator	Edition
1979	Oth.	J. M. de Sagarra	*Otel·lo*, Barcelona: Institut del Teatre–Bruguera (Col·lecció Popular de Teatre Clàssic Universal 2).
1979	Mids.	J. M. de Sagarra	*Un somni de nit de Sant Joan*, Barcelona: Institut del Teatre–Bruguera (Col·lecció Popular de Teatre Clàssic Universal 3).
1980	Sonn.	C. Montoriol	*Sonets*, facsimile of 1928 edition, with prologue by M. Àngels Anglada, Figueres: Banc Industrial dels Pirineus.
1980	Hml.	T. Moix	*William Shakespeare. Hamlet. Príncep de Dinamarca, Traducció directa de l'anglès, pròleg, notes i selecció bibliogràfica de* . . ., Barcelona: Aymà (Quaderns de Teatre ADB).
1980	Mids.	A. Díaz Plaja	*Un somni d'una nit d'estiu*, Barcelona: La Galera (Teatre Joc d'Equip 27).
1980	Mcb.	J. M. de Sagarra	Barcelona: Institut del Teatre–Bruguera (Col·lecció Popular de Teatre Clàssic Universal 4).
1980	Ant.	J. M. de Sagarra	*Antoni i Cleopatra*, Barcelona: Institut del Teatre–Bruguera (Col·lecció Popular de Teatre Clàssic Universal 5).
1980	Wiv.	J. M. de Sagarra	*Les alegres casades de Windsor*, Barcelona: Institut del Teatre–Bruguera (Col·lecció Popular de Teatre Clàssic Universal 6).
1980	Tp.	J. M. de Sagarra	*La Tempestat*, Barcelona: Institut del Teatre–Bruguera (Col·lecció Popular de Teatre Clàssic Universal 7).
1980	All's	J. M. de Sagarra	*A bon fi, tot li és camí*, Barcelona: Institut del Teatre–Bruguera (Col·lecció Popular de Teatre Clàssic Universal 8).
1980	Merch.	J. Voltas	As above, 1973 (2nd edn).
1981	Shr.	A. Díaz Plaja	As above, 1970 (3rd edn).

Appendix A

Year	Work	Translator	Edition
1981	Gent.	J. M. de Sagarra	*Els dos cavallers de Verona*, Institut del Teatre–Bruguera (Col·lecció Popular de Teatre Clàssic Universal 9).
1981	Per.	J. M. de Sagarra	Institut del Teatre–Bruguera (Col·lecció Popular de Teatre Clàssic Universal 10).
1981	JC	J. M. de Sagarra	*Juli Cèsar*, Institut del Teatre–Bruguera (Col·lecció Popular de Teatre Clàssic Universal 11).
1981	Err.	J. M. de Sagarra	*La comèdia dels errors*, Institut del Teatre–Bruguera (Col·lecció Popular de Teatre Clàssic Universal 12).
1981	Rom. Tw.	J. M. de Sagarra	Fragments in J. Vidal i Alcover, 'Josep Maria de Sagarra, traductor', *Estudis escènics*, 23, pp. 87 and 90.
1982	Tit.	J. M. de Sagarra	*Titus Andrònic*, Institut del Teatre–Bruguera (Col·lecció Popular de Teatre Clàssic Universal 13).
1982	Cymb.	J. M. de Sagarra	*Cimbelí*, Institut del Teatre–Bruguera (Col·lecció Popular de Teatre Clàssic Universal 14).
1982	Rom. Merch. Hml. Cor.	M. Morera i Galícia	*Romeu i Julieta, El mercader de Venècia, Hàmlet* and *Coriolà*, in *William Shakespeare. Teatre. Traducció de* . . . revised by Josep Vallverdú, Barcelona: Edicions 62 (Les Millors Obres de la Literatura Universal 15).
1982	Mids.	A. Diaz-Plaja	As above, 1980 (2nd edn).
1982	Merch.	J. Voltas	As above, 1973 (3rd edn).
1982	Sonn.	J. Triadú	*40 sonets de Shakespeare*, Barcelona: Aymà (3rd edn).
1983	Lr.	M. Martines	*El rei Lear, segons l'obra de William Shakespeare, versió de José Luis Giménez Frontín*, Barcelona: Argos Vergara (El drac vermell 11).
1983	Shr.	J. M. de Sagarra	*L'amansiment de l'harpia*, Institut del Teatre–Bruguera (Col·lecció Popular de Teatre Clàssic Universal 15).

Year	Work	Translator	Edition
1983	Cor.	J. M. de Sagarra	*Coriolà*, Institut del Teatre–Bruguera (Col·lecció Popular de Teatre Clàssic Universal 16).
1983	As	J. M. de Sagarra	*Al vostre gust*, Institut del Teatre–Bruguera (Col·lecció Popular de Teatre Clàssic Universal 17).
1983	Wint.	J. M. de Sagarra	*Conte d'Hivern*, Institut del Teatre–Bruguera (Col·lecció Popular de Teatre Clàssic Universal 18).
1983	Mcb.	J. M. de Sagarra	Hecate fragment, *Antologia poètica*, J. Palau i Fabre (ed.), Barcelona: Laie.
1983	Poems	M. Manent	*El gran vent i les heures*. Barcelona: Laertes, 1983. New edition of *Versions de l'anglès*.
1984	Tp.	J. Vinyoli	Ariel's song from II. ii., *Domini màgic*, Barcelona: Empúries.
1984	H4A	J. M. de Sagarra	*El Rei Enric IV. Ia part*, (Revised by J. Costa, A. Mestres and A. Rossinyol) Institut del Teatre–Bruguera (Col·lecció Popular de Teatre Clàssic Universal 19).
1984	Ado	J. M. de Sagarra	*Molt soroll per no res*, (Revised as above) Institut del Teatre–Bruguera (Col·lecció Popular de Teatre Clàssic Universal 20).
1984	H4B	J. M. de Sagarra	*Enric IV. 2a. part*, Institut del Teatre–Bruguera (Col·lecció Popular de Teatre Clàssic Universal 21).
1984	LLL	J. M. de Sagarra	*Treball d'amor perdut*, Institut del Teatre–Bruguera (Col·lecció Popular de Teatre Clàssic Universal 22).
1984	Rom.	S. Oliva	*Romeo i Julieta*, Barcelona: Vicens Vives–TV3 (Obra Dramàtica Completa de Shakespeare I).
1984	R2	S. Oliva	*Ricard II*, Barcelona: Vicens Vives–TV3 (Obra Dramàtica Completa de Shakespeare II).

Appendix A

Year	Work	Translator	Edition
1984	As	S. Oliva	*Al vostre gust*, Barcelona: Vicens Vives–TV3 (Obra Dramàtica Completa de Shakespeare III).
1984	JC	S. Oliva	*Juli Cèsar*, Barcelona: Vicens Vives–TV3 (Obra Dramàtica Completa de Shakespeare IV).
1985	Merch.	J. M. de Sagarra	*El mercader de Venècia*, (Revised as above) Institut del Teatre–Bruguera (Col·lecció Popular de Teatre Clàssic Universal 23).
1985	John	J. M. de Sagarra	*El rei Joan*, (Revised as above) Institut del Teatre–Bruguera (Col·lecció Popular de Teatre Clàssic Universal 24).
1985	Tim.	J. M. de Sagarra	*Timon d'Atenes*, Institut del Teatre–Bruguera (Col·lecció Popular de Teatre Clàssic Universal 25).
1985	Tw.	J. M. de Sagarra	*Nit de reis*, Institut del Teatre–Bruguera (Col·lecció Popular de Teatre Clàssic Universal 26).
1985	Meas.	S. Oliva	*Mesura per mesura*, Barcelona: Vicens Vives–TV3 (Obra Dramàtica Completa de Shakespeare V).
1985	H8	S. Oliva	*Enric VIII*, Barcelona: Vicens Vives–TV3 (Obra Dramàtica Completa de Shakespeare VI).
1985	Tp.	S. Oliva	*La tempesta*, Barcelona: Vicens Vives–TV3 (Obra Dramàtica Completa de Shakespeare VII).
1985	H4A	S. Oliva	*Enric IV (Primera part)*, Barcelona: Vicens Vives–TV3 (Obra Dramàtica Completa de Shakespeare VIII).
1985	Various	S. Oliva, J. Triadú, J. Carner, A. Maseras, J. Vinyoli, J. M. de Sagarra	*Poesia anglesa i nord-americana. Antologia del segle VII al XIX*, Francesc Parcerisas (ed.), Barcelona: Edicions 62–'La Caixa', pp. 113–27. The two S. Oliva sonnets had not been published previously.

Year	Work	Translator	Edition
1986	Ant.	J. M. de Sagarra	*Josep Maria de Sagarra en els seus millors escrits,* Barcelona: Miquel Arimany, pp. 145–9. Death of Cleopatra.
1986	Mcb.	J. M. de Sagarra	*Josep Maria de Sagarra en els seus millors escrits,* as above, 149–54. Conspiracy to kill Banquo.
1986	Err.	J. M. de Sagarra	*Josep Maria de Sagarra en els seus millors escrits,* as above, pp. 154–6.
1986	Meas.	J. M. de Sagarra	*Mesura per mesura,* Institut del Teatre–Bruguera (Col·lecció Popular de Teatre Clàssic Universal 27).
1986	R3	J. M. de Sagarra	*El rei Ricard III,* Institut del Teatre–Bruguera (Col·lecció Popular de Teatre Clàssic Universal 28).
1986	Works	J. M. de Sagarra	*Teatre de William Shakespeare* (3 vols), intro. by J. Coca, Barcelona: Selecta.
1986	H4B	S. Oliva	*Enric IV (Segona part),* Barcelona: Vicens Vives–TV3 (Obra Dramàtica Completa de Shakespeare IX).
1986	H5	S. Oliva	*Enric V,* Barcelona: Vicens Vives–TV3 (Obra Dramàtica Completa de Shakespeare X).
1986	Tw.	S. Oliva	*Nit de reis,* Barcelona: Vicens Vives–TV3 (Obra Dramàtica Completa de Shakespeare XI).
1986	Hml.	S. Oliva	Barcelona: Vicens Vives–TV3 (Obra Dramàtica Completa de Shakespeare XII).
1986	Tim.	S. Oliva	*Timon d'Atenes,* Barcelona: Vicens Vives–TV3 (Obra Dramàtica Completa de Shakespeare XIII).
1986	Cor.	G. Ferrater	*Coriolà,* I–II, in *Papers, cartes, paraules,* J. Ferraté (ed.), Barcelona: Quaderns Crema, pp. 203–97.
1987	Ant.	S. Oliva	*Antoni i Cleopatra,* Barcelona: Vicens Vives–TV3 (Obra Dramàtica Completa de Shakespeare XIV).

Year	Work	Translator	Edition
1987	Err.	S. Mañero/ J. McLucas	*La comèdia de les equivocacions*, Valencia: Consorci d'Editors Valencians.
1987	Wint.	S. Oliva	*Conte d'hivern*, Barcelona: Vicens Vives–TV3 (Obra Dramàtica Completa de Shakespeare XV).
1987	All's	S. Oliva	*Tot va bé si acaba bé*, Barcelona: Vicens Vives–TV3 (Obra Dramàtica Completa de Shakespeare XVI).
1987	Merch.	S. Oliva	*El mercader de Venècia*, Barcelona: Vicens Vives–TV3 (Obra Dramàtica Completa de Shakespeare XVII).
1987	Shr.	S. Oliva	*L'amansiment de la fúria*, Barcelona: Vicens Vives–TV3 (Obra Dramàtica Completa de Shakespeare XVIII).
1987	Mcb.	C. A. Jordana	*Macbeth. William Shakespeare. Adaptació de . . .*, Barcelona: Proa.
1988	Lr.	S. Oliva	*El Rei Lear*, Barcelona: Vicens Vives–TV3 (Obra Dramàtica Completa de Shakespeare XIX).
1988	Wiv.	S. Oliva	*Les alegres casades de Windsor*. Barcelona: Vicens Vives–TV3 (Obra Dramàtica Completa de Shakespeare XX).
1988	Mcb.	S. Oliva	Barcelona: Vicens Vives–TV3 (Obra Dramàtica Completa de Shakespeare XXI).
1988	Troil.	S. Oliva	*Troilus i Cressida*, Barcelona: Vicens Vives–TV3 (Obra Dramàtica Completa de Shakespeare XXII).
1988	Oth.	S. Oliva	*Otel·lo*, Barcelona: Vicens Vives–TV3 (Obra Dramàtica Completa de Shakespeare XXIII).
1989	Mids.	S. Oliva	*El somni d'una nit d'estiu*, Barcelona: Vicens Vives–TV3 (Obra Dramàtica Completa de Shakespeare XXIV).
1989	Mids.	M. Villangómez	*Somni d'una nit de Sant Joan*, Eivissa: Can Sifré.

Year	Work	Translator	Edition
1989	Cor.	S. Oliva	*Coriolà*, Barcelona: Vicens Vives–TV3 (Obra Dramàtica Completa de Shakespeare XXV).
1989	Cymb.	S. Oliva	*Cimbelí*, Barcelona: Vicens Vives–TV3 (Obra Dramàtica Completa de Shakespeare XXVI).
1989	R3	S. Oliva	*Ricard III*, Barcelona: Vicens Vives–TV3 (Obra Dramàtica Completa de Shakespeare XXVII).
1989	Err.	S. Oliva	*La comèdia dels errors*, Barcelona: Vicens Vives–TV3 (Obra Dramàtica Completa de Shakespeare XXXI).
1990	H6A	S. Oliva	*Enric VI (Primera part)*, Barcelona: Vicens Vives–TV3 (Obra Dramàtica Completa de Shakespeare XXVIII).
1990	H6B	S. Oliva	*Enric VI (Segona part)*, Barcelona: Vicens Vives–TV3 (Obra Dramàtica Completa de Shakespeare XXIX).
1990	H6C	S. Oliva	*Enric VI (Tercera part)*, Barcelona: Vicens Vives–TV3 (Obra Dramàtica Completa de Shakespeare XXX).
1990	LLL	S. Oliva	*Penes d'amor perdudes*, Barcelona: Vicens Vives–TV3 (Obra Dramàtica Completa de Shakespeare XXXII).
1990	Sonn.	C. Riba	See 1909, *Serra d'Or*, 363 (March 1990), 49–50.
1991	Tit.	S. Oliva	*Titus Andrònic*, Barcelona: Vicens Vives–TV3 (Obra Dramàtica Completa de Shakespeare XXXIII).
1991	Gent.	S. Oliva	*Els dos cavallers de Verona*, Barcelona: Vicens Vives–TV3 (Obra Dramàtica Completa de Shakespeare XXXIV).
1991	John	S. Oliva	*El Rei Joan*, Barcelona: Vicens Vives–TV3 (Obra Dramàtica Completa de Shakespeare XXXV).
1991	Ado	S. Oliva	*Molt soroll per res*, Barcelona: Vicens Vives–TV3 (Obra Dramàtica Completa de Shakespeare XXXVI).

Appendix A

Year	Work	Translator	Edition
1991	Sonn.	M. Villangómez	*Obres completes. Versions de l'anglès*, Barcelona, Columna.
1992	Per.	S. Oliva	*Pèricles*, Barcelona: Vicens Vives–TV3 (Obra Dramàtica Completa de Shakespeare XXXVII).
1992	Rom. Merch. Hml. Cor.	M. Morera i Galícia	As above, 1982 (2nd edn).
1992	Mids.	J. A. Codina	*El somni d'una nit d'estiu de William Shakespeare. Versió realitzada segons les traduccions i versions respectives de Josep M. de Sagarra i Jaume Batiste.* Typescript in the Biblioteca de l'Institut del Teatre, and has been dated there as 1992.
1993	Sonn.	G. Vergés	*Tots els sonets de Shakespeare*, Barcelona, Columna.
1990s	Works	J. M. de Sagarra	New edition of all 28 volumes of Shakespeare translations – available in boxed edition. Barcelona: Institut del Teatre.
1995	Ant.	E. Mendoza	Unpublished.
1996	Rom.	C. Juan	*Romeo i Julieta*, Valencia: 3 i 4 (Llibres Clau 16).
1997	Hml.	M. Morera i Galícia	*Hàmlet*, Barcelona: Edicions 62–'La Caixa' (MOLU).
1998	Tp.	M. Desclot	*La tempesta*, Barcelona: Proa/Ossa Major.
2000	Hml.	J. Sallent	*William Shakespeare. Hamlet*, Barcelona: Proa.
2001	Mids.	S. Oliva	Fragments in *Comèdies*, ed. Francesc Vernet, Barcelona: Proa. pp. 33–44.
2001	Mids.	N. Oliver	Unpublished translation, performed in Menorca.
2002	Cor.	J. Sallent	*William Shakespeare. Coriolà*, Barcelona: Proa.
2002	Mcb.	M. Desclot	*La Tragèdia de Macbeth*, Barcelona: Columna/Romea.

Year	Work	Translator	Edition
2002	JC	S. Oliva	Publication of excerpts in programme for Teatre Lliure.
2003	Rom.	M. Desclot	Sections published in programme for Companyia Teatre Lliure 2002–3.
2003	Hml. Lr. Mcb.	S. Oliva	*Tragèdies I*, Barcelona: Destino/Universitat Pompeu Fabra.
2003	Sonn.	S. Oliva	*William Shakespeare. Els sonets. Versions en vers i en prosa de* . . .. Bilingual edition. Barcelona: Edicions 62/Empúries.
2003	Tw.	R. Mansell	Unpublished translation performed in Badalona.
2004	Lr.	J. Sellent	Translated for Bieito production.
2004	Merch.	Glòria Castelló	*El mercader de Venècia. Selecció, traducció, glossari i proposta didàctica a cura de* . . . , Valencia: 3 i 4.
2004	Mcb.	P. Fullana	*Adaptació de* . . . *per a Iguana Teatre*, Palma: Fundació Teatre del Mar.
2004	Rom.	M. Desclot	*Romeo i Julieta, Versió de* . . . *Introducció i propostes de treball de Roger Cònsul*, Barcelona: Proa.
2004	Mids. As Tw.	S. Oliva	*Comèdies 1*, Barcelona: Destino/Universitat Pompeu Fabra.
2004	Rom. Oth. Tim.	S. Oliva	*Tragèdies II*, Destino/Universitat Pompeu Fabra.
2005	R2 H4A/B H5	S. Oliva	*Obres històriques I*, Barcelona: Destino/Universitat Pompeu Fabra.
2005	R3	S. Oliva	Selection published in programme for Teatre Lliure.
2005	Mcb.	S. Oliva	Revised edition. Barcelona: Vicens Vives.
2005	Ado	R. Mansell	Unpublished translation in Badalona and Mallorca .

Appendix B

Shakespeare's Works and their Translators into Catalan

Comedies

The Taming of the Shrew

J. Farran i Mayoral (1908), revised (1938)
M. Duran i Tortajada (1928)
E. Giménez Lloberes (1930)
C. A. Jordana (1930)
J. M. de Sagarra (1940s)
A. Díaz-Plaja (1970)
S. Oliva (1987)

The Two Gentlemen of Verona

C. A. Jordana (1930)
J. M. de Sagarra (1940s)
S. Oliva (1991)

Love's Labour's Lost

M. Raventós (1908)
M. Morera i Galícia (1913), fragment
J. M. de Sagarra (1940s)
S. Oliva (1990)

A Midsummer Night's Dream

Josep Carner (1908)
R. Vives y Pastor (1908)
A. Maseras (1923), published (1929)

R. Negre (1927)
J. M. de Sagarra (1940s)
A. Díaz-Plaja (1980)
S. Oliva (1989)
M. Villangomez (1989)
N. Oliver (2001), unpublished

The Merchant of Venice

J. Puig i Ferreter (1909)
M. Morera i Galícia (1924)
J. M. de Sagarra (1940s)
J. Voltas (1973)
S. Oliva (1987)
G. Castelló (2004)

Much Ado About Nothing

R. Pomés Soler (1909)
J. Lleonart (1925)
S. Vilaregut (1929)
J. M. de Sagarra (1940s)
S. Oliva (1991)
R. Mansell (2005), unpublished

As You Like It

J. M. de Sagarra (1940s)
S. Oliva (1984)

Twelfth Night

C. Capdevila (1903), published (1907)
C. Montoriol (1934)
J. M. de Sagarra (1940s)
S. Oliva (1986)
R. Mansell (2003), unpublished

The Merry Wives of Windsor

A. Gual (1905), fragment, published (1913)
J. Carner (1909)
J. M. de Sagarra (1940s)
S. Oliva (1988)

The Comedy of Errors

J. M. de Sagarra (1940s)
S. Oliva (1989)
Sara Mañero/Julie McLucas (1987)

Tragedies

Titus Andronicus

J. M. de Sagarra (1940s)
S. Oliva (1991)

Romeo and Juliet

V. Balaguer (1878)
J. M. Codolsa (1881), parody
M. Morera i Galícia (1920), published (1923)
C. A. Jordana (1932)
J. M. de Sagarra (1940s)
S. Oliva (1984)
C. Juan (1996)
N. Oliver (2000), unpublished
M. Desclot (2003)

Hamlet

Franquisa i Gomis (1880), fragment
O. de Llanza (1884), fragment
A. Bulbena i Tosell (1885), published (1910)
C. Barallat (1890), fragment, published (1896)
A. Masriera (1898)
G. Soler (1898)
M. Morera i Galícia (1918), published (1920)
Johannus (1915), fragment
T. Moix (1978), published (1980)
S. Oliva (1982)
J. Sellent (1999), published (2000)

Othello

A. Coma (1874)
A. Ferrer y Codina (1884), parody
Alfons Par (1904)
J. Massó i Torrent (1906?), unpublished

J. Perpinyà (1929)
C. A. Jordana (1932)
J. M. de Sagarra (1940s)
S. Oliva (1988)

King Lear

A. Torrellas (1908)
A. Par (1912)
S. Oliva (1988)
J. Sellent (2004)

Macbeth

C. Montoliu (1907)
D. Ruiz (1908)
R. Negre (1927)
M. Morera i Galícia (1927), unpublished
C. A. Jordana (1928)
J. M. de Sagarra (1940s)
J. Pujol Cofan (1975)
S. Oliva (1988)
M. Desclot (2002)
P. Fullana (2004)

Histories

Henry VI (Part II)

S. Oliva (1990)

Henry VI (Part III)

S. Oliva (1990)

Henry VI (Part I)

S. Oliva (1990)

Richard III

J. M. de Sagarra (1940s)
S. Oliva (1989)

Richard II

S. Oliva (1984)

King John

J. Martí Sabat (1909)
J. M. de Sagarra (1940s)
S. Oliva (1991)

Henry IV (Part I)

J. Sandaran Bacaria (1907)
J. Farran i Mayoral (1913), fragment
J. M. de Sagarra (1940s)
S. Oliva (1985)

Henry IV (Part II)

J. M. de Sagarra (1940s)
S. Oliva (1986)

Henry V

S. Oliva (1986)

Henry VIII

S. Oliva (1985)

Roman Plays

Julius Caesar

S. Vilaregut (1907)
M. Morera i Galícia (1927)
C. A. Jordana (1930)
J. M. de Sagarra (1940s)
S. Oliva (1984)

Anthony and Cleopatra

F. Torres i Ferrer (1907)
M. Morera i Galícia (1914), fragment

C. A. Jordana (1930)
M. Manent (1934), fragment
J. M. de Sagarra (1940s)
S. Oliva (1987)
E. Mendoza (1995), unpublished

Coriolanus

(Balaguer)
J. Perpinyà (1914), published (1917)
M. Morera i Galícia (1915), published (1918)
J. M. de Sagarra (1940s)
G. Ferrater (1970–71)
S. Oliva (1989)
J. Sellent (2002)

Timon of Athens

C. A. Jordana (1932)
J. M. de Sagarra (1940s)
S. Oliva (1986)

Problem Plays

All's Well that Ends Well

F. Girbal Jaume (1909)
J. M. de Sagarra (1940s)
S. Oliva (1987)

Troilus and Cressida

C. A. Jordana (1932)
S. Oliva (1988)
X. Albertí/L. Cunillé (2002), unpublished

Measure for Measure

Salvador Vilaregut (1928)
J. M. de Sagarra (1940s)
S. Oliva (1985)

Last Plays

Pericles

J. M. de Sagarra (1940s)
S. Oliva (1992)

Cymbeline

C. Montoriol (1930)
J. M. de Sagarra (1940s)
S. Oliva (1989)

The Winter's Tale

V. Caldes Arús (1909)
R. Negre (1927)
J. M. de Sagarra (1940s)
S. Oliva (1987)

The Tempest

J. Carner (1910)
J. Farran i Mayoral (1926), unpublished
R. Negre (1927)
C. A. Jordana (1930)
J. M. de Sagarra (1940s)
J. Vinyoli (1984), fragment
S. Oliva (1985)
M. Desclot (1997), published 1998

Sonnets

R. Font y Presas (1903)
C. Riba (1909)
M. Morera i Galícia (1912)
J. López-Picó (1928)
C. Montoriol (1928), complete
M. Manent (1938)
C. A. Jordana (1937), unpublished
J. Triadú (1958)
M. Villangomez (1977)
S. Oliva (1985)
Vergés (1993), complete
S. Oliva (2003), complete

J. Jaumà (unpublished)
N. Dols (unpublished)

Poems

A. Par (1906), *Rape of Lucrece*
M. Morera i Galícia (1915) *Phoenix and the Turtle*
M. Morera i Galícia (1917) *Venus and Adonis*

Appendix C

Productions

Date	Play	Translator	Place/Details
1873	Otello, il moro di Valenzia	A. Coma	Barcelona: Tívoli/September.
1877	¡Otello o il moro de magnesia!	?	Barcelona.
1879	Les esposalles de la morta	V. Balaguer	Barcelona: Teatre Principal/March, April, May.
1881	Les ventalles de la porta	J. M. Codolsa	Barcelona: Odeon (parody of Les esposalles)/October.
1881	Les esposalles de la morta	V. Balaguer	Barcelona: Romea/December.
1883	Otel·lo o il moro di Sarrià	A. Ferrer y Codina	Barcelona: Tívoli/February, April.
1883	Hamletto, príncipe de Val·licarca	?	Barcelona.
1884	Otel·lo o il moro di Sarrià	A. Ferrer y Codina	Barcelona: Jovellanos/December.
1886	Otel·lo o il moro di Sarrià	A. Ferrer y Codina	Barcelona: Romea/February.
1888	Les esposalles de la morta	V. Balaguer	Barcelona: Romea/October.
1896	Les esposalles de la morta	V. Balaguer	Barcelona: Romea/April.
1898	Hàmlet	G. Soler	Barcelona: various.
1898	Julieta i Romeo	V. Balaguer	Barcelona.

Date	Play	Translator	Place/Details
1904	La festa dels reis	C. Capdevila/ dir. A. Gual	Barcelona: Lírico/ January, then at Vetllades artístiques in Orfeó Gracienc/June.
1905	La festa dels reis	C. Capdevila/ dir. A. Gual	Barcelona: Romea/ October.
1905	Les alegres comediantes	A. Gual	Barcelona (original play incorporating sections from *Wiv.*).
1905	Les esposalles de la morta	V. Balaguer	Barcelona.
1906	Otello ó el moro de Venècia	?	Mataró.
1907	Hamlet	G. Soler	Sant Feliu de Guixols.
1907	Les esposalles de la morta	V. Balaguer	Barcelona: Ateneu Obrer del Districte Tercer.
1907	Les esposalles de la morta	V. Balaguer	Sant Antoni de Calonge: Teatro Rojas.
1907	Julieta i Romeo	V. Balaguer	Monistrol.
1907	Otelo, el moro de Venecia	?	Badalona: Teatre Espanyol.
1907	Hamlet	?	Barcelona: Gràcia Círcol de Propietaris de Gràcia.
1907	Ofelia, Visió	M. Alegre y Mtre. Esquerra	Barcelona.
1908	Les esposalles de la morta	V. Balaguer	Barcelona: Ateneu Obrer Català/Christmas.

Date	Play	Translator	Place/Details
1908	*La feréstega domada*	C. Capdevila	Cassino Ceretá de Puigcerdá/August.
1908	*El somni d'una nit d'estiu*	J. Carner/dir. A. Gual	Barcelona: Novetats/October.
1908	*Otello*	?	Teatre Espanyol de Badalona/October.
1908	*La feréstega domada*	?	Manresa/October.
1908	*Les esposalles de la morta*	V. Balaguer	Cervelló.
1909	*La feréstega domada*	?	Sant Feliu de Guixols/January.
1909	*La feréstega domada*	?	Figueres/March
1909	*Les esposalles de la morta*	V. Balaguer	Vic/April.
1909	*Les esposalles de la morta*	V. Balaguer	Barcelona.
1909	*Otello*	?	Barcelona, Sants: Centre Tradicionalista/26 December.
1909	*Otello o el moro de Sant Gervasi*	A. Ferrer y Codina	Barcelona/December.
1911	*Les alegres comares*	J. Carner/dir. A. Gual	Barcelona: Romea/January/February.
1911	*Hamlet*	G. Soler	Manresa: Joventut Catòlica.
1911	*Various*		Barcelona: Companyia Catalana de Declamació October.
1911	*El somni d'una nit d'estiu*	J. Carner/dir. A. Gual	Barcelona: Romea.
1912	*Otello*	?	Castellbisbal.
1912	*Les esposalles de la morta*	V. Balaguer	Mataró.

Date	Play	Translator	Place/Details
1913	Hamlet	G. Soler?	Reus: Patronat de l'Obrer.
1914	Hamlet	G. Soler	Terrassa.
1915	Juli Cèsar (fragment)	?	Barcelona: Casa de Caritat (Segona Escola d'Estiu de la Diputació)/ August (Mark Anthony's funeral speech).
1920	Romeu i Julieta	M. Morera i Galícia/dir. A. Gual	Barcelona: Teatro Goya (Escola Catalana d'Art Dramàtic). Tours Lleida, Figueres, Casino de Masnou.
1921	Romeu i Julieta (fragments)	M. Morera i Galícia/dir. A. Gual	Barcelona: Escola d'Estiu.
1922	Macbeth, Hamlet, Otello (fragments)	?/dir. A. Gual	Barcelona: Escola d'Estiu.
1925	El marxant de Venècia	M. Morera i Galícia	Barcelona: Romea (Vila-Daví company)/March.
1928	La novícia de Santa Clara	S. Vilaregut	Barcelona: Romea/ August.
1928	La indomable, domada	M. Duran i Tortajada	Barcelona.
1929	Com més petita és la nou	S. Vilaregut	Barcelona: Romea/March.
1931	La mare de Hamlet	J. Millàs Raurell	Barcelona: Romea.
1932	Hàmlet	M. Morera i Galícia	Olesa de Monserrat: Círcol Tradicionalista/ Christmas.

Appendix C

Date	Play	Translator	Place/Details
1935	*La nit de reis*	C. Montoriol	Barcelona: Sala Studium (FNEC youth group)/December.
1938	*La fera amansida*	J. Farran i Mayoral	Barcelona: Teatre de la Comèdia.
1944	*El mercader de Venècia*	J. M. de Sagarra	Barcelona: (private residence of Felix Millet)/29 April (Sagarra played Shylock).
1944	*La tempestat*	J. M. de Sagarra	Barcelona: (private residence of Sagarra).
1953	*Romeu i Julieta*	J. M. de Sagarra	Barcelona: Orfeó Gracienc (Teatre Experimental de Barcelona)/September.
1959	*Les alegres casades de Windsor*	J. M. de Sagarra/dir. F. Roda	Barcelona: Romea (Agrupació Dramàtica de Barcelona)/February; Valls: Cong-Manana-Teatre/July.
1959	*Les alegres casades de Windsor*	J. M. de Sagarra/dir. S. Fité	Sabadell: Grup Palestra/July.
1960	*Enric IV*	J. M. de Sagarra/dir. Andreu Vallvé	Barcelona: (various spaces).
1963	*Romeu i Julieta*	J. M. de Sagarra/dir. Esteve Polls	Barcelona: Romea (Companyia Titular Catalana).
1964	*Otel·lo*	J. M. de Sagarra/dir. S. Fité	Sabadell: Casa Duran.
1964	*Otel·lo*	J. M. de Sagarra	Buenos Aires: Casal Català.

Date	Play	Translator	Place/Details
1964	*Juli Cèsar*	J. M. de Sagarra/dir. E. Polls	Barcelona: Palacio de las Naciones.
1964	*El mercader de Venècia*	J. M. de Sagarra/dir. M. A. Capmany	Barcelona: Palau de la Música (EADAG)/December.
1968	*Juli Cèsar*	J. M. de Sagarra/dir. J. A. Codina	L'Hospitalet de Llobregat: Plaça de L'Ajuntament (Co. Alpha 63)/June–July.
1968	*La nit de reis (El que vulgueu)*	J. M. de Sagarra/dir. Ventura Pons	Barcelona: Teatre Romea (Nova Companyia de Barcelona) / October.
1969	*Otel·lo*	J. M. de Sagarra/dir. A. Carmona	Barcelona: Teatre Romea.
1970	*Somni d'una nit d'estiu*	J. M. de Sagarra/ J. Carner / J. Batiste (dir./adapt.)	Barcelona: Romea then tours (Cavall Fort Cicle de Teatre per a nois i noies VIII).
1971	*Macbeth*	J. M. de Sagarra/dir. R. Ribalta	Sabadell: Auditòrium de la Caixa d'Estalvis.
1971	*Somni d'una nit d'estiu*	Sagarra/ Carner/ J. Batiste (dir./adapt.)	Barcelona: Romea then tours (Cavall Fort Cicle XII).
1972	*La fera sotmesa*	J. M. de Sagarra/ J. Batiste (dir./adapt.)	Barcelona: Romea then tours (Cavall Fort Cicle XIII).
1972	*Les alegres casades de Windsor*	J. M. de Sagarra/dir. A. Chic	Barcelona: Teatre Moratín (Companyia Nacional Angel Guimerà)/December.

Date	Play	Translator	Place/Details
1973	*La comèdia dels errors*	J. M. de Sagarra/dir. J. A. Codina	Barcelona: Romea March Teatre Grec (Escola de Teatre de l'Orfeó de Sants)/August Vilanova (1974).
1974	*Macbeth*	J. M. de Sagarra	Valencia: Teatre del Micalet (Co. Teatre d'Ubú Blau)/December.
1975	*Otel·lo*	J. M. de Sagarra/dir. A. Carmona	Hospitalet/June.
1975	*Macbeth*	J. Pujol Cofan	X. de Roses, Castelló d'Empúries, Sant Pere Pescador.
1976	*Mesura per Mesura*	J. M. de Sagarra/dir. R. Ribalta	Sabadell: Auditòrium de la Caixa d'Estalvis; Barcelona: Teatre Villarroel (Grup 'Palestra' de Sabadell).
1977	*Somni d'una nit d'estiu*	J. M. de Sagarra/dir. J. Mesalles, J. Puigcorbé	Barcelona: Saló Diana/May.
1977	*Coriolà*	J. M. de Sagarra/dir. A. Lucchetti	Barcelona: Teatre Casal Catòlic Sant Andreu (Col·lectiu de Teatre Ignasi Iglesias).
1977	*Amor i Mort de Romeo i Julieta*	?	Terrassa: Església Romànica de Santa Maria d'Egara.

Date	Play	Translator	Place/Details
1977	Romeo i Julieta	J. M. de Sagarra	Valencia: Escoles Professionals Sant Josep.
1977	Titus Andrònic	J. M. de Sagarra/dir. F. Puigserver	Barcelona: Teatre Lliure/ December and into 1978.
1979	Tres sonets de Shakespeare amb música	Composed by J. Soler	Barcelona: Capella de Santa Agata (Dies de Shakespeare a Barcelona)/28 March.
1979	Lectura dels sonets de Shakespeare	M. Manent/ J. Triadú	Barcelona: Capella de Santa Agata (Dies de Shakespeare a Barcelona).
1979	Titus Andrònic	J. M. de Sagarra/dir. F. Puigserver	Madrid: Maria Guerrero.
1979	Hàmlet	T. Moix	Radiotelevisió Espanyola de Barcelona /April – easter Monday and August screenings. First colour Catalan drama.
1979	Hàmlet	T. Moix	Barcelona: Plaça del Rei (Teatre Itinerant Català)/ June, then tours.
1980	Hàmlet	T. Moix	València; Madrid: Teatro de la Comedia (Teatre Itinerant Català, as above).
1980	Els dos cavallers de Verona	J. M. de Sagarra/dir. J. Montañez	Hospitalet (Grup A-71).

Date	Play	Translator	Place/Details
1980	Titus Andrònic	J. M. de Sagarra/dir. F. Puigserver	Barcelona: Teatre Grec as per 1977.
1980	Antoni i Cleopatra	J. M. de Sagarra	Barcelona: Teatre Grec; Romea (Teatre del Trànsit)/August.
1982	Macbeth	J. M. de Sagarra	Barcelona.
1983	La Tempestat	J. M. de Sagarra/dir. J. Lavelli	Barcelona: Romea (Companyia Núria Espert)/May.
1983	Romeo i Julieta	J. M. de Sagarra/dir. J. Ollé	Barcelona: Teatre de Poliorama (Teatre Estable de Sabadell).
1983	Al vostre gust	J. M. de Sagarra/dir. L. Pasqual	Barcelona: Teatre Lliure/October and into 1984.
1983	Enric IV	J. M. de Sagarra	Barcelona: Casal dels Joves Transformadors/June.
1984	La novícia de Santa Clara	S. Vilaregut	Valencia: Teatre Principal de València.
1984	El Duc a Barcelona	Texts from Shakespeare, Brossa, Espriu/dir. J. Montanyés	Barcelona:Romea (La Locomotora Negra).
1985	Les alegres casades de Windsor	J. M. de Sagarra/dir. P. Planella	Barcelona: Teatre Grec (Companyia del Consell Insular de Mallorca)/June/July.
1985	Les alegres casades de Windsor	J. M. De Sagarra/dir. O. Molina	Barcelona: TAC de Granollers.
1985	Textos de Ricard III	P. Cruz	Girona: Teatre Municipal.

Date	Play	Translator	Place/Details
1986	Al vostre gust	J. M. de Sagarra/dir. L. Pasqual	Barcelona: Teatre Lliure/May/June.
1986	Romeu i Julieta	J. M. de Sagarra/dir. E. Polls	Barcelona: Teatre Victòria (Companyia d'Art Dramàtic)/January.
1986	Visanteta de Favara (contains fragments of Ham.)	A. Boadella (arr.)	Barcelona: Teatre Romea (Teatre Estable Pais Valencià)/October.
1987	La comèdia de les equivocacions	S. Mañero/ J. McLucas/dir. J. Leal Duart	Valencia : Centre Teatral Escalante (Co. Teatro de los Sueños)/October.
1987	La Tempesta	J. M. de Sagarra/dir. R. Pereta	Bellaterra: Universitat Autònoma de Barcelona (Aula de Teatre UAB).
1988	Enric IV	J. M. de Sagarra	Sabadell: Teatre del Sol/November.
1989	Somni d'una nit de Sant Joan	M. Villangomez	Ibiza: GAT Teatre.
1989	Els dos cavallers de Verona	J. M. de Sagarra/dir. C. Bieito	Barcelona: Mercat de les Flors (Co. La Infidel)/July, then tours Catalonia.
1990	Nit de Reis	S. Oliva/dir. K. Zschiedrich	Barcelona: Mercat de les Flors (Co. El Talleret de Salt). Tours Catalonia 1990–1.
1991	Timon d'Atenes	J. M. de Sagarra/dir. A. García Valdés	Barcelona: Teatre Lliure.

Appendix C

Date	Play	Translator	Place/Details
1991	*Somni d'una nit d'estiu*	J. M. de Sagarra/dir. C. Bieito	Barcelona: Teatre del Grec (Co. La Infidel)/15–18 July; Mercat de les Flors/ 22 February– 8 March and 24 October–5 November 1992.
1992	*Molt soroll per res*	J. M. de Sagarra/dir. R. Ribalta and J. Fité	Barcelona; Sabadell (Companyia del Teatre del Sol).
1993	*Un Otel·lo per a Carmelo Bene*	X. Albertí (arr./dir.)	Barcelona: Artenbrut (Teatre del Bon Temps)/ December– January, then tours.
1993	*Pericles*	J. M. de Sagarra	Sabadell: Teatre Municipal La Faràndula (Companyia Joventut de la Faràndula)/25 December, then tours in 1994.
1994	*Les alegres casades de Windsor*	J. M. de Sagarra/dir. C. Portacelli	Barcelona: Teatre Grec/July.
1994	*Otel·lo*	J. M. de Sagarra/dir. M. Gas	Barcelona: Teatre Grec.
1994 1995	*El mercader de Venècia*	J. M. de Sagarra/dir. S. Belbel	Barcelona: Romea (Centre Dramàtic de la Generalitat de Catalunya).

Date	Play	Translator	Place/Details
1995	Hamlet	X. Albertí (arr./dir.) based on Shakespeare and Laforge	Barcelona: Teatre Malic (Teatredetext).
1995	Antoni i Cleopatra	E. Mendoza/dir X. Albertí	Barcelona: Teatre del Grec.
1995	El rei Joan	J. M. de Sagarra/dir C. Bieito	Barcelona: Convent dels Angels (Festival Grec) (Co. Focus); then Mercat de les Flors and Teatre Fortuny (Reus).
1995	Treball s d'amor perduts	J. M. de Sagarra/dir F. Madico	Barcelona: Artenbrut/27 September–November, then Reus in 1996.
1995	Tant per Tant Shakespeare (fourteen scenes from different plays)	J. M. de Sagarra S. Oliva	Barcelona: Mercat de les Flors.
1995	Les Obres Completes de Shakespeare (abreujades)	J. M. de Sagarra S. Oliva T. Moix	Barcelona: Artenbrut.
1996	Lear o el somni d'una actriu	S. Oliva/dram. ad. dir. A. Garcia Valdés	Barcelona: Teatre Lliure/May–June.
1996	Macbeth	J. M. de Sagarra/dir. T. Townsend	Barcelona: Pati Manning, then tours in 1996–7 season.
1996	El somni d'una nit d'estiu	J. M. de Sagarra	Vilafranca del Penedès: Cal Bolet; L'Espluga de Francolí: El Casal.

Date	Play	Translator	Place/Details
1996	*A bon fi tot li és camí*	J. M. de Sagarra/ ad. G. J. Graells/dir. J. Mestres	Barcelona: La Cuina (Aula de Teatre de la Universitat Pompeu Fabra).
1996	*La Tempesta*	S. Oliva/dir. A. Rigola	Barcelona: Teatre l'Eixample (Maremagnum Companyia de Teatre)/June 9–30/6.
1996	*Al vostre gust*	S. Oliva/dir. X. Masó	Teatre Municipal de Banyoles, Sala la Planeta and Teatre Principal d'Olot/November.
1996	*Romeu i Julieta. Assaig per a una arquitectura sentimental*	dram. and dir. R. Duran	Bellaterra: UAB; Sala Beckett.
1996	*Romeu i Julieta*	J. M. de Sagarra/dir. M. C. Pujol	Olesa de Montserrat: Font d'en Roure (Co. La Passió d'Olesa).
1996	*Mesura per mesura*	S. Oliva	Mallorca (Iguana Teatre).
1997	*El mercader de Venecia*	J. M. de Sagarra/dir. R. Ribalta	Sabadell: Teatre de Sol/February.
1997	*El somni d'una nit d'estiu*	S. Oliva/dir. F. Carreras Velasco	Barcelona: Centre Moral de Gracia) Grup de teatre el Centre)/May.
1997	*La Tempesta*	M. Desclot/dir. C. Bieito	Barcelona: Teatre del Grec (Co. Focus)/July; then Mercat de les Flors. Tours 1997 and 1998.

Date	Play	Translator	Place/Details
1997	*Macbeth Sempre*	ad. and dir. C. Zulian	Sala Beckett, Festival d'Opera de Butxaca/ November.
1997	*Variacions Hamlet*	S. Oliva/dir. and dram. R. Duran	Bellaterra: Nou Teatre de la Plaça Cívica de la UAB (Co. Aula de Teatre de la UAB).
1997	*Macbeth o Macbetto*	ad. and dir. X. Albertí	Sala Beckett.
1998	*El somni d'una nit d'estiu*	dir. M. Hervàs	Igualada: Teatre de l'Aurora (Grup de joves del taller de teatre)/ February– March.
1998	*Humilment i silencios*	ad. and dir. F. Madico (uses texts by Muller, Pirandello, Chekhov, Shakespeare)	Lleida: Centre Cultural la Caixa (Teatre Estable de Lleida)/March.
1998	*La bohèmia*	arr. and dir. E. Arredondo C. Portacelli, H. Ramada (uses texts by Espriu, Martí i Pol, Shakespeare)	Barcelona: Luz de Gas (Co. Dream's Theatre)/14–28 September; Sala Muntaner in 1999 and Reus
1998	*Nit de reis o el que vulgueu*	S. Oliva/J. M. de Sagarra/dir. P. Planella	Barcelona: Teatre Adrià Gual/12–15 February

Appendix C

Date	Play	Translator	Place/Details
1998	*Romeu i Julieta*	J. M. de Sagarra/dir. Maurice Durozier	(Bitò produccions) Girona/16–18 October; Badalona/ 6 November; Vilanova/ 7 November; Barcelona: Mercat de les Flors/16–28 February.
1999	*El mercader de Venècia*	dir. López París and Mercè Puy	Barcelona: La Cuina (Aula de teatre Abat Oliba)/10 July.
1999	*El somni d'una nit d'estiu*	dir. M. Farreres/ O. Tarragó	L'Hospitalet : Teatre Joventut (Co. Amics integrats)/ 29 November.
1999	*El somni d'una nit d'estiu*	ad. and dir. E. Martin Blanchet	Barcelona: Versus Teatre, 21 January–20 June.
1999	*El somni, imatges d'una nit de Sant Joan*	ad. R. Pla	Perelada: Auditori dels jardins del Castell (Co. Circo Gran Fele)/ 15 August.
1999	*Entrades i sortides*	ad. J. M. Fonalleras/dir. M. Mas (uses texts by Shakespeare alongside Belbel, Zorrilla, Sanchis Sinisterra etc)	Girona: Sala la Planeta (Aula Teatre de la Universitat de Girona)/25–7 May, then Barcelona for Festival del Grec.

Date	Play	Translator	Place/Details
1999	Hamlet	J. Sellent/dir. L. Homar	Barcelona: Teatre del Grec/July–August; then tours Tarragona, Reus, Girona, St Cugat, before Barcelona: Teatre Principal/ May–June 2000.
1999	Hamlet (un projecte)		Barcelona: Convent de Sant Agustí (Moment Teatre).
1999	Mesura per mesura	J. M. de Sagarra/dir. C. Bieito	Barcelona: Teatre Nacional de Catalunya/January–March.
1999	Molt soroll per no res	J. M. de Sagarra/dir. F. Madico	Barcelona: Teatre Grec (Focus Teatre)/July.
1999	Nit de reis	S. Oliva/dir. H. Munné	Barcelona: Abaixadors 10, 13 July–1 August.
1999	Otel·lo	J. M. de Sagarra/dir. P. Pastó i Torelló	Horta: Companyia Foment Hortenc/February.
1999	Peep Show Verona. Variacions Shakespeare	ad. and arr. R. Duran	Barcelona: Artenbrut /March; Convent de Sant Agustí/July.
1999	Macbeth		Associació de Teatre Rodamon (Children's theatre).
1998	Virtual Hamlet	dir. M. Hervàs	Tàrrega: Fira de Teatre al Carrer de Tàrrega (Teatre Nu)/September.

Date	Play	Translator	Place/Details
2000	*El somni d'una nit d'estiu*	dir. E. Pujol	Barcelona: Centre Cívic de Can Felipa (Tàndem Teatre)/February.
2000	*Romeu i Julieta*	N. Oliver/dir. G. Baz	Mallorca: Rafael Oliver Produccions.
2000	*La comèdia dels errors*	J. M. de Sagarra/dir. H. Pimienta	Barcelona: Teatre Nacional de Catalunya/January–April, then tours to Figueres, St Cugat, Reus, Lleida and Madrid.
2000	*Titus Andrònic*	S. Oliva/dir. A. Rigola	Badalona: Teatre Zorrilla, Badalona (Co. Kronos Teatre)/July; then Lliure in April–June 2001. Tours to Reus, Sant Cugat and Lleida in 2002.
2000	*Molt soroll per no res*	J. M. de Sagarra/dir. M. Romero i Tixé	Horta: Co. Foment Hortenc/April.
2000	*Obs*	dir. P. Gatell	Barcelona: Mercat de les Flors (Fura dels Baus)/November–December. Toured internationally.
2001	*H(Amort)3*	dir. M. Puyo (uses texts by Belbel, Durringer, Rostand, Shakespeare, Turrini, S. Kane)	Terrassa: Sala Maria Plana Terrassa/January.

Date	Play	Translator	Place/Details
2001	Les alegres casades de Windsor	J. M. de Sagarra/dir. L. Graells	Reus: Bravium Teatre/28 Jan; Olesa de Monserrat/4–11 March.
2001	Somni d'una nit d'estiu	N. Oliver/P. Pons/dir. Pitus Fernández	Menorca: Rafael Oliver Produccions/La Clota Groc Tours widely in 2002.
2001	Somni d'una nit d'estiu	S. Oliva	Sabadell: Sala Miguel Hernàndez Sabadell (Grup de teatre Barcino)/18 May.
2001	Tot va be si acaba be	J. M. de Sagarra/dir. M. Fernandez	Reus: Teatre Estable de Baix Camp/March.
2001	Shakespeare ¿nuestro contemporáneo?	A. Garcia Calvo (Spanish)/J. M. de Sagarra/dir. P. A. Angelópulos	Barcelona: Teatre de la Riereta/June Mostra del teatre al Raval.
2001	El somni d'una nit d'estiu	Ad. and dir. P. A. Gomez	Barcelona: Teatre Estudi (Aula de teatre de la UPF)/June.
2001	Hamlet, ser o no ser	dir. S. Brotons	Sant Cugat: Centre Cultural de Sant Cugat (Orquesta Simfònica del Vallès), with readings of excerpts from the play by Jordi Boixaderes.
2001	El somni d'una nit d'estiu	ad. A. Diaz/dir. C. Pons	Barcelona: Centre Moral i Cultural del Poble Nou.

Date	Play	Translator	Place/Details
2001–2	El somni d'una nit d'estiu	ad. Teia Moner	Teia Moner (puppets).
2002	Macbeth	M. Desclot/dir. C. Bieito	Barcelona: Teatre Romea/February–April, then tours.
2002	Macbeth	S. Oliva/dir. D. Salgado	Barcelona: Teatre Malic/6–23 June.
2002	Coriolà	J. Sellent/dir. G. Lavaudant	Barcelona: Teatre Nacional de Catalunya/Jan–March 2002, then tours Sant Cugat, Reus, Sabadell.
2002	La Tempesta	S. Oliva/dir. S. Ferrando	Barcelona: Teatre Estudi/February.
2002	Romeo i Julieta	S. Oliva/dir. P. Plana	Jove Teatre Regina.
2002	12 Diuen Shakespeare	Various (Desclot, Oliva)	Barcelona: Espai Lliure/September.
2002	Juli C'esar	S. Oliva/dir and ad. A. Rigola	Barcelona: Lliure de Gràcia/November–January 2003.
2002	Somni d'una nit d'estiu	S. Oliva/dir A. Llàcer	Barcelona: Romea (Companyia Parracs), then tours in 2003.
2002	Shopping, un Hamlet a les rebaixes	dir. J. Duran	Barcelona: Ateneu Barcelonès/April.
2002	Troilus i Cressida	X. Albertí, L. Cunillé, A. Llanas/dir. X. Albertí	Barcelona: Teatre Lliure (Companyia Cae la Sombra, co-production with Bitò Produccions)/July then October–November; Sant Cugat (Auditori)/March 2003.

Date	Play	Translator	Place/Details
2002	*Macbeth*	ad. and dir. P. Fullana	Mallorca: Iguana Teatre, then tours 2003 and 2004.
2003	*Romeu i Julieta*	M. Desclot/dir. J. M. Mestres	Barcelona: Teatre Lliure/March–April.
2003	*Nit de reis*	R. Mansell/ad. N. Oliver/dir. P. Fernández	Badalona: Teatro Zorrilla/June; then tours in 2004.
2003	*Hamlet*	English version/dir. C. Bieito	Barcelona: Romea.
2003	*Molt soroll per res*	S. Oliva/dir. F. Coromina	Teatre de Balenyà (Co. El Mirall de Balenyà).
2004	*Hamlet i el Somni . . . (històries shakespearianes)*	Charles and Mary Lamb trans. and dir. A. Güell	Barcelona: Espai Escènic Joan Brossa/February.
2004	*La comèdia dels errors*	J. M. de Sagarra/dir. R. Molins	Barcelona: Jove Teatre Regina (Zum zum teatre for children).
2004	*La Tempesta*	S. Oliva/dir. J. Sala and F. Bartrina	Girona: Teatre de Salt (Safareig).
2004	*El rei Lear*	J. Sellent/dir. C. Bieito	Barcelona: Romea/June onwards, then tours.
2004	*Juli Cèsar*	S. Oliva/dir. A. Rigola	Barcelona: Teatre Lliure.
2004	*Otel·lo i molt soroll . . . (històries shakespearianes)*	Charles and Mary Lamb trans. A. Güell/dir. A. Lizaran	Barcelona: Versus Teatre; then Planeta in 2005.
2005	*Ricard III*	S. Oliva/ad. and dir. A. Rigola	Barcelona: Teatre Lliure.

Date	Play	Translator	Place/Details
2005	*Molt soroll per res*	R. Mansell/dir. K. Zschiedrich	Badalona: Teatre Zorrilla.
2005	*Al vostre gust*	S. Oliva/dir. X. Masó	Barcelona: Teatre Grec then Romea.

Bibliography

1. Shakespeare Translation Histories, Bibliographies and Chronologies

Birmingham Public Libraries, *A Shakespeare Bibliography. The Catalogue of the Birmingham Shakespeare Library. Part One: Accessions Pre-1932*, III, (Birmingham: Birmingham Public Library/Mansell, 1971).

Birmingham Public Libraries, *A Shakespeare Bibliography. The Catalogue of the Birmingham Shakespeare Library. Part Two: Accessions Post-1931*, VII, (Birmingham: Birmingham Public Library/Mansell, 1971).

Coca, Jordi, 'Presentació', Josep Maria de Sagarra, *Obres completes: Traduccions. Teatre de W. Shakespeare Vol. 1*, Barcelona: Selecta, 1986 (Biblioteca Perenne 34).

Esquerra, Ramon, *Shakespeare a Catalunya* (Barcelona: Institució del Teatre, 1937).

Estudios escénicos 17, Las traducciones de Shakespeare al catalán de José María de Sagarra, (July 1973).

EUTI, *Exposició Bibliogràfica* (Barcelona: EUTI/Biblioteca de la Universitat Autònoma de Barcelona, 1985).

Fàbregas, Xavier, 'Shakespeare a Catalunya', *Estudios Escénicos*, 17 (July 1973), 59–64.

Fàbregas, Xavier, 'Shakespeare als països catalans', *Avui* (3 December 1977), 25.

Fàbregas, Xavier, 'Shakespeare en Catalunya', *Destino*, 2166 (April 1979), 6–7.

Fàbregas, Xavier, 'Notes introductòries a les traduccions catalanes de Shakespeare', in *Miscel·lània Aramon i Serra. Estudis de Llengua i Literatura (Oferts a R. Aramon i Serra en el seu setantè aniversari)*, (Barcelona: Curial, 1979).

Formosa, Feliu, 'La incorporació de textos teatrals a una tradició escènica d'àmbit restringit i amb grans ruptures històriques', *Actes del Congrés Internacional de Teatre a Catalunya 1985*, vol. II section 1, (Barcelona: Institut del Teatre, 1986), pp. 19–33.

Fulquet Vidal, Josep Maria, *Cinc monòlegs i una cançó: Anàlisi comparativa i implicacions teòriques*, Doctoral thesis presented to the Facultat de Filologia, University of Barcelona, April 1996.

Fuster, Joan, *Literatura Catalana Contemporània* (Barcelona: Curial, 1972).

Givanel i Mas, Joan, 'Index per autor de traduccions de teatre estranger al català' *La Revista*, XXI (January–June 1935), 131–44.
González Fernández de Sevilla, José Manuel (ed.), *Shakespeare en España* (Alicante: Universidad de Alicante/Libros Pórtico, 1993).
Guardiola, Carles-Jordi, 'Shakespeare als països catalans', in J. Molas (ed.), *Diccionari de la Literatura Catalana* (Barcelona: Edicions 62, 1979), pp. 673–4.
Juliá Martínez, Eduardo, *Shakespeare en España. Traducciones, imitaciones e influencias de las Obras de Shakespeare en la literatura española* (Madrid: Revista de Archivos, Bibliotecas y Museos, 1918).
Martínez Ascaso, Rosa Maria y Aranzazu Usandizaga Sainz, *Bibliografía de traducciones españolas de las obras de William Shakespeare* (Madrid: Raycar, 1979).
Molas, Joaquim, *Diccionari de la Literatura Catalana* (Barcelona: Edicions 62, 1979).
Palau y Dulcet, Antonio, *Manual del librero hispano-americano*, VI, (Barcelona: Antiquaria; London/Paris: Maggs Bros, 1927).
Palau y Dulcet, Antonio, *Manual del librero español*, XXI (Barcelona: Palau Dulcet; Oxford: Dolphin Books, 1969).
Par, Alfons, *Contribución a la bibliografía española de Shakespeare* (Barcelona: Instituto del Teatro Nacional/Diputación Provincial de Barcelona, March 1930).
Par, Alfons, *Shakespeare en la literatura española*, (2 vols) (Madrid: Victoriano Suárez; Barcelona: Balmes, 1935).
Par, Alfons, *Representaciones shakespearianas en España*, (2 vols) (Madrid: Victoriano Suárez; Barcelona: Balmes, 1936–40).
Pessarrodona, Marta, 'Shakespeare a Catalunya', in *Avui*, 170 (9 May 1984), I–II.
Portillo, Rafael and Manuel J. Gómez-Lara, 'Shakespeare in the New Spain: or, What you will' in M. Hattaway *et al.* (eds), *Shakespeare in the New Europe* (Sheffield: Sheffield University Press, 1994), pp. 208–20.
Ruppert y Ujaravi, Ricardo, *Shakespeare en España; traducciones, imitaciones e influencia de la obra de Shakespeare en la literatura española* (Madrid: Revista de Archivos, Bibliotecas y Museos, 1920).
Serrano Ripoll, Angeles, *Bibliografía shakespeariana en España: crítica y traducción* (Alicante: Instituto de Estudios Alicantinos, 1983).
Serrano Ripoll, Angeles, *Las traducciones de Shakespeare en España: El Ejemplo de Othello* (Valencia: Arcos, 1974).
Institut del Teatre, *Shakespeare a Catalunya*. Exhibition Catalogue, Saló del Tinell, Barcelona, 12 March–6 April, 1979.
Teatre Lliure, *Shakespeare was Here*. Exhibition catalogue, 3rd Santa Susanna Shakespeare Festival/Teatre Lliure, 2005.
Tussetschläger, Eva Maria, *Shakespeare. Aufführungen im spanischen Theater. Madrid und Barcelona* (unpublished Ph.D. thesis, University of Vienna, June 1973).
Vergès, Gerard, Introduction to *Tots els sonets de Shakespeare* (Barcelona: Columna, 1993).
'Vicens Vives inicia la publicació de tot el *corpus* dramàtic de Shakespeare', *La Vanguardia* (17 April 1984), 40.

2. Background and Criticism

Abrams, M. H., *The Mirror and the Lamp. Romantic Theory and the Critical Tradition* (Oxford: Oxford University Press, 1971).
Astrana Marín, Luís, *Obras completas de William Shakespeare* (Madrid: Aguilar, 1941).
Aulet, Jaume, *El noucentisme. Cicle de Conferències fet a la Institució cultural del CIC de Terrassa, curs 1984/85* (Barcelona: Abadia de Montserrat, 1987).
Aulet, Jaume, *Josep Carner i els orígens del Noucentisme* (Barcelona, Curial/Abadia de Montserrat, 1992).
Aulet, Jaume, Jordi Castellanos *et al.*, *Dossier Noucentisme – La Catalunya Perfecta*, *L'Avenç*, 194 (July–August 1995), 15–65.
Bacardí, Montserrat; Fontcuberta, Joan and Francesc Parcerisas (eds), *Cent anys de traducció al català (1891–1990): Antologia* (Vic: Eumo, 1998).
Bacardit, R. and M. M. Gibert, *El debat teatral a Catalunya. Segle XIX* (Barcelona: Institut del Teatre, 2003).
Badia i Margarit, Antoni M., *Llengua i cultura als països catalans* (2nd edn), (Barcelona: Edicions 62, 1966).
Balaguer, Víctor, *Obras de Víctor Balaguer. Tragedias* (3rd edn), (Madrid: Manuel Tello, 1882).
Balaguer, Víctor, *Les esposalles de la morta*, ed. Xavier Fàbregas (Barcelona: Edicions 62, 1968).
Barker, Francis, 'Nationalism, nomadism and belonging in Europe: *Coriolanus*', in John Joughin (ed.), *Shakespeare and National Culture*, pp. 233–65.
Bassnett, Susan, 'The Problems of Translating Theatre Texts', *Theatre Quarterly*, 40 (1981), 37–49.
Bate, Jonathan (ed.), *The Romantics on Shakespeare* (London: Penguin, 1992).
Batlle i Gordó, Ramon, *Quinze anys de teatre català. Els teatres Romea i Novetats de 1917 a 1932* (Barcelona: Institut del Teatre/Edicions 62, 1984).
Batlle i Jordà, Carles, Isidre Bravo and Jordi Coca, *Adrià Gual: mitja vida de modernisme* (Barcelona: Ambit, 1992).
Batlle i Jordà, Carles, *Adrià Gual (1891–1902): Per un teatre simbolista* (Barcelona: Institut del teatre/Curial/Publicacions de l'Abadia de Montserrat, 2001).
Beattie, John, '"Sutil, falso, traidor...". Tres versiones de *Richard III* de Shakespeare', in Soledad González and Francisco Lafarga (eds), *Traducció i literatura. Homenatge a Angel Crespo* (Barcelona: Eumo, 1997), pp. 163–72.
Benet, Josep, *Catalunya sota el règim franquista* (Barcelona: Blume, 1978).
Benjamin, Walter, 'The Task of the Translator' (1923), *Illuminations*, pp. 70–82.
Benjamin, Walter, *Illuminations*, ed. Hannah Arendt, trans. Harry Zohn, (London: Fontana, 1992).

Bennett, Susan, *Performing Nostalgia. Shifting Shakespeare and the Contemporary Past* (London/New York: Routledge, 1996).
Berenguer, Angel, *Teoría y crítica del teatro. Estudios sobre teoría y crítica teatral* (Alcalá de Henares: Universidad de Alcalá de Henares, 1991).
Bergnes, Antoni, 'Influjo que ha ejercido y está ejerciendo Walter Scott en la riqueza, la moralidad y la dicha de la sociedad moderna', *El Museo de Familias*, I (1838), 354–9.
Bergnes, Antoni, 'Shakespeare', *El Museo de Familias*, II (1839), 381–9.
Bergnes, Antoni, 'Comparación entre las literaturas de los diversos países del globo', *El Museo de Familias*, IV (1840), 10–17.
Bilbeny, Norbert, *Eugeni d'Ors i la ideologia del Noucentisme* (Barcelona: La Magrana, 1988).
Birringer, Johannes, *Theatre, Theory, Postmodernism* (Bloomington/Indianapolis: Indiana University Press, 1991).
Bloom, Harold, *The Anxiety of Influence* (Oxford: Oxford University Press, 1973).
Bloom, Harold, *A Map of Misreading* (Oxford: Oxford University Press, 1975).
Bloom, Harold, *Ruin the Sacred Truths. Poetry and Belief from the Bible to the Present* (Cambridge, Massachussets/London: Harvard University Press, 1991).
Bloom, Harold, *The Western Canon. The Books and School of the Ages* (London: Macmillan, 1995).
Bloom, Harold, *Shakespeare: The Invention of the Human* (New York: Riverhead Books, 1998).
Bolla, Peter de, *Harold Bloom: Towards Historical Rhetorics* (London/New York: Routledge, 1988).
Bristol, Michael, *Shakespeare's America – America's Shakespeare* (London/New York: Routledge, 1990).
Bristol, Michael, *Big-time Shakespeare* (London/New York: Routledge, 1996).
Buffery, Helena, 'Speaking in Tongues: The Catalan Coriolanus', in Malcolm Coulthard (ed.), *The Knowledges of the Translator*, pp. 299–323.
Buffery, Helena, 'The meaning of Shakespeare in Catalan: El parany del ratolí', *JOCS (Journal of Online Catalan Studies)*, (1 October 1997), consulted 15 January 2006. http://www.uoc.edu/jocs/1/translation/translation.html
Buffery, Helena, 'Shakespeare and the Cultural Dream in Catalonia', *Tesserae*, Vol. 6, 1 (June 2000), 5–18.
Buffery, Helena, 'Navigating the Tempest: Translation and the Negotiation of Culture in Catalonia', in Bermúdez, Cortijo Ocaña and McGovern (eds), *From Stateless Nations to Postcolonial Spain/De Naciones sin estado a la España Postnacional* (Boulder: Society of Spanish and Spanish-American Studies, 2002), pp. 63–79.
Busquets, Loreto (ed.), *Aportació lèxica de Josep Carner a la Llengua literària catalana* (Barcelona: Editorial Rafael Dalmau, 1977).
Cabot, Just, 'Una veu discordant – Parlem d'"El somni"', *Mirador* (16 January 1936).

Caldera, Ermanno, 'L'Influenza di Shakespeare sul Romanticismo Spagnolo (A proposito di "Romeo y Julieta" di Solis-Ducis)', *Letterature*, III (1980), 41–56.
Caldera, Ermanno, 'Da Menschenhass un Reue a Misantropia y arrepentimiento: Storia di una Traduzione', *Studi Ispanici* (Pisa: Estratto-Giardini, 1980), pp. 187–209.
Camps, Assumpta, 'La incidència dels gèneres en la traducció en català', *Revista de Catalunya*, 97 (April 1995), 109–17.
Capdevila, Carles, 'El mite de l'originalitat', *Mirador* (5 February 1931), 7.
Capmany, Maria Aurèlia, *Cartes Impertinents* (2nd edn) (Palma de Mallorca: Moll, 1980).
Capmany, Maria Aurèlia, 'Noucentisme v Novecentismo', *Lliçons de literatura comparada catalana i castellana segles XIX–XX* (Barcelona: Biblioteca Milà i Fontanals, 1982).
Carbó, Joaquim, *El teatre de 'Cavall Fort'* (Barcelona: Institut del Teatre/Edicions 62, 1975).
Carner, Josep, 'Abans que tot', in *Obres completes de W. Shakespeare. El somni d'una nit d'estiu* (Barcelona: Domènech: 1908), pp. 7–13.
Carner, Josep, 'Respostes a una enquesta sobre el teatre en vers', *Teatralia*, 6 (30 September 1908), 177–8.
Carner, Josep, 'Per començar', in *Obres completes de W. Shakespeare. Les alegres comares*, (Barcelona, Domènech: 1909), pp. i–iv.
Carner, Josep, 'Les persones fines i llur mig català', *Mirador* (16 August 1934), 6.
Carner, Josep, *El reialme de la poesia de Josep Carner*, Núria Nardi and Iolanda Pelegrí (eds) (Barcelona: Edicions 62, 1986).
Carner, Josep, *Epistolari de Josep Carner*, 3 vols, Albert Manent and Jaume Medina (eds), (Barcelona: Curial, 1997).
Carrion, Ambrosi, 'Shakespeare – Divagacions', *El Teatre Català*, 218 (29 April 1916), 154–5.
Castellanos, Jordi, 'El Noucentisme: una proposta de cultura', in Jaume Aulet *et al.*, *Dossier Noucentisme L'Avenç*, 194 (July–August 1995).
Coca, Jordi, *Qüestions de teatre* (Barcelona: Institut del Teatre/Edicions 62, 1985).
Coca, Jordi, 'Sagarra, traductor de Shakespeare', in *Josep Maria de Sagarra en els seus millors escrits* (Barcelona: Miquel Arimany, 1986), pp. 139–44.
Codina, Josep Anton, 'Juli Cèsar' *Estudios escénicos*, 17 (July 1973), 75–86.
Coulthard, Malcolm and Patricia Odber (eds), *The Knowledges of the Translator* (Lewiston/Queenston/Lampeter: Edwin Mellen, 1996).
Crexells, Joan, 'Shakespeare i el bon gust', *La Publicitat* (2 April 1925).
Croce, Benedetto, *Shakespeare*, with translation, preliminary note and appendix by Ricardo Baeza, (Buenos Aires: Editorial Escuela, 1955).
Cruikshank, Don, *Shakespeare in Spain*, Unpublished notes and bibliography (n.d.).
Daniell, David, *'Coriolanus' in Europe* (London: Athlone Press, 1980).

Delgado, Maria, *'Other' Spanish Theatres. Erasure and inscription on the twentieth-century Spanish stage* (Manchester: Manchester University Press, 2003).
Delgado, Maria, 'Journeys of Cultural Transference: Calixto Bieito's Multilingual Shakespeares', *Modern Language Review*, 101 (2006), 106–50.
Derrida, Jacques, *The Ear of the Other. Texts and Discussions with Jacques Derrida*, ed. C. McDonald (Lincoln/London: University of Nebraska Press, 1988).
Dobson, Michael, *The Making of the National Poet. Shakespeare, Adaptation and Authorship, 1660–1769* (Oxford: Clarendon Press, 1992).
Dollimore, Jonathan and Alan Sinfield (eds), *Political Shakespeare: New Essays in Cultural Materialism* (Manchester: Manchester University Press, 1985).
Drakakis, John (ed.), *Alternative Shakespeares* (London/New York: Routledge, 1989).
Dubeux, Albert, *Traductions françaises de Shakespeare* (Paris: 'Les Belles Lettres', 1928).
Emerson, Ralph Waldo, *Hombres representativos*, trans. with prologue by Josep Farran i Mayoral (Barcelona: Iberia, 1960).
Emerson, Ralph W., *La confiança en si mateix. L'amistat*, trans. Cebriá Montoliu (Barcelona: L'Avenç, 1904).
Erickson, Peter, *Rewriting Shakespeare, Rewriting Ourselves* (Berkeley/Los Angeles/London: University of California Press, 1994).
Emerson, Ralph Waldo, *Representative Men: Seven Lectures* (New York: AMS Press, 1968).
Esclasans, Agustí, *Articles inèdits* (Barcelona: 'La Revista', 1925).
Esclasans, Agustí, 'Hamlet, fantasma de bronze', *Revista de Catalunya*, VII, 39 (September 1927), 255–8.
Esclasans, Agustí, *La meva vida (1895–1920)* (Barcelona: Selecta, 1952).
Esclasans, Agustí, *La meva vida (1920–1945)* (Barcelona: Selecta, 1957).
Espasa, Eva, *La traducció dalt de l'escenari* (Vic: Eumo, 2001).
Esquerra, Ramon, *Lectures europees* (Barcelona: 'La Revista', 1936).
Even-Zohar, Itamar, 'The Position of Translated Literature within the Literary Polysystem', in J. S. Holmes and R. van der Broeck (eds), *Literature and Translation* (Leuven: Acco, 1978).
Fabra, Pompeu, *Gramàtica Catalana* (16th edn), with preface by Joan Coromines (Barcelona: Teide, 1993).
Fàbregas, Xavier, 'Joan Puig i Ferrater i la crisi del teatre català (1913–1917)', *Estudios escénicos* 14, 1970.
Fàbregas, Xavier, *El teatre o la vida* (Barcelona: Galba edicions, 1976).
Fàbregas, Xavier, 'Tot buscant Shakespeare amb un llumí', *Avui* (3 December 1977), 25.
Fàbregas, Xavier, *Teatre català d'agitació política* (Barcelona: Llibres a l'abast, 1978).
Fàbregas, Xavier, 'Sir William viene de visita', *El Noticiero Universal* (16 March 1979), 6.
Fàbregas, Xavier *et al.*, 'El teatre a tombant de segle: 1874–1909', *L'Avenç*, 22 (December 1979), 17–41.

Fàbregas, Xavier, 'Shakespeare y los extraterrestres del siglo XVI', *La Vanguardia* (10 May 1983), 46.
Fàbregas, Xavier, 'Las traducciones, codo a codo', *La Vanguardia* (10 May 1983), 46.
Fàbregas, Xavier, 'La más grotesca de las criaturas de Shakespeare', *La Vanguardia* (17 November 1983), 41.
Fàbregas, Xavier, *Teatre en viu (1969–1972)*, ed. Maryse Badiou, (Barcelona: Institut del Teatre/Edicions 62, 1987).
Fàbregas, Xavier, *Teatre en viu (1972–1973)*, ed. Maryse Badiou, (Barcelona: Institut del Teatre/Edicions 62, 1990).
Fàbregas, Xavier, *Teatre en viu (1977–1982)*, ed. Maryse Badiou, (Barcelona: Institut del Teatre/Edicions 62, 1995).
Farran i Mayoral, Josep, 'El teatre i els poetes', *La Revista*, 9 (15 February 1916), 7.
Farran i Mayoral, Josep, 'L'educació política del poble' (1917), in *Labor dispersa* . . . (1928), pp. 53–7.
Farran i Mayoral, Josep, 'Les humanitats i la nostra candidesa', *La Revista*, 36 (1 April 1917), 129–32.
Farran i Mayoral, Josep, *La renovació del teatre* (Barcelona: 'La Revista', 1917).
Farran i Mayoral, Josep, *Lletres a una amiga estrangera* (Barcelona: 'La Revista', 1920).
Farran i Mayoral, Josep, *Labor dispersa. Articles-Pròlegs-Discursos* (Barcelona: 'La Revista', 1928).
Farran i Mayoral, Josep, 'Mesura, responsabilitat i . . . traduccions directes', *La Veu de Catalunya* (29 August 1928).
Farran i Mayoral, Josep, *Homes, coses, polèmiques* (Mataró: 'Diari de Mataró', 1931).
Ferrater, Gabriel, 'El enigma de la personalidad de Shakespeare', *Destino*, 1421 (October 1964), 15.
Ferrater, Gabriel, *Papers, cartes, paraules*, Joan Ferraté (ed.) (Barcelona: Quaderns Crema, 1986).
Ferrer i Gironès, Francesc, *La persecució política de la llengua catalana*, (5th edn), (Barcelona: Edicions 62, 1986).
Foix, J. V., *Catalans de 1918* (Barcelona: Edicions 62, 1986).
Fontcuberta i Gel, Joan, 'Als cinquanta anys de l'art de traduir de C. A. Jordana', *Revista de Catalunya*, 36 (December 1989), 119–30.
Fuster, Jaume, *Breu història del teatre català* (Barcelona: Bruguera, 1967).
Gallén, Enric, 'El teatre' in Joaquim Molas (ed.) *HLC*, vol. VIII, 1986, pp. 379–448, and vol. IX, pp. 413–62.
Gallén, Enric *et al.* (ed.), *L'art de traduir. Reflexions sobre la traducció al llarg de la història* (Vic: Eumo, 2000).
Gallofré i Virgili, Maria Josepa, *L'edició catalana i la censura franquista (1939–1951)* (Barcelona: Abadia de Montserrat, 1991).
García Márquez, Gabriel, *Cien años de soledad* (Buenos Aires: Ed Sudamericana, 1967).
George, David and John London (eds), *Contemporary Catalan Theatre. An Introduction* (Sheffield: The Cromwell Press, 1996).

George, David, *Theatre in Madrid and Barcelona* (Swansea: University of Wales Press, 2002).
Grady, Hugh, *The Modernist Shakespeare* (Oxford: Clarendon Press, 1991).
Gual, Adrià, *Mitja vida de teatre*, with prologue by Maurici Serrahima, (Barcelona: Aedos, 1960).
Gual, Adrià, *Scherzo tràgic de Romeo i Julieta*, Barcelona: manuscript in Institut del Teatre.
Hattaway, M. *et al.* (eds), *Shakespeare in the New Europe* (Sheffield: Sheffield University Press, 1994).
Hawkes, Terence, *Meaning by Shakespeare* (London/New York: Routledge, 1992).
Hawkes, Terence (ed.), *Alternative Shakespeares 2* (London/New York: Routledge, 1995).
Heylen, Romy, *Translation, Poetics, and the Stage. Six French Hamlets* (London/New York: Routledge, 1993).
Holderness, Graham and Christopher McCullough (eds), *The Shakespeare Myth* (Manchester: Manchester University Press, 1988).
Hulme, Peter (ed.), *'The Tempest' and its Travels* (London: Reaktion Books, 2000).
Hunter, Lynette and Peter Lichtenfels (eds), *Shakespeare, Language and the Stage: The Fifth Wall* (London: The Arden Shakespeare and Thomson Learning, 2005).
Illas, Edgar, 'Visca la mort del català! Una proposta modesta per a les llengües minoritàries', *Dissidences. Hispanic Journal of Theory and Criticism*, 1. On line. Internet: 15/09/05 http://www.dissidences/MortDelCatala.html
Jordana, Cèsar August, *Què cal llegir?*(Barcelona: Catalònia, 1928).
Jordana, Cèsar August, *Resum de literatura anglesa* (Barcelona: Barcino, 1934).
Jordana, Cèsar August, 'Josep Carner, traductor', in *L'obra de Josep Carner. Volum d'homenatge...*, pp. 194–7.
Jordana, Cèsar August, *El món de Joan Ferrer* (Barcelona: Proa, 1971).
Joughin, John (ed.), *Shakespeare and National Culture* (Manchester: Manchester University Press, 1997).
Junyent, A., 'De Paris estant – Shakespeare, agitador subversiu', *Mirador* (22 February 1934), 5.
Kamps, Ivo, *Shakespeare Left and Right* (London: Routledge, 1991).
Kamps, Ivo (ed.), *Materialist Shakespeare. A History* (London/New York: Verso, 1995).
Kennedy, Dennis, *Looking at Shakespeare* (Cambridge: Cambridge University Press, 1993).
King, Stewart, *Escribir la catalanidad. Lengua e identidad culturales en la narrativa contemporánea de Cataluña* (Woodbridge: Tamesis, 2005).
Kott, Jan, *Shakespeare our contemporary* (London: 1964).
Kott, Jan, *Apuntes sobre Shakespeare* (Barcelona: Seix Barral, 1969).
Lamuela, Xavier and Josep Murgades, *Teoria de la llengua literària segons Fabra* (Barcelona: Quaderns Crema, 1984).
Lehmann, Courtney, *Shakespeare Remains. Theater to Film, Early Modern to Postmodern* (Ithaca/London: Cornell University Press, 2002).

Ley, Pablo, 'Jugando con Shakespeare', *El País* (21 October 2002), 46.
Lleonart, Josep, 'Cada manuscrit té la seva història' and fragments of *Molta remor i poca saó* (Much Ado about Nothing) in *La Revista*, XI (1 May 1925), 129–35.
Llopis, Artur, 'Un erudito barcelonés de Shakespeare: Alfonso Par Tusquets', *Destino*, 1421 (October 1964), 33.
Llúria, Rossend, 'Del amor al art del teatre', *De tots colors*, V (15 March 1912).
'Loge', 'Qui espera desespera.–L'amich X . . . que ve de Stratford.– No hi vagis noy! Shakespeare explotat.– In extenso!', *De tots colors*, IV (1 September 1911), 546–8.
Loomba, Ania and Martin Orkin (eds), *Postcolonial Shakespeares* (London and New York: Routledge, 1998).
López-Picó, Josep Maria. 'Tècnica i cultura', *La Revista*, 23 (15 September 1916), 1–5.
López-Picó, Josep Maria, 'Dietari espiritual', *La Revista*, 31 (16 January 1917), 60.
López-Picó, Josep Maria, *Moralitats i pretextos* (Barcelona: 'La Revista', 1918).
López-Picó, Josep Maria, 'Lectures' *La Revista*, (16 October 1919), 316.
Man, Paul de, 'Conclusions: Walter Benjamin's "The Task of the Translator"', in *The Resistance to Theory* (Manchester: Manchester University Press, 1986).
Manent, Albert, *Escriptors i editors del Nou-cents* (Barcelona: Curial, 1984).
Manent, Albert, *Josep Carner i el noucentisme* (Barcelona: Edicions 62, 1969).
Manent, Albert and Joan Crexell, *Bibliografia catalana dels anys més difícils (1939–1943)* (Barcelona: Abadia de Montserrat, 1988).
Manent, Albert and Joan Crexell, *Bibliografia catalana: cap a la represa (1944–1946)* (Barcelona: Abadia de Montserrat, 1988).
Manent, Marià (trans.), *John Keats. Sonets i Odes* (Barcelona: 'La Revista', 1919).
Manent, Marià, *Dietari dispers (1918–1984)*, ed. José Muñoz Millanes, (Barcelona: Edicions 62/'La Caixa', 1995).
Manyé, Josep, 'Per què Shakespeare en català?', *Avui* (18 March 1979), 29.
Maragall, Joan, *Obras completas. Serie castellana*, 6 vols (Barcelona: Gustau Gili, 1912–13).
Maragall, Joan, *Obres completes*, 25 vols (Barcelona: Edició definitiva, 1929–55).
Maragall, Joan, 'Hamlet', in *Obres completes*, vol. XV, (Barcelona: Edició definitiva, 1929–55), pp. 131–6.
Maragall, Joan, 'Othello', in *Obres completes*, 25 vols., (Barcelona: Edició definitiva, 1929–55).
Maragall, Joan, *Elogi de la paraula i altres assaigs* (Barcelona: Edicions 62/'La Caixa', 1978).
Martínez Ascaso, Rosa Maria, 'Dos catalans i un anglès: Shakespeare', *Avui* (31 March 1979), 24.

Martínez Ascaso, Rosa Maria, 'Shakespeare o el superhombre', *La Vanguardia* (8 April 1979), 53.
Martínez Ascaso, Rosa Maria, 'Las 10 musas de Shakespeare', *Diario de Barcelona* (5 April 1979), I.
Martínez Ascaso, Rosa Maria, 'Diàriament, periòdica, sempre Shakespeare', *Cuadernos de traducción e interpretación/Quaderns de traducció i interpretació*, 5–6 (1985), 137–51.
Masoliver, J.R., 'Què cal traduir?', *Mirador* (27 April 1933).
Mata, Jordi, *La segona mort de Shakespeare* (Barcelona: Columna, 1999).
Meschonnic, Henri, *Pour la poétique II: Épistémologie de l'écriture. Poétique de la traduction* (Paris: Gallimard, 1973).
Minguet i Batllori, Joan, 'Els altres noucentistes. Ramon Rucabado', *Estudis de llengua i literatura catalanes XIX, Miscel·lània Joan Bastardas 2* (Barcelona: Abadia de Montserrat, 1989), pp. 233–46.
Mira, Alberto, 'La tradición, la traducción, el tiempo: versiones del canon (el ejemplo de *Hamlet*)', *Donaire*, 8 (June 1997), 43–8.
Moix, Terenci, 'Shakespeare–Sagarra, el regreso de la maestría', *La Vanguardia* (21 November 1979), 47.
Molas, Joaquim (ed.), *Història de la literatura catalana. Part moderna*, vols VII–XI (Barcelona: Ariel, 1986–8).
Molas, Joaquim, *La literatura catalana d'avantguarda 1916–1938* (Barcelona: Bosch, 1983).
Molins, Manual, *Una altra Ofèlia* (Barcelona: Assaig de Teatre, 2003).
Montoliu, Cebrià, 'Pròleg', *Macbeth* (Barcelona: L'Avenç, 1907), pp. vii–xxxix.
Montoliu, Manuel de, 'Moviment assimilista de la literatura catalana en els temps moderns. Conveniencia que's fassin moltes traduccions i esment ab que cal fer-les', *Primer Congrés*, pp. 569–73.
Montoliu, Manuel de, 'Beatriu – Assaig de crítica dantesca', *Empori*, 8 (February 1908), 48.
Montoliu, Manuel de, *Breviari Crític I 1923–1924* (Barcelona: Catalònia, 1926).
Montoriol, Carme, Introduction to *Cimbelí* (Barcelona: 'La Revista', 1930).
Montoriol, Carme, Introduction to *Nit de reis* (Barcelona: 'La Revista', 1935).
Montoriol, Carme, 'L'escriptor i el moment actual' in *Escriptors de la revolució* (Barcelona: September 1937), pp. 155–61.
Morató, J., 'Per la nostra escena. El sentit nacional', *Catalunya* I (18 July 1914), 460.
Morera i Galícia, Magí, 'Homenatge a Magí Morera i Galícia', *Bibliofilia*, I (1911–14), 402.
Morera i Galícia, Magí, 'Proemi a la *Selecta de sonets de Shakespeare*', *Catalunya*, 7 (10 January 1914), 23–6.
Morera i Galícia, Magí, *Macbeth*, translated into Castilian (Madrid: Estrella, 1919).
Morera i Galícia, Magí, *Nou i vell* (Barcelona: Oliva de Vilanova, 1921).
Morera i Galícia, Magí, *Consideracions sobre els personatges de Shakespeare* (Barcelona: Escola Catalana d'Art Dramàtic, 1921).

Morera i Galícia, Magí, *Els poetes d'ara: Magí Morera i Galícia*, prologue by Carles Riba (Barcelona: 'Omega', 1924).
Morera i Galícia, Magí, *Vida Lleidatana, Número extraordinari dedicat a Magí Morera i Galícia*, II, 28 (15 June 1927).
Morera i Galícia, Magí, 'La mort del poeta Magí Morera i Galícia' in *La Veu de Catalunya* (5 May 1927).
Murgades, Josep, 'El Noucentisme', chapter 1 of Joaquim Molas (ed.) *HLC* IX, pp. 9–72.
Munt, Albert, *L'escorxador, Elsinore (1601)* (Barcelona: AADPC, 2004).
Oliva, Salvador, *Introducció a la mètrica* (Barcelona: Quadern Crema, 1986).
Oliva, Salvador, Prologue to *William Shakespeare. Hamlet* (Barcelona: Vicens Vives/TV3, 1986).
Oliva, Salvador, Prologue to *William Shakespeare. Coriolà* (Barcelona: Vicens Vives/TV3, 1989).
Oliva, Salvador, 'Shakespeare en catalán: problemas y soluciones' in González Fernández de Sevilla (ed.) *Shakespeare en España* (1993), pp. 193–218.
Oliva, Salvador, 'Sobre els elements suposadament intraduïbles de la traducció literària' in Marco Borillo, *La traducció literària* (1995), pp. 81–92.
Oliva, Salvador, *Introducció a Shakespeare* (Barcelona: Editorial Empúries, 2000).
Oller, J., 'D'En Carner i les seves darreres traduccions', *Catalana*, 2 (21 October 1909), 28–9 and 7 (25 November 1909), 102.
Olwer, Nicolau d', 'El centenari de Shakespeare–Cervantes', *La Revista*, 34 (1 March 1917), 102–4.
Ors, Eugeni d', *Glosari 1906 ab les gloses a la conferencia d'Algeciras y les gloses al viure de Paris* (Barcelona: Francesch Puig, 1907).
Ors, Eugeni d' (Xenius), 'La Donzella curiosa llegeix una traducció d'en Josep Carner', *La Veu de Catalunya* (8 September 1909).
Ors, Eugeni d', *Gualba, La de mil veus* (Barcelona: Catalònia, 1935).
Ors, Eugeni d', *Obra completa* (Barcelona: Selecta, 1950).
Ors, Eugeni d', *Glosari*, ed. Josep Murgades (Barcelona: Edicions 62/La Caixa', 1982).
Palau i Fabre, Josep, *La tragèdia o el llenguatge de la llibertat* (Barcelona: Rafael Dalmau, 1961).
Palau i Fabre, Josep, *El mirall embruixat* (Palma de Mallorca: Moll, 1962).
Palau i Fabre, Josep, 'Consideracions sobre el Shakespeare de Josep Maria de Sagarra', *Estudios escénicos*, 17 (July 1973), pp. 65–74.
Palau i Fabre, Josep, *Teatre de Josep Palau i Fabre* (Barcelona: Aymà, 1976).
Palau i Fabre, Josep, 'Shakespeare a l'abast', *Avui* (14 December 1979), 5.
Palau i Fabre, Josep, *Avui, Romeo i Julieta seguit de El porter i el penalty* (Barcelona: Institut del Teatre/Mall, 1986).
Palau i Fabre, Josep, *L'Alfa Romeo i Julieta precedit per Aparició de Faust, El Porter i el penalty, Els mots de Yorik* (Barcelona: Edicions 62, 1990).
Par, Alfons, 'Shakespeare; sa concepció y sa obra', *XXV Conferències dades en la Associació Wagneriana* (Barcelona: Verdaguer: 1908), pp. 157–91.

Par, Alfons, 'El forçament de Lucreça', *XXV Conferències dades en la Associació Wagneriana* (Barcelona: Verdaguer, 1908), pp. 470–92.
Par, Alfons, *Vida de Guillem Shakespeare. segons les millors biografies angleses y compte habut dels darrers documents desarxivats* (Barcelona: Verdaguer/Domènech, 1916).
Par, Alfons, *Shakespeare y el folklore español* (Palma: Círculo de Estudios, 1931).
Permanyer, Lluís, *43 respostes catalanes al qüestionari Proust* (Barcelona, 1967).
Permanyer, Lluís, *Sagarra vist pels seus íntims* (Barcelona: La Campana, 1991).
Perpiñà, Joan, Introduction and notes to *La tragedia de Coriolanus* (Barcelona: La Renaixensa, 1917).
Perucho, Joan, 'Sheyton Barrett, el fantasma de Shakespeare', *Obres completes 3. Narracions* (Barcelona: Edicions 62, 1987), pp. 30–4.
Pessarrodona, Marta, 'Shakespeare en catalán', *La Vanguardia* (22 November 1979), 44.
Pessarrodona, Marta, 'Mr.W.H.', *Avui* (25 October 1980), 20.
Pessarrodona, Marta, 'Shakespeare a Catalunya', *Avui* (9 May 1984), I–II.
Pessarrodona, Marta, 'Les traduccions en la producció editorial catalana: un comentari', *Serra d'Or* (April 1986), 29–31.
Piñol, Rosa Maria, 'Salvador Oliva tradueix mantenint el mateix nombre de versos del text original anglès', *La Vanguardia* (17 April 1984), 39.
Prat de la Riba, Enric, 'Importancia de la llengua dins del concepte de la nacionalitat', *Primer Congrés . . .*, pp. 665–9.
Prat de la Riba, Enric, *La Nacionalitat Catalana* (5th edn) (Barcelona: Edicions 62, 1978).
Primer Congrés Internacional de la Llengua Catalana, Barcelona Octubre de 1906 (Barcelona: Joaquim Horta, 1908).
Puig i Ferreter, Joan, *Diari d'un escriptor. Ressonàncies 1942–1952* (Barcelona: Edicions 62, 1975).
Puig i Ferreter, Joan, *Textos sobre teatre*, ed. Guillem-Jordi Graells, (Barcelona: Institut del Teatre/Edicions 62, 1980).
Raventós, M., 'Sobre Schiller en el 150 aniversari de son natalici', *Catalana* 7 (25 November 1909), 102.
Riba, Carles, 'Venus i Adonis' (1917), *Obres completes*, II, 1.
Riba Carles, 'Elogi del poeta traductor' (1918), *Obres completes*, II, 1, pp. 85–7.
Riba, Carles, 'Al marge de *Sonets i odes* . . . ' (1920), *Obres completes*, II, 1, pp. 149–50.
Riba, Carles, 'Al marge de *Hamlet*', (1920), *Obres completes*, II, 1, pp. 151–2.
Riba, Carles, prologue to *Els poetes d'ara* volume III on Magí Morera i Galícia, selection made by Tomàs Garcès (Barcelona: Omega, 1924).
Riba, Carles, *Plutarc. Vides paral·leles. Coriolanus. Alcibiades* (Barcelona: Fundació Bernat Metge, 1928).
Riba, Carles, *Obres completes II, Crítica 1*, ed. Enric Sullà (Barcelona: Edicions 62, 1985).
Riba, Carles, *Obres completes III, Crítica 2*, eds Enric Sullà and Jaume Medina (Barcelona: Edicions 62, 1986).

Riba, Carles, *Obres completes IV, Crítica 3*, ed. Enric Sullà (Barcelona: Edicions 62, 1988).
Riba, Carles, *Cartes de Carles Riba I: 1910–1938*, ed. Carles-Jordi Guardiola (Barcelona: La Magrana, 1990).
Riba, Carles, *Cartes de Carles Riba II (1939–1952)*, ed. Carles-Jordi Guardiola (Barcelona: La Magrana, 1991).
Riba, Carles, *Cartes de Carles Riba III (1953–1959)*, ed. Carles-Jordi Guardiola, (Barcelona: La Magrana, 1993).
Riquer, Martí de, Antoni Comas and Joaquim Molas (eds), *Història de la literatura catalana*, 11 vols (Barcelona: Ariel, 1964–88).
Robinson, Douglas, *The Translator's Turn* (John Hopkins University Press, 1990).
Rossi, Ernesto, *Discorso improvvisato nell' Ateneo di Barcellona – La sera di lunedi 3 de mese di agosto del 1868, sopra il teatro di Shakespeare, e specialmente sopra la tragedia Hamlet, sua interpretazione, sua esecuzione; per Ernesto Rossi, Artista drammatico* (Bilbao: Eduardo Delmas, 1868), with translation by Oscar Camps y Soler.
Rovira i Virgili, Antoni, *Nacionalisme i federalisme* (Barcelona: Edicions 62/La Caixa', 1982).
Rovira i Virgili, Antoni, *Antoni Rovira i Virgili: Textos polítics*, Josep-Lluís Carod Rovira (ed.) (Barcelona: Generalitat de Catalunya, 1995).
Ruiz, Dídac, *Lo boig Macbeth, sacerdot* (Barcelona: 1907).
Sagarra, Josep Maria de, 'Ofelia', *La Ilustració Catalana*, IX (19 March 1911), 143.
Sagarra, Josep Maria de, 'Zacconi–Otello', *La Publicitat* (28 January 1923).
Sagarra, Josep Maria de, 'Shakespeare, Zacconi', *La Publicitat* (7 February 1923).
Sagarra, Josep Maria de, 'Hamlet a l'escena', *La Publicitat* (8 February 1923).
Sagarra, Joan de, Introduction to *Shakespeare. Ricard III ". . . El meu reialme per un cavall!'*, trans. Josep Maria de Sagarra (Barcelona: Selecta, 1969).
Sagarra, Joan de, 'Mis almuerzos con Shakespeare', *Tele-eXprés* (11 April 1979), 26.
Sagarra, Josep Maria de, Preface to *Tragèdies Romanes* (Barcelona: Alpha, 1958).
Sagarra, Josep Maria de, Preface to *Romeo i Julieta, Otel·lo, Macbeth* (Barcelona: Alpha, 1959).
Sagarra, Josep Maria de, *Antologia poètica*, ed. Josep Palau i Fabre (Barcelona: Laie, 1983).
Sagarra, Josep Maria de, Introduction to *Shakespeare. Teatre. Coriolà* (Barcelona: Institut del Teatre–Bruguera, 1983).
Sagarra, Josep Maria de, *Josep Maria de Sagarra en els seus millors escrits* (Barcelona: Miquel Arimany, 1986).
Sagarra, Josep Maria de, *Crítiques de teatre 'La publicitat' 1922–1927*, edited by Xavier Fàbregas (Barcelona: Institut del Teatre/Edicions 62, 1987).
Said, Edward, *Culture and Imperialism* (London: Vintage Books, 1993).

Salvat, Ricard, *Escrits per al teatre* (Barcelona: Institut del Teatre/Edicions 62, 1990).
Samsó, Joan, 'El mecenatge cultural de postguerra. Benèfica Minerva', *Revista de Catalunya*, 37 (January 1990), 41–52.
Samsó, Joan, *La cultura catalana entre la clandestinitat i la represa pública* (2 vols) (Barcelona: Abadia de Montserrat, 1994).
Samsó, Joan, 'L'activitat editorial en català entre el 1939 i el 1951', *Afers*, 22 (1995), 555–69.
Sardà, Joan, *Obras escogidas. Serie castellana* (Barcelona: Francisco Puig y Alfonso, 1914).
Sellent, Joan, 'Traducció teatral i traducció audiovisual', in Montserrat Bayà (ed.), *VI Seminari sobre la Traducció a Catalunya: La traducció teatral* (Barcelona: AELC, 1998), pp. 47–62.
Sellent, Joan, 'Nota del traductor', in *William Shakespeare, Coriolà* (Barcelona: Proa, 2002).
Serrahima, Maurici, *Del passat quan era present* (Barcelona: Edicions 62, 1972).
Soldevila, Carles, 'El Teatre Català', *D'Ací D'allà*, XVI (June 1927), 229–30.
Soldevila, Carles, 'En la mort de Magí Morera i Galícia', *D'Ací D'Allà*, XVI, 114 (June 1927), 165.
Soldevila, Carles, *Què cal llegir?* (Barcelona: Catalonia, 1928).
Solé de Sojo, V., 'Orientacions perilloses', *Gaseta Catalana d'Art Dramàtic*, 3 (June 1917), 1.
Spivak, Gayatri, *Outside in the Teaching Machine* (London/New York: Routledge, 1993).
Steiner, George, *After Babel* (Oxford: Oxford University Press, 1975).
Still, Judith and Michael Worton (eds), *Intertextuality: Theories and Practices* (Manchester: Manchester University Press, 1990), pp. 27–8.
Taylor, Gary, *Reinventing Shakespeare. A Cultural History from the Restoration to the Present* (London: Vintage, 1991).
Teatre Lliure 1976–1987 (Barcelona: Institut del Teatre, 1987).
'Terenci Moix traduce *Hamlet* al catalán', *La Vanguardia* (28 November 1978), 17.
Torreño, Antoni, *L'ombra de Hamlet* (Alzira: Edicions Bromera, 2000).
Toury, Gideon (ed.), *Translation Across Cultures* (New Delhi: Bahri Publications, 1987).
Toury, Gideon, *Descriptive Translation Studies – and Beyond* (Amsterdam: John Benjamins, 1995).
Triadú, Joan, *Llegir com viure* (Barcelona: Fontanella, 1963).
Vallcorba, Jaume, *Noucentisme, Mediterraneisme i Classicisme. Apunts per a la història d'una estètica* (Barcelona: Quaderns Crema, 1994).
Vallverdú i Aixala, Josep, 'Fortuna de Magí Morera i Galícia (1853–1927)', *Serra d'Or* (October 1977).
Venuti, Lawrence, *The Translator's Invisibility. A History of Translation* (London/New York: Routledge, 1995).
Vidal i Alcover, Jaume, 'Josep Maria de Sagarra, traductor', *Estudis escènics*, 23 (June 1983), 69–94.

Vilà i Folch, Joaquim, 'Shakespeare de butxaca: text i didàctica dels clàssics', *Avui* (8 March 1980), 27.
Vila San-Juan, Pablo, 'La última tragedia de Shakespeare', *La Vanguardia* (14 April 1973), 54.
Vinyes, Ramon, 'De la tragedia', *Revista Teatralia* 3 (1908).
Vinyes, Ramon, *Hamlet, dramaturg*, Catalunya Teatral, 189 (Barcelona: Millà, 1983).
Vinyoli, Joan, *Tot és ara i res* (Barcelona: Ed. 72, 1973).
Vinyoli, Joan, *Domini màgic* (Barcelona: Empúries, 1984).
Worthen, W.B., *Shakespeare and the Authority of Performance* (Cambridge: Cambridge University Press, 1997).
Worthen, W. B., *Shakespeare and the Force of Modern Performance* (Cambridge: Cambridge University Press, 2003).
Yates, Alan, *Una generació sense novel·la?* (Barcelona: Edicions 62, 1975).

Index

acculturation 108, 115–116, 131
  see *anostrament* and
    domestication
adaptations 19–20, 22, 35, 46–47,
  50, 112, 119, 131, 140–141
  n.73–74, 154, 170, 176
  n.56, 219 n.7
aesthetic paradigms 6, 10–11, 32,
  64, 69, 90, 102, 104, 112
Agrupació Dramàtica de
  Barcelona 36, 40
Albertí, Xavier 14, 29, 36, 48, 49,
  50, 133
Alcover, Joan 183
Alomar, Gabriel 138, 155, 162, 174
  n.22
amateur theatre groups and
  stagings 24, 29, 30, 49, 51,
  54, 60 n.84, 119, 166, 170,
  176 n.54, 180, 218 n.3
Amyot, Jacques 185, 198
anglophilia 157–158
Antony and Cleopatra 141, 185
anostrament 70–71, 72, 74,
  106–107, 136, 138 n.12,
  214
anthologies 46
anxiety of influence 29, 104–105,
  114, 125, 135 n.7–8, 144,
  207–209, 212–214, 215,
  225

arbitrariness 78, 103, 104, 105,
  110, 111
Aristophanes 75
As You Like It 41, 59
Astrana Marín, Luis 36, 174
author function 63–64
authorship 134–135
Babel story 147–149, 173 n.7
Balaguer, Víctor 26–28, 40, 152
  Coriolanus 27–28, 181, 185, 219
    n.9
  Les esposalles de la morta 27, 30,
    40, 119, 226
Balearic Islands 23, 49–50, 52, 154
Bandello, Mateo 27, 235
bardolatry 101
Barcelona 19, 24, 108, 118, 186,
  187, 217
  Madrid, and 24
BBC 38, 41, 44
Beethoven, Ludwig van 82
Belbel, Sergi 14, 41
Benjamin, Walter 14 n.11
  afterlives in translation 1, 12,
    21, 62, 151, 169, 224
  'The Task of the Translator' 9,
    136 n.9, 179
Bergnes de las Casas, Antonio
  5–7, 15 n.18–19, 19, 62–63,
  93 n.2
Bible 114, 128, 147–149, 190
Biblioteca Popular de l'Avenç 30

Biblioteca Popular del Grans
    Mestres 30–33, 74, 102,
    107, 114–115, 126–129
Bieito, Calixto 42, 43, 47–51, 59
    n.81, 104
  Macbeth 99n.74, 216, 223–224
  Tempest, The 92–93
Bloom, Harold 13 n.11, 91,
    103–105, 135 n.7–8, 144,
    194
  see anxiety of influence
Boadella, Albert 22, 30
Borràs, Enric 26, 57 n.46
Boulangisme 195
bourgeoisie 27, 39, 64, 81, 120,
    137, 189
Branagh, Kenneth 44, 45, 49
Brecht, Bertolt 91, 130, 188
Bristol, Michael
  types of Shakespeare, on 10
Brook, Peter 48, 91
Browning, Robert 83
Bulbena i Tosell, Antoni 28, 31,
    152, 155, 182
Byron, George 83
Calderón de la Barca, Pedro 139
    n.55, 219
Canals i Gordó, Josep 119
canon 1, 4, 5, 11, 65–66, 71, 73,
    80, 83, 86, 99 n.75,
    103–105, 106, 111–112,
    135 n.7, 138 n32
  see also classics
  canonicity 20, 96 n.25, 224
  canonization 21, 74, 77
  theatre canon 21, 68, 73, 75, 88
Capdevila, Carles 31, 56 n.33, 74,
    124–125, 176 n.54
Capmany, Maria Aurèlia 14 n.15,
    35–36, 40, 262
Carlyle, Thomas 73, 96 n.20, 133
Carner, Josep 32, 74–76, 83, 95
    n.15, 126–127, 128,
    132–134, 152, 161–162,
    165, 169, 183, 184, 224
  'Del Shakespeare en llengua
    catalana' 106–108,
    112–116,126–128, 152, 189
  alegres comares de Windsor, Les
    75–76, 175 n.35, 230
  Catalan language, and 160–161,
    175 n.33–4, 183, 198
  Noucentisme, and 107, 126,
    130–131
  somni d'una nit d'estiu, El 32–33,
    75, 97 n.38, 107, 118, 125,
    129, 162, 164–167, 168,
    222 n.59, 223, 225
  Venus and Adonis, on 79, 128,
    163, 168, 169
Castilian
  versions of Shakespeare in
    25–26, 33, 34, 46, 49, 51,
    154–155
Catalan culture 1–4, 13 n.6, 64,
    68, 83, 101, 107–108,
    110–111, 114, 126–127,
    144–145, 151, 190–191
  Shakespeare and 1, 5–12,
    19–20, 21, 29, 42, 64, 66,
    83, 89, 101–141, 143–145,
    161, 169, 215–216,
    225–226
  Spanish culture, and 2–3, 24,
    51, 115, 123, 146, 154, 190
  translation and 4–8, 11–12, 14
    n.14, 42, 40–47, 60, 114,
    116, 131, 150–151, 166,
    185, 215–216, 226
Catalan identity 1–3, 4, 24, 52 n.1,
    116, 146, 147–149, 216,
    225
Catalanitat 27, 144–146
Catalan language 113, 143–177
  aptitude for translation of
    Shakespeare 145, 160–163,
    165, 168–169, 198–199

attitudes to 51, 207, 214
bilingualism 54 n.11, 146, 153,
    182–183
Castilian, and 54 n.11, 57 n.46,
    64–65, 79, 93, 118, 146,
    153–155, 162, 204
Catalan culture, and 169–172,
    216–218
Catalan identity, and 141–150,
    155–156, 158, 199–207,
    216–218
co–officiality of 183
dialects 156, 160, 168–169, 175
    n.33, 198
diglossia 54 n.11, 153–154
elocution 122, 166, 172
English, and 49, 51, 128, 153,
    157–159, 161–162, 163,
    165, 167
grammar 108, 149, 153–4,
    156–157, 174 n.16
Franco regime, and 19–21, 24,
    37–39, 51, 57 n.55, 88, 138
    n.32
Italian, and 26, 161–162, 163,
    198, 204
language of culture, as 66, 143,
    151, 154–157, 164, 168,
    205
linguistic conflict 51
orthography 35, 108, 153, 157,
    159–160, 175 n.30, 199
prosody 164–165, 166
suppression of, 186
see also censorship
working class, and 174 n.22
Catalan literature 4, 12, 14 n.12,
    14 n.14, 25, 31, 37, 68,
    113, 144, 162
    importance of translation for
    74–75, 113–114, 116, 150,
    151
Catalan Shakespeare 1–2, 101–141

Catalan–speaking regions 2, 4, 29,
    52 n.1, 122
Catalan theatre 74, 105, 107
    actors 47, 57 n.46, 109, 119,
    122, 172
    audiences 118
    canon 30, 88
    Castilian-language theatre, and
    118
    Catalan culture, and 51, 118,
    225
    children, for 41
    crisis in 7, 30, 32–33, 117–118,
    debate on shape and direction
    of 33, 89, 106, 117–119,
    121, 143, 167
    entry point for Shakespeare, as
    25
    film, and 44
    language versus visual effects in
    92, 93–94, 117, 152, 164,
    166, 167, 169–170, 172
    lectures on 75, 121
    limited infrastructure of 48,
    124, 167, 170
    magazines 33, 75, 82, 119, 120
    Noucentisme and 80–82, 84, 112,
    118, 120, 167
    paradigm shift in 50
    politics, and 126, 130, 131, 172,
    193, 194, 196, 206, 216,
    222 n.54
    popular 30, 50, 121, 152
    post-Civil War recovery of 40,
    117
    professionalization of 119, 121
    projects to renew 31, 106, 118,
    119, 138 n.38
    public funding of 36
    repertoire 40, 45, 117, 124–125,
    132
    reviews 85, 126, 216
    Shakespeare's importance for 5,
    21, 32, 68, 84, 88, 89, 105,

118–119, 120, 121, 122, 133, 224
    theatrical genius to, importance of 117, 121, 122, 123–124, 132
    translation, and 118, 119
Catalonia 2–4, 6, 24, 25, 30, 35, 37, 39, 42, 51, 54 n.11, 83, 99 n.71, 105–108, 119–120, 126, 129, 133, 134, 143–144, 146–149, 151, 159, 170, 189, 216–217, 224–226
Cavall Fort 41, 46
censorship 24, 37, 86, 88, 108, 187
Cervantes, Miguel de 15–16 n.22, 154–155
Cheek by Jowl 48, 59 n.61
children
    versions of Shakespeare for 22, 35, 36, 41, 42, 49, 90, 127, 131, 140 n.68, 224, 239, 272, 276
Chomsky, Noam 166
clandestine editions 20, 24, 37–39, 57–58 n.55, 58 n.59
Classicism 66, 68–69, 109, 111, 126–127, 136 n.16, 138 n.16, 143, 157, 184–185, 190
classic translators 43, 45, 117, 167–168, 183–184
classics 11, 47, 57, 74, 77, 82, 83, 85, 86–87, 121, 125, 162–163
    translation of 30, 42, 43, 45, 59 n.78, 112, 118, 138 n.52, 169, 190
Coca, Jordi 99 n.74, 122
Coleridge, Samuel Taylor 68, 72, 77, 78, 79, 83, 96 n.18, 112, 133, 196
colonialism 1–3, 79, 103, 150, 151, 154, 224

decolonization, and 52, 110
comedies 25, 26, 30–34, 47, 50, 86, 102, 180
    see also individual comedies
community 2, 113, 126–127, 156–157, 186, 190–191, 192–193, 214, 217
comparative literature 6, 20, 116
Complete Works 7, 28, 34, 36, 38, 42, 44, 83, 87, 102 133, 152, 174, 182, 199, 219
Complete Works of Shakespeare (Abridged) 41
Coriolanus/ Coriolà 27, 34, 41, 48, 51, 54–55 n.21, 126, 151, 179–222
    see also Balaguer; Morera; Oliva; Perpiñà; Sagarra; Sellent
    Belly tale 194
    Classicism 184–185
    Comédie Française performance 130, 180, 189, 191, 195
    courage 192
    custom, attitudes to 213–214
    delegation 206–207
    fascism, symbology of 217
    imperialism 205
    language 194–195
    monument 188
    'Most sweet voices' speech 209–214
    99 n.74, 180
    politics 129–130, 179, 186–187, 188, 193–194, 200–201, 217
    pride/orgull 190, 191–192, 221 n.48
    productions 99 n.74, 180, 216–218
    reviews 186–187, 197–198
    rhetoric 200, 205, 207

storytelling 179–180, 201–203, 207–208
struggle for city 217–218
women in 216–217
Costa i Llobera, Miquel 183
creativity/ *creació* 68, 79, 80, 85, 108, 111, 126, 133, 143, 185–186, 193
emancipation, and 80
Crexells, Joan 85–86
critical readings of Shakespeare 61–99
Cruz, Pep 46
Cruz, Ramon de la 25
cultural contact 2, 4, 115–116
Cunillé, Lluïsa 36, 48
Cymbeline 35, 86
dance versions of Shakespeare 170
Dante 65, 87, 103, 111, 126, 129, 163
Desclot, Manuel 14, 153
Díaz Plaja, Aurora 36, 41
Dies de Shakespeare a Barcelona 42, 43, 91
Dols, Nicolau 49–50
domestication 224
  see *anostrament*
difference 4, 10, 39, 105, 110–111, 135–136 n.9, 146, 149, 173 n.7, 200, 224, 225
dramaturgy 41–42, 45, 59–60 n.82
dreams 31–32, 68, 76, 118–120, 125–126, 128, 143, 152, 170–172, 173–174 n.15
  materialization versus idealization 169–170, 171–172
Editorial Catalana 188–189
Emerson, Ralph Waldo 70–71, 80, 82, 85, 96 n.20, 104, 112, 133, 139–140 n.58
Escola catalana d'art dramàtic 32
Espert, Núria 36, 40, 46, 50, 58 n.64, 92

Esquerra, Ramon 5, 16 n.24, 62, 67, 86–87, 163, 198
Shakespeare a Catalunya 7–8, 20–21, 54 n.14, 57 n.51, 138 n.31, 184, 189
Europe 36, 51, 65, 115, 116
European theatre companies and directors 25–26, 36, 48–49, 52, 60 n.84, 97 n.29, 216
Euripides 82
Even-Zohar, Itamar 57 n.50
exile 38, 39, 58 n.62
Fabra, Pompeu 108, 146, 149, 153, 156–157, 174 n.16
Fàbregas, Xavier 21, 27, 41, 42, 43, 118, 122–123, 125, 135
Farran i Mayoral, Josep 80–81, 85, 107, 111, 112, 126, 129–130, 139–140 n.58, 153, 163, 194
Lletres a una amiga estrangera 82, 83, 98 n.51, 129–130, 140 n.70, 145, 172–173 n.3, 193–194, 198–199
Fascism 188, 195, 217
Ferrater, Gabriel 46, 134–135, 165, 182, 214
Coriolà 22, 41, 167, 192, 208, 211–214, 219 n.15, 222 n.68
festivals 47
  Año Shakespeare 8
  Festival Grec 48, 49, 51, 172, 218 n.3
  Santa Susanna Festival 21, 50, 51, 92
First World War 33, 56 n.43, 109, 111, 137 n.22, 186, 188, 189
Foucault, Michel 11, 101
Forum of Cultures, International 51, 172, 217
Fundació Bernat Metge 109
Fura dels Baus, La 48, 52, 223

Garavaglia, Ferruccio 102
Gaudí, Antoni 71
Generation of 1898 28
genius 66, 68, 71, 72, 77, 79, 80, 85, 90, 96 n.18, 112, 131, 154–156, 157, 158, 168, 193, 195
   theatrical genius 74–75, 117–118, 120, 123–125, 132, 195–196, 206, 216
Godard, Barbara 3
Goethe, Johann Wolfgang von 31, 65, 66, 73, 94 n.10, 104
Gual, Adrià 30–33, 34, 119, 120, 122, 123–124, 132, 133, 138, 183, 184, 186, 187, 222 n.59
   Somni d'una nit d'estiu 31–33, 118–119
Guimerà, Angel 94 n.11, 122
Hamlet 8, 28–30, 34, 36, 40, 41, 49, 50, 51, 58 n.64, 65, 72, 85, 92, 102, 144, 151, 152, 166, 170, 180, 182, 223, 224
   advice to players 166–167, 172
   complex 37, 55 n.23
   materialism v idealism 39
   politics 39
   silence 39, 55 n.28
Hazlitt, William 77
Herder, Johann Gottfried von 96 n.18
hermeneutics 179
Història de la Literatura Catalana 4, 14 n.12
Homer 65, 121, 129
Homar, Lluís 40, 48, 50, 51, 216
Hugo, Victor 73
humanism 65, 76, 69–70, 74, 81–85, 109, 111, 126–127, 217
Ibsen, Henrik 73, 75, 94
identity, see Catalan identity

Ideological keywords 72, 82, 89, 106–108, 115, 129
   see arbitrariness; *creació*; dreams; genius; imperialism; inspiration; *joia*; *seny*; mediterraneanism; universalism; voluntarism
Iglésias, Ignasi 22, 29
imperialism 1–2, 4, 10–12, 13 n. 9, 51, 72, 79–80, 87–88, 91, 102, 108–111, 113–116, 116–117, 125, 143, 147–151, 154, 188, 189, 190–191, 195, 215–216, 225–226
   British Empire 11, 87–88
   cultural imperialism 90
   English imperialism 102–103, 109–111, 114, 148, 184–185, 188
   Spanish colonialism, and 28, 79, 111, 146
inspiration 73, 118, 132, 143, 145, 152, 164, 177
Institut d'Estudis Catalans 108
Institut del Teatre 24, 32, 40, 41, 42, 50
Instituto Shakespeare 49, 52, 91
intellectual, role of 113, 114, 126, 128, 155–156, 218
   see also *Noucentisme*
Ireland 111, 148
Jaumà, Joan 49–50
Jocs Florals 25
Johnson, Samuel 66
joia 71–72, 79–83, 85, 89, 98 n.51, 106, 109, 112, 116, 143, 193, 194, 225
   serenity versus 71–72, 81, 111
Jonson, Ben 69, 78, 123
Jordana, Cèsar August 4–5, 23, 36, 37, 83, 86, 131, 133, 137

n.30–31, 140 n.68, 151,
    152, 163, 223
Julius Caesar 27, 28, 32, 34, 40, 45,
    48, 75, 127, 185
Keats, John 81–82, 112
King Lear 33, 34, 47, 50, 76, 160,
    161
King John 41, 42, 45–46, 48
Kott, Jan 91, 188
Lamb, Charles 35
language
    see Catalan language
    English 76, 158, 159, 162, 163
    French as mediating language
        28, 32, 46, 54, 160,
        169–170, 172, 185, 216
    relation, and 26, 149, 157, 158,
        215, 217
Lavaudant, Georges 51, 99 n.74,
    180, 182, 216
Lavelli, Jorge 92
Lizaran, Anna 36
Llàcer, Angel 50, 170–171
Lleonart, Josep 35, 83, 98 n.52,
    168, 182, 198
Lliga Regionalista 109, 183, 187,
    189, 201, 220
Lope de Vega 123
López-Picó, Josep-Maria 67, 80,
    82, 84, 121, 132
Love's Labour's Lost 39, 48
Luhrmann, Baz 49
Macbeth 45, 47, 50, 72, 130, 140
    n.68, 180, 216, 223–224
Macià, Francesc 29, 55 n.27
Maeterlinck, Maurice 73, 94
Man, Paul de 179
Mancomunitat 108, 201
Manent, Marià 37, 39, 109–110,
    113
Maragall, Joan 65–66, 122, 188
Marlowe, Christopher 98 n.62,
    123
Mascaró, Joan 91

Maseras, Alfons 23, 32, 34, 46, 175
    n.44
Masriera, Artur 28, 166
Mediterraneanism 71, 109, 136
    n.16
Mendoza, Eduardo 14, 45, 46, 153
Merchant of Venice, The 33, 34,
    38–39, 41, 85
Merry Wives of Windsor, The 30, 32,
    40, 57 n.49, 75, 94 n.7,
    170, 175 n.35, 184
Meschonnic, Henri 1, 3–4
metatheatre 121, 140–141,
Michelangelo 80, 82
Midsummer Night's Dream, A 31–32,
    33, 34, 37, 47, 170–172,
    184
    see also Carner
Milà i Fontanals, Manuel 6, 19
Millàs-Raurell, Josep 22, 29, 35
Millors Obres de la Literatura
    Universal 44, 213, 214
minority culture 1–2, 101, 111,
    138, 150
minority literature 68, 99 n.71,
    111, 150
Modernism 24, 221
Modernisme 31, 53 n.9, 55 n.29,
    65–66, 73, 74, 108
Moix, Terenci 8, 14 n.15, 29, 41,
    42, 46–47, 163, 164, 177
    n.55
Molas, Joaquim 8, 151
Molière 126
Molins, Manuel 22, 29–30
Montoliu, Cebrià 67, 72–74, 80,
    109, 128, 132, 136 n.12,
    162–163, 175 n.32, 181
    Macbeth 30, 33, 72–74
Montoliu, Manuel de 94–95 n.13,
    121, 125, 132, 173 n.8
Montoriol, Carme 35, 41, 86
Moratín, Leandro Fernández de
    25, 152

Morera i Galícia, Magí 15 n.22,
    23, 33, 29, 34, 40, 79, 113,
    119, 151, 164, 166, 167,
    168, 180, 182–184, 187,
    189, 190
  Shakespeare, on 77–79, 94, 220
    n.21
  Coriolà 83, 151, 181, 212–214
Much Ado about Nothing 35
Munt, Albert 30
Napoleon 194
nationalism 107–109, 110–111,
    147–148, 154, 201, 204
New Shakspere Society 15 n.21
Nietzsche, Friedrich 110, 111, 112,
    137 n.22, 195
Normalization, cultural and
    linguistic 32, 47, 59 n.73,
    91–92, 104, 108, 110, 116,
    144–146, 149, 153,
    156–157, 161, 174 n.16
Noucentisme 10, 11, 16–17 n.28,
    34, 66, 67–68, 72, 74, 78,
    95 n.15–16, 107–109,
    111–112, 125, 126,
    130–131, 144–145, 152,
    157, 167, 172 n.1, 184,
    190, 191–195, 215–216,
    221 n.38, 225
Novell, Rosa 138 n.35, 217
Novelli, Ermete 31, 94 n.7
Oliva, Salvador 29, 41, 42, 43, 48,
    49, 92, 99 n.75, 102, 152,
    161, 164–166, 168, 169,
    171, 177,
  Coriolà 182, 208, 212–214, 222
    n.68, 224
opera 26, 65, 94 n.7, 172 n.2
Ors, Eugeni d' 22, 32, 33, 67, 83,
    109
Othello 26, 40, 50, 65, 67, 119
Palau i Fabre, Josep 29, 88,
    117–118, 121
Pan–Catalanism 115–116

Par, Alfons 5, 6–7, 8–9, 15 n.25, 16
    n.22, 20–21, 33–34, 56
    n.43, 67–72, 74, 82, 83, 90,
    93–94 n.4, 103, 132, 159,
    160–161, 162–163, 181,
    184
  Gualba, la de mil veus 33–34
  Lo rei Lear 15 n. 25, 152, 182
  Shakespeare's life, on 15–16
    n.22
parodies 27
Pasqual, Lluís 48, 50, 51, 172
performance history 23–24,
    25–27, 28–29, 30, 31–34,
    36, 40–42, 45, 46–49,
    50–52, 52 n.2, 92–93,
    169–172, 184, 216–217,
    223–224, 257–277
Perpiñà, Joan 34
  La tragèdia de Coriolanus 181,
    184, 212–214, 215
Perucho, Joan 86, 98 n.62
Pessarrodona, Marta 21, 91
Pimienta, Helena 48, 52, 170
Plutarch 27, 181, 185, 186
Popular editions 30–34, 36–37, 42,
    44–45, 74, 137–138 n.30
Poems 49, 71
Portaceli, Carme 57 n.49
postcolonialism 24, 52, 135 n.9,
    150
Prat de la Riba, Enric 79–80, 107,
    112–113, 147, 154, 187
  La nacionalitat catalana 108–110,
    154
pride/*orgull* 4–5, 131, 185,
    190–193, 199, 213–214,
    216, 221 n.40, 225
  see also *Coriolanus*
Primer Congrés de la Llengua
    Catalana
    146–147
Primo de Rivera 17 n.28, 33, 34,
    84, 108

Puig i Ferreter, Joan 33, 74, 175 n.44, 176 n.57, 188
Puigserver, Fabià 41, 50
Racine 112
Renaixença 5, 13, 52 n.1, 68, 114, 146
revolution 109
  evolution, versus 109, 135 n.15
Riba, Carles 73, 81–82, 85, 103, 168, 183, 184, 189–190
  'Elogi del poeta traductor' 83, 114, 127, 131, 189, 190, 197
Richard III 39, 40, 45, 50, 93
Rigola, Alex 30, 45, 47, 50, 51, 55 n.28, 93
Romanticism 6, 7, 15 n.20, 19, 21, 25, 61–62, 65–66, 68, 72–73, 76, 77, 81, 90, 92, 96 n.18–20, 109, 112,115, 143, 155, 156, 184
Roman tragedies 182
  characteristics of Shakespeare's Romans 188, 220–221 n.36
Romea 216
Romeo and Juliet 15 n.20, 27, 31, 34, 40, 42, 44, 48, 144, 163, 166, 180, 226
Rossi, Ernesto 28, 101, 105, 135 n.1
Rovira i Virgili, Antoni 79, 183
Royal Shakespeare Company 48, 94 n.6, 119
Sagarra, Josep Maria de 8, 21, 22, 23, 24, 37–39, 40, 41, 42, 43, 45, 46, 48, 49, 50, 58 n.65, 83, 85, 87–88, 89, 122, 133, 138 n.35, 139 n.49, 152, 155, 163, 165, 166–167, 168, 170, 176 n.56,
  Coriolà 182, 187, 208, 212–214
Sainets 25
Sardà, Joan 64–65

Schlegel, Friedrich von 72, 96 n.18
Schlegel–Tieck translations 21
Scott, Walter 6
Sellent, Joan 46, 48, 49, 50
  Coriolà 182, 212–214, 216
seny 83, 131, 134, 140 n.70, 187, 192–193, 200–203, 223
Setmana Tràgica 32, 102, 108, 189, 201
Shakemyth 101
Shakespeare
  alternative Shakespeares 1
  authenticity of 15 n.21, 105, 117, 134–135, 184
  biographies 64, 77, 82, 90, 131
  body of works, as 9–10, 63–63, 143–144
  classic status of 43, 47, 77
  contemporaneity of 86–87, 89, 93, 121, 224
  cultural symbol, as 2, 9–11, 86, 93, 104
  cultural value 59 n.68, 61–63, 96 n.25, 104, 128, 184, 217
  criticism 8, 61–99
  didactic role of 70, 74, 129, 139 n.54, 187
  Englishness of 90, 102–104, 134
  film, on 36, 44, 49
  humanity of 65–66, 69–70, 71, 75–76, 83, 85–86, 87–88, 89, 93, 103–104, 105, 116, 125, 188, 189, 221 n.47, 224
  imagination of 76, 79
  imperialism, and 1–3, 11–12, 17 n.29, 90, 102, 111, 117, 125, 143, 151, 226
  industry, The 11, 89–92, 94 n.6
  institutional 11–12, 17 n.29, 76, 77, 90, 103, 225
  irony of 69–70

lack, as 6–7, 29, 55 n.25, 63–64, 88–90, 103, 133–134, 144, 215
linguistic prestige and compexity of 10, 47, 76, 89, 105, 159–160, 224
literary prestige of 47, 89
man, as 62, 76–77, 82, 94, 128, 179, 217
man of the theatre, as 64, 119, 143
meaning by 12, 179
mirror to nature, as 79, 105, 143, 224
misspelling of 120–121
modernity, and 15 n.21, 64, 70, 86–87, 105
morality of 72, 78, 81–82, 128–130, 131
objectivity of 68–69, 72, 89, 129, 189,195–196
organic nature of 68–70, 78, 83, 96 n.18–19, 159–160
originality of 124, 126, 143, 145, 180
personal Shakespeares 76, 78, 83, 99 n.75, 106, 126, 131–133, 223
politics 187
Prospero, as 92–93
sincerity of 65–66
sources 69
translator, as 66, 112, 119, 124–125, 195
theatrical authority 112, 119, 121–122, 143, 166–167, 194, 224
women, and 35–36, 86, 129, 216–217
Shelley, Percy Bysse 73
Soler, Gaietà 28
Soler, Lluís 138 n.35
Sonnets 33, 35, 39, 46, 64, 77–78, 90, 94, 113, 177 n.60

Sophocles 81, 109, 126, 163
Spivak, Gayatri Chakravorty 135–136 n.9
Spain 115, 123, 190
Spanish Civil War 5, 8, 13 n.6, 23, 37, 39, 87, 112, 116, 132, 222 n.54
speech act 215
Stratford 64, 94 n.6, 134
Strehler, Giorgio 48, 91
Symbolism 31–32, 167
Taine, Hippolyte Adolphe 68
Taming of the Shrew, The 31, 32, 33, 37, 119
Teatre Intim 31–32
Teatre Lliure 14 n.15, 21, 41
Teatre Nacional de Catalunya 182, 209, 216, 217
Tempest, The 2, 32, 36, 39, 51, 52, 60, 70, 72, 75, 92, 112, 138 n.54, 158, 172
theatre
  see Catalan theatre
  Elizabethan and Jacobean 69, 74, 95 n.14, 123
  society, and 26, 121, 123
  identity, and 225
Thomas, Sir Henry 38, 58
Titus Andronicus 41, 45, 50
Toury, Gideon 1–2
townsend, Tamzin 49, 223–224
tragedies 27, 75, 80, 224
Transition 14, 41, 170
translatability 9, 105, 179, 224, 225
Translator
  invisibilty of 5, 46
  duty of 126–127, 131, 185–186
  ideal poet– 168, 190
  list of Shakespeare translators by play title 249–257
Translation
  adaptation, as 66, 112, 124, 131, 190, 216
  adequacy 91–92

Index

afterlives
see Benjamin
appropriation, as 107, 121, 127, 130
audiovisual translation 41, 44, 59 n.74
children, for 52
choice 101–102, 106, 124, 137, 149, 150, 191
chronological table of translations and adaptations of Shakespeare 243–258
collaboration, as 11, 33–34, 46
communication, as 166, 215, 225
concordance, as 11, 33
correspondence 153
creation, as 127
cultural 11–12, 62, 108, 124
cultural intervention, as 5, 7, 11, 34, 35, 42, 101, 107, 128, 131, 150, 187
cultural memory, as 11, 42, 185–186, 217
domestication, as 50, 71, 72, 74, 82, 87
see also *anostrament*
equivalence in 150
evaluation 5, 20, 21, 45, 59 n.74, 88, 89, 107, 150, 213
foreignization 135–136 n.9
fidelity in 27, 45, 46, 73, 78, 122, 149, 208
fixing of language, and 5, 35, 112, 144, 145, 151, 153
free 46, 73
function 44, 150
history 5, 11, 14 n.14, 19–25, 46, 151, 215
imperialism, and 1–4, 11–12, 114, 151
interpretation, and 12, 73, 90, 92, 105, 114

keywords 191
literal 73
metacommentary on 72–73, 79, 92, 107, 185
minority, and 150
naturalization, as 128, 136
negotiation 78, 157–158, 226
norms 2, 113, 150–151, 152
page versus stage 34, 48, 50, 52, 59 n.76, 102, 117–118, 121, 151, 161, 166–167, 176 n.51
poetic translation 46, 49, 59 n.74, 112, 158, 160, 164–166, 167, 222 n.68
policy 2, 5, 14 n.14, 66, 101, 111–112, 116, 119, 124, 129, 144–145, 150–151
politics of 11, 102, 123, 124, 129, 130, 150–151, 180, 187
polystems theory, and 36, 47, 150
power, and 3, 11–12, 105, 109–111, 130, 135–136, 149–150, 215
practice 2, 5, 151, 152, 163–164 169–170
process, as 11, 76, 112
professionalization of 91
regeneration, as 43, 112, 114, 128, 131, 150, 185
repetition, as 89, 224
representation, as 10–11, 218, 223–224
resistance, as 11, 13 n.8, 38, 116–117, 131, 138 n.32, 151
rhetorical process, as 9, 11–12, 13–14 n.9, 47, 66, 78, 89, 106, 146, 149, 151, 179, 194, 208, 212–214, 215, 223–224
speakability 50, 138 n.35, 153

studies 4–5, 14 n.14, 20, 99 n.71, 145
target context, and 145, 157, 161, 165, 182
theory 49
tradition, and 11, 35–36, 46, 107, 214
transculturation, and 9, 47, 143
transparency 3, 4, 145
unpredictable effects of 4, 9
transfiguration 9, 64, 146, 225
travesties 27
Triadú, Joan 39, 41
Troilus and Cressida 36, 48, 87
tropes 105, 143, 194, 212
TV3 41, 47
Twelfth Night 30, 35, 56, 60, 86, 138 n.42, 184
Two Gentlemen of Verona 47
Ulysses 190
universalism 10, 72, 82, 104, 125, 113, 131, 134, 143, 188, 193, 215
unpublished translations 22–23
Valencia 36, 49, 52, 91, 154, 214
Valle-Inclán, Ramon del 29
Venus and Adonis 79, 80, 128, 163, 168, 169, 183
Venuti, Lawrence 3
  Translator's Invisibility 13, 173
Vergés, Gerard 49, 164
Vilaregut, Salvador 35, 39, 56, 74, 120, 127, 133, 166
Villangómez, Marià 52
Vinyes, Ramon 29, 35, 39, 58 n.62, 75
Voltaire 66, 85
voluntarism 110, 111, 114
Wagner, Richard 68–69
working class 189
Xirgu, Margarita 57 n.46
Yeats, William Butler 83
Zola, Émile 73